The Great American Outlaw

The Great American Outlaw

A LEGACY OF FACT AND FICTION

By Frank Richard Prassel

UNIVERSITY OF OKLAHOMA PRESS : NORMAN AND LONDON

By Frank Richard Prassel

The Western Peace Officer: A Legacy of Law and Order
 (Norman, 1972)
Introduction to American Criminal Justice (New York, 1975)
Criminal Law, Justice, and Society (Santa Monica, 1979)
The Great American Outlaw: A Legacy of Fact and Fiction
 (Norman, 1993)

Library of Congress Cataloging-in-Publication Data

Prassel, Frank Richard, 1937–
 The great American outlaw : a legacy of fact and fiction /
by Frank Richard Prassel.
   p.   cm.
 Includes bibliographical references and index.
 ISBN 0-8061-2534-9 (alk. paper, hardcover)
 ISBN 0-8061-2842-9 (alk. paper, paperback)
  1. Outlaws—United States—History.   I. Title.
 HV6446.P7   1993
 364.1′092′273—dc20   93-14675
                                                          CIP

The paper in this book meets the guidelines for permanence and
durability of the Committee on Production Guidelines for Book
Longevity of the Council on Library Resources, Inc. ∞

2 3 4 5 6 7 8 9 10 11

Utlagatus est quasi extra legem positus;
caput gerit lupinum.

An outlaw is placed outside the law;
he bears the head of a wolf.

Contents

Illustrations

Preface

DEEP within American folklore rides a mysterious and significant figure. He comes to us through mists of fact and fiction, an incarnate mixture of right and wrong. On the one hand, this ever changing image represents crime, violence, and fear. On the other, it represents fearlessness, independence, and dedication. The figure poses a number of contradictions, including the true meanings of justice and freedom. Surrounded by legend, the outlaw endures as an enigma in our heritage.

He gallops toward us on a magnificent black horse, alone. His face is obscure, for his head is turned to look behind for pursuers. He holds a smoking revolver in one hand, and his saddlebags appear to be bulging with loot. This ominous rider may pose a grave danger; he threatens our security and safety. However, the outlaw also represents resistance to oppressive authority; he defies odious burdens imposed by corrupt society. The horseman should pass us by and disappear into the darkness, but he will certainly leave behind a feeling of excitement and a confused memory.

This apparition occupies no clearly defined place or time. We may easily associate him with the American Southwest and a century past. However, our outlaw could come from any part of the country, any generation. With simple modifications the image can be transformed to that of a colonial pirate, an urban gangster, or an adventurer in outer space fighting an evil empire.

Among the perplexing aspects of this legendary image is that of truth. What we think we know as history blends into myth. And what was once accepted as fiction merges with that now treated as fact. To confuse the issue still more, individual outlaws have long been of great interest to a multitude of writers. Their efforts range from entirely admirable to beyond lamentable, but today they are sometimes difficult to distinguish.

The American outlaw myth spans artificial boundaries and distinctions of race, education, and wealth. While wholly individualistic, it remains essentially democratic. In pure form the legend is born of injustice and reflects a wish for rebellion, yet it often has elements of savagery, suffering, betrayal, and doom. These themes, however frequently used, never seem to go out of date, for they are really very old.

To attempt an understanding of the heritage of the great American outlaw requires a careful backward look to a time long ago and a place far away. It begins more than a thousand years ago in countries which no longer exist.

FRANK RICHARD PRASSEL

An Outlaw Chronology

1071 Hereward the Wake vanishes from England.
1100 William II killed by a mysterious forest archer.
1247 Robin Hood dies at Kirklees Nunnery, Yorkshire.
1324 Lady Alice Kyteler investigated, Kilkenny, Ireland.
1404 Owain Glyn Dwr summons an independent parliament, Wales.
1593 Grace O'Malley meets with Elizabeth I.
1597 Transportation of convicts to America authorized.
1600 Anthony Munday completes *The Downfall of Robert Earl of Huntington*.
1603 James I condemns witchcraft and enchantment.
1610 John Day depicts the *Madde Pranckes of Merry Moll*.
1637 Anne Hutchinson banished from Massachusetts.
1649 James Hind named "that grand thief of England."
1670 William Pope writes *Memoirs of Monsieur Du Vall*.
1671 Henry Morgan attacks and loots Panama.
1684 Alexander Exquemelin describes *The Buccaneers of America*.
1692 Witchcraft trials, Salem, Massachusetts.
1698 William Kidd captures the *Quedah Merchant;* Parliament authorizes piracy trials in the colonies.
1718 Blackbeard killed at Ocracoke Inlet, Carolina.
1724 Jack Sheppard escapes from Newgate Prison; Daniel Defoe writes *A General History of the Pyrates*.
1728 John Gay's *The Beggar's Opera* premieres outside London.

1739   Dick Turpin rides Black Bess to York; Stono Revolt, South Carolina.

1763   John Wilkes publishes issue 45 of *The North Briton.*

1771   William Tryon crushes rebellion in North Carolina.

1781   The Doans loot a county treasury, Pennsylvania.

1797   Sam Mason occupies Cave-In-Rock, Illinois.

1809   Meriwether Lewis dies mysteriously along the Natchez Trace.

1815   Jean Lafitte's Baratarians help defeat the British at the Battle of New Orleans.

1821   Frederick Waldo writes *Captain Lightfoot.*

1830   Indian Removal Act drives tribes into exile.

1831   Nat Turner leads slave revolt, Virginia.

1834   Virgil A. Stewart exposes the "Great Western Land Pirate," John Murrell.

1838   Mormons outlawed from Missouri.

1842   "Destroying Angel" Porter Rockwell shoots Missouri's governor.

1850   Edward Bonney exposes *The Banditti of the Prairies;* 6,737 in prison.

1853   John Rollin Ridge writes *Joaquin Murieta.*

1859   Billy the Kid born, New York City; John Brown attacks Harpers Ferry, Virginia.

1862   Thirty-eight Santee Sioux simultaneously executed, Minnesota.

1863   William Clarke Quantrill raids Lawrence, Kansas.

1864   John Plummer lynched by vigilantes, Montana.

1873   The Benders vanish from Kansas; Alfie Packer devours his companions, Colorado.

1875   Thomas Hurley of Pennsylvania becomes "fugitive number one."

1876   Texas forbids outlawry forever; James-Younger gang attacks Northfield, Minnesota.

1877   John Newman Edwards's *Noted Guerrillas* published.

1878 Sam Bass killed and Satanta dies in prison, Texas.

1880 30,659 in prison.

1881 Billy the Kid escapes from jail and is killed, New Mexico.

1882 Jesse James killed by Bob Ford, Missouri; Pat Garrett writes *The Authentic Life of Billy the Kid.*

1883 Black Bart captured, California; Howard Pyle's *The Merry Adventures of Robin Hood* published.

1885 Teton Jackson escapes from prison and disappears, Idaho.

1886 Geronimo contacted by Apache scouts, Mexico.

1889 Richard Fox publishes *Bella Starr, the Bandit Queen.*

1892 The Daltons end their rampages at Coffeyville, Kansas.

1894 The Apache Kid vanishes, Arizona.

1896 *The Life of John Wesley Hardin as Written by Himself* published.

1901 Gregorio Cortez pursued across Texas; Butch Cassidy, the Sundance Kid, and Etta Place flee to South America.

1902 Federal Train Robbery Act passed; Augustin Chacón executed, Arizona.

1903 Harry Orchard assassinates former Gov. Frank Steunenberg, Idaho; Edwin S. Porter directs *The Great Train Robbery.*

1906 Stackalee blows down San Francisco, California.

1907 Emerson Hough writes *The Story of the Outlaw.*

1910 68,735 in prison.

1914 William S. Hart stars *On the Night Stage.*

1915 Frank James dies at family farm, Missouri; Bill Tilghman tours with *The Passing of the Oklahoma Outlaws.*

1916 Pancho Villa attacks Columbus, New Mexico.

1920 Douglas Fairbanks makes *The Mark of Zorro.*

1921 Terrible Tommy O'Connor escapes execution, Chicago.

1926 Walter Noble Burns writes *The Saga of Billy the Kid.*

1931 James Cagney stars as *The Public Enemy.*

1933 Pretty Boy Floyd conducts the Kansas City Massacre.

1934   John Dillinger proclaimed Public Enemy No. 1; FBI given police power.

1935   Ma Barker and her son Freddie killed, Florida.

1940   165,585 in prison; Richard Wright's *Native Son* published.

1941   George Hendricks writes *The Bad Man of the West*.

1942   Japanese-Americans driven from West Coast.

1943   Howard Hughes produces *The Outlaw*.

1950   FBI begins "Ten Most Wanted" list.

1958   Charles Starkweather and Caril Ann Fugate pursued across Nebraska.

1963   David Janssen flees in television's "The Fugitive"; John Toland describes *The Dillinger Days*.

1967   Arthur Penn directs *Bonnie and Clyde*.

1969   *Butch Cassidy and the Sundance Kid* most popular western.

1970   198,831 in prison.

1971   D. B. Cooper parachutes into myth, Washington State.

1974   Patty Hearst kidnapped by Symbionese Liberation Army, California.

1976   Last state outlawry statute declared unconstitutional.

1982   *E.T.* goes home.

1988   Lumbees seize hostages as protest against injustice, North Carolina.

1990   Manuel Noriega surrenders, Panama; 774,375 in prison.

1992   Clint Eastwood is *Unforgiven*.

Dates shown for the various subjectively selected events are those most frequently given. Some incidents are dubious and others spurious, but most occurred in reality as well as in imagination.

The Great American Outlaw

CHAPTER 1

The Bandit

Outlaws are made, not born.

—WYATT EARP

EVERY society has its outlaws. They may be numerous or few, notorious or honored, powerful or weak. And as surely as the existence of crime itself, each society appears to develop its own outlaw tradition. The long ancestry of the American concept reaches directly back to the British Isles, before the Norman conquest.

During the fifth and sixth centuries, several waves of invaders crossed the English Channel from northern Europe. Variously called the Angles, Saxons, and Jutes, these immigrants tended to push earlier arrivals, such as the Gaels and Picts, to the west and north. Many separate tribal areas developed, with strong family and village allegiances.

The concept of justice was primarily one of approved vengeance, by and against the clan as well as the individual. Crime was not a major problem and typically led to informal reaction by kinsmen or local villagers, but major offenses sometimes led to far more serious consequences. At that time in history, a freeman's status and value, or worth, was called his *laga*. Should a victim die, his clan could demand payment for the loss incurred from those responsible. Retribution was the foundation for law.

If an accused killer escaped, however, no means of direct compensation existed. As a consequence, the fugitive was considered to have lost his *laga,* or position as a freeman. He no longer possessed status or worth to society; he became *utlagatus,* a term which eventually was transformed into the word *outlaw*. The meaning remained clear, the consequences dire. The fugitive was deprived of all the protection normally afforded by primitive law. He could be hunted and slain as a wild animal, by anyone. Symbolically, the outlaw carried "the head of a wolf," *caput lupinum,* and he deserved death.

Since the time of the British druids, church and state were essentially one, so outlawry remained linked to excommunication. The early fugitive lost not only all legal rights, but the blessings of God. He became "a spiritual leper," doomed to live in the woods until ultimately found and destroyed.

Primitive British concepts of outlawry derived in part from practices of northern Europeans, but the precise ancestry remains unknown. There appear to have been two applications of outlawry on the Continent, and perhaps both found application across the English Channel.

In early Germanic law, a serious crime might be punished by casting the offender out into the wilds. The *bandit,* for one banished, paid for misdeeds through the loss of contact with society; he became a forest rover, or *wargus.* The Scandinavians, on the other hand, had a somewhat different approach. They deemed refusal to submit to justice a separate violation which could be punished by outlawry. Such a fugitive then became a proper subject for revenge by injured parties.[1]

Little is known about the actual outlaws of Anglo-Saxon days. Writing was very rare; laws of various small kingdoms were based essentially on local customs. Slowly, however, an embryonic nation called England (from *Angle-land*) began to develop. Among the several forces contributing to the end was the unifying influence of the Christian church and the successes of kings bent upon expanding their individual realms. But the foremost cause of consolidation came from abroad.

For most of the ninth century, the British Isles were the target of raids and invasions by the Norsemen, or Danes. This led to resistance to alien oppressors and prepared a foundation for later creation of an outlaw folklore. Just as the Celts had battled the Saxons, the English fought the Danes.

It became quite possible to view the outlaw as more than an

ordinary criminal; he might also be seen as a free man hunted by unjust authority. The word *brigand* even came into use indicating a roving bandit. It carried connotations of strife, fighting, and plunder. But it also signified independence, strength, and honor.

Among the foremost of the foreign raiders was a mysterious Norse chieftain usually known as Rollo the Ganger. This ambitious leader eventually became the first duke of Normandy, and an ancestor of the present British royal family. The Ganger also contributed to the English language, as *gang* developed a criminal meaning. And Rollo, in various northern European tongues, was called Rolf or Hrolf, for wolf.

One consequence of a unified English kingdom was the legal refinement, and considerably extended use, of outlawry. Prior to the tenth century the practice was rare and apparently reserved for unusual offenses, such as murder or betrayal of a lord. With development of a nation came the power to outlaw for any felony.

Under King Canute, who ruled in England from 1017 to 1035, a number of significant legal developments occurred. Outlawry remained a local process, but its effect was now applied throughout the country. A fugitive could not escape simply by going to another district. Under Canute, only the king could remove the designation of outlaw and thus restore the status and peace enjoyed by a freeman. Furthermore, a confusing question of responsibility was resolved. King Canute proclaimed that a declaration of outlawry released the fugitive's kinsmen from all obligations which would routinely apply for criminal acts of a family member. In short, an outlaw not only was legally placed beyond protection of state and church, his ties to the clan for past or future misdeeds were dissolved. He became a man with neither lord nor kin.[2]

England underwent its most fundamental change in 1066 when William of Normandy, a descendant of the raider Rollo, crossed the channel to begin his campaign of conquest. Never again would the British Isles experience a successful invasion. William placed Norman nobles in control of the country, centralized government and justice, separated church and state (offenses against one no longer being regarded as offenses to both), and created a strong class system which still endures. The ruthless conquest met considerable opposition, however, and led to an antagonism between Anglo-Saxons and Normans which lasted for generations.

At least in legend, the greatest defender of the oppressed and leader of the resistance was an outlaw. The people called him Hereward the Wake, "the Last of the English." Born in Lincolnshire, rejected by his father, and banished from the country in 1062, he returned years later to fight against William the Conqueror. Hereward led a large band of outlaws based on the Isle of Ely in Cambridgeshire and burned the nearby town of Peterborough. By 1071, however, well-equipped Norman forces proved too strong. Hereward faced eventual defeat and, as a truly legendary brigand often does, simply disappeared.[3] He is the earliest English outlaw to have a complete story, based in part on fact.

The legend of Hereward, now almost a thousand years old, contains essential elements of an enduring image. Driven to outlawry by injustice, he fought against oppression. Bold and reckless, he was nevertheless doomed, yet he somehow managed to escape and remain a symbol of rebellion.

These basic themes reach only some aspects of the outlaw image, but they provide a vital basis upon which violence and robbery may be both rationalized and justified. They became a pattern, perhaps rooted in Celtic tales, that was endlessly repeated. The desperate brigand could, at least in myth, resist oppression. Thus the outlaw emerged as a peculiar mixture of good and evil, threatening yet at the same time reassuring. Usually without the slightest intention, he represented a dream of personal independence and hope. Anglo-Saxons had no reasonable expectations of overthrowing the Normans, but the legendary outlaws might at least harass them in popular ballads.

The English tradition was, of course, similar to those of other lands. Outlaws often ignore national and even cultural boundaries. Their forms, however, display rather distinctive characteristics. In Iceland and Denmark, with Germanic and Scandinavian heritages not too different from that of Britain, the outlaw tradition focused upon the individual and his destiny. Fate and doom were paramount features in the ancient Norse ballads. "In England the outlaw represented to the people the champion of freedom. . . . [H]e became a social type."[4]

Still, the bandit of any land committed many obvious wrongs. He murdered, robbed, and pillaged. The poor might not be primary victims, but even they suffered some crimes. Furthermore, the outlaw remained the apotheosis of social disorder. He stood damned by the state and sometimes forsaken by the church. Even sympathetic legend routinely involved the brigand's ultimate disappearance or death.

Whatever medieval ballad might rightly or wrongly recall, there is no question about the prevalence of outlawry. Employment of the practice clearly increased under the Norman rulers. Many of the earliest recorded cases in the heritage of common law concern political enemies of the king faced with outlawry.[5] But for every demonstration of governmental power, resentment endured. It is perhaps of no little significance to future legend that in 1100 the unpopular William II (son of the Conqueror) died while hunting in a royal forest. He was assassinated by an unknown skilled archer. To the common people, the mysterious bowman may have seemed the finest man in all the land, but, although never caught, he did not reverse the tide of tyranny.

During the twelfth century the central government and its courts were greatly strengthened. Primitive versions of the jury system appeared, and criminal law emerged as a set of distinctive rules for the supposed protection of the "king's peace." Major criminals were deemed to have directly offended the crown, not just the immediate victim. During the reign of Richard I, a reward of two marks was routinely paid for each brigand's head literally severed and brought to the king at Westminster.[6]

As concepts of personal vengeance waned, outlawry became an almost routine practice, apparently intended to compel appearances by fugitives from justice. Eventually the process was extended to certain misdemeanors, although the consequences usually led to seizure of the accused's property rather than a virtual sentence of death. But the formal process of outlawry became more than a means of dealing with brigands; it was a particularly vicious instrument for abuse. The kings of England and their appointed judges turned a measure once meant to fight crime into an instrument of greed. Prospective enemies of the crown could be terrified into fleeing and, because they were then declared outlaws, all their property could be taken arbitrarily. King John engaged in precisely this practice against Robert Fitz Walter and Eustace de Vesci in 1212.[7]

During this turbulent era the most famous of all legendary outlaws is believed to have appeared. Eight centuries later his image remains ineffably linked to the positive aspects of banditry. Despite an almost total lack of clear historical evidence, he endures as a symbol far greater in significance than ever possible in life. His story is the first to demonstrate the peculiar flexibility extended the outlaw. For we confront not a single brigand but three, and for hundreds of years they have confused one another.

This fugitive is perhaps a figure of history, but he might really be a mythic composite of disputable reality while at the same time he probably remains best known to all of us through fiction. Today, no man knows precisely where fact ends and fantasy begins. Nothing is more suitable for the outlaw image. If a real person, dark mystery yet surrounds him. This greatest of all outlaws could only have been a brigand of rare tactical skills and leadership abilities. From deep forests in central England he directed raids by a band of loyal followers throughout a region notorious for its corrupt authorities. Feared for his expertise at arms and admired for his daring, he remained a fugitive for years. There was doubt about his true identity, and he became known by a pseudonym engrafted in history, legend, and folklore: Robin Hood.

The popular story of this outlaw is most easily explained as a patchwork of tales crafted in various ways over many centuries. Most accounts can be neither proved nor disproved by documentation. Therefore they have come to serve most satisfactorily as a foundation for countless legends surrounding later fugitives.

Robin Hood's story is far more than an early example of the outlaw myth, however; it has become the principal ancestor of a distinguished genealogy of portrayed brigandage.

Apart from passing references to a Yorkshire fugitive usually identified as Robert Hod early in the thirteenth century, documentary sources offer no clues to the historical reality of Robin Hood,[8] but the absence of reliable information has never been a hindrance to legend. It may, in fact, serve as a means of support. When little can be determined with certainty, myth more easily conforms to contemporary or individual demand. Robin Hood, for example, has attraction for the rightist (he supported the true monarchy), the leftist (he fought for the oppressed), or the anarchist (he undermined existing authority).[9]

Much of what we think we know about this famous outlaw comes from dozens of unwritten ballads performed by yeoman minstrels of the thirteenth and fourteenth centuries. The "rymes of Robyn Hood" served, in turn, as sources for the earliest known recorded version of the story. *A Gest of Robyn Hode,* composed about 1400, contained several of the essential elements still associated with the outlaw legend after more than five centuries.

In 456 verses this lengthy ballad portrays Robin Hood as a proud and crafty leader who is eventually pardoned by the true king. With the aid of devoted followers such as the giant Little John, Much (Midge) the Miller's Son, and Will Scarlock (Scarlet), the great archer fights the villainous sheriff, steals from the rich, and defies the venal clergy. *A Gest of Robyn Hode* opened with these lines:

> Lythe and listin, gentilmen,
>   That be of frebore blode;
> I shall you tel of a gode yeman,
>   His name was Robyn Hode.
>
> Robyn was a prude outlaw,
>   Whyles he walked on grounde;
> So curteyse an outlawe as he was one
>   Was never non founde.

> Robyn stode in Bernesdale,
> And lenyd hym to a tre;
> And bi hum stode Litell Johnn,
> A gode yeman was he.

In many respects, the story is still being written.

For several generations after their inception, the tales of Robin Hood probably meant quite different things to different social classes. By the sixteenth century, however, the myth began a significant transformation. It was deliberately modified to meet changing conditions. "Robin became all things to all men."[10] He emerged in the festive May Games as a popular figure who not only stole from the rich but gave to the poor and defended the downtrodden. Furthermore, this unusual outlaw acquired a most attractive female companion. Maid Marian did not exist in the early ballads, but she soon became an indispensable element in the expanding and increasingly romantic legend.

In 1521, John Major's *History of Greater Britain* arbitrarily assigned Robin Hood to the late twelfth century and the reign of John and Richard I. The choice of time, which some historians suspect to be a century before the likely fact, proved indelible. Robin Hood thus became the dedicated enemy of evil King John and the loyal supporter of Richard the Lionhearted.

The next figure to add significantly to the legend was an English draper and playwright named Anthony Munday. About 1600 he completed and soon experienced the success of two imaginative efforts, *The Downfall of Robert Earl of Huntington* and a sequel, *The Death of Robert Earl of Huntington*. With these plays Robin achieved a claim to the English peerage which, while fictional in origin, eventually received formal recognition. Munday also fixed the outlaw's place of birth as Locksley and, still more important, the general area for his adventures as "merrie Sherwodde" forest near Nottingham.[11]

As years passed a variety of specific locations became closely associated with the story. Various wells, caves, stones, and hills north of Nottingham were identified with the legend of Robin and his band of merry men. The area fit well with the legend that the Normans' rigid restrictions against hunting and gathering wood were unjust and led to resistance by the innocent poor. Nothing in the original ballads tied the outlaws to Sherwood Forest, but the story flourished in the chosen region.

By far the most important of the exact locations was a particular grave and its marker. Existence of an old stone slab at Kirklees Nunnery, originally carrying the name Robert Hude, could not be denied. Any further inscription on the marker had, however, been worn away and seemingly lost forever. Then, early in the eighteenth century, an apparent copy of the marker was discovered among the papers of the deceased dean of York, Thomas Gale. Easily deciphered today by phonetic reading, it stated:

> Hear undernead this laitl stean
> Lais Robert earl of Huntington
> Nea archir ver as hei sae geud
> An pipl kauld im robin heud
> Sick utlaws as hi an is men
> Vil England nivr si agen
> Obit 24 kal dekembris 1247

Accepted as an accurate representation of Robin Hood's grave marker, this seemed clearly to authenticate the legend and even support the portion relating to his final betrayal and burial by a prioress. But the documentation was false. Authorities hold that the language used is quite unlike early English, and as the dean of York surely knew, the date shown did not exist in calendars followed at that time.[12] The truth, however, means very little when compared to legend. In outlaw mythology, fiction often appears to supplant fact.

By the middle of the eighteenth century, Robin Hood had received a proper name, Robert Fitz Ooth. The outlaw also acquired a fictitious ancestry, supporting the previous claim to nobility. It should be noted, however, that invented pedigrees, sometimes accompanied by forged church records and fake portrait paintings, were not unusual among those accepted as members of the English peerage.[13]

Sherwood Forest's famous archer, from Joseph Ritson, *Robin Hood,*
1795.

Although Robin had been given credit for protecting and
giving aid to the poor centuries before, it remained for Walter
Scott's *Ivanhoe,* published in 1819, to add defense of the Anglo-
Saxons against tyrannical Normans. But fame during the nineteenth century really came through popular versions of the tale
designed for younger readers. In England, this occurred primarily through Pierce Egan's *Robin Hood and Little John,* first published in 1840.[14] Generations of American readers found the
outlaws of Sherwood Forest through Howard Pyle's words and
wonderful illustrations in *The Merry Adventures of Robin Hood,*
which began its multiple printings in 1883.

Some authorities assert that the world's most famous outlaw
is entirely mythical, completely without historical basis.[15] Robin
has been associated with the Germanic woodland deity Wode or
Hode.[16] Interesting conjecture also relates him to the Green
Man, an ancient symbol for English inns and rural public
houses,[17] yet only similarities connect the legendary outlaws to
the forest fairy people.

It is certain that Robin's story cannot be severed from those of other early English fugitives. The ballads clearly borrowed from one another. "The Outlaw's Song" and "The Tale of Gamelyn" were only two which told of wronged men hiding in the medieval forests. It is certainly possible that Robin Hood is a composite of many individuals, real and fictional.[18] Whatever its origin, there is no doubt about the significance of the legend in the continuing myth of banditry. It represents the most appealing part of truth because "at one and the same time it illuminates and distorts."[19] Legend transforms the outlaw into a figure of lasting significance, it turns the concept of justice into a moral issue, it spans the gulf between crime and charity, and it simplifies complex social problems through violence and vengeance.

Robin Hood is greater than history. We really do not care whether much that is believed about him apparently is based upon compounded works of fiction; we *know* that he represents right against wrong. Robin lives on, forever fighting the agents of bad King John from the depths of Sherwood Forest. Today, Nottingham proudly advertises itself as "Robin Hood Country." A statue in his honor stands in the city's major park. Brave and innocent, unjustly outlawed, Robin represents freedom and courage. Whatever its basis, this romantic image is not fiction. An endless succession of famous fugitives has been, and continues to be, compared with this legend. Its significance in the development of the American concept remains beyond dispute.

While questions will never be answered concerning the historical existence of Robin Hood, no doubt remains about other notable fugitives of the era. Fulk Fitz Warin, a distinguished baron of the Welsh marches, was outlawed in 1200 and became a respected leader in the struggle to limit the abuses of King John. Another who battled long against the crown was the legendary but also very real figure known as Eustace the Monk. The younger son of a minor noble, he renounced his monastic order after his father was murdered. Eustace, who could have been a model for Robin Hood's companion Friar Tuck, eventually led a group of outlaws which seized the island of Sark and raided England for many years. He was finally captured and beheaded in 1217.

The tales surrounding the renowned fugitives of medieval England shared several common traits. These became important details in outlaw legend. The famous brigand was, initially, the subject of some injustice, often involving a loved one. He possessed an almost supernatural skill at arms and frequently resorted to disguise. He attacked only the rich and powerful, and he faced ultimate destruction through treachery. Such characteristics have endured as vital ingredients of a story retold with numberless personalities and leaping geographic barriers for scores of generations.

Outlawry was a very significant reality during the reign of King John. Furthermore, it clearly reflected abuse of royal power as well as serious crime. Perhaps at no other time in English history did ordinary people identify more closely with fugitives from justice. The practice of simply outlawing those differing with the king caused great personal suffering and natural resentment. This was one of many varieties of mistreatment which led, early in the thirteenth century, to a collective uprising against the king.

Angry nobles, dissatisfied churchmen, and the growing merchant class joined to force concessions of royal power. The movement culminated in 1215 when John was forced, "in the meadow that is called Runnymead," to recognize the Magna Carta. This list of limitations on the crown had no clear precedent in world history. It meant, quite simply, that the king must abide by established rules; his authority was not absolute.

One of the most famous clauses in the Magna Carta, which remains a part of common law, forbade the arbitrary placing of fugitives beyond ordinary processes of justice. The relevant portion provides that "no free man shall be . . . outlawed or exiled . . . except by the law of the land."[20] This protection is the ancestor of the subsequent American guarantee of due process and has been carried on directly through several constitutions of the United States.

The requirement that outlawry could only be accomplished "by the law of the land" naturally led to increased formalities. English courts gradually developed specific rules and restrictions upon them. Most important was the determination that only males of twelve or more years could be outlawed. Women and children enjoyed total immunity from the practice. Furthermore, after 1329 the law did not permit the outlaw to be arbitrarily slain without court proceedings. His risk of being summarily killed theoretically ended with capture.[21]

Outlawry was medieval law's ultimate though clumsy weapon. The process required a series of "exactions," or proclamations at successive sessions of court calling upon the fugitive to "come in to the king's peace." The original custom probably demanded three such announcements, but eventually neither the first nor the last was counted, thus increasing the required number to five. This really meant that outlawry could not be accomplished quickly. It usually took several months.

There was ample opportunity for escape. "Except for the sentence of outlawry for those who ran away, as everybody did when there was the slightest ground for suspicion or prejudice, executions and personal punishment for crime were extremely rare,"[22] wrote J. W. Jeudwine. And Edward James Watson notes:

At Gloucester in 1221 the justice inquired into about 330 cases of homicide [not necessarily murder], and as a result one man was mutilated, about 14 were hanged, and about 100 orders of outlawry were given. . . . The Northumberland Assize Roll . . . [for] 1256, records 77 murders; 72 of the murderers escaped with outlawry, one murderer abjured the realm, and only in four cases did the felons receive their just punishment. The Assize Roll for the same county . . . [in] 1279, shows that of 68 murderers, two were hanged, 65 escaped with outlawry, and one murderer abjured the realm.[23]

A man might be outlawed yet be innocent of any crime. Exactions sometimes occurred in a distant county without knowledge of the suspect. Technically, once the dreaded sentence of outlawry was pronounced, he might be hunted down and, if necessary, killed. Many instances of obvious injustice resulted, and as a consequence many royal writs "inlawing" individual outlaws were issued.[24]

An ordinary citizen bore a responsibility to protect the community against criminals. The law expected him to pursue out-laws, yet he acted at his peril. Ordinances which commanded all men to hunt down fugitives offered no protection in the event of a mistake, and this probably contributed to a natural reluctance to join actively in the search for outlaws. With only widely scattered sheriffs and constables to enforce the law, apprehensions did not occur with great frequency.

If arrested, the outlaw might still avail himself of several defenses. These did not deal with the original crime charged but with the process by which he was placed outside the usual protections of justice. The courts demanded absolute accuracy in all relevant proceedings. For example, "if the day and year of the king be inserted in the 1, 2, 3 and 5 exactus, but omitted in the 4th exactus, it is erroneous."[25] Legal technicalities for the benefit of defendants are by no means a product of the twentieth century; they were widely known in medieval England.

Charges of outlawry also could be defeated by evidence that the accused was not the individual exacted but another of the same name. The defense might also be established that the subject was underage or that he was in prison or "beyond the sea" when outlawed. Should these efforts fail, the courts issued a warrant to the local sheriff for legal execution. The original charge was no longer relevant.

The outlawed fugitive lost all rights to hold property. His lands and goods were taken by the king; any contracts he had made were dissolved. Children of those who "bear the wolf's head" could not inherit property from anyone, and those found to have aided the outlaw in his effort to escape justice might themselves be executed. Such harsh penalties had absolutely no effect on crime. According to the rolls of the bench, "from 1216 to 1272 . . . the bad police of the country was an obstacle to improvement; and rendered all communication dangerous, and all property precarious. . . . [M]en were never secure in their houses . . . whole villages were often plundered, by bands of robbers."[26]

It was a violent age, and resistance to English domination continued to fuel the flames of legend. One prominent outlaw of the era was Scotland's great hero William Wallace. According to tales still told, in 1297 he avenged his beloved Marion by killing the sheriff of Lanark. Wallace led a large band of fighters and controlled a significant portion of Scotland until defeated at the Battle of Falkirk. The chivalrous and daring Wallace was eventually betrayed, convicted of treason, and beheaded in 1305.[27]

The fourteenth century found England beset by a multitude of organized bands of brigands, many of whom enjoyed some degree of protection from powerful local barons. Such nobles often employed outlaws against their personal enemies. Eustace, Robert, and Walter Folville led a gang of fifty robbers in Leicestershire. James Coterel concentrated his activities in Derbyshire, and William Beckwith was reputed to have a gang of several hundred outlaws in Yorkshire.

Large groups of brigands were not the rule, however. Most outlaw bands in medieval England had only a few members, often from the same family. The common people apparently regarded these gangs with a mixture of fear and admiration. Ordinary bandits seldom sustained their criminal activities for more than a few years despite close ties to those in positions of local power.[28] While the nobility rarely became brigands themselves, they sometimes hired brutal and vicious men to suppress peasant uprisings. Outlaws were typically arrested if located, rather than slain during the pursuit.[29] With some frequency they even managed, probably through the instigation of their powerful friends, to obtain pardons and appointments as minor local officials.

Outlawry became a common means of dealing with all types of fugitives. Its extension to routine offenses, such as trespass, was even followed by eventual recognition in civil courts. The process permitted legal seizure of another's property. Outlawry in civil matters endured in England for hundreds of years and was not formally abolished until 1879.[30]

The court records of Lincolnshire reveal some of the practices of fourteenth-century criminal justice. Between 1381 and 1396, 483 felons were indicted. Eighty-one eventually went to trial, twenty-three apparently were convicted, five received death sentences, and outlawry was the outcome in all of the remaining cases. Lesser offenders received similar treatment. On the charge of trespass, with 589 accused, almost half were outlawed.[31]

The overall efficiency of justice was deplorable, and in at least one respect it was similar to that in the United States today: only a small minority of criminals eventually were caught and punished. As stated in a famous exposition of early common law, "we are speaking of no rarity; the number of men outlawed at every eyre is very large; ten men are outlawed for one who is hanged."[32]

The prevalence of crime in medieval England was probably paralleled by offenses against the church. These violations were judged by canon rather than common law, with an ultimate extreme sanction of excommunication. Beside deprivation of all Christian rites and anticipated damnation, this meant isolation from society. No one was permitted to pray, eat, or even talk with the excommunicate.

However severe its own penalties, the church offered a very important benefit to fugitives from the king's justice. It provided sanctuary, a concept descended from ancient doctrines allowing a chieftain to prevent disorder in his immediate presence. Once marked by the distance of a spear throw, the limits were gradually expanded and endured until the seventeenth century. Sanctuary extended two thousand paces, about one mile, in all directions from cathedrals and one thousand paces from consecrated churches. These points were sometimes marked by stone crosses along major roads, and heavy penalties attached to anyone breaking the ecclesiastical peace and seizing a fugitive under its protection.[33]

Sanctuary, however, remained a limited privilege. Neighboring villagers had a duty to prevent escape while a coroner attempted negotiations. The fugitive could, during a period of forty days, agree to plead innocence and stand trial. If he remained within sanctuary at the end of the time permitted, all food was denied him. Hunger would then force surrender.

But there was another choice: the fugitive might admit guilt and "abjure the realm":

Should he choose the latter course he swore to go forth from the realm of England, and not to return thither except with the licence of the lord the King or of his heirs. The criminal might name the port from which he was to pass to another country. Dressed in pilgrim's garb—barefooted, bareheaded, ungirt, and clothed only in his shirt, and in his hand a wooden cross, the warrant of Holy Church—he was compelled to journey in the King's highway, deviating only in case of great necessity or for a night's lodging, never delaying anywhere for two nights, and refraining from entertaining himself, so that he might reach the port by the appointed day. Arriving there, he was to cross the sea as soon as he found a ship, unless delayed by the weather. No ship being obtainable, each day he had to wade into the sea up to his knees or his neck to show that although willing he was unable to cross. He had to sleep on the beach, and if he failed to sail by the appointed time it became necessary to find fresh sanctuary. The act of abjuration worked a forfeiture of his chattels, and caused his lands to be escheated. Should he return he was treated as an outlaw. But every man clings sturdily to a whole skin; for while life remains all is not lost. Hanging is a sharp argument, and one jumps not at the humour of it. Strange figures must these proscripts have cut in the eye of the rude villagers; these ragged, barefooted, bareheaded wayfarers, posting along the King's highway, in rain or sun, among the downs and tillage. For themselves, rural loveliness had lost its charm. Their eyes dwelt not on flowers and green fields, but furtively would spy for hideous scaffolds around which screamed the wind and the birds. And their cheeks would blanch as they hurried by these gibbets with their human burdens swinging helplessly in the blast,—for had they themselves not shaved the gallows?[34]

The grim lot of the fugitive stands in sharp contrast to the daring life portrayed in outlaw legend. Then, as now, fact and fiction reveal completely different worlds. Those facing outlawry in medieval England were typically common criminals, not romantic rebels.[35] Yet legend never died; it merely changed to fit different social needs. New refuges for outlaws seemed ever destined to appear, whether geographic or marked only by the borders of imagination.

Early in the fifteenth century the story of Owain Glyn Dwr (Owen Glendower) added credence to the enduring myth of the downtrodden rising against foreign oppression. According to legend, this educated Welsh gentleman was wronged by an English noble and finally accepted leadership of the resistance. Supposedly possessed of supernatural powers, Glyn Dwr took mighty Conway castle, besieged Caernarfon, and summoned an independent parliament for Wales at Machynlleth in 1404. The English, nevertheless, finally proved too strong and crushed the dream of the Welsh freedom. Glyn Dwr followed the route of Hereward into outlaw legend: he disappeared from history and became part of a national culture. Use of outlawry decreased during the fifteenth and sixteenth centuries. Tens of thousands underwent the formal process annually in the reign of Richard II, while only a few hundred did so yearly under the Tudors.[36] Meantime, the legendary bandit grew in stature. The outlaw of myth was a man of the people who fought oppression and turned to crime because of persecution and provocation. This daring trickster had a good heart, enjoyed widespread support, and attempted to right wrongs. He was betrayed when routine methods failed to bring him to corrupt justice. Yet he survived under an assumed name, or through supernatural means, as both a moral warning and a model of resistance to tyranny.

By the end of the medieval times, basic elements of the outlaw legend had become well entrenched. The story of Owain Glyn Dwr was but one of many illustrations. A long line of distinguished fugitives graphically illustrated the enduring strength of this antihero epic. From Hereward through Robin and Wallace to Glyn Dwr stretched the myth of the wronged man fighting oppression.

Although contradicted by evidence of numerous criminals committing serious crimes, the legend has never died. The outlaw may well represent danger and deviance, but he also signifies independence and strength. Coming centuries would bring changes to these themes, as would the crossing of seas and oceans. Throughout, the peculiar myth of the good-bad man was destined to survive in ballad and book, play and film, confounding concepts of justice, contributing to disorder, and preserving ideals of freedom.

CHAPTER 2

The Pirate

Rogues will swear anything.

—WILLIAM KIDD

OVER the west gate of Galway appears an inscription: "From the fury of the O'Flaherties, good Lord deliver us." Dating from 1549, this prayer referred to the greatest threat faced by trading centers: pirates. In this instance the danger came from a notable clan of robbers who dominated much of Connaught for three hundred years.

Raiders from the sea were not unique to Ireland. For centuries isolated ports throughout the world lived in fear of attack by pirate captains, and ships often sailed in danger of seizure by rovers. These oceanic outlaws struck terror seldom equaled by their counterparts on land and cast a peculiarly dark and lingering shadow on the bandit image.

Late in the eighth century the Britons first encountered the horror of vicious, organized raids from the sea. The attackers came from Scandinavia and relied on surprise, force, and ruthlessness for success. The English called them Vikings, from the Norse word *vikingr,* for "sea rover" or "pirate." These raiders plundered, almost at will, for generations.

The Vikings founded many of Ireland's cities and ravaged the country until they were defeated by the legendary high king Brian Ború in 1014. In England they achieved even greater success, systematically terrorizing and collecting enormous sums through extortion. Furthermore, they expanded the scope of the Western world. Vikings occupied Iceland, and in 982 an outlaw banished to that new colony sailed farther across the Atlantic to discover Greenland. His son, Leif Eriksson, then helped extend the line of settlement another thousand miles to North America. Thus the Vikings who began as pirates became the first Europeans to discover the New World.

Political design and piracy were often difficult to distinguish. The Vikings appeared as a separate society, but to their victims they seemed to be criminals intent upon pillage and destruction. Their legacy was one of fear.

Viking raids stopped by the eleventh century, but new forms of piracy soon appeared. The English Channel became a favorite hunting ground for sea rovers. As trade developed, opportunities for robbery increased, and with it the new and related variety of crime called smuggling grew in significance.

Taxes on imported goods were onerous and annoying, so shadowy and somewhat sinister figures with ways of avoiding these duties emerged as major factors in local economies. In some circumstances these men operated on the edge of illegality; in others they served as essential connections between pirates and powerful merchants. Both patterns were to be repeated frequently for centuries.

Before the Norman Conquest, Edward the Confessor granted special privileges to the harbors of Hastings, Romney, Hythe, Dover, and Sandwich in southeast England. In return for maintenance of ships, freedom from taxation was extended. The villages became known as the Cinque Ports and played a major role in the development of smuggling and piracy for eight centuries. Norman and later kings not only continued to recognize these privileges, but gradually increased the number of Cinque Ports until there were thirty-two.[1]

Smuggling was probably the major means of commerce through the harbors of Kent and Sussex from the eleventh through the fourteenth centuries. Illegally imported alcohol became a common item of trade, and those responsible for contraband were treated with respect or even honor by local people.[2] As smuggling became socially acceptable, attitudes toward piracy also began to change. So long as sea raiders attacked only others, they might be tolerated, and when they brought financial opportunities, their ships were most welcome. The pirates had begun the strange process of transformation from a pure source of terror to one mixed with romantic appeal. They became a special, privileged criminal class. Furthermore, a peculiar pattern of indirect government approval developed. It confused issues for hundreds of years.

During the 1280s, Edward I began issuing letters of marque, authorizing private ships to make reprisals against the trade of other nations. These commissions were little more than an approval of piracy, so long as it targeted the intended political objectives. The term *privateer* came into use to distinguish a captain operating under such an authorization. Collectively, they turned piracy into both a business and an instrument of national policy.

Sea raiders had a pronounced influence on history. English pirates accidentally captured James Stuart, heir to the Scottish throne, and Henry IV held him hostage for nearly twenty years. On the other hand, Scotland employed its own pirates against England, the best known of whom was Andrew Barton, with his name changed to Henry Martin in one of the oldest surviving outlaw ballads.[3]

The sixteenth century brought dramatic changes. Piracy flourished throughout the British Isles, with hundreds of crewmen organized under powerful captains. John Callice maintained his headquarters at Cardiff in Wales. It was a convenient location; Callice's father-in-law served as high sheriff.[4] And in the farthest reaches of Ireland the real pirate chieftain Grace O'Malley (Donal O'Flaherty's widow) held sway. Her meeting with Queen Elizabeth I in 1593 still remains a subject of mystery and legend.[5]

One reaction to flourishing piracy was the first English statute covering the subject. Admiralty courts had assumed criminal jurisdiction in the fourteenth century, and they regarded robbery at sea as an offense against all countries and men; principles of Roman, rather than common, law applied. In 1536 this system was modified, with depredations on the high seas made a statutory crime.[6] Admiralty courts were strengthened and reorganized to deal with various accusations and retained jurisdiction in England until 1834.

Although not specifically defined, piracy was clearly accepted as a unique crime properly punishable by any country:

Pirate, in Latin, pirata, from the Greek . . . as transcendo mare, of roving upon the sea; and therefore, in English, is called a rover and robber upon the sea. . . . [T]hey are in the law hostes humani generis, enemies, not of one nation, or of one sort of people only, but of all mankind. They are outlawed . . . by the laws of all nations; that is, out of the protections of all princes, and of all laws whatsoever. Everybody is commissioned, and is to be armed against them as rebels and traitors to subdue and root them out. That which is called robbing upon the highway, the same being done upon the water, is called piracy.[7]

In the peculiar heritage of outlawry, however, formal action seems partly contradicted by social force. Piracy was denounced and prosecuted while being encouraged and praised in a different guise. Sixteenth-century England may have publicly despised its pirates, but it dearly loved its privateers.

As Spain occupied and developed a vast empire in the New World, fantastic opportunities for sea rovers appeared. Slow-moving shipments of incredible value were sent routinely from such ports as Cartagena and Vera Cruz. Such cargoes proved a temptation impossible to resist by captains from the Netherlands, France, and England, who turned the Caribbean into a breeding ground for piracy's golden age.

Of all of England's daring sixteenth-century sea dogs, the name of Francis Drake stands supreme. This "deare Pyrat" of Queen Elizabeth I may be best remembered for his role in the defeat of the Spanish Armada in 1588, but as a privateer his fantastic three-year voyage around the world stands unsurpassed.[8] Between 1577 and 1580, Drake crossed the Atlantic, plundered Spanish settlements on the Pacific coast of South and North America, destroyed ships, visited the bay near San Francisco that bears his name, and became the first Englishman to circumnavigate the globe. By the time his ship, the *Golden Hind,* finally returned to England, she reportedly had carried thirty-five tons of gold and silver and repaid the voyage's secret backers at a rate of forty-seven to one.[9]

Drake and his fellow privateers cut a brilliant swath through English maritime history and left a popular image of at least one type of sea rover who could easily be considered heroic rather than criminal. Portrayed as not only bold and successful but also courtly and gallant, they contrasted totally with the raiders operating around the British Isles. Here was the romantic good contrasted with the frightening bad. During the seventeenth century the sometimes artful distinction between privateer and pirate became still more confused. Each period of warfare among the colonial powers seemed to leave a legacy of disorder in the Caribbean, and the wealth of the Spanish Main continued to tempt privateers to cross the thin line to outright piracy. A new name was then applied to these robbers of the sea.

The Indians on Hispaniola had long used small structures called *boucans* to smoke meat. Colonists, hunters, and herdsmen resorted to the same places and methods for preparing their food. Early in the seventeenth century some of them used canoes to attack passing ships; this conduct gradually expanded into the routine business of piracy, and its practitioners became known as buccaneers. When Spain attempted to crush these assorted French, Dutch, and English outlaws, they established centers of operation on Tortuga and Jamaica. The buccaneers organized the Brethren of the Main and became a powerful force in the Caribbean, answerable to no country, for two generations.

The pirates functioned with far more control than is generally believed. They usually had a commission issued by the local colonial governor, who typically received 10 percent of all profits in return. Payments or proportions due members of the crew were specified in formal articles of agreement, with special provisions for those suffering loss of limbs. The captain did not rule with iron discipline; outside actual battle, a form of democracy prevailed. Crews consisted of an assortment of deserters, mutineers,

escaped slaves, discontented indentured servants, and men simply in search of personal gain. Buccaneers attached little significance to race or nationality; individual ability was paramount.

The giant galleon beloved in fiction rarely served as a pirate
vessel. A typical ship used by English buccaneers was a low-
decked brigantine, clean and fast. She carried an average crew of
sixty and about seven guns. The men on board probably included
veterans of three navies, many wars, and countless battles at sea.
Sometimes operating in association with other pirate ships, they
wreaked havoc on Spanish shipping and ports and in time preyed
on victims from all nations.[10]

The buccaneers thrived on Tortuga and then dominated Jamaica, with Port Royal emerging as their principal market for
stolen goods. It also served as a convenient location for arranging
ransom for prisoners. While torture to extract information frequently occurred, no clear evidence of wholesale brutality and
abuse exists. Female prisoners normally were treated with civility
and handled as items of potential value. Buccaneering was a business, but one of unusual risk and danger. The pirates seldom surrendered; they knew death would almost surely result.[11]

One name became almost synonymous with exploits on the
Spanish Main: Henry Morgan. He was born in Wales and became
a notorious privateer with a particular knack for plundering wealthy Spanish communities. Morgan looted Puerto Principe in
Cuba, Maracaibo in Venezuela, Portobelo and Panama City in
Panama, but his notorious activities clearly went beyond the limits expected of buccaneers. Arrested for piracy, he was sent to
England in chains. There, Charles II granted him a pardon and
added a knighthood. In 1675, Morgan returned to Jamaica in
triumph as deputy governor. During the next several years he
assisted, to a questionable degree, in the hunt for his former
pirate colleagues. He died quietly in Jamaica in 1688 and
became a basis for the popular tale of the pardoned and rewarded
outlaw.

As Morgan enjoyed his position and notoriety, the image of
the buccaneer was abruptly frozen in the public mind; the view
has remained unchanged for three hundred years. This occurred

because of a remarkable and controversial book. It first appeared in Amsterdam in 1678 as *De Americaensche Zee-Rovers* under the authorship of Alexander Oliver Exquemelin. Within three years the book was translated into Spanish as *Piratas de la America* and three years after that into English as *The Buccaneers of America*. The London edition anglicized the author's name to John Esquemeling and quickly became the standard reference on seventeenth-century buccaneering.

Exquemelin, "who himself, of necessity, was present at all these acts of plunder" according to the original title page, remains a figure of mystery. The book revealed little of the author but clearly focused on the Spanish Main from 1666 to 1675. Today Exquemelin is generally believed to have gone from the Netherlands to Tortuga as an indentured servant of the French West Indies Company. When freed, he worked for several years with the pirates as a barber and surgeon. Returning to the Netherlands, Exquemelin then published his remarkable book, blending events he witnessed with those of which he had indirect but still uncommon knowledge.

The Buccaneers of America was widely accepted as providing an unprecedented and accurate view of piracy. Through it, many English and American readers saw the buccaneer as an oceanic Robin Hood, preying upon the rich and wicked supporters of the Spanish Inquisition—targets remarkably similar to those of Sherwood Forest's own legendary bandit. Moreover, this popular book was no dry treatise on crime. It contained many titillating descriptions of sex and sadism, qualities which undoubtedly contributed to its enduring popularity.

Exquemelin dealt to a considerable degree with "Henry Morgan's inflamed lust."[12] The buccaneer chieftain was described as having more than a natural interest in beauteous, chaste, and unclad Spanish *señoritas*. But such portrayals led to problems; Exquemelin soon found himself named as a defendant in a libel suit, with the "reformed pirate" as plaintiff.

Despite its exaggerations and capitalizations on the public's possibly base interests, the book achieved a sustained and resounding success. In addition to unending reprints, *The Bucca-*

neers of America has served as an essential source, acknowledged or not, for scores of later writers. Through it "the buccaneer has become established as a stock figure in our romantic mythology. Anarchistic, untrammeled, extravagant, sadistic, a crack shot and wildly courageous."[13]

Exquemelin, perhaps consciously, provided relatively few specific details of historic note. Those furnished have proved quite accurate when compared with documentary records. Yet *The Buccaneers of America* became a key link in the complex outlaw image and itself an integral part of popular history. Exquemelin's exposition substituted for reality and obviously met an enduring demand. As a knowing disciple wrote nearly a century ago, "it is generally difficult to find any actual data, any tangible history of the popular villain-hero. . . . [A]s a rule any positive material passes quickly away and is lost in the oblivion of past things. . . . [I]t is only in popular romance and fiction that their name and fame is embalmed and preserved."[14]

Whether or not Exquemelin's book served as a significant cause, its publication coincided with increasing efforts to curtail piracy in the Caribbean. James II dispatched a squadron of warships under Robert Holmes to the West Indies with orders to destroy the buccaneers. A new governor of Jamaica, Thomas Lynch, began an active campaign of eradication. Port Royal, the favorite haunt of pirates for decades, was destroyed in 1692 by an earthquake, only to be followed by a particularly violent series of storms. These natural disasters led, incidentally, to the sea's claiming the grave of Henry Morgan.

Then, in 1698, Parliament passed a significant statute entitled "An Act for the More Effectuall Suppression of Piracy." This law made those encouraging, aiding, or concealing pirates triable as accessories. Furthermore, it permitted the establishment of admiralty courts with criminal jurisdiction in the colonies and clarified the question of privateering by providing that "if any of his Majesties . . . subjects . . . shall commit piracy or robbery . . . upon the sea under color of any commission from any forreigne prince . . . such offender . . . shall be . . . taken to be pirates felons and robbers."[15] The combined result of these efforts was not an end to piracy, but an important relocation of activities away from the Caribbean to the north. Colonial trials offered convenience and apparent efficiency, but they also opened the way to corruption and conspiracy. A Rhode Island court once acquitted a pirate who accidentally pleaded guilty.[16] The buccaneers took their ships to new, welcoming ports in the Bahamas, Carolina, Pennsylvania, New York, and Massachusetts. Organized crime had come to the North American mainland.

At the end of the sixteenth century, England's colonies along the Atlantic coast were small, isolated, weak, and poor. Threatened by foreign powers, throttled by restrictive trade laws, and governed by political appointees, they viewed the pirates with favor rather than fear. They offered the sea robbers little property to plunder but ample protection from authority. Colonial governors, such as Benjamin Fletcher in New York, William Markham in Pennsylvania, and Philip Ludwell in Carolina, competed with one another in their greed to exchange illegal aid for criminal profit. Many captains of the Royal Navy also displayed notable reluctance in destroying piracy; they commonly received a percentage of cargoes in return for protection during passage. Colonial merchants and local citizens delighted in the contraband made available by the sea raiders. The pirates even provided much needed forms of currency. Before the American Revolution, the most common type of money in the colonies was Spanish coins, nearly all of which had been stolen and illegally imported by the buccaneers.

Frank Brown and John Gerassi tell us: "Pirates were often simply regarded as gentlemanly outlaws."[17] Virtually all of the famous English sea rovers of the period had close associations with the American colonies. Thomas Tew, best known for his exploits in the Indian Ocean, maintained an estate in Rhode Island. James Brown married the governor's daughter and gained a seat in the Pennsylvania assembly. And two other captains were by parallel combinations of events elevated to the ranks of outlaw mythology: John Avery and William Kidd. Their careers as pirates, though brief, became foundations of legend.

John Avery, alias Henry Every and nicknamed Long Ben,

was born in Devon. As a sailor he apparently followed an increasingly popular path leading from mutiny to piracy and departed the Caribbean for the Indian Ocean. There he acquired an enormous treasure by capturing the *Rampura,* an Indian vessel bound with pilgrims to Mecca. Within a few months, Avery became a pirate of rare fame and wealth. He went to Massachusetts and secured the governor's protection in 1696. Shortly thereafter, Avery vanished.

This "Grand Pirate" naturally became a popular subject for conjecture. One story found him living under an assumed name on a huge estate in Ireland. Another version left him to enjoy his wealth on New England's frontier. But the most imaginative and best remembered tale crystallized in an influential play, *The Successful Pyrate,* first performed in 1712 at London's Theatre Royal in Drury Lane. Avery was portrayed as having captured with that treasure ship an enchanting Indian princess (daughter of the Great Mugul) who naturally became his loving bride. Together they reigned as king and queen on Madagascar (an actual pirate refuge at the time).

Daniel Defoe added to Avery's fame by 1720 making him the hero of two books: *The King of Pirates* and *The Life of Captain Singleton.* No one can be certain as to the true end of the story. Today, authorities tend to accept a far from romantic climax. It has Avery returning to England in secret, exhausting his treasure with bribes to officials, and dying in poverty near his place of birth.[18] The theatrical version naturally proved more appealing.

William Kidd will probably always remain the most controversial of all pirates. A native of Scotland, he became a respected ship's master in Atlantic trade. Kidd married Sarah Oort in New York and operated a packet line between the American colonies and England. Then, about 1695, he was approached by Richard Coote, the earl of Bellomont, with a peculiar proposal. Coote apparently represented several notable secret partners in England who sought a captain for a specially built privateering vessel, the *Adventure.* Kidd accepted the position, probably with a promise of protection, and embarked for the Indian Ocean in 1696. His mission may have been to seek and destroy actual pirates, to take prizes representing powers not friendly to England, or to gain fortune in any possible way. Within two years, ships returning from the region brought disquieting rumors. Perhaps confused by recent exploits of Avery, the public came to view Kidd as an outrageous pirate destroying vessels of all flags.

He undoubtedly seized a Moorish ketch, the *Quedah Merchant,* with a great deal of treasure, but then ran the *Adventure* aground on Madagascar. When most of the crew deserted, Kidd sailed on in the captured ship. This he exchanged for a small sloop at Hispaniola and proceeded with only twelve remaining men up the Atlantic coast. Rumors of the pirate's coming spread throughout the colonies. When Kidd reached Boston in 1699, the earl of Bellomont, now a colonial governor, placed him under arrest.[19]

Sent to London, he faced trial in atmosphere of political tension and much public interest. Drunk during testimony, Kidd claimed that the *Quedah Merchant* carried French passes which made his action privateering rather than piracy. But no such documents were produced, and several witnesses appeared against him.[20] Convicted along with six of his crew, the "Great Rogue Kidd" was executed in 1701. Outlaws ordinarily faced hanging at Tyburn (now Marble Arch), but in this instance a special gibbet at Wapping found use. According to the traditional practice, Kidd's corpse was chained to a post until the tides flowed over it three times. Next, the pirate's body was coated with tar, placed in a metal harness, hung once more on the gibbet, and allowed to remain there until eventually destroyed by sun and rain, with assistance from hungry birds.

Captain Kidd's story did not end. Most of the pirates convicted with him were promptly pardoned or bribed their way to freedom. A ballad, using the name Robert rather than William and reflecting the cruelty perhaps falsely associated with him, achieved remarkable popularity. Sarah, the pirate captain's widow, married a prominent politician and moved to New Jersey. Countless reports of buried treasure and ghostly sightings began to appear from Florida to Massachusetts.

"For some inexplicable reason," wrote John S. C. Abbott, "while hundreds of other events of vastly greater movement have passed in oblivion, the name of Captain Kidd, from that hour to this, has been almost a household word in both England and America."[21] A final note: the missing documents so important to the defense (possibly hidden by the earl of Bellomont) were discovered in London's Public Record Office in 1911. History had its greatest pirate, who was an innocent dupe or incredibly inept and was almost never portrayed as either.

Captain Kidd inaugurated an era of pronounced criminal activity in the waters just off the American Atlantic coast. Some fifteen hundred pirates were soon at work, typically slipping out to sea in small, fast sloops to attack passing merchant vessels. They could not contend with English men-of-war, but their shallow draft permitted escape into rivers and inlets when challenged. The pirates kept these fleet ships (commonly and significantly named *Revenge*) in excellent condition, careening them with frequency and sometimes removing all possible structures above deck. And they employed a special flag to indicate their criminal vocation.

Derived from an old English symbol for death, the skull and crossbones on a black background was a simplification of entire skeletons employed on some earlier banners. An interesting but almost certainly false legend has the pirates' flags traditionally made by a sailmaker's widow in Nassau. Moreover, the emblem was not originally called the Jolly Roger, a term probably derived from *joli rouge* and used in reference to the red ensigns of French *filibusters* operating from Martinique.

The colonial pirates became particularly active in Carolina some fifteen years before the division of the colony into North and South Carolina. For a time, Charles Town became host to the foremost outlaws of the Western world. Furthermore, they began to acquire an increasingly widespread reputation for cruelty while losing the romantic aura enjoyed by the buccaneers. These changes may well be related to attention focused upon the most feared of all American pirates: Blackbeard.

His true name may have been Thatch or Tach or Teach or Hyde or Drummond. He may have been born in England or Virginia or Jamaica. He may have been incredibly wanton or the

Blackbeard, America's most feared pirate, from
Daniel Defoe, *History of the Pyrates,* 1724.

crafty creator of a frightful image. Active under his assumed and
cultivated nickname for only two years, Blackbeard added an
ugly facet to American piracy. An insolent, lustful, brutal, and
calculating drunkard, he still enjoyed obvious encouragement
and support from corrupt Carolina authorities. Stories about him
abounded, even in his time. He routinely killed and buried
someone with treasure so that a ghost would guard the spot. He

was married fourteen times but kept one sixteen-year-old bride in chains before giving her to the crew. The pirate wore smoldering fuses in his wild hair and beard to resemble even more closely a figure from hell.[22]

Whatever the bases of truth in such tales, the nearby colony of Virginia finally had enough of Blackbeard. In 1718, Gov. Alexander Spotswood dispatched two hired sloops on a secret mission. Lt. Robert Maynard, borrowed from the Royal Navy, was to command an attack on Blackbeard's protected stronghold at Ocracoke Inlet in Carolina. The battle lasted only a few minutes but resulted in terrible carnage. Blackbeard "stood his ground and fought with great fury till he had received five and twenty wounds and five of them by shot."[23] His head was severed and placed on a bowsprit (the decapitated body reportedly swam away when thrown in the water). Taken to Virginia, the large and rotting skull hung for years on a pole by the Hampton River at a place still known as Blackbeard's Point. In time, it was removed and fashioned into a punch bowl for use at Williamsburg's Raleigh Tavern. Blackbeard's demise attracted attention throughout the colonies; none other than Benjamin Franklin wrote and printed for sale a song celebrating the event.[24]

Papers recovered after the battle clearly established the corruption of Carolina's governor, Charles Eden, and its chief justice, Tobias Knight. Neither was convicted, while disputes over recovered booty and claims for rewards continued for years. Blackbeard's ghost, usually without head, is still often reported along the Carolina coast. Hunts for his buried treasure continue to this day.

Blackbeard's chief gunner, Israel Hands, provided evidence after the battle at Ocracoke Inlet and received a pardon. He is believed to have died a beggar in London, but he lived on in literature. Robert Louis Stevenson made Hands a major character in his classic *Treasure Island*. As for the pirate captain, J. C. Cross featured him in *Black Beard; or, the Captive Princess,* a popular London play of 1798. It allowed a maiden to be rescued from the fiend by her fiancé. Even drama could not make Blackbeard a hero.

Colonial America featured many other pirates. Edward Low, Samuel Bellamy, and Stede Bonnet each achieved his own branch of notoriety, but the strange machinations of legend relied to a surprising degree on the exploits of two women, Anne Bonny and Mary Read. They established the thin foundation for the gorgeous female pirate theme so much beloved by writers of fiction.

Despite the presence of some seventy crews, the tide was beginning to run against sea rovers in American waters. Woodes Rogers, a former privateer, served as unsalaried governor of the Bahamas from 1717 until his death in 1732. He skillfully combined an aggressive campaign of elimination with the offer of a general pardon. This encouraged many pirates to abandon lives of crime and keep their loot without fear of legal reprisal.[25]

Still, the most significant step toward reduction of the menace was taken through an act of Parliament in 1721. Striking at the roots of crime, it used a method that has proved to be singularly effective over the centuries. A provision in the law permitted all people knowingly trading with pirates to be tried and punished as such; indirect profiteers from robbery at sea might be given the death penalty. For the first time, respectable merchants, who had often encouraged and even financed the sea rovers, faced a serious threat of prosecution.[26]

Revocation of proprietary charters in the colonies apparently led to the appointment of honest officials. Meanwhile, pirate attacks on ordinary shipping caused a gradual change in public attitude. Settlers became irritated when even letters to and from their home countries were routinely lost at sea,[27] and so, gradually, "England and her colonies put behind them the idea that they could afford crime better than they could afford an adequate police force . . . once a congenial atmosphere was eliminated, piracy collapsed of its own weight."[28]

It did not, however, quickly disappear. The pirates of the Atlantic coast left a vivid and lasting impression on history through fact and fiction. Without doubt, they were the first great American outlaws, associating England's colonies with crime and violence of a particularly dramatic and romantic visage. The brigand had become an integral part of the American scene generations before the birth of the United States.

The enduring image of the dashing but terrifying pirate was fixed in large part, and probably forever, by a book entitled *A General History of the Pyrates*. First published in 1724 by the firm of Charles Rivington in St. Paul's Churchyard, London, it soon became popular throughout the Western world and the only rival to *The Buccaneers of America*.

A General History of the Pyrates, with subtitles of more than two hundred words, concentrated on the period from 1717 to 1724 and artfully surveyed dramatic instances of American piracy. In truth, the volume was rather deficient on fact and remarkably strong on fiction. It soon appeared in several languages and a succession of new and expanded editions.[29] *A General History of the Pyrates* thus emerged as a singularly important reference, although it was riddled with errors and misinterpretations. Virtually all subsequent portrayals of American sea rovers begin, and many also end, with this book.

It has been said that "pirates mostly died young and left few descendants."[30] They purposefully maintained almost no written records, and reliable contemporary accounts of their activities are rare. Consequently, a well-written popular volume appearing at an opportune time easily determined the flow of interpretive history. As has happened on many occasions in the course of the outlaw legend, a journalistic publication with little scholarly pretention emerged as the source of unending myth. *A General History of the Pyrates* contained images and generalizations which are now assumed as unquestionably authentic. Of just such is the brigand's story.

A Captain Charles Johnson was recorded as the author of *A General History of the Pyrates*. Today, authorities tend to believe it to have been a pen name for one of the greatest English authors of the time, Daniel Defoe. There was, however, a real Captain Charles Johnson who hunted buccaneers in the Caribbean in the late seventeenth century.[31] It is possible that he either wrote the book or at least contributed to Defoe's efforts.

Whatever its true authorship, *A General History of the Pyrates* created an outlaw archetype. The bloodthirsty and picturesque pirate occupied a principal role in the ongoing development of a darkening myth. His gory specter haunts the collective memory with a strange mixture of horrifying excitement and romantic fascination. He represents, perhaps better than any other, an imagined time when might could indeed become right and the mutineer transform himself into a captain of the ocean waves with a treasure-laden vessel and a seductive princess lying just beyond the horizon.

In fact, "pirates were a sorry lot of human trash."[32] Preying upon the weak and innocent, they caused great suffering and loss, yet their undeniably daring life of adventure and their relentless quest for wealth continue to hold a perplexing appeal. Perhaps more clearly than with any other type of outlaw, the pirate poses the elemental question of why we are attracted to banditry. The clearest answer may still be found in the 1891 rhetorical queries of a master of the image, Howard Pyle:

Why is it that the pirate has, and always has had, a certain lurid glamour of the heroical enveloping him round about? Is there, deep within the accumulated debris of culture, a hidden groundwork of the old-time savage? Is there even in these well-regulated times an unsubdued nature in the respectable mental household of every one of us that still kicks against the pricks of law and order?[33]

Bases for obvious conclusions on such issues are, however, as poorly defined as the brigand's trail. The pirate is known to us less by his acts than by the efforts of writers to promote and capitalize upon his fame. He has become, as have other notable outlaws, a figure shrouded by myth and a part of legend.

Such was uniquely true of William Kidd. The American Revolution helped transform him from a crazed brigand of the seas into a mysterious dreamer linked to the spirit of independence. He began the new nation's continuing line of preeminent outlaws. Between 1824 and 1849, Washington Irving, J. S. Jones, Edgar Allan Poe, Samuel Judah, and James Fenimore Cooper made Kidd a favorite figure in stories, plays, and novels. He was identified as the "Wizard of the Sea" and the "Flying Dutchman of the Western World," usually seen in conflict with a handsome naval officer attempting to save the lovely young heroine. The pirate captain's ballad became a hymn of lament at concerts and camp meetings. As "Billy Kidd, King of the Kikaroos," the sea rover even appeared in humorous popular song in minstrel shows and music halls.[34] Subsequent generations would hear much about an outlaw from the American Southwest with a remarkably similar name.

CHAPTER 3

The Highwayman

Life is a jest and all things show it.
I thought so once, and now I know it.

—EPITAPH OF JOHN GAY, WESTMINSTER ABBEY

CRIME was a major problem in the British Isles for centuries. Robbery, perjury, and corruption were common during the Tudor era; Wales retained its reputation as a haven for outlaws. According to John Coatman, "with the destruction of the monasteries [under Henry VIII and Elizabeth I] . . . the flood-gates of vagabondage, and its attendant crimes of every kind were opened. Legislation against sturdy mendicants and rogues became common."[1]

Of the many tales of crime, perhaps the most appalling came from Scotland early in the seventeenth century. Over a score of years, there had been rumors of an outlaw band led by Sawney Beane and of the mysterious disappearance of numerous citizens. Finally, as king of Scotland, James I personally directed a great manhunt involving hundreds of searchers and hounds. South of Glasgow they discovered a cave containing dried and pickled human limbs. Sawney Beane and his extended family, including fourteen children and thirty-two grandchildren, "all born in incest," were captured and convicted of robbery, murder, and cannibalism. The hands and legs of the men were amputated and they slowly bled to death. The women were forced to witness this punishment, then executed by burning.[2] Stories of Sawney Beane were modified over the years and probably contributed to the false legend of Sweeney Todd, London's "demon barber."

The late seventeenth and early eighteenth centuries were distinguished by the rise and popularity of a new and important variety of outlaw. He haunted the developing road systems of England, stopped public stagecoaches, and committed highway robbery. Well dressed, often polite, and mounted on a fine horse, this "gentleman bandit" had a major influence on the brigand's image. A great favorite of balladeers and poets and novelists, the English highwayman would become a preeminent model for portrayals of American outlawry.

The so-called knights of the road gained prominence during the Cromwellian Protectorate and were frequently pictured as disillusioned former royalist officers. Perhaps most notable among them was "that grand thief of England," James Hind. The son of a saddler in Oxfordshire, he reputedly assisted in Charles II's escape to France. Hind remained in England, cultivated the manners of a gentleman, and acquired singular fame as a highwayman. His polite and considerate treatment of victims was combined with daring and wit; in fact, he once ambushed the Lord Protector himself, Oliver Cromwell. Hind also became the subject of a popular ballad, "Captain Hind's Progress and Ramble."

One story of this noted highwayman deserves retelling, for it illustrates both the esteem in which he was held and the durability of themes in outlaw legend. Briefly, Hind discovers a poor innkeeper who is unable to repay twenty pounds he owes a Warwick moneylender and therefore is facing arrest as a debtor. The kindhearted highwayman provides the necessary sum from his own frequently replenished purse. Later, Hind waylays the usurer and regains his twenty pounds with a large additional amount to boot.[3]

The familiarity of this tale is in itself illuminating. The poor innkeeper actually appeared some five centuries earlier as a destitute knight in *A Gest of Robyn Hode*. Then, it was the famous forest bandit who first provided funds, only to rob them back from a greedy abbot. More than 220 years after Hind's adventures, the innkeeper and knight became a poverty-stricken Missouri widow, with the highwayman's role being taken by Jesse James; the abbot and moneylender had become a heartless banker. The same basic story has been and undoubtedly will be told of many other brigands. While no reliable evidence ever appeared to indicate that Robin Hood, James Hind, or Jesse James actually took part in such an escapade, the tale is self-perpetuating. Despite any basis in fact, it has become accepted history, with the poor and the greedy easily altered to meet changing social conditions.

As for the real James Hind, his career as a highwayman was quite brief. After participating in an abortive effort to restore the monarchy, he was discovered in London living under an assumed name in 1651. He was promptly tried, convicted, and executed. Significantly, however, he died under the charge of treason rather than robbery.

Ensuing decades saw no decline in the activity of highwaymen. They infested the roads outside London, often enjoying the sporting activities available in the city, but "no thoroughfare was free from the tyranny of the fraternity of highwaymen, who were allowed to terrorize whole districts, and who enjoyed almost unlimited freedom from interference."[4]

Outstanding among the new wave of "road inspectors" was the romantic figure of Claude Duval (or Du Vall). The background of this colorful, dashing character remains a mystery. According to a favorite version, Duval was born in Normandy in 1643 and came to England as a page of Charles II with restoration of the monarchy in 1660. Within a few years, he turned to a life of crime, but one properly spiced with Gallic charm.[5]

Duval supposedly delighted women of all classes, ages, and degrees of wealth. The dashing highwayman once danced with a lady during a coach robbery on Hounslow Heath (now Heathrow Airport). But his love of women and wine, combined with the offer of a large reward, eventually led to his capture: the rogue was found drunk in a London tavern. Many of his female acquaintances reportedly visited him in prison and sought to secure a pardon in his name, without success. Duval was executed in 1670 and buried in a churchyard at Covent Garden. His epitaph reads in part:

Here lies Du Vall. Reader, if male thou art,
Look to thy purse. If female, to thy heart.
Much havoc has he made of both for all
Men he made stand, and women he made fall.

Within weeks of the highwayman's execution, a professor at
Oxford, William Pope, published a biography describing his
exploits. *Memoirs of Monsieur Du Vall* was, perhaps, written as a
satire on the notoriety accorded criminals; if so, its irony has been
deeper than ever intended. Pope's book became accepted as the
source of virtually all details on Duval's life. Furthermore, *Memoirs of Monsieur Du Vall* initiated a steady flow of popular publications intended to profit from the careers of noted fugitives.

The site of Duval's capture provides another link in the strange
chain between outlaw myths of the distant and recent past. Seizure of the highwayman occurred at a London drinking establishment called Hole-in-the-Wall, a name that extended back in
time to the end of the feudal period and eventually crossed the
Atlantic.

With the development of artillery, medieval fortifications were
rendered obsolete. City walls no longer served as defenses. They
continued as a limited means of social control, providing barriers, especially at night, to denizens of the forests, including
bands of outlaws. But the cities outgrew the walls, and the old
ramparts fell into disrepair. Finally, chinks appeared or were
made in them, allowing people to slip in and out at any hour.
These locations frequently acquired a rather sinister but still fascinating reputation, and such a passage was commonly referred
to as Hole-in-the-Wall.

Vestiges of these locations may yet be found. Half a block
from the traditional site of investiture for princes of Wales, in
Caernarfon, and just outside the castle itself, Hole-in-the-Wall
Street runs parallel to the preserved remains of the city's former
defenses. Five centuries ago the areas adjacent to these narrow
entrances were much frequented by those associated with crime
and vice, for they provided obvious routes of escape. The name
was then transported to new cities, regions, and countries.

During the nineteenth century the most notorious saloon in New York City bore the title Hole-in-the-Wall. Two generations later the name achieved its greatest American fame in an isolated, sparsely populated section of central Wyoming. Hole-in-the-Wall again had come to indicate a place for criminals and outlaws. Despite repeated efforts to associate the designation with some truly unusual geographic phenomenon, it probably related directly back through a dozen generations in a way unknown to the outlaws who used the term.

Derivation of the name of the tavern (Wyoming also had a Hole-in-the-Wall saloon) where a particular highwayman was captured naturally seemed of little significance to anyone actually involved with crime. England confronted a continuing problem of disorder, violence, and robbery. Writes Colin Wilson: "By 1688 the English working classes were alcohol starved. The consumption of gin rose steadily, from half a million gallons around 1690 to . . . nineteen million gallons [by 1750]. The result was a crime wave."[6] Lack of an adequate police system, growth of cities, and a variety of disruptive religious and economic forces provided additional causes. The situation also appeared to be exacerbated by public sympathy, if not actual support, for criminals. To members of the upper class, fugitives from justice were simply disturbing examples of rabble; "the darling of their hearts was the highwayman."[7]

There were many logical reasons for such regard. As portrayed, the highwayman usually had a less-than-genteel background, yet he enjoyed the money and social graces of the privileged few. Furthermore, the highwayman seemed a romantic, daring, and crafty figure. He robbed, and perhaps raped, but very seldom murdered. His victims represented power, wealth, and education. The highwayman was simply a man of the people bettering himself in a most expedient manner and doing no significant harm to ordinary people. At times, he was even thought to demonstrate some of the traits of Robin Hood.

This view had little to do with reality, but it was extremely popular and adeptly cultivated by many writers. The most active and versatile of these is today recalled as the author of *Robinson*

Crusoe, Daniel Defoe. His contribution to the outlaw image, however, remains far less known. Defoe, born the son of a London candle merchant about 1660, failed as a businessman before beginning a remarkable career as an author. During a period of forty years he wrote scores of books and hundreds of lesser items, usually under assumed names.

The "father of the English novel" encountered many serious problems, including erratic earnings and political controversy. In 1702 he published a satirical study entitled *The Shortest-Way with the Dissenters.* For this, Defoe spent several months in prison and received a sentence of exposure in the pillory for three days. The penalty was extremely harsh. Pillorying meant physical abuse by the mob as well as ridicule. Defoe's reaction was to write the most important composition in his career, the bitter and ironic *Hymn to the Pillory.* Its publication had an immediate consequence for the author: upon his appearance in the pillory, Londoners greeted him with cheers and pelted him with flowers instead of garbage and stones.

Nevertheless, punishment apparently had a pronounced if unintended effect. Many of Defoe's later literary efforts concerned criminals, whether highwaymen, pirates, thieves, or prostitutes. His imprisonment gave him access to England's underworld and an unprecedented empathy for its denizens. Biographer Thomas Wright tells us: "Defoe took upon himself to impress his readers how intensely wretched is the career of even the most prosperous rogue. . . . [H]e also points out that it is not sufficient for the criminals themselves to reform, the whole country must reform. . . . [H]is rogues get punished . . . but Defoe feels for them."[8]

In dozens of books Defoe portrayed the most notorious of outlaws, real and imaginary.[9] His casual regard for factual details combined with a truly remarkable writing facility. Furthermore, he knew the nature of crime and fugitives better than any other author of his time. He died in hiding from creditors in 1731.

Some of Defoe's attitudes are reflected in the words of his most famous heroine, the amorous adventuress Moll Flanders (whose husband was a highwayman, transported to America):

I have been told, that in one of our neighbour nations, whether it be in France or where else I know not, they have an order from the king, that when any criminal is condemned, either to die, or to the galleys, or to be transported, if they have any children, as such are generally unprovided for, by the forfeiture of their parents, so they are immediately taken into the care of the government, and put into an hospital called the House of Orphans, where they are bred up, clothed, fed, taught, and when fit to go out, are placed to trades, or to services, so as to be well able to provide for themselves by an honest, industrious behavior.

Had this been the custom in our country, I had not been left a poor desolate girl without friends, without clothes, without help or helper, as was my fate; and by which, I was not only exposed to very great distress, even before I was capable either of understanding my case or how to amend it, but brought into a course of life scandalous in itself, and which in its ordinary courses tended to the swift destruction both of soul and body.[10]

Moll's comments remain as meaningful today as they were in 1722.

Defoe was clearly fascinated by all aspects of crime and directed his interest toward many noted highwaymen. Of these, Jack Sheppard occupies a very special, if personally undeserved, place. He appears to have been a rather common thief, burglar, and robber. But Sheppard did possess an incredible ability to escape from authorities; he broke out of prison on at least five occasions, sometimes with the aid of his accomplice, Elizabeth ("Edgeworth Bess") Lyon. By the time of his final incarceration, the twenty-three-year-old Cockney was a celebrity. As the subject of ballads, stories, and a Drury Lane pantomime, *Harlequin Sheppard* by John Thurmond, he became more widely publicized than any previous highwayman.

Sheppard's 1724 execution at Tyburn drew a crowd of two hundred thousand. Visitors to the condemned's cell at Newgate Prison had included painters William Hogarth and James Thornhill, Defoe (who promptly produced *The History of the Remarkable Life of John Sheppard*), and an aspiring poet named John Gay. The latter would soon elevate the image of the outlaw to yet another level of public acclaim.

Gay, who came from Devon, attempted to earn a living as a silk merchant in London while dabbling in drama and poetry. A friend, Jonathan Swift, humorously proposed that he write a "Newgate pastoral among the Whores and Thieves." Gay turned the suggestion into an innovative comedic play with music, *The Beggar's Opera*. Its radical technical approach, biting social satire, and obvious opportunity for censorship caused London producers to refuse serious consideration. Only through the sustained efforts of Gay's patroness, the Duchess of Queensbury, did *The Beggar's Opera* reach the stage, just outside the city, in 1728.[11] The play achieved phenomenal, widespread, and enduring success. It became a standard theatrical presentation, undergoing numerous revivals and revisions. It initiated the distinguished tradition of musical comedy in New York in 1750 and was largely responsible for development of a vast "robber school" among novelists and dramatists.

As anticipated, *The Beggar's Opera* attracted the censors' ire. It was denounced as glorifying crime and causing improper behavior. Pressure from the courts eventually caused the ending to be modified, with transportation substituted for the martyrdom of hanging, and authorities prevented the production of a sequel, *Polly,* during the remaining years of Gay's life. Still, there is no doubt that "whatever else we may want to say about the much-played piece, *The Beggar's Opera* was written under a lucky star."[12]

Gay had based his characters on real personalities, particularly the accomplices of Jack Sheppard. The most famous role in *The Beggar's Opera* was that of Macheath, a bold highwayman and glamorous rogue. It proved appealing to audiences and actors for generations. Yet, strangely enough, the most acclaimed Macheath was the portrayal offered by a stunning actress, Eliza Bertolozzi Vestris. She first played the role in London in 1820, wearing costumes skillfully designed to reveal "her perfect legs, in the tightest of tight hose."[13] A century later, Bertolt Brecht rewrote *The Beggar's Opera* as *Die Dreigroschenoper,* or *The Three-penny Opera.* Through the music of Kurt Weill, Macheath became famous once again—as Mack the Knife.

John Gay's score for *The Beggar's Opera* was itself quite significant. He based the music on old airs and folk tunes of the British
Isles. One of these, "Lillibulero," has its own distinguished heritage. Apparently first sung and whistled as a kind of a code during the Ulster Rising of 1641, the words were altered to reflect
anti-Irish and anti-Stuart sentiments during the Glorious Revolution of 1688 and its aftermath. Gay then cleverly adapted the
music as a rebel song in *The Beggar's Opera*.[14] The tune eventually
became popular as a military march, particularly for the Royal
Marines and various army regiments during the Napoleonic
Wars. Still later, British engineers adopted it as their anthem.
Today, more people probably listen to "Lillibulero" than any
other music on earth. It is the signature theme for the World Service of the British Broadcasting Corporation. Any shortwave lis-
tener can hear it on the hour immediately following the proudest
announcement on radio: "This is London!"

Daniel Defoe and John Gay developed great public interest in
the romanticized highwayman. Within a few years after their
death, the foremost outlaw of the type dashed upon the scene.
Dick Turpin, the "Prince of Highwaymen," was a handsome
gentleman who dressed in scarlet, carried arms encrusted with
silver, and rode a magnificent black horse.[15] It is, perhaps, a pity
that such a glorious image contains such little truth.

He was in fact a brutal lout described by one reward publication in the following manner: "Richard Turpin, a butcher by
trade, is a tall fresh colored man, very much marked with the
small pox, about five feet nine inches high . . . wears a blue grey
coat and a light natural wig."[16] Nevertheless, he acquired a reputation as an active and daring highwayman throughout Essex and
all of London.

Historical records indicate that Turpin's four-year career ended
rather strangely. He had assumed a name and moved to Yorkshire. Then, under circumstances never satisfactorily explained, a
former teacher recognized the highwayman's handwriting on a
letter mailed to a relative. This led to Turpin's identification,
conviction for horse stealing, and execution at York in 1739. He
walked bravely to the gallows and then affirmed the image of the

Dick Turpin on Black Bess, from *Turpin's Ride to York,* 1839.

outlaw's defiance of death. According to reports of the time, Turpin spoke a few words to the hangman and threw himself off the ladder.[17]

Those with faith in legend know the true story, however. Turpin's end is directly related to that of his great horse, Black Bess. Together they set out upon an epic run to establish an alibi, with authorities in pursuit, from the vicinity of London to York. The distance of nearly two hundred miles was accomplished in one day, but as they approached their destination, Black Bess collapsed and died. As a result, Turpin was captured and hanged.

Doubters point out that no contemporary account of such an event exists. Furthermore, they indicate that a similar ride was ascribed to an earlier highwayman, usually identified as John Nevison and nicknamed Swift Nicks. And some even suggest that Turpin's 1676 journey was an invention of Daniel Defoe.[18] As for the epic ride to York, it has been duplicated, but only by using a succession of many mounts. However, fact matters little in a world dominated by myth.[19] Future generations were destined to sing of a man and a horse on a timeless journey:

> Then one halloo, boys, one loud cheering halloo,
> For the swiftest of coursers, the gallant, the true,
> For the sportsman inborn shall the memory bless
> Of the horse of the highwaymen, Bonny Black Bess.[20]

Another strange tale of Turpin concerns his involvement with a former pirate and the archbishop of York, Lancelot Blackburne, who really were one and same. Legend has the highwayman working as the butler of this notably experienced ecclesiastic.[21] And that, in turn, probably contributed to persistent rumors of a buccaneer turned pastor who secretly acted as a smuggler! Russell Thorndike eventually crystallized the story in his novel *Dr. Syn.*

In the established pattern, the Turpin legend developed immediately after his death through a popular publication. In this instance a Richard Bayes of Essex wrote *Life of Richard Turpin* within months of the highwayman's hanging. It contained, or created, many of the stories about the robber. Then, in 1834, Harrison Ainsworth (who popularized the term *double-cross*) made Turpin the hero of a successful novel, *Rookwood.* England had her favorite highwayman, and with him a.beloved horse.

The great ride became another staple for outlaw fare. It was adapted, although never bettered, for the careers of several noted fugitives. According to Pat Garrett, "[Billy] the Kid made his famous trip of eighty-one miles in a little more than six hours, riding the gray the entire distance."[22] The Kid, incidentally, has also been reported as having had a mare named Black Bess.[23]

Nevertheless, the Turpin legend enjoys an unequaled conclusion. The highwayman is buried in an unusually large double grave at York, with no record of who (or what) may share it. The faithful know well the answer: Dick Turpin lies with his own Black Bess.[24] At night in London's Hampstead area, people still sometimes report hearing the sounds of a galloping horse going north. It is, without question, the ghosts of the highwayman and Black Bess, once more making their ride to York.

They carry with them a significant part of the outlaw image because the English highwayman is the clearest direct antecedent of the romanticized American robber. By the late eighteenth century the myth of the dashing bandit, or road inspector, was soundly established. With the benefit of gifted authors such as Defoe, Gay, and Ainsworth, tales of Duval, Sheppard, and Turpin provided a grand background for later embellishment. American writers would use them freely. Every generation created new opportunities for application of "the deeds of ancient robber outlaws and highwaymen—what a treasure house pierced with windows for the imagination."[25]

As usual, myth promptly divorced itself from reality. Highwaymen probably never committed a large portion of crime in Britain, and even that eventually began to decline. A system of rewards instituted in the late seventeenth century had little effect, but increasing road use meant more witnesses or even help for victims. Authorities also struck at a vulnerable contributor to robbery by denying licenses to public houses and inns long thought to provide the highwaymen with information on travelers as well as refuge during pursuit. Finally, an efficient police system with high personnel standards and centralized control slowly evolved.

Crime continued as a massive social problem, however. Vice flourished in rapidly growing urban areas, and near the sea entire village populations were involved in coast wrecking. In one instance "it was proved that a woman had bitten off the earlobes from a female corpse for the sake of the earrings."[26]

The basic reaction of the courts involved frequent and severe punishment. Some 156 felonies carried the death penalty, and public hangings were regular occurrences. "Between 1749 and 1771, Peter Newark tells us, "more than 250 highwaymen were executed at London's Tyburn gallows, not to mention hundreds of other poor souls, men, women, and children (the age of criminal responsibility being seven)."[27] The English had a partial solution to this carnage, however, and one of particular importance to their colonies. It commenced with an act of 1597 allowing magistrates to banish "Rogues, Vagabonds, and Sturdy Beggars

. . . unto such parts beyond the Seas as shall . . . be Assigned."[28] While seldom used, it followed the pattern of transporting offenders established several decades earlier by nations on the Continent. In 1666 a new statute in England made it lawful "to transport [notorious thieves and spoil takers] . . . into any of his Majesties dominions in America, there to remain, and not to return."[29] Thirteen years later, another provision extended the possibility of such punishment for any convicted felon upon request.[30] Such petitions became matters of routine; the usual alternative was hanging.

Unfortunately, statutory language does not offer a clear guide to actual practice. Transported criminals frequently appeared in the colonies without notice to authorities and under the control of contractors empowered to sell their labor. The status of such offenders proved a problem for colonial governors, and several attempted to have the practice eliminated, curtailed, or at least clarified. In 1644, Johan Printz of New Sweden pleaded in a report for any information as to "what difference there was between the free people and those who had been sent here on account of crimes, how long each one of the criminals should serve here of this crime and when his time was past how he should either be sent from here or kept here."[31]

Transported offenders never constituted a large proportion of the population in any colony. Moreover, they do not appear to have ever posed a significant problem in social control. For many, transportation probably meant severe punishment, but it also could mean the possibility of a second chance.

What began as a trickle became a steady stream.[32] According to Alan Frost, "by the early 1770s, the British were transporting some 1000 convicts annually across the Atlantic, mostly to Virginia and Maryland."[33] About 75 percent were between the ages of fifteen and twenty-nine, a proportion almost identical with that in the present United States inmate population. From available reports it would appear that most of the convicts shipped to the colonies came from small towns and rural areas. Scotland (which allowed an accused to petition for banishment) provided few for transportation, Ireland a great many.[34]

Surprisingly, about one in five criminals sent to America was a woman, a proportion much higher than that found in most contemporary prisons. Theft, manslaughter, and vagabondage were typical offenses, but perhaps one-fourth of those transported had life sentences. Still, a large number received early releases, and almost none returned to Britain.[35] During a single year more than a thousand felons faced trial at Old Bailey, London's central criminal court. More than half were acquitted, but transportation served as a common sentence for those convicted.[36] Lesser felons usually obtained discharges after no more than seven years of servitude.

Between 1718 and 1775, at least fifty thousand British convicts arrived in the New World.[37] James Oglethorpe promoted the future state of Georgia as a utopian penal colony, primarily for debtors. Although the plan never went into full effect, it illustrates the significance of transportation to America.

The colonies received a vast assortment of people, including many who had sympathy with fugitives. In 1776 a numerical majority of residents consisted of transported convicts, slaves, and indentured servants, together with their children. They certainly considered themselves as constituting separate lower classes, but many of them shared one thing: resentment of authority, an attitude exemplified by one of England's most bizarre and influential outlaws.

John Wilkes was certainly not a highwayman. A witty and eccentric member of Parliament known for his questionable morality, he seemed destined for a life of dissipation. But in 1763 the thirty-six-year-old spendthrift anonymously wrote a monograph attacking the policies and practices of the king. Appearing as issue 45 of *The North Briton,* it turned Wilkes into a controversial celebrity. Outlawed through the ancient writ of *capias utlagatum,* he fled to Europe but eventually returned to face conviction for having "most audaciously, wickedly and seditiously . . . published a certain scandalous book and libel."[38]

Wilkes went to prison for twenty-two months and became a hero to common people in England and to many Americans.

Symbolic toasts of "forty-five" and "twenty-two" were frequently heard in taverns and at parties; Pennsylvania named a town in Wilkes's honor. He represented liberty to criticize authorities, freedoms of speech and press, and a right against compulsory self-incrimination. In addition, his case involved the privilege of voters to select representatives of their choice, as well as their protection against political and judicial coercion.

Wilkes proved to be stubbornly devoted to his principles. For years he repeatedly underwent arrest, imprisonment, and even torture. Parliament expelled him on six different occasions, only to have the people of Middlesex promptly re-elect him. Wilkes later became sheriff and then lord mayor of London. In these offices he brought an end to the practices of trying prisoners in chains and charging spectators fees for visiting the courts.

During the American Revolution, Wilkes opposed the British government's policy of oppression. He died insolvent in London and was buried quietly at Grosvenor Chapel, his simple marker reading "The Remains of John Wilkes, a friend to liberty." In the United States his accomplishments are reflected in the Bill of Rights, undoubtedly devised with him clearly in mind.

Meanwhile, in England, both highway robbery and the procedure of outlawry were in decline. Crime remained, but it took new forms in reaction to new technology. Adequate lighthouses evolved, and the last instance of coast wrecking occurred in Devon in 1842.[39] Fast trains appeared, and William Pierce robbed one in 1855. Stagecoaches and carriages no longer held great attraction, so highwaymen moved on to other things and other places. Some literally took their trade to the United States or Australia.

Outlawry fell into disuse as a formal legal process but found far broader application to indicate any fugitive without requirement of court procedure. Anyone hunted by authorities could fit within the term. The last traditional use of outlawry in England took place in 1859. In 1938, Parliament finally decreed: "Outlawry proceedings . . . are hereby abolished."[40] Such a rejection applied only to England, however. It was not until 1949 that the

Scots received such protection, along with abolition of drawing and quartering![41] The British have not yet seen fit to bring an end to outlawry in Northern Ireland.

The highwayman rode off into literature. He remains the illusion of a robber with courtesy, color, and nerve—not a Robin Hood, perhaps, but certainly not a pirate. The highwayman could never be confused with the ordinary, crude, and simple criminal. This robber had intelligence, education, manners, and taste. For writers, he did not die on the gallows at Tyburn. Alfred Noyes skillfully captured his spirit in a poem "The Highwayman," written in 1906. In very romantic terms it recounts the love between the doomed robber and the lovely innkeeper's daughter. Although they are both killed, Noyes tells us:

> And still of a winter's night, they say,
>   when the wind is in the trees,
> When the moon is a ghostly galleon tossed
>   upon the cloudy sea,
> When the road is a ribbon of moonlight
>   over the purple moor,
> A highwayman comes riding—Riding—riding—
> A highwayman comes riding up to the old
>   inn-door.

In Noyes's poem, incidentally, the heroine's hair is black and her name is Bess.

CHAPTER 4

The Desperado

*Most that is now current about them among the credulous
is derived from unreliable babblers, who have circulated
the idle rumors of the street, or the fables of their own invention.*

—CHARLES GAYARRÉ

THE early American colonists perched on a narrow strip of land
between the ocean and the wilderness. Pirates roved the sea,
while marauding Indians lurked in the forest. Violent sudden
attack from France or Spain remained an almost constant danger.
It was an inhospitable social environment destined to influence
life on the edge of civilization for nearly three centuries.

Colonial communities were small and widely scattered. People
knew one another; mutual dependence provided the only reasonable way of survival. Under such conditions, ordinary crime remained a relatively minor problem. Piracy flourished but found
its victims at sea, originally vessels of hostile nations. On occasion the buccaneers even appeared as saviors; Francis Drake rescued the Roanoke settlers from almost certain death in 1586.
Later, when pirate ships operated from friendly ports, the sea
rovers made few enemies while on shore.

Faced with danger on all sides, the colonies were quite orderly
and peaceful:

The most important conclusion that can be drawn about crime in all
jurisdictions in America before 1660 is that there was very little of it.
On the average, only one person out of every 750 appeared in court in
any given year accused of any crime or misconduct. From the perspec-

tive either of seventeenth century England or twentieth century America, this is a low rate of incidence.[1]

Today, approximately one person out of every twenty-five in the United States faces criminal charges in a year. Historical comparisons involving rates of offenses are notably difficult, but it would certainly appear that the likelihood of specific kinds of crimes is far higher now than in early colonial times. With adjustment for the difference in population, homicide, assault, and theft now occur many times more frequently.[2]

The crime problem naturally varied, in both nature and magnitude, from one colony to another. The pronounced role of religion among the Puritans had an obvious effect: it increased the frequency of offenses against morality.[3] Enforcement of such laws sometimes had unexpected consequences. The banishment of heretics such as Roger Williams and Anne Hutchinson from Massachusetts led directly to the creation of Rhode Island, with relative religious freedom, by 1644.

Meanwhile, some six hundred miles to the south, slavery affected crime. Many forms of perceived misbehavior by blacks were considered legal violations punishable by the government. Much crime was viewed as caused by slaves, and harsh codes were drafted specifically to curtail and punish offenses by blacks. Such statutes seldom received rigid enforcement, however; even in colonial days, whites simply expected and tolerated some misbehavior among blacks.[4] While crime was considered to be a problem, it usually could be controlled by the local community: "There was little conspicuous wealth. . . . Theft was a casual act, and a career in crime was impossible. . . . If the success of a criminal justice system is judged by recidivism, all of the colonial jurisdictions receive high marks . . . the rate of recidivism was virtually nil."[5]

Another aspect of disorder appeared and tore the society of colonial Virginia apart in 1676. It began in an atmosphere of anxiety caused by the outbreak of major Indian attacks in New England, known there as King Philip's War. A series of battles also occurred on Virginia's frontier, and these led a young but prominent planter named Nathaniel Bacon to demand a general commission against the Indians from the colonial government. The governor, William Berkeley, responded by proclaiming existence of a rebellion and attempting to raise troops for its suppression. Bacon countered with his "Declaration of the People" and denounced the colony's administration.

The rebellion ended when its principal leader presumably died of dysentery. Fourteen of his lieutenants were hunted down, captured, and executed, but one, Richard Lawrence, could not be found. Excepted from a general pardon issued by the king, he remained at large. For decades rumors persisted that this outlawed rebel was about to return from the wilderness and once more ignite insurrection.[6]

Bacon's Rebellion may be seen in three lights. It has been portrayed as the first effort to achieve independence in the colonies, a forerunner of the American Revolution. Second, it can be depicted as a demonstration of the need for maintenance of order on the frontier and against an ineffective colonial administration. Finally, it was viewed by English authorities as a combination of criminal acts by people interested in seizing power and exploiting friendly Indians. Whatever the original motives of Bacon, Lawrence, and their followers, they left an atmosphere of tension, and the frontier began its long association with outlawry. It came to indicate a region where ordinary law failed to function and fugitives could seek escape.

Meanwhile, the formal process required for outlawry, as developed in England, supposedly applied in the colonies. After a series of exactions at court, a fugitive felon could be hunted and killed by anyone. Those sought for misdemeanors forfeited their property after a similar procedure. But American courts seldom insisted on details and formalities: "Colonists left the technical apparatus of process behind in England. . . . When it became clear that a suspect had fled, he might in fact be outlawed."[7] By the end of the seventeenth century, the Americans were beginning to develop their own indigenous customs and laws.

Colonial life was changing. Increasing population, growing cities, improving transportation, and expanding backcountries brought gradual alteration in the nature and degree of crime. Isolation and mutual dependence diminished. Urban areas appeared and emerged as centers of misconduct. "Over the course of the century," writes Douglas Greenberg, "the volume of serious crime—and especially violent crime—became a more difficult problem in New York after 1750 than it had before."[8]

Fugitives like robber Tom Bell and counterfeiter Owen Sullivan found it possible to operate across colonial borders and maintain themselves for years. To the south, the specter of slave revolt began to haunt white settlers. The Spanish in Florida consciously encouraged these fears by welcoming escaped slaves at Fort Moosa near Saint Augustine. One consequence was the Stono Revolt in 1739, in which some twenty whites were killed near Charles Town in South Carolina.

Rumors concerning large bands of criminals operating in the colonial backcountry circulated. Runaway slaves, renegade whites, mulattoes, and "women deep in the deeds of darkness" reputedly were led by an outlaw identified as Caesar.[9] Raids on plantations in South Carolina, combined with governmental inactivity, eventually caused settlers to take action. The pardoning of stock thieves in 1767 led to formation of the Regulators, a force totaling perhaps four thousand men intent on bringing justice of their own making to the frontier.

Unintentionally following a pattern created by the Irish Whiteboys of County Tipperary, the South Carolinians launched America's first large vigilante movement. The colonial government reacted by organizing companies of rangers, as Maryland and Virginia had done earlier. The troops then joined the Regulators in fighting outlaws. A more adequate means of law enforcement finally evolved. South Carolina's single provost marshal, a London playwright named Richard Cumberland, was replaced by county sheriffs throughout the backcountry.[10]

The situation in neighboring North Carolina reached a far less satisfactory resolution. The basic problem there was not a lack of law enforcement, but an institutionalized abuse of justice. In North Carolina, "as soon as counties were organized on the frontier sheriffs, clerks, registrars, and lawyers swooped down upon the defenseless inhabitants like wolves."[11] Backcountry settlers in what became the central portion of the state were aggrieved by dishonest officials, excessive fees, and widespread corruption. Local disturbances began, and a Regulator movement appeared just as that in South Carolina commenced its decline. Vigilantes terrorized appointed authorities, interrupted court sessions, and demanded representation in the colonial assembly.

North Carolina's governor was neither inept nor inactive. A professional soldier, William Tryon responded with oppression. The legislature passed a statute allowing for the outlawing and execution of people assembling in groups of ten or more,[12] and the governor set forth with a powerful trained militia force to crush the rebels.

The "first battle of the American Revolution" took place on the Alamance River of North Carolina in May 1771. Although the Regulators enjoyed a numerical superiority (approximately two thousand to twelve hundred), they had no chance for victory. Tryon's professionally directed army had a company of rangers, a cavalry detachment, and artillery. The battle became a rout, with the "Great Wolf of North Carolina" directing a ruthless pursuit of the defeated Regulators. Tryon then issued a decree against the rebel leaders:

Whereas, Harmon Husband, James Butler, Rednap Howell, and William Butler are outlawed and liable to be shot by any person whatever, I do therefore proclaim that they are to be punished for the Traitorous and Rebellious crimes they have committed . . . hereby offering a reward of 100 pounds sterling and 1000 acres of land to any person or person who will take dead or alive and bring into mine or General [Hugh] Wadell's camp either or each of the above-named outlaws.[13]

Several men believed to be prominent Regulators were captured and promptly convicted. Martin Howard, the colony's chief justice, sent six to their deaths under the dreadful sentence prescribed for traitors, ordering that the prisoner should be carried to the place from whence he came; that he should be drawn [dragged] from thence to the place of execution and hanged by the neck; that he should be cut down while yet alive; that his bowels should be taken out and burned before his eyes; that his head should be cut off, and that his body should be divided into four quarters . . . and may the Lord have mercy on your soul.[14]

Governor Tryon gave personal attention to the actual infliction of the death penalties, assembling his army as an audience. He then proceeded to devastate much of the backcountry, requiring all male inhabitants to take an oath of allegiance. But many Regulators slipped away into the wilderness with their families. Legend has hundreds of them crossing the Appalachians, moving westward to the new lands of Tennessee and Kentucky.

The British were pleased with Tryon's efficiency and made him governor of New York, but the legacy of the outlawed Regulators became the prelude to revolution and independence of the entire United States. Years later, North Carolinians attempted to erase the memory of Tryon. They took the rare but thoughtful step of obliterating from the map a county named in his honor.

The fate of North Carolina's Regulators would have been extended to many American revolutionists had they lost. There is probably no clearer example in the history of the United States of outlawry determined by political power. In some instances the distinctions between criminal, rebel, revolutionary, and national hero are determined simply by winning or losing and history is then written to justify the outcome.

During widespread social disorder, crime depends essentially on point of view. In the American Revolution, the same activity was often looked upon in totally opposite ways. One example may be found in the "cowboys" who operated in New York's "neutral ground," a part of Westchester County, from 1777 to 1783. To some they were a "worthless and criminal element . . . governed by neither law or mercy" and to others "dedicated Loyalists . . . principled men fighting to regain their homes and their rights."[15]

Moses Doan fights Pennsylvania militiamen, from *Piratical Times,* 1846.

In regard to the law of outlawry, America's revolution had a clear effect because independence provided an opportunity to restrict the arbitrary use of the process. Outlawry remained as a function of state criminal law, but one routinely limited by written constitutional standards. Officials and judges were not to outlaw fugitives without adhering to specific formalities. The Massachusetts Constitution of 1780 provided that "no subject shall be . . . put outside the protection of the law . . . but by the judgment of his peers, or the law of the land."[16] Similar language, derived from England's Magna Carta but not routinely applied to the colonies, subsequently was accepted throughout the United States.

Protection against arbitrary outlawry affected the most notable American bandit gang of the eighteenth century. The Doans became the new nation's first prominent crime family. Six Doan brothers and several other men, including the daring James ("Sandy Flash") Fitzpatrick, were active robbers in Pennsylvania and New Jersey between 1780 and 1788. They looted a county treasury, falsely claimed to be Loyalist supporters, and reportedly used various caves as hideouts.

Before hangmen finally decimated the Doan gang, significant legal questions concerning outlawry reached the Pennsylvania Supreme Court. The old process was upheld, permitting a judicial act alone to serve as a conviction and allowing forfeiture of life as well as property. But the court insisted on precision:

To take away the life of a man without a fair and open trial, upon an implication of guilt, has ever been regarded as so dangerous a practice that the law requires all the proceedings in such a mode of putting to death to be "exceedingly nice and circumstantial."[17]

Both of the great conflicts which tore the United States apart, the American Revolution and the Civil War, left chaos in their wake. But each of these periods corresponded with another aspect of national life, the frontier. The American Revolution and the Civil War ended as new lands opened to the west, and because of this the image of the outlaw became closely involved with that of the frontier. In reality the connection was tenuous; in myth it is forever linked.

Something unique happened when the frontiersmen pushed out beyond the Appalachians. For the first time in American history the West became clearly separable from the previously settled areas nearer the Atlantic. In the public's perception, life and attitudes toward it were very different for those settling beyond the mountains. Such views held sway for two centuries and still exert a significant influence.

In one common attitude, pioneers are viewed as an assorted collection of social misfits, nomads, fugitives, and greedy adventurers. In truth, the great majority were brave people seeking a better life. The West undoubtedly provided a kind of escape, but it also meant hardship and danger. The percentage of criminals among the pioneers crossing the mountains was probably never higher than that to be found among the people remaining in Europe or the East.

Those moving to Kentucky, Ohio, Tennessee, or Mississippi usually found themselves living in a great forest, dark and mysterious. Communication and transportation remained severely restricted for decades, and physical danger was very real. But it was far less likely to come from outlaws than from peoples called Miami, Chickasaw, Creek, or Shawnee. These images became confused as the savagery of one was associated with the other.

Since the seventeenth century, Americans had pondered the threats posed by hostile Indians. These consisted of more than the possibility of death or torture; they were a menace to morality. Indian captivity emerged as a peculiar kind of literature, with references to sexual temptation, cannibalism, rape, and demonology. The savages endangered not just lives, but souls!

Such considerations probably mattered little to the pioneers venturing along the Cumberland and Wilderness roads, but Americans fortunate enough to enjoy both leisure and literacy made natural associations. Depictions of outlaws on the frontier borrowed from the barbarian imagery associated with marauding Indians. There was an element not just of crime, but of deviltry—savage, barbarous, and evil. This confused and overlapping imagery became compounded with visions of the frontiersman themselves. When John Filson wrote a real-estate brochure entitled *The Discovery, Settlement and Present State of Kentucke* in 1784, he unknowingly inaugurated a powerful myth. It popularized the colorful figure of "Col. Daniel Boon," which in turn served as a model for the long line of frontier heroes.

In more general terms, the theme may be seen in relation to a far older myth, for the frontier also was viewed in terms of innocence, simplicity, and a rejection of unreasonable discipline. Its heroes have been related to the greatest of outlaw myths, "Robin Hood or Robin of the Wood a traditional English version of the archetypal 'King of the Woods,' and a figure of increasing importance in the Americanized literature of the colonies. Daniel Boone and Leatherstocking are his lineal descendants."[18]

Such colorful backwoodsmen were mixtures of positive and negative features. The violent, independent pioneer frequently appeared in a quite unfavorable light. Richard Slotkin tells us:

American writers of conservative sympathies (like Fenimore Cooper) associated this type of Western hero with demagogic politics, Jacobinism, philistinism, savage anarchy, and disrespect for social position and private property. In the West the same type of hero—common in origin and speech, materialistic, and skilled in all arts of hunting and speculative economics—was presented as the quintessential representative of local spirit and virtu.[19]

While often portrayed with characteristics resembling those of a criminal, the frontiersman was also seen as courageous, possessing a native intelligence, and remarkably self-sufficient. He rejected complex regulations, had contempt for unearned authority, and would act promptly when a perceived need arose. If beset with outlawry, he resorted to his own extended form of self-defense. As Frederick Jackson Turner wrote:

The frontiersman was impatient of restraints. He knew how to preserve order, even in the absence of legal authority. . . . [A] crime was more an offense against the victim, than a violation of the law of the land. Substantial justice, secured in the most direct way, was the ideal of the backwoodsman. He had little patience with finely drawn distinctions or scruples of method.[20]

The term usually applied to such simple justice was "lynch law," and whether derived from the name of Charles Lynch, a notorious Virginia justice of the peace, or James Lynch Fitz Stephen, a County Galway magistrate who hanged his own son, the practice often met the immediate need for justice on the frontier.

Lynch law probably seemed the only practical recourse to some kinds of crime in the West. Those responsible for such acts were given a name clearly revealing their perceived ancestry: river pirates. Their rise and fall related directly to available means of transportation. After 1787 the Northwest Ordinance encouraged settlement on the frontier. These pioneers had no reasonable means of transportation to the East, so they soon developed trade routes, using rafts and boats to ply the great rivers flowing south toward the Gulf of Mexico.

The most popular path of commerce ran down the Ohio and

Mississippi rivers to the towns of Walnut Hills (later Vicksburg) and Natchez. Goods were then transhipped through Louisiana to New Orleans, while the Americans returned home by land with money obtained by trade. This vulnerable traffic attracted a particularly vicious new variety of brigand. Writes Paul I. Wellman: "The deviltry introduced by the river pirates was different, a deviltry so vicious, cruel and bloodthirsty, that it eclipsed all other forms of terror and appalled even the callous frontiersmen."[21] These criminals, with such nicknames as Bully Wilson and Colonel Plug, haunted particular areas along the rivers, including sections near present-day Henderson, Kentucky, and Cairo, Illinois. They preferred to entice the boatmen on shore with liquor and women; robbery and murder would follow. Should diversion fail, the river pirates might simply ambush the cautious travelers from canoes or small boats.

Most notable among the brigands was Sam Mason, a native of Virginia and veteran of George Rogers Clark's campaigns against the British. After the revolution this experienced woodsman and soldier turned to crime. Mason's career lasted for several years and made him a legend on the frontier. There were even tales of what were, perhaps, calculated efforts at terrorism. The following message would be carved in a tree at the grisly scene of a crime: "Done by Mason of the Woods." About 1797 he helped establish the most renowned center for the river pirates. Today it is a quiet state park, still carrying the infamous name of Cave-In-Rock, in Hardin County, Illinois. A large cavern adjoining the Ohio River, it served as a sinister and dominant location of criminal activity for forty years.

Shortly before Mason moved on, Cave-In-Rock had visitors whom even the river pirates deemed contemptible. They probably identified themselves by the same chilling announcement reportedly used to frighten victims, "We are the Harpes!" This was not a statement to be ignored; it often constituted a death sentence. The Harpes originally came from North Carolina and are assumed to have been brothers. There is considerable doubt about their racial heritage. "Their tawny appearance and dark curly hair betrayed a tinge of African blood."[22] Micajah, or Big

Harpe, was born in 1768; his brother Wiley, Little Harpe, arrived in 1770. Their family reportedly favored the defeated Loyalist side during the revolution and the boys drifted into clearly deviant ways. In 1795 they crossed into Tennessee, accompanied by Susan and Betsey Roberts, and may have lived for a time among the Cherokees. Two years later the four occupied a piece of land near Knoxville, and Wiley married Sally Rice, a parson's daughter.

Within months there were ugly rumors of the Harpes' involvement with a number of thefts and arsons. A posse captured the brothers, but they promptly escaped and embarked on a reign of murder and robbery rarely if ever equaled on the frontier. The Harpes reportedly developed what became a trademark of the river pirates: in a reasonably successful effort to hide their dead victims, believed to number in the dozens, they would rip open and disembowel a body, fill the cavity with rocks, and drop the remains into a nearby river or stream. No one associated them with Robin Hood, although many later frontier outlaws were rumored to be relatives of the notorious Harpes.

Otto A. Rothert tells us: "They lived like man-eating animals."[23] Micajah reportedly tired of his child's crying on one occasion and ended the problem forever by dashing the baby's head against a tree. All five members of the Harpe band were captured near Danville, Kentucky, in 1799. Once more the brothers escaped, this time leaving the three women (all pregnant) behind, but the Kentuckians were determined to rid the frontier of this particular scourge. A small posse of woodsmen, under the leadership of a justice of the peace named Silas McBee, was assembled; it included two men previously associated with the brigands. The trackers followed the Harpes westward toward Cave-In-Rock and finally caught them near the present site of Dixon, Kentucky. Wiley escaped capture, but a member of the posse shot Micajah. The wounded Big Harpe probably died as his head was severed from his body and placed in the fork of a large tree. For many years the skull remained as a landmark for pioneers going west; legend has it eventually removed and powdered to make medicine. The location is still known locally as Harpeshead.

One hesitates to ponder on the fate of the Harpe women had they been tried a century or two earlier. But Kentucky was not Massachusetts and the West was already developing its own unique jurisprudence. The women, each of whom gave birth while awaiting trial, eventually were released. Sally returned to live with her father near Knoxville; Betsey married John Hufstetter and settled in Russellville, Kentucky; Susan became a weaver and moved to Christian County.[24] On the frontier, people thought of the future and forgave the past.

Meanwhile, the master of Cave-In-Rock, Sam Mason, shifted his operations far to the south. He quickly seized upon the opportunity offered by an important new road running from Nashville to Natchez. Mason now became a "land pirate," robbing travelers along former Indian trails which served as routes to the old southeastern frontier.

Mason's victims were often boatmen making their way home with the profits of trade. He obtained a Spanish passport and committed no crimes west of the Mississippi, thus maintaining a safe refuge where he supposedly buried his ill-gotten gains. His skill as a woodsman and his expertise at duplicity seemed unequaled. In 1803, two lesser members of his gang, John Setton and James May, were released from custody for the purpose of seeking the frontier's chief land pirate. They succeeded, returning with Mason's head carefully preserved in blue clay to prevent putrefaction.

Then the story took a bizarre twist. John Setton was recognized by his true identity, the infamous fugitive Wiley Harpe; both treacherous bounty hunters died by hanging near Natchez. Their bodies were taken down, decapitated, and buried in shallow graves. The executioners placed the heads on long poles to serve as a warning to other land pirates. According to legend, increasing traffic along the road leading north eventually exposed the bones of the dead, at which time dogs or wolves dragged them away.[25]

The brigands of Cave-In-Rock appeared in stories and poems of the frontier. By 1833, James Hall featured them in his book of fiction, *Harpe's Head,* and in 1845, N. E. Paxton, using the pseudonym Orlando, wrote *The Brigand, or, A Tale of the West Done into Rhyme.* With characters borrowed from Lord Byron's *The Corsair* of 1814, it told of Spanish outlaws operating from "Rock Cave" on the Ohio and featured a leader's desire to kill a female captive, foiled only by "the timely intervention of his own son, who nobly rescued her."[26] A steady procession of equally grotesque distortions followed, and then, in 1923, Otto A. Rothert produced a remarkable volume entitled *The Outlaws of Cave-In-Rock.* This scholarly, comprehensive, and well-written book immediately became the only acceptable source of information on the subject.

The demise of Sam Mason and Wiley Harpe brought no end to frontier brigandage, despite increasingly romanticized portrayals. The era of river piracy was, however, drawing to a close. Steamboats, organized resistance, and increasing traffic on the Mississippi caused the outlaws to focus their attention elsewhere, and an outstanding target of opportunity developed. Treaties with Indian tribes allowed more use of an old Chickasaw and Choctaw trail and development of the Natchez Trace. It flourished from 1800 until 1820, winding several hundred miles from Nashville to Natchez, and became a major route for migrants moving south.

Land pirates made the Natchez Trace a favorite stalking ground. It was—and still is in certain preserved portions—a lonely and strangely sinister road. Meriwether Lewis, at that time governor of Louisiana, died mysteriously along it in 1809. That and many other events made the Natchez Trace an infamous haunt of thieves, robbers, and murderers. At the southern terminus of the trail could be found the most notorious center of crime in the United States during the first half of the nineteenth century. Natchez-Under-the-Hill was a narrow strip of land less than a mile long below a high bluff along the Mississippi River. It teemed with taverns, brothels, gambling dens, and docks. In dramatic contrast, some of the most beautiful homes in North America were built in the area just above the bluff.

Natchez-Under-the-Hill attracted an incredible variety of boatmen, prostitutes, gamblers, and thieves. Undermined by a great hurricane in 1840 and ravaged by a series of epidemics, it finally declined in significance. Today, Natchez-Under-the-Hill (much reduced in size) is a tourist center, but on occasion, when one of the giant riverboats pays a call, a little imagination can still transform it into its infamous image of long ago.

The old Southwest gave America a new and lasting name for outlaws. Borrowed from the Spanish, the term *desperado* signified a particularly bold, reckless, and violent criminal. Such a designation, however, did not necessarily imply the evil associated with certain earlier brigands. No, the qualification applies most clearly to the region's most famous fugitive, one of very few American criminals to have affected the course of history directly, and almost everything about him remains a mystery.

In one of those strange twists of legend, only one of two brothers is widely remembered, perhaps for no significant reason. Jean and Pierre Lafitte came from France, Haiti, or somewhere else. They either did, or did not, receive military training in the Caribbean and then drift into piracy, presumably under the leadership of Dominique You. What can be stated with a degree of certainty is that by 1809 the Lafittes had established a blacksmith shop on Saint Philip Street in New Orleans. "They were men of a limited education, but intelligent, active; their manners were cordial and winning. . . . [B]oth were tall and of commanding presence."[27] Apparently, the brothers were accepted as Frenchmen who had come to Louisiana by way of the West Indies.

Within a few years they began acquiring somewhat dubious reputations as associates of the region's criminal element. Finally they left New Orleans and established themselves in the bayous of Barataria, which conveniently reached to the Gulf of Mexico. Perhaps with the assistance of the able Captain You, and unquestionably with the aid of prosperous Louisiana merchants, they became major participants in the flourishing business of smuggling and piracy. Of course the Baratarians claimed to be privateers operating under commissions from the "Republic of Cartegena," attacking only Spanish vessels.

The exasperated governor of Louisiana, William Claiborne,

Jean Lafitte meeting with Governor Claiborne and General Jackson, from Charles Ellms, *The Pirates Own Book,* 1837.

finally posted reward notices throughout the area offering five hundred dollars for the delivery of "John [Jean] Lafitte and associates." Two days later, these proposals were more than matched. Reward notices appeared in the name of Jean Lafitte, the "Boss of Barataria," offering five thousand dollars for the delivery of William Claiborne.[28]

Soon thereafter international politics entered the story. The War of 1812 was drawing to a close and the British hoped to seize control of New Orleans and the mouth of the Mississippi. They sent a large military force to accomplish the task, and in late 1814 two officers were dispatched on a very special mission to Barataria. The British offered Jean Lafitte the rank of captain and land to all of the pirates; in return, they expected aid, primarily in the form of guidance through the swamps, to prepare for battle with a diverse force of American Indian fighters led by Andrew Jackson.

Lafitte promised to consider the offer but secretly contacted John Blanque, a member of the Louisiana legislature. Why he did so remains an unanswerable question. Myth supplies the solution: he was a patriot. Outlaw help seemed absurd to Claiborne, but Jackson knew the military reality. The pirates might mean the difference between victory and defeat, between retention and loss of Louisiana, between American and British control of the entire Mississippi region.

The Battle of New Orleans proved disastrous for the British. Whether the pirates reversed the outcome cannot be determined with certainty, but they certainly played a major role, particularly with information. More obviously, the Baratarians used their artillery with telling effect. The pirates were, after all, "the best cannoneers in the western hemisphere."[29]

Andrew Jackson quickly changed his view of the "hellish banditti" of the bayous, making them "privateers and gentlemen." At his request, President James Madison issued a proclamation granting "a full and free pardon of all offenses . . . touching the revenue, trade or commerce of the United States with foreign nations at any time before the 8th of January 1815, by any person or persons . . . being inhabitants of the island of Barataria."[30]

Many of the pirates took advantage of their opportunity and settled into a peaceful life in Louisiana. Dominique You ran a tavern on Saint Anne Street in New Orleans and was buried with full military honors upon his death in 1830. But Pierre and Jean Lafitte once more drifted into a life of crime. They established a community of outlaws they called Galvez Town (Galveston) in Texas and again attacked ships in the Gulf of Mexico. Times were no longer auspicious for piracy, however. The United States came to regard the Lafittes as a threat and in 1821 sent them a stern warning: the pirates must leave their stronghold or face attack. Shortly thereafter, the Lafittes burned their fortress and sailed away into the mists of legend.

Where did they go? What did they do? What became of

them? No one really knows, but stories are still told. There is strong indication that Pierre eventually made his way up the Mississippi to the Saint Louis vicinity, dying peacefully in 1844.[31] As for Jean, whose direct descendants were still living in New Orleans more than a century after his departure from the city, the usual version of the story has him drifting, forgotten, about the Caribbean until his death in Yucatán in 1826.[32] But far more interesting variations exist: Lafitte was murdered by his own men at sea. He died in a battle with a British man-of-war. He changed his name and married a wealthy woman in North Carolina. The Spanish captured him and he died in Cuba. His ship was wrecked and his body washed ashore near the two Louisiana communities which preserve his name.

The handsome pirate also accomplished a remarkable rescue prior to his demise. After leaving Galvez Town, he sailed to the island of Saint Helena and secretly exchanged a double for the exiled Napoleon! Furthermore, Lafitte captured a Spanish ship, the *Santa Rosa,* loaded with silver. The pirates buried most of this vast treasure somewhere along the Sabine River, or in Bayou Lafouche, or perhaps on Barataria Bay. It has never been found, although searches continue.

Lafitte's ghost (or sometimes his entire ship) still appears along the Gulf Coast. Perhaps more than any other American outlaw, he has become legend. Jean Lafitte is certainly the only one, to date, with a national park named in his honor. But he will probably always remain much as he appears in the only painting of his likeness: a dark and slender figure seen only at a distance, in the shadows.

It seems clear that many of the legends associated with one pirate were freely applied to others. Some of the Lafitte tales sound suspiciously similar to those related to other sea rovers, such as Vincent Gambi or Edward Low. Myth is remarkably flexible. Lafitte, for example, may well have served as one basis for Florida's favorite but apparently quite mythical pirate, José Gaspár. To Tampa residents who celebrate during the annual Gasparilla Festival, his absence from historical record may be an asset. After all, real pirates are often far less appealing than fictional ones.

Driving the Lafittes from Galvez Town was part of a major American effort against sea rovers. The Constitution granted Congress authority to "define and punish piracies and felonies committed on the high seas, and offenses against the law of nations,"[33] and the basic statute dealing with the subject, which remains in effect, was duly passed in 1790.[34] A generation later, however, conditions required more drastic action. A special squadron of naval vessels under a commodore was sent to the West Indies to protect shipping.

In 1819, Congress strengthened the statute outlawing piracy, providing that "if any person . . . shall on the high seas, commit the crime of piracy, as defined by the law of nations and . . . shall afterwards be brought into or found in the United States, every such offender shall, upon conviction thereof . . . be punished with death."[35] The following year, in the first of many cases brought under the statute, the Supreme Court upheld such general language and the required penalty against citizens of all countries.[36]

The legal process of outlawry remained a function of state courts and clearly degenerated. In some states it became a common device to obtain control of property. An outlawed fugitive was subject to forfeiture, after which the government routinely disposed of his lands and goods by auction. On occasion an innocent individual might be accused and driven into hiding simply to seize his property.

Outlawry no longer routinely indicated a serious offense, such as murder, rape, or robbery. In certain states the process commonly applied to a wide variety of lesser charges. In Virginia during 1821, for example, appellate courts approved of outlawry in such matters as assault, battery, larceny, and ordinary trespass.[37] Practices like these led to curtailment and finally abolition of forfeiture later in the nineteenth century.

Where courts no longer relied upon outlawry as a means of eliminating offenders, less formal practices applied. A direct method was banishment from the community. In much of the new nation it remained an effective penalty for criminals considered as deserving of more than whipping and less than death. In parts of the South, "slaves convicted of capital crimes were more likely to be banished than executed."[38] Travelers along the overland trails resorted to expulsion from wagon trains for offenses ranging from slander and fraud to lesser forms of homicide. "In those circumstances, short of murder, where antisocial conduct necessitated some action, the pioneers . . . sought . . . the most simple expedient available to them—banishment."[39] Informal and formal agencies of justice frequently informed malefactors of the wisdom of prompt and permanent departure. Thus the renowned San Francisco Vigilance Committee of 1851 "notified undesirables to 'leave this port.' "[40] Whether exile encouraged desperadoes to reform or permitted them to circulate may never be known.

Meanwhile, American outlaws were making their way into the popular press, following the route established a century before in England. The United States had its own highwaymen, and they too could be made into figures of note. Michael Martin, Captain Lightfoot, was one of the first to undergo the process. Originally from Ireland, he worked as a highwayman in New England from 1819 until his final capture in 1821. Prior to his execution, Martin supposedly told his life story to an enterprising writer named Frederick Waldo. This led, naturally, to a biography entitled *Captain Lightfoot, the Last of the New England Highwaymen.*

A few years later another prominent road agent, Joseph Hare, received similar acclamation. He had been a robber along the Natchez Trace before spending five years in prison. Released in 1818, Hare held up a stagecoach near Baltimore, Maryland. His subsequent capture led to trial and execution, with a diary then reportedly discovered in his cell. It served as the foundation, however questionable, for a number of publications, including 1847's influential *The Life and Adventures of Joseph T. Hare,* presumably by H. R. Howard.

Such imaginative books, forerunners of the dime novel, were significant milestones along the road of American outlaw mythology. They became primitive procreators in the long chain of misinformation. For the first time, what was written about fugitives made them widely known and then served to support subsequent embellishment. In many instances, fiction begat fact. Within a few decades that pattern became more established as far greater American outlaws rode into the scene.

CHAPTER 5

The Rebel

Oh, what was your name in the States?
Was it Thompson or Johnson or Bates?
Did you murder your wife and fly for your life?
Say, what was your name in the States?

—ANONYMOUS

AMERICA'S fascination with outlaws changed markedly during the 1830s as a consequence of a series of strange happenings in the southern Mississippi Valley. After a century and a half, the exact sequence of events and the precise roles played by individuals cannot be determined, but their existence and notoriety are quite significant. They occurred because of dark social conditions and exemplified the deliberately created myth, which became a hallmark of outlaw legend.

The most obvious personality in this peculiar episode was probably born just south of Nashville, Tennessee, in 1804. His mother is usually portrayed as a prostitute and tavern operator. His father has been variously described in forms ranging from that of an itinerant Methodist minister to a former pirate and colleague of Jean Lafitte. Whatever his actual parentage, John A. Murrell (often spelled Murrel or Murel) drifted into a familiar pattern of crime before he was twenty. He received such assorted sentences as a year in jail, whipping, the pillory, and branding on the thumb (for horse theft) while sometimes functioning as a revivalist.

Murrell subsequently became involved in the lucrative practice of slave stealing, which typically meant combinations of kid-

John Murrell disposes of a body along the
Natchez Trace, from *Life and Adventures of John
Murrell,* 1847.

napping, fraud, and murder. Stolen slaves would be promised
eventual freedom, resold several times, and finally killed. Murrell apparently prospered in this vicious game, gaining a notable
reputation in an interstate underworld reaching from New
Orleans to Nashville:

He had . . . courage, a precise mind, a seeing eye, and the ability to
judge, organize, and handle men. He attained a polished manner as by
instinct, . . . grasped abstruse points of law and theology . . . a ready

and fluent speaker. . . . When you add to these things an intense hatred of humanity, and a satanic instinct to do evil, you have the ingredients for a super-criminal.[1]

And then a young traveler in eastern Tennessee named Virgil A. Stewart set in motion the events destined to create a unique tale. He claimed to have been taken by Murrell on an amazing trip across the Mississippi, discovering a vast conspiracy which went far beyond ordinary slave stealing. The reception of this tale undoubtedly reflected deep and real fears prevalent in the South.

Tennessee vigilantes arrested Murrell, who escaped but was soon recaptured, in 1834. With Stewart appearing as the principal witness, he was convicted of slave stealing and given a ten year prison sentence. Shortly thereafter John A. Murrell became "one of the most fantastic outlaws of an era which apparently specialized in fantasy."[2]

A few months after the trial, Stewart presumably published (under the name of Augustus Q. Walton) an astonishing little book entitled *A History of the Detection, Conviction, Life and Designs of John A. Murel, the Great Western Land Pirate.* Quickly revised and expanded, the volume told of a vast "mystic clan" reaching from Texas to Maryland, with hundreds of members planning an enormous slave uprising to begin in 1835. The "united banditti" had secret headquarters (which Stewart had visited with Murrell) near the present town of Marked Tree, Arkansas.

The consequences of the book's revelations manifested themselves almost immediately. Several suspected white clansmen were lynched and many slaves hanged in Mississippi. Affidavits and confessions indicated that the South, by fortunate coincidence and prompt action, had narrowly averted disaster. This appeared to be promptly verified in such publications as H. R. Howard's *The History of Virgil A. Stewart, and His Adventures* of 1836. The story of Murrell's great plot to promote a massive slave rebellion in order to plunder the innocent became part of history. Members of the mystic clan reportedly fled the region, spreading organized outlawry into Iowa, Missouri, and Texas.

Objective analysis of the Murrell legend raises very serious doubts as to its credibility. The affidavits supporting Stewart's story appeared after publication of his popular book. The confessions of suspected conspirators probably all resulted from torture, and no members of the "Grand Council of the Mystic Clan," supposedly men of power and social standing, ever went to trial. Had Stewart cunningly created the entire conspiracy, cleverly combining fears of a great slave uprising (the Virginia rebellion led by Nat Turner occurred in 1831) with common suspicion of the secret Masonic Order? Could the plot have been only a grandiose dream of Murrell, lacking any rational basis or support? Or was the conspiracy real, involving the murder of hundreds over a period of years and spawning crime all along the frontier, as many people sincerely believed?

Meanwhile, the pivotal player languished in prison, gradually deteriorating mentally and physically. To the public, Murrell had a "monstrous lust for blood and suffering, and a hate of humanity that was diabolic. One almost imagines there may have been a smell of sulphur on this breath."[3] The noted phrenologist O. S. Fowler examined the outlaw's head in prison and somberly announced findings of pronounced secretiveness, self-esteem, and misdirected natural abilities.[4] But time routinely softens attitudes toward individual criminals. Murrell received a pardon in 1844 and was discharged from prison several months before the end of his sentence, probably with tuberculosis and perhaps syphilis. Many sources recite that he then disappeared, an imbecile. In fact, Murrell quietly settled in Pikesville, Tennessee, working as a blacksmith. He died a short time later, and grave robbers disinterred the corpse. According to legend, the head was severed and displayed at fairs for a fee.[5] Another variation has the body taken to a medical school in Nashville and eventually destroyed in a fire.[6]

Virgil Stewart dropped out of public view shortly after the trial and publication of his book. Some sources say he sailed for Europe, presumably to enjoy the profits of his story. Other claimed that he assumed another name to live in obscurity somewhere in the United States. And still others assert that members of the mystic clan found and killed him.[7]

In the usual fashion, stories of Murrell's buried treasure soon appeared, with scores of charts and maps circulated among ever hopeful hunters.[8] These guides to hidden wealth were fully as dubious as the infamous legacy created by Stewart. Murrell's biographer had, however, accomplished two things in the growing literature of outlawry: he introduced the concept of a vast criminal conspiracy directed toward society itself, and he developed the internal exposé of misconduct. Stewart claimed to reveal a network of American outlawry through his personal observations; it would prove to be a successful technique adopted by many, many others.

An example of this method was *The Secret Band of Brothers,* written by Jonathan H. Green and published in 1847. In it the "reformed gambler" reveals through his own twelve-year involvement an enormous secret organization of "The American Outlaws." Founded in 1798 at "Hanging Rock, Virginia," it was reportedly directed by "some two hundred Grand Masters," generally men of wealth and respectability, often connected with a "learned profession." Scattered throughout almost every town in the nation, these sinister villains controlled a far more numerous inferior order of "pickpockets, thieves, gamblers, horse racers, and sometimes murderers" who wandered about enjoying the protection of their profiteering masters.[9] The band of brothers covered the nation, but they flourished along the southwestern frontier. The author took special care to describe conditions in Texas settlements, where "drunkenness, debauchery, and murder walked abroad," and in that "wild and mysterious refuge" of criminals, the Choctaw Nation.[10] With such publications it should be no surprise that in the public mind the West became closely associated with lawlessness and outlawry.

According to common belief, fugitives from eastern cities drifted to the frontier, continuing their lives of violence, but no clear evidence of such a trend exists. Urban centers have always had higher rates of crime than small towns or rural areas, and this situation surely applied in the United States before the Civil War. As Emerson Hough correctly observed, "the most lawless parts of America are the most civilized parts."[11] Among the tens of thousands of people going to the frontier, the proportion of criminals probably did not exceed that among those staying east of the Mississippi, where opportunities for many offenses were greater.

Yet the association of outlaws and the West became an integral facet of the American myth. There were undoubtedly many men and some women who left the East to escape justice. The phrase "gone to Texas," often abbreviated "G.T.T.," even came into use signifying those departing for a region with a less-demanding system of justice. An ironic song appeared, perhaps during the California gold rush, asking "What Was Your Name In the States?" The majority of those to whom such a question might have been humorously addressed became responsible citizens rather than outlaws. Although often using assumed names, most created new lives for themselves. Ramon Adams succinctly explained and illustrated the practice with a quotation: "The West don't care what you call yourself. It's what you call others that lets you stay healthy."[12]

In 1850 the vision of the lawless West, combined with references to another great criminal organization, was dramatically reinforced: Edward Bonney's *The Banditti of the Prairies; or, The Murderer's Doom!!* appeared. Needless to say, care must be taken to avoid confusion with William Bonney and *The Banditti of the Plains,* both of which were to have significant effects on later western history. Edward Bonney's book, first published as a newspaper serial, told of the author's discovery of and efforts to combat criminal elements threatening the welfare of the Middle West. The New Yorker moved to the Illinois frontier in 1844 and soon found himself involved with counterfeiters, stock thieves, robbers, and killers. In Bonney's words:

Organized bands, trampling upon right and defying all law human or divine, have so annoyed the peaceful and quiet citizens of this great [Mississippi] valley that in the absence of a sufficient judicial power the aid of "Judge Lynch" has been but too frequently called in, and "a short shrift and strong cord" been the doom of those who have ever pled vainly for mercy at his bar.[13]

The author of *The Banditti of the Prairies* sought to expose these "reckless and blood-stained men" through his own investigation, testimony, and publication. Not a peace officer or a private detective, "Bonney . . . was more the bounty-hunter type, seeking reward either in money or notoriety or both . . . a snooper, a spy, a lover of blood money."[14]

The Banditti of the Prairies was a readable account of the author's experiences in ferreting out criminals. Its specific, factual details are generally reliable, although assumptions made by the writer remain quite doubtful. The book proved very popular, appearing in at least six editions in the span of only eight years. Bonney, meanwhile, continued his strange crusade along the edge of the law, eventually being charged (not convicted) of counterfeiting and murder. He died in Chicago in 1864.

While *The Banditti of the Prairies* provided a fascinating portrayal of crime on the frontier, it may be best remembered for its observations of what can be properly if unjustly described as an American outlaw subculture. Bonney pictured the then mysterious Mormons as instrumental in the lawlessness he sought to combat. Although not vituperative, *The Banditti of the Prairies* clearly viewed the Church of Jesus Christ of Latter-day Saints as a sinister force. In this the author reflected the common suspicion and fear directed toward all Mormons, especially the dreaded Danites. "The Danite Band, a secret order organized in Missouri in 1838 . . . exemplified border outlawry. Danites were reputed to be pledged to follow the wishes of the Prophet regardless of law or accepted morality."[15]

Between 1833 and 1890, the Mormons shared what virtually amounted to an outlaw religion, leading to their creation of Deseret and eventually the state of Utah. While it may seem peculiar to consider these believers together with notable criminals, such was precisely the prevailing public attitude throughout much of nineteenth-century America.

Opposition to the Mormons reached a crisis in Missouri in 1838. Different beliefs, a secretive subculture, attitudes toward slavery, economic difficulties, and rumors of polygamy led to a dramatic confrontation. Amid mass violence Gov. Lilburn W.

Boggs issued an order that all Mormons leave the state or be exterminated. Technically, this declaration of outlawry remained a part of Missouri law until 1976.

The Mormons moved north along the frontier to establish the community of Nauvoo, Illinois, where Edward Bonney encountered them during what is sometimes called the Mormon War. Once more mob violence and widespread disorder occurred. Finally, in 1846, the Mormons deserted Nauvoo and began their epic trek of more than one thousand miles to the valley of the Great Salt Lake. Intolerance, suspicion, secrecy, conflict, and violence continued, however, for several more decades. Misunderstanding led to hysteria and murder, exemplified by Utah's Mountain Meadows Massacre in 1857.

Throughout much of the nineteenth century the Mormons served as unique villains for writers of frontier fiction. Depictions of immorality and depravity then, as ever, attracted readers. Members of the outlaw sect made almost ideal scoundrels. "Included in this rogues' gallery were Mormon elders, all of them lecherous sex fiends seeking innocent virgins (usually the hero's sister) for their harems; 'pirates of the prairies' who had adopted all the vices of both whites and Indians."[16]

If the Latter-day Saints were bad, those admitted to the mysterious band of Danites (Sons of Dan) were even worse. This secret organization, about which church leaders consistently denied all knowledge, reportedly acted on orders from the highest circles. Many Americans regarded them as sinister fanatics and calculating assassins, veritable devils of the frontier. Of all the Danites, the most feared was the mysterious Porter Rockwell. He was born in Massachusetts, became a Mormon as a young man, and moved to the West with the steadily growing sect. In 1842, Rockwell, presumably on an assigned mission, shot former Missouri Governor Boggs, held responsible for the "extermination order."[17] For more than a generation the "Sword of the Prophet" and the Mormon's primary "Destroying Angel" remained at large, a phantom of the frontier, the West's foremost avenger. Precisely what he did, and upon whose instructions, will never be known.

Rockwell undoubtedly enjoyed protection from highly placed, powerful men in Deseret. He sometimes worked, very effectively, as a peace officer. And if he was an outstanding Danite, Rockwell remained a most peculiar Mormon. He never paid his tithing, he rejected polygamy, and he drank to excess.[18] Yet no one ever questioned his standing in the church; Porter Rockwell knew too much. He died quietly in 1878, having been arrested on a murder charge and promptly released on bond.

Porter Rockwell and the Danites certainly never considered themselves criminals. They viewed their activities as defensive efforts to protect the church and as a means of approaching justice through retaliation. In this, killings occurred not as murders but as necessary means of achieving retribution. When the formal law of the nation failed to protect rights and liberties, informal justice took its place. In the pattern established a century before, frontiersmen simply took matters into their own hands.

Prior to the Civil War, those acting informally against miscreants commonly called themselves regulators, but their efforts were not always outside the law. In frontier Indiana, for example:

Offenders were frequently punished by "regulators" without resort to the courts, and by an act of March 9, 1852, the legislature approved the formation of societies for the purpose of arresting horse thieves, counterfeiters and other offenders. The first society, the La Grange County Rangers, was organized in 1856. By 1859, thirty-seven companies with a membership of about two thousand had been formed.[19]

The term *regulator* fell into disuse after much publicity accorded the San Francisco vigilance committees of 1851 and 1856. Thereafter, *vigilante,* borrowed directly from the Spanish word for watchman, clearly indicated self-appointed citizens acting against criminals. The term would be freely applied, particularly in the West, to mean almost any quick, unofficial form of justice.

There were (and still are) two radically different interpretations of the American vigilante. He commonly appears as a manifestation of frontier violence. The vigilante simply relies upon force, imposing his will without regard to law. He acts as a member of a mob, a criminal, killing the innocent along with the guilty. The other view of the vigilante takes an opposite perspective. Through it he is seen as reluctantly taking essential steps against criminals to preserve order and obtain justice. The vigilante therefore represents natural law, to which citizens must resort in the absence of adequate formal agencies of government.[20]

Western history offers ample support for either attitude. On the frontier, however, evidence of the latter dominates. In blunt terms, "the depreciation of lynch law, and the whining cry that the law should be supported, that the courts should pass on the punishment, is in the first place the plea of the weak, and in the second place, the plea of the ignorant."[21] To a female traveler from England the frontier system appeared extreme but effective:

In the West, when things reach their worst, a sharp and sure remedy is provided. Those settlers who find the state of matters intolerable, organize themselves into a Vigilance Committee. . . . [W]arnings are issued to obnoxious people. . . . A number of the worst desperadoes are . . . "strung up," and ignominiously buried.[22]

In truth, the vigilante often performed a necessary function duly recognized by law. When the Independent District of Gilpin County, Colorado, was created in 1861, the miners gave primary authority to an elected president. That official in turn relied directly upon selected citizens for law enforcement. According to the code:

It shall be the duty of the President to appoint a Vigilance Committee, consisting of four persons, to examine into and report all criminal violations of the Laws of this District . . . and said committee shall receive one-half of fines arising from their investigations. . . . Any person found guilty of wilful murder shall be hanged by the neck till dead, and then given to his friends if called for, and if not to be decently buried; and all other crimes not enumerated in these laws [perjury, theft, salting claims, setting fires, nuisances] shall be punished as the Court or jury of men may direct.[23]

A Colorado incident illustrates the expedience with which westerners dealt with fugitives. When soldiers and local sheriffs failed to capture Juan and José Espinosa, wanted for theft and murder, officials offered a reward of five thousand dollars. Frontiersman Tom Tobin, attracted by the money, set out in the winter of 1862 on the brothers' trail. A few days later he appeared at Fort Garland with a mysterious sack. In the presence of the garrison's commanding officer, Tobin rolled out the heads of the Espinosas. The reward, as often occurred, was never paid. Tobin remained in the area for more than forty years, however, a living and respected example of simple justice.[24]

One of the better-known instances of vigilante activity occurred in distant Montana (then part of Idaho Territory) during the Civil War. It illustrated, perhaps more clearly than any other incident, the western reaction against official misconduct, for the outlaws and the lawmen had become one and the same. Henry Plummer, elected sheriff at Bannack in 1863, was chief of a large gang of brigands terrorizing the region. According to Thomas J. Dimsdale, "it was found that one hundred and two people had been certainly killed by those miscreants. . . . [S]cores of unfortunates had been murdered and buried, whose remains were never discovered nor their fate definitely ascertained."[25] When rumors and finally evidence of the criminal organization appeared, the vigilantes quickly organized and acted. Within a few months the episode ended, with twenty-two desperadoes executed; in many instances a famous and direct message was left with the hanged bodies: "Road Agents, Beware." Wrote Dimsdale: "The Vigilantes, for the sake of their country, encountered popular dislike, the envenomed hatred of the bad, and the cold toleration of some of the unwise good."[26]

The "Road Agent Chief," Henry Plummer, went to his death on a bitterly cold Sunday evening in January 1864. His pleas for a jury trial or exile were denied. Decades later, Sheriff Plummer would reappear in numberless western novels, serials, and films. He became the model for the outwardly respectable official revealed in the dramatic conclusion as the secret mastermind of the criminal organization. Such versions, however, do not ordinarily end with a vigilante hanging.

At least one of those lynched in Montana did not have any direct involvement with the Plummer gang. Joseph A. ("Jack") Slade died because of his notorious reputation and general defiance of the vigilantes. Often the foe of stage robbers in his supervisory position with the Overland Express, he was well known for brutality, a terrible temper, and frequent drunken interludes. The citizens of Virginia City finally had enough and decided to hang him along with members of Plummer's gang. Said Dimsdale: "The execution of Slade had a most wonderful effect upon society. Henceforth, all knew that no one man could domineer or rule over the community. Reason and civilization then drove brute force from Montana."[27] As a final bizarre touch, Slade's widow, Virginia, attempted to preserve her husband's body by having it sealed in a tin coffin filled with raw alcohol. Her objective of shipping the remains to his native Illinois for burial failed, however. The body putrefied and Jack Slade was quietly put to rest in a Mormon cemetery at Salt Lake City, Utah.

The practice of obtaining justice through direct action could nevertheless encourage a vast range of behaviors. Amid pronounced social disorder, as seen during great emotional disturbance, right became indistinguishable from wrong. And justice for some became crime for others. No place and time illustrated such dilemmas more clearly than the Kansas-Missouri border at the beginning of the Civil War.

An unfortunate sequence of events made the region famous as a breeding ground of outlawry for three generations. It began, of course, in a controversy over slavery and the admission of Kansas as a state. This led to a series of tragedies and several of the nation's most famous fugitives. One of these still remains one of the more controversial figures in American history.

John Brown was born in Connecticut in 1800. His parents took him as a child to frontier Ohio, where his mother soon died. Brown received an education in his native New England and then returned to the Middle West. Whether an abjectly inept businessman or a reasonably successful swindler and embezzler, he gradually acquired a less than admirable reputation. By 1854 he had experienced bankruptcy in four different states, as well as fatherhood on twenty occasions. Logic might indicate a possible relationship.

Brown had long been an opponent of slavery, but this grew into outright militancy with passage of the Kansas-Nebraska Act. By 1855 he had settled with several of his sons near Pottawatomie Creek, about forty-five miles southwest of Kansas City. "Surrounded by pro-slavery communities, the radical Brown came with a wagon load of guns."[28] Within a year, tension turned to disorder and violence to murder. John Brown became a fugitive from federal authorities, so he used a number of aliases, as well as disguises, and moved in secret throughout the country. Finally, in 1859, his small band of followers struck the arsenal at Harpers Ferry, now in West Virginia, approximately forty miles up the Potomac from Washington, D.C. His wild scheme of inciting a massive slave uprising had no chance of success. The government reacted quickly, dispatching a force of marines led by a promising army colonel named Robert E. Lee. Needless to say, the little group of dedicated antislavery activists met a quick defeat.[29]

John Brown was captured and promptly put on trial for treason. Previously he had been regarded primarily as a bandit turned terrorist, but attitudes in the North began to change at this time and the brigand acquired heroic stature. Brown's conduct during the trial and execution created a foundation for an essential legend. He was not to be regarded as an opportunist and killer, but a dedicated proponent of personal liberty. To a significant degree, the factor of slavery in the subsequent Civil War may be attributed to the actions of this outlaw.

Less than two months after the attack at Harpers Ferry, John Brown went to the scaffold and martyrdom at Charleston. Cadets from the Virginia Military Institute were assembled to witness the execution; within months, most of them would be involved in the terrible conflict between North and South.[30] Some years after the Civil War, the primary arsenal building was dismantled to serve as a sideshow attraction at local fairs and expositions. By that time "John Brown's Body" had become part of the nation's musical heritage, to the tune of a ribald old army song now more closely associated with "The Battle Hymn of the Republic."

Brown's reputation along the Kansas-Missouri border soon had a notable equal, although of an individual with precisely opposite opinions. Born in 1837, he too was raised in Ohio. One writer has described his father as an embezzler, his brothers as thieves, and his remarkable mother as a "diabolical creature."[31]

William Clarke Quantrill (often identified as Charles Quantrell) moved to Utah at the age of twenty, then to Kansas by 1859. Quiet, mannered, intelligent, and articulate, he sometimes earned a living teaching school. There was no indication that this slender young man, to whom young ladies seemed most attracted, would shortly become the most feared outlaw on the Kansas-Missouri border.

Precisely when, where, and why Quantrill became a criminal will never be known. In the ominous months before the outbreak of the Civil War, however, he obviously began a career of calculated lawlessness. Quantrill later invented and spread a false tale, similar in plot to those sometimes crafted to depict Indian fighters, concerning this period of his life. He claimed to be a Southerner whose family's wagon train was attacked by Kansas Jayhawkers (an Irish word for shrikes), those militant antislavery exponents, such as John Brown, haunting eastern Kansas. Quantrill survived the massacre to be rescued and restored to health by friendly Indians. He then set out on a road of vengeance, eventually tracking down, stalking, and killing thirty of the murderous Jayhawkers.[32] This story contained no element of truth, but it was widely accepted and undoubtedly contributed to the much used later theme of a lonely avenger on the trails of the American West.

Secession transformed Quantrill from a horse thief and slave stealer into an independent fighter for the Confederacy. Operating outside the normal chains of military command and often behind enemy lines, both Northern and Southern sympathizers were known as guerrillas (a term adopted from Spanish during the Napoleonic Wars). With personal plunder perhaps as much an objective as military victory, such raiders frequently played a role similar to that of privateers in earlier centuries. The analogy even applied to the flags employed and the styles of dress chosen.

Quantrill, a military tactician of rare ability and imagination, gradually assembled a large group of rebels from western Missouri. Their "uniform" consisted essentially of a large overshirt with several pockets and a diverse assortment of weapons. They became known as Quantrill's Raiders, and their ranks included several men who subsequently emerged as the nation's most notorious outlaws. Without design, the former schoolteacher ran a school for crime.

By 1862 the Confederacy's Partisan Ranger Act allowed selected officers to form bands of guerrillas operating behind Federal lines. The border raiders were duly sworn into service, with Quantrill elected as captain. Operating in Missouri, Kansas, and Arkansas, they began a campaign of systematic destruction. As a contemporary of Quantrill stated, "his mission was not to kill, alone, but to terrify."[33] To attain this objective, he developed techniques which became hallmarks of noted American outlaws. He relied on patience and planning, sudden and surprise attack, and the use of great force and violence.

Quantrill's Raiders gained a fearsome reputation as woodsmen, horsemen, and marksmen, and so the legends began to form. Among the multitude of guerrillas supporting the Confederacy, Quantrill became noted as a particularly daring, cruel, cunning, and charismatic leader. In April 1862 he and his men were formally outlawed by the Union, a step which seemed only to encourage young men to join his band.[34] Soon after that, Quantrill undertook a journey to Richmond, Virginia, in a vain effort to obtain a commission as a colonel in the Confederate army. James A. Seddon, secretary of war, personally denied the request.

Quantrill returned to his guerrillas and began a campaign of increasing ferocity. One of the fascinating explanations for the change concerned his horse, Charley. This mount was Quantrill's favorite, and only he could ride him. Charley would neigh a clear warning if strangers approached camp and thereby saved the rebel gang on several occasions. When a blacksmith accidentally hamstrung the horse, Quantrill became a bitter and vicious man.[35]

A tragic sequence of events then transpired. In an effort to combat the guerrillas, Union forces began systematically to arrest and imprison female members of families suspected of Southern sympathies. To add to this clearly unconstitutional practice, the women and girls were crowded into a crumbling three-story building in Kansas City. A military surgeon urged the district's commanding officer, Gen. Thomas Ewing, to have the hostages moved. He refused, and one August afternoon "the building suddenly collapsed with a thunderous crash. . . . [F]rom the rubble rescuers pulled the crushed and mangled bodies."[36] Within a few days, William Clarke Quantrill put into motion a bold plan destined to make his name a household word along the frontier.

Quantrill assembled approximately 450 guerrillas, including Bill Anderson, Frank James, and Cole Younger, and promptly crossed the border into Kansas. The column moved very quickly toward its objective, a prominent center of operations for Jayhawkers. According to a notably unsympathetic writer, "they were the best horsemen in America at that time and as a military organization perhaps the world has not surpassed that band led by Quantrill to Lawrence."[37] Such a statement might well be contested by followers of the First Virginia Cavalry or the Quahadi Comanches, but Quantrill's Raiders certainly were a very formidable fighting force and they undoubtedly rode for revenge.

On August 21, 1863, just before the dawn attack, "for the first time the black banner was unfurled. In the center of it, and neatly worked with red silk was the single word 'Quantrill.' "[38] Then, writes William A. Settle, Jr.,

a few minutes later the most fiendish massacre of the Civil War was underway.

In the next two hours, at least 150 defenseless victims—mostly men, but also a few boys—died at the hands of the raiders from Missouri. No women were harmed, but . . . houses and building were looted and burned, sometimes with the occupants hiding inside.[39]

Union reaction to the raid on Lawrence was swift and drastic. On August 25, General Ewing issued his renowned Order Number 11:

All persons living in Jackson, Cass, and Bates Counties, and in that part of Vernon included in this district [of Missouri] . . . are hereby ordered to remove from their present places of residence within fifteen days from the date hereof.

Those who within that time establish their loyalty . . . will be permitted to remove to any military station in this district. . . . All others shall remove out of the district. . . .

All grain and hay in the field or under shelter . . . within reach of military stations . . . will be taken to such stations and turned over to the proper officers. . . . All grain and hay found . . . not convenient to such stations, will be destroyed.[40]

The practical effect of the order was to drive into immediate exile and poverty virtually all residents of approximately three thousand square miles south of Kansas City. In most instances, Federal troops or Jayhawkers set fire to the fields and destroyed the houses. For decades the region was called the burnt district, marked by lonely chimneys of former homes.

Nearly a century later, author Paul I. Wellman advanced the theory that Ewing's drastic action against the people of western Missouri, most of whom probably never helped the Confederate guerrillas, created a legacy of resentment of authority which spawned an outlaw dynasty.[41] While such an analysis can never be proved, there is ample evidence to support it. No region of the nation may be more accurately called outlaw country than the western foothills of the Ozarks, including the desolated burnt district.

Several months after the raid on Lawrence, Quantrill shifted his operations to Texas. His force dwindled rapidly as some guerrillas (such as Bill Anderson) stayed on to fight in Missouri and others (such as Cole Younger) joined the regular Confederate army. Meanwhile, Quantrill had acquired a mistress and probable common-law wife. A farmer's daughter, Katherine King usually used the name Kate Clarke to avoid identification; "sometimes, dressed in men's clothing, she rode with his band as it roamed the hills and brush."[42]

As the end of the war approached, Quantrill suddenly moved far to the east. One explanation for this strange behavior is that the guerrilla leader planned to assassinate President Abraham Lincoln in Washington. If so, he delayed too long in Kentucky. There, in May 1865, his small band (still including Frank James) joined in battle with plundering Union forces and Quantrill was mortally wounded. He died several days later at the age of twenty-seven and was quickly buried in Louisville in an unmarked grave. Legend has him leaving a bequest to Kate Clarke, with which she subsequently established a prominent Saint Louis brothel.[43] Twenty-two years after Quantrill's death, his mother had her son's remains disinterred, presumably for reburial in Ohio. According to a particularly grisly although plausible variation, however, she sold the bones as souvenirs![44]

In the normal pattern for renowned outlaws, Quantrill did not die. His disappearance from the Kansas-Missouri area added credence to the idea of survival, and reports of death in Kentucky were widely disbelieved. In fact, men claiming to be Quantrill eventually appeared in Arkansas, Colorado, and Mexico. Decades after his death, many people believed that "after the war he went with a few of his most bloodthirsty companions to Brazil. He is now back in the United States, he is poor in pocket and teaching school in winters."[45]

Quantrill seems always to have been viewed in great extremes. To some he was a gallant defender of the Southern cause, a "gloriously romantic cavalier of the border, the bravest of the brave."[46] This attitude, based on such commentaries as John N. Edwards's influential 1877 book *Noted Guerrillas,* had a natural audience. Quantrill's Raiders held annual reunions until 1920 and attracted far more claims to membership than could ever be justified. Throughout the South and much of the West, men took pride in having ridden "under the black flag."

The opposite view of Quantrill "pictured him as a 'degenerate' and a 'depraved' monster who was motivated solely by 'blood-madness' and a lust for 'plunder' and 'fallen women.' "[47] William Elsey Connelley fueled such attitudes in his 1909 volume *Quantrill and the Border Wars*. This carefully noted diatribe found the personification of evil in Quantrill:

> In cruelty he towered above the men of his time. Somewhere of old his ancestors ate the sour grapes which set his teeth on edge. In him was exemplified the terrible and immutable law of heredity. He grew into the gory monster whose baleful shadow falls upon all who share the kindred blood. He made his name a Cain's mark and a curse to those condemned to bear it.[48]

Whether a demon from hell or a bold Robin Hood of the Confederacy, Quantrill became something for everyone. Both extreme views were reflected in a popular ballad describing the raid on Lawrence (see the Appendix). He could also be transported easily to fit the needs of writers. One frequently employed theme found the guerrilla leader going west instead of east, to Colorado instead of Kentucky, as the Civil War ended. There the rebels might fight Indians or turn to outright banditry. Such versions typically conclude with Quantrill (almost always portrayed as a man of middle age) dying bravely, allowing the audience to reach a personal conclusion about his essential good or evil. The hero, perhaps a youthful member of the gang, is then permitted to begin a new life with the lovely ingenue; such a version does seem better than having a mother sell the bones of her son.

This scenario, while quite lacking in fact, apparently derived from a quite dissimilar episode in Colorado history. Shortly before the Civil War began, a founder of the mining town of Fairplay, Jim Reynolds, became a robber.[49] He then went to Texas and several years later undertook a bold raid back into the Rockies. In 1864, Reynolds led about fifty Southern sympathizers to Colorado with a plan of robbing gold shipments in the mountains west of Denver. The scheme failed. Most of the guerrillas promptly defected, while posses and U.S. Cavalry detachments hunted down nearly all of the remainder. These were tried and convicted, given life sentences, and quickly "shot dead while trying to escape." They had managed to hold up one stagecoach and never harmed anyone, but legend still has them burying a huge treasure somewhere in the mountains.[50] If he knew of the escapade, Quantrill must not have been impressed. On the other hand, the performance of John Wilkes Booth surely received his sincerest admiration.

The shooting of President Lincoln on April 14, 1865, was the American crime of the century. It led to an extensive manhunt throughout several states and the death of twenty-six-year-old actor John Wilkes Booth in a burning Virginia barn twelve days after the assassination. One myth has him escaping to France. Nine other individuals were implicated in the conspiracy, eight of whom soon faced military trial. In July, four convicted accomplices were hanged. One of these, Mary Surratt, in whose rooming house the murder was planned, became the first woman to die on a gallows in the United States. Four others, including Dr. Samuel Mudd, who had treated the injured Booth, received long prison sentences.

One of the suspects in the assassination escaped. John H. Surratt, Mary's son, made his way to Canada, Europe (to serve in the Vatican Guard), and eventually Egypt. He was finally caught and returned to the United States for trial. The hysteria resulting from Lincoln's murder had ended, however, and it was impossible for the prosecution to convict Surratt, who settled peacefully in Baltimore as an auditor. By 1869, President Andrew Johnson had pardoned Dr. Mudd and two other convicted conspirators; a third had died of yellow fever in prison.

The Civil War's end set the stage for America's greatest era of outlawry. Within a generation, important new properties had been added to the production, and these inaugurated a succession of features which broadened the significance of the fugitive criminal. Instead of individuals or isolated small groups, the new brigands represented organizations masked by secrecy and possessing great power. Furthermore, such groups as Murrell's "mystic clan" threatened far more than occasional acts of violence or against property. They seemed to constitute a grave danger to the very fabric of society. John Brown's terrorists were of little consequence by themselves, but they attempted to ignite the same great horror posed by John Murrell: a massive slave revolt. That could destroy the culture of the South.[51]

These outlaws obviously were something more than a problem for peace officers or even vigilantes. Quantrill did not come alone or with a few skulking felons. He rode at the head of a rapidly moving column of experienced and hardened guerrillas. No sheriff or constable could seriously impede their sudden assault, and such outlaws left utter destruction in their wake.

At least some of the rebel forces represented a dire threat toward people's concepts and beliefs. They challenged social institutions with the strength of their own convictions. Porter Rockwell and the Danites did not kill for profit; they had a cause. Whatever their initial motives may have been, John Brown and William Quantrill undoubtedly attracted followers clearly dedicated to a goal, a mission, a faith. More than opponents of a government, these were society's rebels.

Such desperadoes would be called degenerates, fiends, demons, and fanatics. Evil in and of themselves, they exemplified ancient concepts of outlawry and so must be hunted down and exterminated. But of course such public attitudes only disguised deep and often unstated fears. Slave revolt, secession, and Mormonism were perceived as terrible threats for many reasons, including suppressed personal doubts and a lack of confidence in established social institutions.

Those representing strong, mysterious, desperate agencies of fear became images of disorder. They appeared often to have association with the frontier, a region already perceived as wild, primitive, and violent. With the Civil War's conclusion, a new background for development appeared and the American outlaw found a new home: the West.

CHAPTER 6

The Bugheway

No citizen shall be outlawed, nor shall any person be transported out of the State for any offense committed within the same.

—TEXAS CONSTITUTION, ARTICLE I, SECTION 20

ONE popular theme of Western fiction involves a community cowered by the threats of an outlaw gang. Only the efforts of a valiant hero restore order—after the climactic gunfight, of course. The basic story has been used in some truly distinguished motion pictures, but it is essentially false. However useful to writers of fiction, the very concept contradicts the nature of the American frontier.

Pioneers of any age, sex, race, denomination, or nationality were by nature courageous, hardy, and self-reliant. On the frontier, virtually all men, and many women and children, viewed firearms as essential tools. Winchester's "gun that won the West" and Colt's "peacemaker" were more than advertisements. A large percentage of men had served in the Civil War for the North or the South (and a few for both). Many had battled Indians, and most undoubtedly viewed the native tribes as a danger far surpassing that ever posed by any gang of outlaws. Cowards tended not to tarry long on the American frontier.

What happened when a group of gunmen actually threatened Buffalo, Wyoming, in 1892?

When . . . it was learned that the invaders were on their way . . . a feeling of alarm and determination at once took possession of the people. Robert Foote, the leading merchant . . . dashed up and down the streets calling the citizens to arms. . . .

"It is the duty of every citizen to protect and uphold the laws of his country. . . . An armed body of assassins . . . is now marching on our village with open threat to murder our citizens and destroy our property. . . . I call upon you to shoulder your arms and come to the front to protect all that you hold dear. . . . If you have no arms, come to my store and get them free of charge. . . . Fall in line."

The venerable appearance of Mr. Foote . . . had the desired effect. In less than one hour a hundred brave men were under arms. . . .

They were all sworn in as deputy sheriffs and systematically organized, the city marshal co-operating with them in every detail. Pickets were mounted and stationed well out on all the approaches to the town, and order and discipline everywhere established and maintained. The churches and school houses were opened as quarters for the men, and the good women volunteered their services as in the old colonial days of our country. [?] As flying couriers carried the news to the country districts, the settlers came pouring in, each man with his gun and pistol, and a look of determination on his face that boded no good to the outlaws who dared to invade their homes.[1]

It was all quite efficient—only three troops of cavalry from Fort McKinney rescued the invaders. Smaller though better known gangs of desperadoes experienced similar receptions in Northfield, Minnesota, and Coffeyville, Kansas. Criminals just did not terrorize western towns. In some instances their escapades seemed only to provide the frontiersmen with opportunities for diversion.

There can be no doubt that self-defense and vigilante justice played significant roles in the early West, and the tradition lingered for several decades. The importance of expedient forms of trial and retribution in crime control remains conjectural, but the classic ingredients of penology were hallmarks of the system: rapidity, certainty, and severity. In addition, as on the Klondike in Alaska, vigilantes rejected many characteristics associated with mob rule.

When a crime was committed it was reported to the recorder of the mining camp. A complaint was then written out. If they had no paper they would use birch bark. The accused was then arrested by order of the recorder, and a miners' meeting was held. A jury of twelve men was summoned. The recorder would appoint one prominent man to defend and one to prosecute the defendant. He would get a fairer trial than any man is allowed under our laws in the States. But if he were found guilty of a capital crime, such as murder for the purpose of robbery, or stealing grub from a cabin, his punishment was terrible, swift, and sure.[2]

The author of these words, whether called Frank Canton or by his real name, Joe Horner, should be taken seriously. He knew justice personally from both sides, as outlaw and as peace officer.

On the early frontier, "the entire absence of jails and prisons reduced available penalties to three—banishment, whipping, and death."[3] Perhaps as a consequence, lynching flourished throughout the West. The lives of those accused of serious offenses often were terminated summarily. By legend, repeated hangings left a large Cottonwood tree in Pueblo, Colorado, almost constantly skinned of bark.[4]

The number of lynchings will never be known because the execution of outlaws frequently received little publicity. As an early pioneer slyly commented, "it is sometimes amusing to hear people say that the murderers of so-and-so in those days were never caught. Well, ignorance is bliss."[5] For a full century historians have delighted in pointing out that more individuals on the frontier died by mob violence than through legal execution.[6]

But such a fact can be somewhat misleading. Throughout the United States, more people died by mob violence than through legal execution until about 1900. And the West by no means led the nation in lynchings; ten times more such killings occurred in the South, with Mississippi and Georgia heading the list. With the exception of New England, lynchings transpired with frequency in all parts of the country.[7]

Nevertheless, westerners certainly had their own informal means of social control and their own language to describe those in need or correction. Thus an individual of ill repute might be variously referred to as "bad medicine," *cabrón* (from the Spanish for the he-goat or cuckold), high-line rider (who can look for lawmen), "curly wolf," road agent, "sticky rope" (for rustler), snake, or "man with wool in his teeth" (for one suspected of stealing sheep). Another unique descriptive term was "bugheway," apparently a corruption of French *bourgeois* but implying a dangerous and mysterious blackguard.[8]

Pioneers remained remarkably forgiving and tolerant of those with questionable histories. In some instances they knowingly accepted outlaws, so long as the fugitives took care to commit no local crimes. But a bugheway threatening his neighbors could expect little sympathy. In one instance from the early 1900s the residents of southeast Utah's Robbers Roost region had a problem. A local drunkard known as Shoot-Em-Up-Bill Hatfield, believed to be a descendant of the famous feuding West Virginia clan, earned a reputation as a troublemaker who posed a significant danger to the area's children. After two years of patience, a delegation of citizens visited Hatfield and shot him to death. The case eventually reached a coroner's jury, which was convened in a store. Although promptly discharged, the primary suspect was reprimanded by the presiding judge, who "remarked he ought to throw the book at him for his lack of civic pride in letting the matter drag on all this time."[9] Penalties in the West were sometimes related to how much a victim deserved to die. Incidentally, Len McCarty served as a particularly well informed juryman in this case. His father, Tom, was at the time a known outlaw associate of Butch Cassidy's fabled Wild Bunch.

There was, of course, an ugly side to such events. "What with presumption of guilt, inability to compel witnesses, acceptance of prejudicial jurors, carelessness about the rules of evidence, and lack of competent and watchful judges, trial as performed by vigilantes has been deficient in many of the safeguards against error and abuse,"[10] John W. Caughey asserts. The same valid criticisms, of course, may be addressed to modern criminal courts throughout much of the United States.

Seemingly barbaric punishments inflicted by vigilantes upon those deemed guilty must be viewed in relation to their time. Whippings were commonly applied, and to extreme degrees. Thus a California thief found guilty of taking provisions from a tent in 1850 received seventy-five lashes. The victim administered some of the specified strokes, followed by the sheriff and several citizens apparently anxious to take a hand.[11]

For more serious offenses a common penalty was death. Lynchings did not attract much attention or indication of public alarm. Consequently, in 1879 the *Weekly New Mexican* at Santa Fe only briefly and quite casually noted the murder of an unknown man at Piedra, followed by successful pursuit of the killers: "The same night the two murderers, who in the meantime had made full confessions, were taken from the jail and hung."[12]

But one should keep the punishments inflicted by vigilantes of the West in perspective. In 1987, Arkansas prisoners, including pregnant women, were found chained to trees. A few years before authorities of that same state's unconstitutional penal system tortured inmates with electric shock while encouraging extortion, homosexual rape, and homicide.[13] Frontier vigilantes could only have regarded such practices with contempt. While not always exemplary, their actions usually sprang from perceived need.

Vigilantes had varying relationship with formal agencies of justice. In many places, they formed willing alliances. Some of those responsible for exterminating fifteen or more rustlers in Montana in 1884 held special commissions as deputy federal marshals or stock inspectors. The next year, Arizona Gov. F. A. Tritle recommended that Congress authorize fifty-six hundred dollars to reimburse the citizens of Cochise County for taking action against southwestern cattle thieves.[14]

At other times and places, vigilantes demonstrated the contempt they held for courts. In 1880, for example, the citizens of Fairplay, Colorado, were displeased with a sentence of only eight years for homicide, so townsmen simply hanged the killer, John Hooper, from the second-story window of the courthouse. The vigilantes also took care to place a noose on the judge's desk.

Fairplay's jurist took the hint and promptly left town. In 1953, incidentally, a likely hangman's rope was discovered during remodeling of Colorado's "court that never adjourned."[15]

The notion that crime declined as formal agencies of justice appeared lacks clear foundation. A defender of early western vigilantism presented quite the opposite view:

> With the rise of legislative assemblies, the adoption of a constitution, and the election of state and county officers, the administration of affairs in the more settled parts was taken from the hands of the merchants, mechanics, and miners, and placed under the direction of the officers of the law and legal tribunals. Then the wicked took heart. Hitherto there had been an absence of those legal and political juggleries which primarily are devoted to defeating the ends of justice. Now might crime weave round itself the threads of law, as the larva spins the protecting cocoon. Most strange and paradoxical was it that the elevation of law should have subverted legal authority, and that the cultivation of morals should have so demoralized the community. . . . [T]he establishing of courts tended to encourage crime rather than prevent it. . . . Police officers connived with professional house-breakers and shared the spoil.[16]

The quality of crime, and of criminal justice, apparently has changed little during the last century. Then, as now, the vast majority of offenses were misdemeanors, less serious violations now typically punished by fines or short jail sentences but once commonly penalized by whipping or banishment. Arrest statistics reveal striking similarities and some significant variations.

A survey of Arizona Rangers' activities during a four-year period may be compared with recent national figures. The territorial officers reported felony charges in approximately one of every four apprehensions, a proportion almost identical to that found throughout the United States at present. Most arrests were for misdemeanors relating to alcohol, disorderly conduct, fighting, and petty theft, reflecting general conditions which show little change.

Among the felony charges, some interesting variations have occurred. The Arizona Rangers arrested suspects for murder and grand larceny (primarily of livestock) much more frequently than current peace officers do. On the other hand, burglary and crimes associated with fraud appeared far less often than in modern arrest statistics. Apprehensions for aggravated assault, robbery, and rape occupy proportions showing no significant change. Drug violations appeared rarely in arrest records as occasional misdemeanor charges of "keeping and frequenting opium resorts." And instances of driving while intoxicated (of horses) were then typically treated as ordinary drunkenness. [17]

The distinction between felonies and misdemeanors was just as significant a century ago as it is at present. Those arrested for more serious crimes faced possible indictment by a grand jury, a contested trial, and the likelihood of long prison sentences. Those apprehended for misdemeanors were usually processed with scant regard for procedural formality. Early judges in Colorado sometime traveled with a peace officer and clerk, enabling arrest, trial, conviction, and sentencing in one rapid and continuing action. [18]

A misdemeanor trial, seldom by jury, often consisted of nothing more than a plea of guilty and nearly automatic assignment of a fine. From 1882 to 1885, for example, the police court in Boulder, Colorado, acquitted defendants in only about one case in a hundred, a percentage not unlike that of today's municipal tribunals. Most of Boulder's misdemeanants, nearly always charged with public intoxication, disturbing others, or prostitution, promptly paid their apparently predetermined fines of three to five dollars. [19]

It was quite different with serious felonies. In most jurisdictions these went to a grand jury, a body exercising considerably more discretion than is typical at present. Prosecutors had to present convincing evidence of guilt to obtain the true bill required to take the case to trial, and that often proved a difficult task on the frontier. A change in attitude had transpired since the preceding generation held sway. Westerners' suspicion of formal authority emerged as a very significant factor. Instead of punishing wrongdoers, they sought to protect the accused from arbitrary government. Grand juries could dismiss cases for virtually any reason or none at all. The panel for the Second Judicial District in Indian Territory in 1893 rejected nearly one-third of all applications for indictment presented to it. The grand jury routinely returned true bills for gambling and false pretense while looking with considerable suspicion upon accusations of importing liquor.[20] Westerners apparently liked bootleggers more than swindlers.

Occasionally a grand jury would take upon itself the duty of denouncing corruption in government or what was perceived to be an improper emphasis by lawmen. The latter often concerned concentration on vice offenses instead of those against person and property. Some New Mexicans complained in 1877: "With reference to the Justices of the Peace and Constables of the County of Santa Fe, this Grand Jury feel that it is their imperative duty to call attention to the laxity of these officers, which endangers the personal liberty of our citizens and which at the same time we believe allows criminals to go unpunished."[21]

Next, prosecutors faced the task of taking felony cases to trial, where their problems continued. Less than 10 percent of indictments for murder and assault with intent to kill led to conviction in the Texas Republic.[22] A review of court records from selected federal jurisdictions in the West from 1896 to 1904 indicates that felony cases concluded with findings of guilt about half the time, including pleas to reduced charges. The percentage of acquittals and dismissals is much lower in today's criminal courts.[23]

The western outlaw enjoyed a substantially greater likelihood of release than his modern counterpart. Hubert Howe Bancroft reported: "As a matter of course all criminals were strong law and order men. 'Only give us a trial,' they said, 'it is all we ask,' meaning thereby a trial in the courts, with one of their colleagues as judge, another as sheriff, and the jury-box well filled with sympathizing friends."[24] Furthermore:

So simple a thing as the impanelling of a jury was profitable if one understood one's business. Likewise witnesses were always at hand who would testify on either side of any case, even though they never heard of it before trial. . . . [P]ersons who waited at the proclamation posts set up by sheriffs at their doors and haunted the purlieus of the courts ready to swear to anything for a consideration. There was always money in office for judges ready to sell state morals by auction, as well as for sheriffs, who bought truth cheap and sold falsehood high.[25]

During the 1870s, California juries routinely demanded payment of their fees before handing in a sealed verdict to be read by the courts.[26] It was, in short, a good time and place for criminal defendants. And when their interests coincided with a large portion of the public, such as sometimes occurred when small ranchers were accused of cattle rustling, conviction became virtually impossible. The frustrated secretary of a Wyoming stockmen's association wrote as follows: "We have thrown away thousands of dollars in the past [four years] in sincere efforts to stop thieving on the range, and the only result has been that we have been thrown ignominiously out of court."[27]

Conviction by no means meant punishment. Appeals to higher state courts often proved successful, for many reviewing judges protected defendants' rights. A favorite device demanded strict construction of indictments, with any variation or possible exception leading to prompt reversal. Texas took the technique to incredible degrees. Thus to "kill by drowning" was deemed insufficient; "by immersion in water" should have been added. Homicide by shooting also failed, lacking the specification "by gun." And "stomping to death" was incomplete because it did not state "by the feet."[28]

Western feelings toward the death penalty reflected a change in attitude. Somehow, lynching by vigilantes had more appeal than execution by authorities. Michigan began the movement toward abolition of capital punishment in 1846, but the West led the way by the end of the nineteenth century. When the nation entered World War I, thirteen of the United States had abandoned the death penalty, including Colorado, Kansas, Washington, Oregon, Arizona, North and South Dakota, Minnesota, and Missouri. Although California and Texas continued to execute large numbers, New York remained the state most often relying on the death penalty.[29]

Tolerance for people with troubled backgrounds continued. Such acceptance extended to individuals convicted for serious crimes. Former outlaws probably encountered less negative reaction in the West than anywhere else in the country. On the frontier, people focused upon the dreams of tomorrow, not the failures of yesterday. Consequently, a New Mexico newspaper quite casually announced that "John Kinney the terrible bandit of the Rio Grande has settled down to peaceful habits and opened a meat market in La Mesilla. Success to you, John."[30]

Perhaps most significantly, attitudes toward the ancient concept of outlawry underwent pronounced change. The United States had followed fundamental outlines of the common-law process after the American Revolution, with certain additional safeguards. In some instances, recognition and restriction of outlawry appeared in state constitutions. Thus while the Revolution still raged, Massachusetts provided that "no subject shall be . . . put out of the protection of the law . . . but by the judgment of his peers, or the law of the land."[31] Tennessee adopted more sweeping protections, stating: "No man [freeman until 1870] shall be taken or imprisoned, or disseized of his freehold, liberties or privileges, or outlawed, or exiled, or in any manner destroyed or deprived of his life, liberty or property, but by the judgment of his peers or the law of the land."[32] Provisions similar to these appeared in the constitutions of several other states, including New Hampshire, Maryland, North Carolina, and Arkansas.

Outlawry, while neither endorsed nor forbidden by the Constitution of the United States, was used in the federal courts.[33] That did not, of course, hinder its recognition by the sovereign states. Individuals might be outlawed, but only in accordance with constitutional provisions and statutory guidelines intended to prevent arbitrary application. The process was rarely used on the early frontier, although sometimes it was accompanied by offers of suitable rewards.

After the Civil War, an obvious trend toward abolition of outlawry began. This goal could be achieved in any of three ways. Virginia followed the obvious course of repealing the appropriate statutes. The Alabama Supreme Court simply declared outlawry repugnant to the state's constitution and institutions. Texas took an even more dramatic course. In 1876, with the end of Reconstruction, a new state constitution was adopted; its opening declaration of fundamental rights forbade the practice of outlawry forever.[34]

Texas's unique constitutional protection saw rare but interesting use. In one politically inspired instance the town of Weatherford attempted to enforce a local prohibition against the renting of private property to a "lewd woman." The Texas Supreme Court held the action to be in violation of the constitutional protection against outlawry and "in contradiction of common right."[35] While the lady in question probably did not consider herself in the same category as Jesse James and Billy the Kid, she enjoyed some of the same legal rights.

Outlawry as a technical process against fugitives vanished from the West. It lingered on, largely forgotten, in parts of the East for almost another century. The last three states to maintain the legal concept bordered on the Atlantic: New York, Pennsylvania, and North Carolina. Each had its own distinctive form, illustrative of the variations which once existed throughout the nation.

The New York statute on outlawry applied only to fugitives who had pleaded guilty or had been convicted of treason. Its consequences included placing the subject completely outside the scope of the law, declaring him civilly dead, and forfeiting all his property to the state. New York's provision fell into disuse generations ago and was finally repealed in 1970.[36]

Pennsylvania's statute, based on an act of 1791, closely paralleled common law: it allowed outlawry of any fugitive indicted for "treason, felony of death, robbery, burglary, sodomy or buggery." The process really consisted of a finding of guilt and sentencing without trial. A Pennsylvania outlaw could be legally executed upon capture. The detailed statute remained part of the law, although long ignored, until it was repealed in 1978.[37]

North Carolina has the distinction of being the last state in the nation to outlaw fugitives from justice. The statute, although varying significantly from common law, still permitted dire consequences:

> In all cases where any justice or judge . . . shall . . . receive information that a felony has been committed by any person, and that such person flees from justice . . . the justice or judge is hereby empowered and required to issue proclamation against him . . . at the door of the courthouse . . . and as the justice or judge shall direct; and if any such person against whom proclamation has been thus issued continues to stay out, lurks and conceals himself, and does not immediately surrender himself, any citizen of the State may capture, arrest, and bring him to justice, and in case of flight or resistance . . . by him, after being called on and warned to surrender, may slay him without accusation of any crime.[38]

The statute, in slightly different form, was a reaction to conditions in North Carolina shortly after the Civil War. Escapades of the notorious Lowry (also spelled Lowery) gang, rumored to be of mixed Indian and black ancestry, led to enactment of the outlawry provision. North Carolina's statute, based on precedents extending back to the colonial period, enjoyed sporadic use until recent times. In 1960 for example, Robert Tyson, an escaped prison inmate separately wanted for murder and rape, was formally outlawed. He probably never knew of his unusual legal status, however, because he committed suicide the day after the proclamation of outlawry.[39]

Time and changing concepts of due process eventually undermined North Carolina's unique statute. By the 1970s it faced repeated challenges based on requirements of probable cause, notice, the possibility of cruel and unusual punishment, and a danger of arbitrary application. Finally, in 1976, a federal court ruled the outlawry provision unconstitutional,[40] but the North Carolina legislature declined to remove the outdated section from the state's general statutes.

Abolition of outlawry as a legal process did not, of course, remove all related consequences. Authority to kill a fugitive certainly diminished, but slaying a felon attempting to escape or posing a threat to another was still considered justified. The law continued to permit, or even encourage, private citizens to join in the pursuit of fugitives, even when suspects could not be readily identified. In some instances appropriate officials authorized such action by proclamation. The acting governor of New Mexico (Gov. S. B. Axtell naturally being in attendance at the Philadelphia Exposition) took such a step in 1877:

> Whereas it has been officially represented to this office that organized lawlessness prevails in Doña Ana and adjoining counties, that the people are powerless and terrorism prevails . . . any and all good citizens are hereby authorized to pursue and arrest either or both of said men [two unnamed murderers of Benito Cruz]. This proclamation shall be a warrant of authority to any such citizen making such arrest and delivery, and to use such force as necessary.[41]

Common law, routinely expanded by statute, recognized the power of posse comitatus, by which peace officers could request assistance from citizens in arrests. In the West, such authority was often broadly construed to authorize widespread manhunts.

Even as outlawry disappeared from the language of the law it took on far broader popular meanings. Instead of individuals formally outside legal protection, it became descriptive of notorious fugitives from justice. Indeed, any lawless person or habitual criminal might be called an outlaw. In the West the term was also applied to untamable horses or wild steers. It carried implications not invariably bad, with hints of adventure and independence, and it proved remarkably flexible in application. Groups, faiths, places, and even things were sometimes called outlaw, westerners demonstrating considerable imagination in such respects. Consequently, the Cheyenne Dog Soldiers, Mormonism, the Oklahoma Panhandle, and certain cattle brands shared on various occasions the appellation *outlaw*.

Broad and indefinite usage naturally led to some confusion. Simply describing a wanted man as an outlaw could promote questions of classification: "A man might be rated by his own contemporaries as both a badman and a goodman. Warrants might be out for his arrest in one town while he was serving, and ably, as peace officer in another."[42] All three of the West's most famous lawmen were, at one time or another, fugitives from agencies of justice. James Butler ("Wild Bill") Hickok fled Hays City, Kansas, in 1870 after killing a soldier and seriously wounding another. Wyatt Earp, previously wanted for horse theft, escaped from Arizona in the aftermath of Tombstone's gunfight at the O.K. Corral. Even Sheriff Pat Garrett of New Mexico was sought for defying a court's writ of habeas corpus in 1882, one year after he killed Billy the Kid.[43]

The identification of major criminals as outlaws still remained quite clear. They eventually received recognition as symbols of a time and place best known through imagination. In fact, most were not significantly different from criminals of any age or nation. Their fame rests largely upon legend rather than fact. Very, very few of the West's most renowned outlaws were ever outlawed, and many never had a clear reason for committing their crimes. Most led rather short and unromantic lives marked by loneliness and fear, posing danger to others only on rare occasions. As an old frontiersman and scout recalled, "a cold, wet, starving, hunted human being comes far from being a happy individual."[44]

Most fugitives from justice were accused of crimes against property, not violence. A survey of extradition papers issued by the territorial secretary for New Mexico from 1900 to 1905 reveals that horse and cattle thieves made up half the men sought. Less than 20 percent were wanted for murder, with a slightly higher proportion sought in connection with larceny and embezzlement.[45] Nevertheless, it cannot be denied that the western outlaw enjoyed a special mystique that was destined to transform his image. A perceptive detective commented in 1882:

The criminal of the Far West is a man who displays himself most thoroughly in times of emergency. It is when he comes face to face with the officer that he is desperate and difficult to deal with. He will always fight, and the officer who hunts him down may in four cases out of five count upon having to take his man at the muzzle of his revolver. It is this fact which makes the Western narrative of more thrilling interest than that of the more conservative Eastern localities.[46]

During the nineteenth century, however, the western desperado did not occupy the position of importance indicated by present beliefs. Perceptions at the time came far closer to reality than those of today. For example, the *New York Times* of the era contained a wealth of crime news, replete with articles carrying such titles as "Bold Robbery in Hotel," "Accused of Wife Murder," "Opera Singers Robbed," "A Son's Terrible Crime," and "Murdered with An Axe," in addition to continuing columns relating phases of crime throughout the nation. Yet these reports relate to the West in only about one instance in ten, a ratio almost exactly the same as population distribution of the period. The five articles mentioned above, incidentally, came from New York City, Norwich, Chicago, Cincinnati, and Milwaukee. It is also of interest that western newspapers then contained less local crime news, preferring politics and agriculture, than is generally found in current publications.[47]

Frontier bandits, viewed as rather primitive, enjoyed no special prestige. The nation's most notorious criminal class consisted of skilled craftsmen concentrating on safecracking, fraud, and counterfeiting. They were often portrayed as sophisticated, successful, and wealthy, with proven abilities to avoid and frustrate agencies of justice.

The most wanted men in America did not steal cattle or rob trains. Billy the Kid, John Wesley Hardin, and Butch Cassidy ranked well down on the nation's list of famous outlaws. Between 1875 and 1900, "fugitive number one," by Pinkerton record, was Thomas Hurley. He stole no horses and held up no banks. Thomas Hurley was believed to be the chief assassin for the secret labor organization known as the Molly Maguires, once active in the coal fields of Pennsylvania. He was described in 1879 as twenty-five, five feet eight inches tall, about 160 pounds, with sandy hair, and rumors had him committing suicide in Colorado, sailing to England, or continuing to avenge the fabled "Mollies."[48]

Even in the West the now notorious bandits received relatively little attention. Officials concerned themselves primarily with ordinary local criminals. Those few subjected to extensive pursuit most frequently had attracted the persistent attention of powerful social and economic forces. Between 1877 and his death in 1887, the most wanted man in the American West was John Taylor. He did not rustle cattle or rob stagecoaches. John Taylor was the third president of the Mormon church, following Joseph Smith and Brigham Young. He spent most of a decade of leadership in hiding, protected by the faithful in defiance of federal efforts to suppress polygamy.[49]

The western desperado did, however, receive considerable recognition for particularly brazen or spectacular crimes. This was particularly true of train robbery. Although the first of such offenses occurred in England in 1855 and the earliest American instance (apart from military actions in the Civil War) took place in Indiana in 1866, the West gained renown for such crimes. For a generation, "train robbery was an American phenomenon. In no other country did it become a problem. . . . [T]he crime was endemic to the American West."[50]

On one occasion the train robbers were thought to pose an indirect danger to the very security of the nation itself. In 1892 the United States experienced a severe financial panic that led to a run against the dollar. In fact, major banks and the government itself faced the immediate likelihood of lacking sufficient gold to support the currency, without which the economy might collapse. The desperate solution involved a secret "gold train" racing from San Francisco to New York. It carried the equivalent in bullion of several billion current dollars and was guarded by armed railway mail clerks, at that time correctly considered the federal government's most reliable agents. Despite several mysterious incidents, there were no attempts to rob the train.[51]

Railroads and express companies resorted to various means to combat robbers, spending far more in their efforts than was ever stolen. A technique favored by the Union Pacific involved groups of carefully chosen officers waiting to travel by train to the site of the holdup and begin the chase on fast horses. Another, preferred

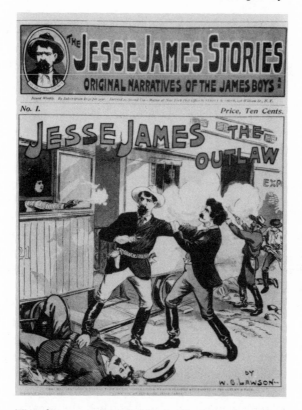

The dime novel and Missouri's legendary train robber, circa 1890.

by Wells Fargo in the Southwest, used accomplished trackers employed for their skill and endurance; Apache Indians proved uniquely successful in such work. Even so, the robbers could usually scatter and resume their identity as cowboys on remote ranches.

More traditional investigative methods also were employed. Detectives would flood an area with operatives, hoping to infiltrate criminal gangs; these efforts would be combined with offers of rewards and promises of immunity from prosecution.[52] Nevertheless, a decline in the frequency of robbery resulted from a combination of factors apart from the police. Mining shipments and payrolls decreased, traveler's checks became popular, telephone and telegraph systems expanded, and fast mail trains replaced the vulnerable express cars. Such developments frustrated robbers' efforts.

Perhaps the most powerful weapon against the bandits came through law. In 1902, Congress passed the Federal Train Robbery Act, making entry of railway cars to commit murder or robbery a federal offense. It constituted a precedent through assumption of criminal jurisdiction over acts not clearly related to operation of the national government.[53] The train robbers quickly noted a flaw in the statute, however: they could avoid its reach by striking at railroad stations and post offices rather than the trains. Eight months later, Congress closed the loophole with a separate law making the violent entry of such structures a federal crime.[54] Robbers continued to violate such provisions, but with less frequency.

If western outlaws earned their reputation for robbing trains, such was untrue with regard to banks. In an era of "professional" banditry, the frontier occupied a minor stage.[55] Of one hundred bank robberies recorded in the United States and Canada between 1862 and 1885, only eighteen occurred west of the Appalachians. New York, Massachusetts, and Pennsylvania dominated the list of popular locations and also furnished the great bulk of all sums stolen.[56] Banks of the frontier rarely reached sufficient size to tempt a knowing robber.

Myth has greatly changed reality. Today a minuscule number of white western desperadoes from the generation following the Civil War dominate not only works of fiction but those of apparent fact and academic respectability.[57] Through the years, the frontier criminal was transformed from simple bugheway to social bandit, a stereotyped figment of imagination rather than a creature of recorded history.[58] False ascriptions of idealism, generosity, cheerful virtue, superior intellect, and defeat through treachery changed the image of bad men fit for lynching into descendants of Robin Hood supposedly beloved by those they actually victimized. A succession of creative writers and artists catapulted a handful of troublesome thieves and devious killers, selected by fate rather than achievement or social condition, to lasting fame as dubious heroes.[59]

Without coincidental understanding, the outlaw's fabled days of glory drew to a close; at the same time, and with slowly growing comprehension, his era of romantic attention began. The frontier faded away, replaced by a golden myth. The desperado's ghost galloped into the new scene to achieve a prominence far exceeding any prophecy. His image bore slight resemblance to truth but proved infinitely more appealing than reality. The western outlaw was not about to disappear; he was about to become a legend.

CHAPTER 7

The Hoodlum

Outlaw fashions change, but lawlessness runs on forever.

——EMMETT DALTON

PERCEPTIONS of the American frontier have long been distinguished by contradiction. Extreme and varied portrayals applied quite clearly to the pioneers in general and to the outlaws in particular. Frontiersmen were seen as independent, crude, courageous, violent, greedy, and smart. On many occasions they appeared as a blend of eastern refinement and Indian savagery illuminated by flashes of gross materialism and great nobility. They could, in fact, be both good and bad. And some of these paradoxes had sound bases, as Lewis Garrard noted on his travels along the Taos Trail in the 1840s:

My companions were rough men . . . whose manners are blunt, and whose speech is rude—men driven to the western wilds with embittered feelings—with better natures shattered—with hopes blasted—to seek, in the dangers of the warpath, fierce excitement and banishment of care. . . . Yet these aliens from society, these strangers to the refinements of civilized life, who will tear off a bloody scalp with even grim smiles of satisfaction, are fine fellows, full of fun, and often kind and obliging.[1]

Decades later the buffalo hunters of the Great Plains were frequently pictured as brutal, treacherous exterminators who looked and acted like desperadoes fleeing from the vestiges of respectability. But Emanuel Dubbs, a Texas judge, recalled them quite differently:

116

There has never been a better, braver, nobler set of men lived. They were God's true noblemen, loyal, brave, honest, and true. A woman's honor as sacredly preserved as if she had been in paradise. Such a thing as petty theft was entirely unknown. You could leave any kind of property exposed and unprotected [in their camps], and it was safe as if locked up in a New York City vault. . . . [S]uch a thing as a fist fight rarely if ever occurred. If trouble did come up they used the gun and not the fist, this made a man careful how he treated his fellow man.[2]

Contradictory characteristics also applied to outlaws. A perceptive observer could find elements of right and wrong in a single individual. Such was the case with the English lady Isabella Bird and her strange friend the Colorado desperado Mountain Jim Nugent. When that plucky woman reported on her remarkable 1873 travels through the Rocky Mountains, she revealed more than a passing concern with the brigand soon to be killed near Estes Park:

One eye was entirely gone, and the loss made one side of the face repulsive, while the other might have been modeled in marble. "Desperado" was written in large letters all over him.

• • •

He is a man for whom there is now no room . . . and the fame of many daring exploits is sullied by crimes which are not easily forgiven here. . . . [H]e is a desperate character, and is subject to "ugly fits," when people think it best to avoid him. . . . "When he's sober Jim's a perfect gentleman; but when he's had liquor he's the most awful ruffian in Colorado."

• • •

His life, in spite of a certain dazzle which belongs to it, is a ruined and wasted one, and one asks what of good can the future have in store for one who has for so long chosen evil?

• • •

Lately a child in the other cabin was taken ill, and though there were idle men and horses at hand, it was only the "desperado" who rode sixty miles in "the shortest time ever made" to bring the doctor. . . . May our Father which is in heaven yet show mercy to His outcast child![3]

Obvious paradoxes of character, depicted objectively by Miss Bird, could also be utilized, or even created, for a variety of purposes. When the lady traveler made the acquaintance of Mountain Jim in Colorado, other outlaws were at work some five hundred miles to the east, and their portrayal had a profound effect on American myth.

Writers of the time were quite familiar with depictions of brigands from earlier times and other places. Early nineteenth-century literature abounded with useful examples, romanticizing with considerable skill both real and fictional outlaws. Some works enjoyed not only popular success but critical acclaim as well. They included all types of writing. Sir Walter Scott provided *Ivanhoe* (with a sympathetic portrayal of Robin Hood) in 1819 and *Rob Roy* (based loosely on the exploits of the Scottish bandit Robert Macgregor) two years earlier. Lord Byron wrote *The Corsair,* a lengthy poem glorifying pirates, in 1814. Johann von Schiller produced a drama entitled *Wilhelm Tell,* relating the story of Switzerland's legendary hero, in 1804; twenty-five years later, Gioacchino Rossini transformed it into the opera *Guillaume Tell,* the overture of which was destined for unique fame in the twentieth century as the "Lone Ranger" radio and television theme.

Newspapers and magazines frequently reported on the fascinating exploits of notorious Italian outlaws, such as Angelo Duca (Angiolillo), Domenico Tiburzi, Rinaldo Rinaldini, and Gaetano Ricca. General and youthful audiences delighted in Pierce Egan's *Robin Hood and Little John* and Harrison Ainsworth's *Rookwood* (featuring tales of highwayman Dick Turpin). It was, quite simply, a great period in outlaw literature.

American authors may have been frustrated by the success of such works, but writers in the United States found few domestic models worthy of real effort. No one could make heroes of the dreadful Harpes and John Murrell. Other plausible candidates may well have been slighted for racial or ethnic reasons; their day would come. And then, through a combination of conditions, events, and personalities, America suddenly produced outlaws comparable in stature to any in the world. They sprang from a natural setting already associated with violence and daring: the western frontier. Although neither time nor place showed any unusual frequency of crime, its imagined perpetrators came to represent both a region and an era.

Exploits of these brigands reached a growing audience through rapidly developing media. For the first time in American history, tens of millions of people could read. Popular newspapers, magazines, and inexpensive books catered to demand. Imaginative, if not always creative, writers provided the necessary material, often imposing old themes upon current figures for contemporary consumption. The western outlaw became transformed from a criminal into a myth.

The means employed was neither completely original nor without justification, but it had probably never before achieved such immediate impact or lasting effect. In the course of a single decade the West spawned at least a dozen bandits destined to be accorded legendary status. Several of them became world famous and symbols of a contradictory American character.

In this same era the nation created a new term to describe tough troublemakers. It appeared first in northern California about 1872 and spread across the entire nation within a decade. The word *hoodlum* indicated a young ruffian, disorderly and violent. While the term obviously originated in the West, its derivation remains a mystery. It could have been a corruption of a family name, an abbreviation of the phrase "huddle 'em," an allusion to efforts to hide the face, or even a reference to Robin Hood. Whatever the actual derivation of *hoodlum*, it carried the connotation of annoyance along with danger and fascination rather than fear.

At almost precisely the same time, northern California also gave birth to a quite remarkable outlaw folk figure, "the Bad Man from Bodie." First publicized in 1878 by E. H. Clough of the *Sacramento Bee*, he became a western myth in one decade. Whether loosely based on some real character, a composite of several desperadoes, or entirely imaginary, this frontier brigand appeared as much a demon as a human. For a generation "almost every gunfighter or rough was said to be a badman from Bodie."[4]

He symbolized an infamous mining town perched high in the Sierras about one hundred miles southwest of Lake Tahoe and once described as a "sea of sin, lashed by tempests of lust and passion." It boomed for only a few years, but the inhabitants undoubtedly found humor in a grotesquely exaggerated reputation for violence and debauchery. It was all summed up by a little girl's reported and sorrowful prayer, "Goodbye, God, I'm going to Bodie." The town's supporters (perhaps increasing her age a few years) insisted that the proper quote was, "Good, by God, I'm going to Bodie!"[5]

Early descriptions of the community's famed desperado leave little doubt about an original tongue-in-cheek intention.[6] He was incredibly profane, cowardly, vulgar, murderous, and perhaps a descendant of the "boasting chants" associated most often with boatmen of the Ohio, Mississippi, and Missouri rivers. If half the stories of the colorful badman from Bodie had been true, citizens would have quickly terminated his career with vigilante justice. Instead, he emerged as an imaginary spirit in a frontier dream.

The West had no monopoly on legendary outlaws. One destined for a special kind of immortality came from North Carolina; his name was Thomas C. Dula. He returned home after the Civil War to find a schoolteacher named Grayson having an affair with his girl. Dula killed the fickle young lady and attempted to escape from pursuers across the Blue Ridge to Tennessee. But Grayson predicted his route, caught the fugitive, and returned him for trial and eventual execution at Statesville. The culprit supposedly wrote a haunting song as a confession shortly before his hanging.[7] Time changed the name of Thomas Dula to Tom Dooley, and nearly a century later the Kingston Trio transformed his musical folk tale into the best-selling record in the nation (see the Appendix).

In the aftermath of the Civil War many border regions produced outlaws of considerable regional fame and significance. These included the Reno brothers in Indiana, Cullen Baker in Arkansas, William P. ("Wild Bill") Longley in Texas, the Farrington brothers in Tennessee, Dutch Henry Borne in Kansas, and Beanie Short in Kentucky.

Desperadoes of the era appeared in many guises: good and bad, alone and together, men and women, brazen and devious. Some became infamous evildoers with reputations that endured for decades. Such was the strange case of a family sometimes later called the Hell Benders. Where they came from and where they went, no one can say, but it is known that a family of four settled in southeast Kansas near the community of Cherryvale in 1871.[8] Old John (or Pa) Bender and his wife Old Kate (or Ma) had two children. Young John (or Geiger) was assumed to be retarded, but the daughter, Johanna (or Kate), who worked as a waitress in Cherryvale, proved the most provocative member of the family. Young and pretty, she attracted several suitors and gained a reputation locally as a spiritualist and healer.

The Benders lived in a large cabin, offering food and shelter to travelers. For many months no one associated the family with a number of mysterious disappearances in the area. Then, in 1873, inquiries concerning a missing doctor from Fort Scott led to chilling discoveries. Neighbors found the Bender home deserted, then noticed peculiar signs of digging in and around the cabin. Excavations revealed several buried bodies, all with crushed skulls.

As pieced together from reports of numerous witnesses, the story was spread by newspaper throughout the nation. The Benders had systematically killed and robbed lonely travelers. According to contemporary reports, "it is certain that they have murdered over one hundred people,"[9] and the fiends had vanished. Posses and detectives scoured the region, with discoveries reported from points as far away as Mexico, Utah, and Iowa. These all proved false. Souvenir hunters destroyed the cabin, taking pieces that reportedly were sold from San Francisco to New York.

Investigations produced an assortment of clues and possibilities. Ma and Pa supposedly spoke with pronounced German accents, although some claimed it was Dutch. They may have come from Texas with a family name of Liefen. In any event, they became a legend on the frontier, with anyone giving his name as Bender likely to be viewed with suspicion.[10]

In 1884 the continuing hunt appeared to have some success. An old man was jailed at Salmon, Idaho, in the Bitterroot Range, for a murder committed by means similar to that employed by the Benders. Witnesses from the Cherryvale area were summoned. Before they arrived, however, the suspect cut off his own foot in an attempt to escape ankle chains and bled to death. The body deteriorated so badly that identification could not be made. "Pa Bender's skull," however, was carefully preserved for permanent display in a local saloon.[11]

Five years later, aggressive detective work led to the arrest of a mother and daughter in Michigan. When extradited to Kansas, a number of witnesses identified them as Ma and Kate. Then the case fell apart. Defense attorneys for the women produced documentary evidence indicating their presence in Michigan at the time of the murders, so charges were dropped.

Early in the twentieth century another plausible end developed. Several dying men claimed to have been members of an 1873 posse which found the Benders, burned them alive, and secretly buried the bodies in a well. Still, if all such tales were true, posses slaughtered several innocent families. By the best historical evidence, "it has never been proved that the Benders were ever apprehended nor is it certain that they ever made a successful escape."[12] Cherryvale had the final solution; its citizens built a replica of the cabin in 1961 and opened a museum in memory of the murderers and their victims.

While the hunt for the Benders continued, an equally bizarre outlaw tale developed in southwest Colorado. In the winter of 1873 and against the advice of local Indians, a guide named Alfred (also identified as Alferd and Alfie) Packer led a small group of prospectors from the Salt Lake area into the rugged San Juan Mountains. Several weeks later the guide came back alone. Packer claimed his companions had abandoned him, but suspicions soon developed. Several months later searchers found five bodies along the trail, some with their skulls crushed. An even more grisly discovery followed: signs indicated that flesh had been systematically removed from the dead.[13] Packer was arrested and began to tell conflicting stories about events. He then escaped, leaving a trail through Wyoming and Utah. Nearly ten years later the guide was finally apprehended and returned for trial in Colorado.

Packer's defense, essentially a claim that one of the prospectors had turned to cannibalism in their snowbound camp and that he had finally killed in self-defense, failed. He received a sentence of forty years for murder. But even then "the man who ate Democrats" (for the political affiliations of the victims) was becoming a legend. He served only a small portion of his sentence and then obtained a position as a doorman in Denver. Until his death in 1907, Alfie had a quiet existence, although no one seemed anxious to join him on camping trips into the Rockies. Today a monument to Packer stands in Slumgullion Pass near the site of the homicides.[14] And in a bit of perverse sophomoric humor, the cafeteria in the student union at Boulder's distinguished University of Colorado carries his name.

The Benders and Packer were notorious fugitives hunted throughout the West for many years, but they represented a hideous, accurate side of crime impossible of serving as the basis for any kind of romantic outlaw tale. Systematic murder of innocents and cannibalism had no popular appeal. The West, however, offered a wide variety of offenders, including those naturally attracting far more sympathy. Among them must be ranked an American outlaw poet, "Black Bart, the Po-8."

He first robbed the California stages of Wells Fargo in 1875, establishing a pattern successfully repeated on more than a score of occasions over a period of eight years. Always working alone and wearing a mask, he used a now presumably unloaded shotgun. His robberies were carefully planned, involving a sudden appearance and use of the valuable draft horses as shields. He took the contents of coach strongboxes but never stole from the passengers. And this mysterious robber displayed a unique histrionic flair. He sometimes left notes in rhyme for his pursuers, providing his own sobriquet. The best known of the refrains read as follows:

> I've labored long and hard for bred
> For honor and for riches
> But on my corns too long you've tread
> You fine-haired Sons of Bitches.
>
> Let come what will, I'll try it on
> My condition can't be worse
> And if there's money in that box
> 'Tis munny in my purse.
>   Black Bart, the Po-8.

The robber almost dared Wells Fargo to stop him, but routine investigation proved fruitless. Offers of rewards and undercover operations produced nothing. Then, in November 1883, Black Bart finally made a mistake. Slightly wounded during a robbery near Reynolds Ferry, he managed to escape from the scene, as usual, but he left behind a number of useful clues. Among these was a handkerchief upon which Wells Fargo detectives found a laundry mark, "FX07." This, in turn, led them to a man known as Charles E. Bolton who was living quietly in San Francisco.[15]

Under intense and extended questioning the slight, dapper New York native, former miner, and Civil War veteran confessed to the last robbery, leading detectives to its hidden proceeds. Within days he pleaded guilty to that single crime and received a sentence of six years at nearby San Quentin Prison.

Nine days later Wells Fargo's chief of detectives, James B. Hume, notified agents throughout the system that although no other prosecutions would be made, "the man Chas. E. Boles [alias Charles E. Bolton] . . . is 'BLACK BART, the Po-8.'" He served a little over four years and promptly dropped out of sight. Within a few months a new rash of familiar crimes began. After the stage to Nevada City was held up in November 1888, Hume notified his detectives that "we have reason to believe that the

. . . robbery was committed by the notorious C. E. Boles . . . alias Black Bart."[16] The evidence did not permit issuance of an arrest warrant, however, and no specific proof of the outlaw-poet's activities appeared. He may have continued his career into the twentieth century because rumors of his exploits persisted throughout the nation.[17] As a final mystery, an obituary notice for Boles appeared in a New York City newspaper in 1917. That item could well have been deliberately planted by an aging Black Bart.

The stage robber, an obvious descendant of England's high-waymen, met many requirements for lionization by the press. Black Bart hurt no one, and he carefully selected a large, profit-able company for a victim. Such an approach tended to produce a receptive audience, if not secret sympathy and support. The technique also worked well against many banks and railroads throughout the West. "At that time," writes William M. Breakenridge, "the Southern Pacific and the Wells-Fargo Com-panies were rather unpopular with people. It was claimed that their freight and express charges were exorbitant, and whenever a train was held up a great many sympathized with the robbers."[18]

This perception of accord, approaching affection, contributed significantly to further development of the outlaw myth. The nec-essary components in a fictionalized and explosive formula were present, they required only figures of romantic potential and an imaginative alchemist. In the 1870s these appeared primarily in the form of two Missouri brothers and a journalist named John Newman Edwards. The latter, a native of Virginia, had served with the Confederate forces of General Joseph O. ("Jo") Shelby in the Civil War. He then became a reporter and later editor for var-ious newspapers in and around Missouri. Edwards remained admittedly sympathetic to the South and to those suspected of continuing to fight after hostilities came to a formal end. That provided an essential key to his contribution to the story of the American outlaw.

Edwards's now renowned subjects were, of course, Alexander Franklin James (born in 1843) and his younger brother Jesse Woodson James (born in 1847). Their parents, an aspiring Baptist preacher and a bride of only sixteen from a Catholic convent, had come from Kentucky and settled in Clay County, Missouri, about twenty miles northwest of Kansas City. After the birth of four children, Robert James, the father, left the family to join the California gold rush but soon became ill and died. Zerelda, his young widow, quickly remarried but then promptly separated from her second husband, whose own demise transpired with alacrity. The roles played by Frank and Jesse in this familial chaos and the possibility of the two brothers' having different fathers long remained subjects for local rumor, if not humor.

Meanwhile, Zerelda married once again, this time to Dr. Reuben Samuel, and bore four additional children. The family apparently stabilized around her because Frank and Jesse spent their adolescent years in relative peace and quiet. The Civil War undoubtedly began the transformation of their lives from ordinary to remarkable. The foundation of America's greatest outlaw myth was about to be laid.

Frank, later joined by Jesse, participated in the bloody guerrilla struggles which raged between Confederate and Union factions throughout the Ozarks during the Civil War. Although the brothers achieved no particular distinction, they undoubtedly proved able pupils in subjects of great value to them in future years.[19] Frank participated in William Clarke Quantrill's infamous raid on Lawrence, Kansas, in 1863. Jesse joined in the massacre of dozens of unarmed Union soldiers at Centralia, Missouri, in 1864. Perhaps the clearest although indirect evidence of the Samuel-James family view of the war was less dramatic. In the midst of such violent conflict, Frank and Jesse gained a new baby sister; her second given name was Quantrill.[20]

The end of the Civil War brought only a qualified form of peace to western Missouri. Reconstruction extended animosities; fears and hatreds fanned by years of disorder lingered. Most veterans returned to ordinary lives, but some turned to crime. Frank and Jesse chose the latter path. Together with the fabled Younger brothers (Cole, James, John, and Robert) of Lee's Summit, Missouri, they formed the nucleus of a criminal gang which operated for more than a decade.

Although this group originated neither bank nor train robbery, they unquestionably perfected such offenses. Careful preparation, sudden and violent attack, followed by planned escape, proved a remarkably successful formula. But with little doubt a primary basis of their ability to frustrate investigators existed in the mixture of sympathy, admiration, and fear accorded the robbers by many ordinary citizens: "Never before, or since, has there been the public support of an outlaw gang's activities as these men were given during the early years of their operations."[21] Such a condition resulted in part from the deep antagonism engendered by oppressive authorities during and after the Civil War. The outlaws consciously used these attitudes. They struck at institutions of wealth and power, avoiding crimes against neighbors and acquaintances, and they eventually benefited from the cultivation of public support through the press, most particularly the efforts of journalist John Edwards.

The pattern crystallized with the robbery of the Kansas City Fair on September 26, 1872. Three men held up the ticket office, wounding a little girl, and escaped with $978. The fair, incidentally, had another famous visitor the following day. James Butler ("Wild Bill") Hickok, already renowned as a peace officer, was in attendance and broke up a disturbance of unruly Texans. If his visit had occurred one day earlier, the perceived history of the Wild West might have taken a different turn.[22] Instead, John Edwards, editor of the *Kansas City Times,* took a hand.

Edwards quickly reported the robbery, praising the offenders for their daring and nerve. Two days later he followed up with an editorial under the headline "The Chivalry of Crime." This remarkable piece compared the outlaws with the knights of King Arthur and with English highwaymen. To Edwards, the robbers were already mythic figures:

Men who have carried their lives in their hands so long that they do not know how to commit them over into the keeping of the laws . . . and these men sometimes rob. But it is always in the glare of day and in the teeth of the multitude. With them booty is but the second thought; the wild drama of the adventure first. . . . What they did we condemn.

But the way they did it we cannot help admiring. . . . It was as though three bandits had come to us . . . with the halo of medieval chivalry upon their garments and shown us how the things were done that poets sing of.[23]

This was followed within weeks by publication of a supposed letter from the bandits in which they claimed to kill only in self-defense while robbing the rich and giving to the poor and signed the names of England's most famous highwaymen: Jack Sheppard, Dick Turpin, and Claude Duval.[24] In addition, there appeared notes, allegedly from Jesse James himself, denying guilt and pointing out the difficulty of ever obtaining a fair trial. Whether such publications were actually Edwards's remains a question, but he most certainly established contact with the gang while emerging as its most apparent defender.

Over a period of years the reputation of this criminal organization attained national recognition. The James-Younger gang was apparently a rather loose association of as many as twenty-eight men, including several sets of brothers. Only five or six members normally participated in a single robbery, after which they would separate into still smaller groups, assuming false names and the roles of ordinary travelers. Sometimes seeking shelter with relatives or friends, these outlaws rarely found it necessary either to fight or hide from pursuers. Months of planning and preparation might proceed the next crime, while the bandits resumed their ordinary lives as quiet farmers.[25] These methods proved very successful, resulting in fifteen or more robberies in Missouri and adjoining states between 1866 and 1875.

Frank and Jesse James were soon suspects, but substantial proof of guilt could not be obtained. Descriptions of the robbers revealed marked discrepancies, photographs were not generally available, no simple means of tracing stolen money existed, and local police agencies could not catch the calculating mobile bandits. But in 1873 the gang went beyond its practice of striking small and isolated banks and began attacking trains. These actions caused the railroads to assign the case to the Pinkerton National Detective Agency.

Investigators soon appeared near the homes of the James and Youngers as operatives attempted to infiltrate the gang. The robbers promptly detected the menace, however, and a number of deaths resulted, including those of John Younger and three Pinkerton agents. In such an atmosphere, Jesse and Frank married their sweethearts and briefly dropped out of sight. The surviving Younger brothers sought refuge in Texas, sometimes volunteering their able services as lawmen. And then in January 1875 occurred an event of major significance in American outlaw legend: a group of Pinkerton agents secretly approached the Samuel-James homes and threw an incendiary device through the window. Whether by design or accident, the resulting explosion killed the nine-year-old half brother of the absent James brothers and maimed their mother, causing the loss of her right hand. It was not an act in keeping with the yet-to-be-invented Code of the West. Sympathy for the robbers reached unprecedented heights. The Missouri legislature seriously considered—and almost passed—a general grant of amnesty.

According to a plausible tale, Jesse set forth on a journey of revenge. He stalked Allan Pinkerton for several months but never got an opportunity to kill the founder of the famous detective agency.[26] A Samuel neighbor who was suspected of being an informant for the investigators fared less well: someone killed him on his doorstep.

Meanwhile, rumor had the Jameses and Youngers robbing or in hiding from West Virginia to Texas to Wyoming. They were, in fact, on their way to Northfield, Minnesota, and their encounter with destiny. In September 1876, eight men attempted to rob the First National Bank in that quiet farming community about thirty miles south of Saint Paul. For the outlaws, it was a disaster. A brave but foolhardy cashier refused to open the vault and the robbers slashed his throat. The wounded teller escaped to spread the alarm. Within minutes the peaceful but armed townsmen decimated the nation's most famous outlaw gang. Within days, Cole, James, and Robert Younger were captured, wounded, cold, and hungry; three other outlaws were dead; and two had escaped: Frank and Jesse James. Posse members had to sue the state of Minnesota to collect even a small portion of the proffered reward.[27]

The Younger brothers pleaded guilty and received life sentences, thereby entering the special limbo occupied by indefinitely imprisoned outlaws. Such a status usually means a deflation of reputation far greater than that caused by either death or disappearance. To some degree, this pattern occurred with the Youngers. Before the Northfield raid they enjoyed a notoriety matching that of the James brothers, but those who got away had no immediate equals in its aftermath. Publishers created as well as catered to the market.

Missouri newspapermen capitalized on events, attitudes, and their own journalistic skills to produce books appearing to deal with contemporary brigands. Augustus Appler of Osceola was the first to fulfill this mission. In 1875 he produced a small volume entitled *The Guerrillas of the West: or the Life, Character, and Daring Exploits of the Younger Brothers*. Poorly written and inaccurate, it concentrated on Cole's adventures as a Confederate soldier, presenting his siblings as brave and innocent young men forced into outlawry by oppressive Reconstruction.

John Edwards then entered the market with a far more lasting impact. Six months after the Northfield raid, his *Noted Guerrillas, or the Warfare of the Border* appeared. This book proved to be a mine of misinformation for later writers and the obvious source for many unfounded but widely accepted tales. In it the Jameses and Youngers receive no more attention than a multitude of now largely forgotten outlaws, such as Oll Shepherd and Arthur McCoy. Edwards is now generally believed to have based portions of *Noted Guerrillas* on often unreliable information provided by contacts in the bandit gangs. But he also embellished these, whether unconsciously or by design, with bits of traditional outlaw lore. He unquestionably capitalized on the exploits of wanted and notorious fugitives. Although such a practice did not originate with Edwards (Alexander Exquemelin and Daniel Defoe had done precisely the same thing centuries before), he is primarily responsible for developing the technique on a successful scale in the United States.

Noted Guerrillas was reprinted on many occasions, and because of its apparent authenticity, it firmly established many unlikely stories as now accepted facts. Such was particularly true in regard to the James brothers. In one favorite episode, for example, Jesse is seen attempting to surrender peacefully at the close of the Civil War, only to be shot without cause by Union soldiers—justifying his subsequent criminal activity. Such an incident could have transpired, but no evidence has been discovered.

Edwards also confidently included many certain errors. He places Jesse with Frank among Quantrill's Raiders at Lawrence, Kansas, and regarding the same attack he states, in typical florid fashion, that "Cole Younger saved at least a dozen lives that day. Indeed, he killed none save in open and manly battle."[28] In a still more obvious mistake, Edwards revealed where the fugitive brothers were supposedly located. According to *Noted Guerrillas*, "Jesse and Frank James are outlaws and trading in cattle along the lower Rio Grande river, sometimes in Texas and sometimes as far in-land in old Mexico as Monterey."[29]

In fact, Frank and Jesse were living quietly under the assumed names of B. J. Woodson and Thomas Howard with their growing families in Tennessee. They avoided crime for some time but eventually organized a new gang that concentrated on train robbery. In 1879 they struck at Glendale, Missouri, and two years later robbed a train near Winston, about sixty miles northwest of Kansas City, with serious eventual consequences. One of the bandits deliberately and pointlessly murdered the conductor, train crewmen were beaten, and one passenger was killed. This was not the work of a frontier Robin Hood, and the nation reacted. The *New York Times* reported the robbery with banner headlines, and articles identifying the criminals dominated front pages for days:

There is considerable evidence to show that the train robbery on the Rock Island Road last Friday evening was done by the notorious James gang, and it may prove that one or both of the James boys were present with the gang. The horses used by the robbers were thorough-bred animals, in the best condition for the work on hand.[30]

The governor of Missouri, Thomas Crittenden, realized that the gang had to be stopped. He secured promises of some fifty thousand dollars for rewards and expenses. Only a portion of these sums and activities were publicized; the full story of what followed has never been revealed.[31] Meanwhile, the search continued throughout the country. The brigands had been sought in many areas, and false reports of their deaths sometimes followed. At times these stories were strangely prophetic, as illustrated by an 1879 article from New Mexico:

The notorious Jesse James is reported to have been killed near Joplin, Missouri, by an old companion of his who joined the detective force and ingratiated himself again with Jesse, whom he shot in the back of the head with a revolver. . . . During the last spring James was reported to be operating in Lincoln county in this Territory.[32]

In 1882, Jesse would be killed almost precisely as described. Lincoln County, New Mexico, meanwhile, found its own unique niche in outlaw legend.

Newspapers throughout the nation headlined Jesse's death:

Killed by one his confederates who claims to be a detective. A great sensation was created in this city [Saint Joseph, Missouri] by the announcement that Jesse James, the notorious bandit and train robber, had been shot and killed. . . . Crowds rushed to the quarter of the city where the shooting had occurred. . . . [Kansas City] Police Commissioner [Henry] Craig started for St. Joseph with a heavily armed posse of men to guard James' body and give protection to the man who killed him. Bob Ford . . . is a young man, almost 22 years of age, and looks like a verdant youth from the country. In appearance he is a mere boy, and the last person in the world to be taken as the slayer of the famous outlaw.[33]

A new recruit of the James gang, Robert Ford, killed for the reward, using a revolver Jesse had given him a few days earlier. Needless to say, he was not regarded as much of a hero. Within two weeks he and his brother Charles were indicted for murder,

That dirty little coward (Bob Ford) shoots Mr.
Howard (Jesse James), *Police Gazette,* 1882.

entered guilty pleas, and received death sentences. Governor
Crittenden's full pardon followed within hours.

The Fords attempted to profit from their notoriety, with
mixed success. Charles committed suicide in 1884. Bob became
an itinerant entertainer in *The Outlaws of Missouri* and *How I
Killed Jesse James,* giving performances which fixed details of a
martyr's death while receiving audiences' pronounced disap-
proval. Later he toured as a somewhat pathetic attraction with

the shows of P. T. Barnum. Eventually he became a saloonkeeper in Creede, Colorado. There, in 1892, a relative of the Youngers named Ed O. Kelly shotgunned him to death.

The rented house in Saint Joseph where Jesse died first became a kind of shrine but eventually fell into disrepair. By 1938 it had been sold for back taxes, moved, and converted into a filling-station attraction.[34] Authorities seized the personal goods and managed to return a considerable amount of stolen property to rightful owners. After an auction, the James family regained the remaining items, including a copy of John Edwards's *Noted Guerrillas.*[35] America's outlaw myth had already begun to feed directly upon itself.

Additional purported histories of the outlaws soon gained popularity. *Life and Adventures of Frank and Jesse James and the Younger Brothers* by J. A. Dacus appeared in some sixteen editions, but James William Buel's *The Border Outlaws* probably enjoyed even more success. Like the competitors, it had to be rapidly revised and reissued to cover Jesse's death.[36] The strangest reaction in publishing occurred within a few weeks of the outlaw's demise in the form of *The Life, Times and Treacherous Death of Jesse James,* supposedly dictated to Frank Tripplett by the desperado's widow and his maimed mother. Both women subsequently denied their involvement with the book, and Governor Crittenden ordered copies destroyed, guaranteeing great rarity in outlaw literature.

Jesse's remarkable mother had her son buried on the family farm a few yards from the site of the bombing incident and perhaps with a view toward preventing desecration. Within a few months she began the practice of charging visitors and offering for sale countless shoes from Jesse's horse as well as pebbles from the grave. The latter souvenirs were, according to local wags, replenished whenever necessary from a nearby stream. In 1902 the exhumed body was reburied in the family plot in nearby Kearney; within a generation its marble marker had disappeared, gradually chipped away by vandals.[37]

Frank James remained at large for six months after Jesse's murder. Then a dramatic and prearranged meeting transpired at the governor's office in Jefferson City, Missouri. Frank, accompanied by none other than John Edwards, surrendered before a group of invited reporters. He spent more than two years in various courts facing charges of murder and robbery, but was never convicted—of anything. The tide had clearly turned; outlaw had become legend.

But life is not necessarily easy, even for a legend. Frank James became a shoe salesman in Dallas, Texas, and later a doorman for a burlesque theater in Saint Louis. He also sometimes worked as a starter at local race tracks and fairs. Such positions were, of course, provided primarily for advertising purposes. Frank's major disappointment came in 1901 when his efforts to secure the eminently suitable appointment as doorkeeper for the Missouri legislature failed. He then turned to acting, traveling in such plays as *The Fatal Scar* and *Across the Desert*. It was not until 1903 that he attempted specifically to use his bandit background in collaboration with a former and equally notorious colleague.

For a quarter of a century the Younger brothers remained in the Minnesota penitentiary at Stillwater, where, incidentally, they participated in the founding of the nation's oldest and most highly regarded prison newspaper. Robert Younger, a model inmate, died of tuberculosis in 1889. This led to increased efforts to secure the release of his two surviving brothers, and finally, in 1901, they received limited pardons, which prevented them from leaving the state.[38] The two former convicts sold tombstones for a time. James committed suicide only a few months after his release from the prison where he had spent nearly half his life. Soon thereafter Cole, the oldest and "last of the famous Younger brothers," was allowed to leave Minnesota.

He promptly joined Frank James in the entertainment field. Together the two reformed outlaws established the James-Younger Wild West Show! It did not enjoy great or lasting success, however.[39] Frank returned to the farm, operating it as a tourist attraction much as his mother had done. The family even attempted to maintain a golf course on the grounds. Frank died quietly in 1915. Cole Younger remained active on the lecture circuit for some time, telling appreciative audiences about the evils of crime. He eventually retired to his birthplace at Lee's

Summit. Younger died in 1916 at the age of seventy-two, weighing 260 pounds and carrying the scars of some twenty bullet wounds.[40]

The Samuel-James farm continued under family ownership for many years, Frank's widow surviving until 1944. By 1978 it had fallen into disrepair and was taken over by Clay County for careful restoration. Visitors again may tour the premises and visit Jesse's well-tended original grave. The guides (who report no ghosts) do not sell souvenir pebbles, however, and the golf course has long since vanished.

Only one known member of the James-Younger gang managed to escape. Jim Cummins had the good sense to move far away (to Wyoming) and start a new life. Decades later he indicated that many knew but kept secret his real identity, and he offered a practical explanation: "If the reward had been $500, no doubt somebody would have killed me for it; but $5000 was so big that they had no confidence in its ever being paid."[41]

Meanwhile, the story of Missouri's "long riders" surpassed plausible limits. Jesse, Frank, and Cole emerged as symbols of a violent and romantic era. They became popular characters in a vast number of books, weeklies, and dime novels.[42] Between 1901 and 1903, the Street and Smith publishing house alone sold some six million copies of 121 Jesse James novels.[43] In addition, the bandits were favorite figures in plays for generations, culminating with Broadway's *Missouri Legend* in 1938.

Very soon after his death, Jesse received an ultimate homage accorded the greatest of outlaws. A ballad honoring his name appeared in Missouri and has endured as probably the most well known of such songs in the United States. Its many verses and variants include obvious parallels to the Robin Hood myths and have left a lasting image of the "dirty little coward" who killed Mr. Howard, and "laid Jesse James in his grave" (see the Appendix). The ballad contains its own unique mystery. A closing stanza identifies the composer as Billy Gashade, but no reliable evidence of such an individual has been found.[44]

As is true of many famous outlaws, Jesse was reborn frequently. More than two dozen individuals claimed to be the original, usually asserting that someone resembling the renowned bandit died at Saint Joseph in a successful plot to mislead the police, and at least one bogus Frank James arose while the real one still lived. So long as close relatives survived, such tales came to fairly rapid conclusions, but several misguided individuals continued to assert their assumed identities until after World War II.[45]

Other routine trappings of outlaw lore developed. Numerous locations, particularly caves, are identified as hideouts used by the James brothers, even though one of their more reliable biographers asserts without apparent fear of contradiction that "the Boys never hid in a cave at any time."[46] And the hunt for their buried treasure continues, although evidence indicates that the gang never got a great amount of loot from their robberies. After division of the spoils, routine living expenses probably consumed everything.

Articles and books offering historical analyses of the James-Younger band abound. These typically fall into two diametrically opposed groups. One views the outlaws as terrifying and bloodthirsty monsters who killed without cause and stole out of simple greed. The other sees them as courteous Robin Hoods driven to crime by unjust persecution of their relatives. Many writers simply perpetuate false stories, mixing fact with sufficient fiction to ensure sales. One common error concerns rewards offered for the outlaws dead or alive. No bounty of this nature was ever announced for the Jameses or the Youngers, although souvenir posters heralding such may still be purchased.

The proliferation of repeated error makes serious efforts to interpret the truth about the outlaws fraught with difficulty.[47] Many writers, under a mere pretense of history, seize upon any convenient tale, thus rendering a multitude of purported biographies absolutely useless from the standpoint of reliability. As an obviously frustrated Ramon Adams accurately wrote of one relatively recent work on Jesse James: "The author's many errors begin with his foreword and end only with the end of the book. It does not seem possible that any person trying to write history could make so many errors of fact, dates, and statistics."[48]

Those who might have told the true story probably saw little to gain in doing so. Creation of the James-Younger Wild West Show in 1903 coincided, conveniently, with the appearance of *The Story of Cole Younger, By Himself*. It was only a short, moralistic autobiography in which "himself" concludes that crime does not pay (except perhaps through royalties). The pattern remains popular, of course, with the reformed but still profiteering brigands of today.

The great interest shown and sustained in the Jameses and Youngers has many possible explanations. These include a Reconstruction background, the remarkable duration of their criminal activities, the rapid expansion of a popular press, and convenient stretching of a frontier setting. The mere alliteration in the name Jesse James is not without significance, but the most apparent reason comes in the form of people (such as John Edwards) willing and able to popularize stories to suit their own ends.

Ultimately, Jesse's son could not resist entering the act. Once tried and acquitted for train robbery, he became an attorney in Kansas City. Jesse James, Jr. (as he preferred to be called), wrote a book entitled *Jesse James, My Father* in 1899, portraying the bandits as misunderstood victims. The author took a bit of license, incidentally. Jesse, Sr., had the middle name of Woodson (which he used as an alias while hiding in Tennessee). Jesse, Jr., born at that very time, had the middle name of Edwards (the source of which should be obvious). He eventually left Missouri for California, much as his grandfather had done, but seeking his gold through a career in motion pictures. By that time a clear relationship existed: the outlaws had recognized opportunities in show business, and show business had most certainly recognized opportunities in the outlaws.

CHAPTER 8

The Gunman

¿Quién es?

—BILLY THE KID

THE Jameses and the Youngers had many rivals in the popular press of their day. Texas provided several. While none of these caught the national fancy in quite the same manner as the Missouri outlaws, several achieved significant regional fame. They also helped to add another dimension to the bandit's image by blending it with that of the cowboy and later that of the gunfighter. Most could be described as ill suited to the role.

"Sam Bass was not much of an outlaw as outlaws go. He was no gunman, nor was he a killer,"[1] says Charles L. Martin. Legend made him quite different. Samuel Bass was born in 1851 and spent the early years of his life in Indiana.

Up to the time of the death of his father and for two or three years afterward, young Bass maintained an excellent character, but after that he began to associate with bad companions and soon acquired evil habits. . . . In 1869, tired of the restraints of his guardian or longing to see more of the world, he left his Hoosier home and went to St. Louis, a very bad place to go to at any time.[2]

He soon drifted to North Texas and found work as a farmhand, teamster, and cowboy. He was apparently a good rider and became noted for his fast mount, "the Denton mare." By 1876 the still-illiterate Sam had become involved with horse theft, moved north to Nebraska and the Black Hills of Dakota, failed in a mining venture, and turned to robbing stagecoaches. His little gang then moved on to trains and returned to Texas. A series of robberies near Dallas prompted creation of a special force of Rangers, sheriff's deputies, railroad detectives, marshals, and Pinkerton agents. The end followed rather quickly. Jim Murphy, a member of the gang, betrayed his colleagues for a promise of leniency. Texas Rangers ambushed the outlaws during an attempted bank robbery at Round Rock on July 19, 1878. Bass was seriously wounded in the battle and died two days later on his twenty-seventh birthday.[3] The engraving on his grave marker was simple, but somehow fitting:

> Samuel Bass
> Born July 21st 1851
> Died July 21st 1878
> A Brave Man Reposes in Death Here.
> Why Was He Not True?

He had already become a subject of note, far exceeding the significance of actual exploits. Four books—Thomas E. Hogg's *Authentic History of Sam Bass,* Alfred Sorenson's *Hands Up!* Charles Martin's *A Sketch of Sam Bass,* and an anonymous work, *Life and Adventures of Sam Bass*—were in print by 1880. By 1956 the number of biographies had grown to two hundred.[4]

The ballad of Sam Bass quickly appeared and became a favorite on the range (see the appendix). Jim Murphy, the betrayer, died rather strangely in 1879 after swallowing atrophine, an eye medicine; some chose to regard it as an act of suicide. And Sam Bass, represented by a wax figure carried about Texas for exhibition, became known as a jovial, horse-loving, generous, friendly, and brave young man who had sadly gone astray. "In folklore . . . he was remembered as the 'beloved bandit.' . . . [H]is ghost was heard riding through the oak woods of Denton County at night. Negroes . . . knew Sam had come back to reunite his gallant band and dig up his buried gold and avenge his betrayal."[5]

Caves and groves of trees throughout central Texas were identified as favorite hiding places of the Bass gang, although the

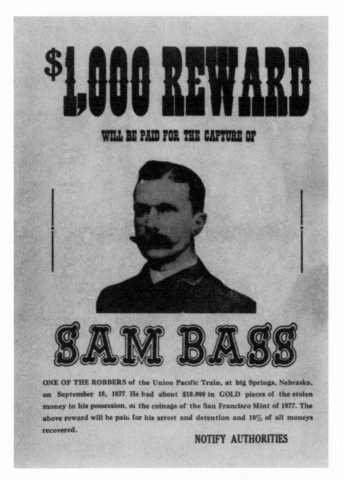

Bogus wanted poster for Texas' "beloved bandit."
(Author's collection)

bandits had in most cases never been near such sites. And, naturally, these places served as logical places to look for hidden treasure. "As long as the Sam Bass legends persist, no Texan can be sure that he will not awake some morning to find a ton of earth removed from his front yard by some romanticist who has just come into possession of the one authentic treasure map."[6]

Although Sam Bass apparently never killed anyone, he was associated with the cult of the gunfighter. Virtually all noted outlaws of the period seemed automatically to acquire unusual skill with firearms, perhaps in emulation of the archers of Sherwood Forest. Early in the 1870s, journalist John Edwards so provided for Jesse James: "Looking at his small white hands . . . one would not imagine that with a revolver they were among the quickest and deadliest hands in all the west."[7] And Sam Bass, in another absurd but assigned achievement, "shot his initials at full speed" in a landmark live oak tree near Belton.[8] Even the smooth running Denton mare must have wondered at that trick.

Another Texas cowboy and outlaw had a far more realistic claim to the gunfighter image: John Wesley Hardin. A product of Reconstruction and the son of a Methodist preacher (hence his given name), he probably became a killer in 1868 at the age of fifteen. During the next nine years he roamed from Kansas to Florida, escaping from custody on several occasions. Since he was never known as a robber or thief, Hardin's fame rested primarily on a willingness to kill. In his own words, "be the consequences what they may, I propose to take life" to avenge friends and family members.[9]

In 1877, Texas Rangers captured Hardin near Pensacola, Florida, having traced him through intercepted letters to relatives. Curious crowds besieged the train returning him for trial and conviction. He served sixteen years at Texas's Huntsville prison, first attempting to escape and then studying law! Hardin received a pardon in 1894, became an attorney, married, and drifted west to El Paso. There in August of 1895 a local constable and former outlaw named John Selman shot him in the back of the head. Hardin had been shaking dice at the bar of the Acme Saloon. His killer died by gunfire within a year. The bullet which finished Hardin's sad life remained a curiosity at the Acme for many years, preserved in a glass jar which only valued customers were permitted to handle.

Within a year of his death, *The Life of John Wesley Hardin as Written by Himself* appeared. It was supposedly based on a manuscript discovered among the desperado's papers and has been generally accepted as both authentic and reasonably accurate. The book, reprinted on several occasions, is the primary source used in all Hardin biographies and a foundation for his reputation as a leading gunfighter. But even that has become the subject of great exaggeration.

Like those of most other desperadoes of the era, the number of killings attributed to Hardin depends entirely on the source. To one, "he claimed to have slain 44 men—and his reckoning was probably not far off."[10] To another, "John Wesley Hardin was the epitome of the gunfighter with over 40 men falling to his guns."[11] Scholarly sources are somewhat more cautious. A leading encyclopedia on American crime states that "even the most skeptical will grant him 34 or 35."[12] An academic tome focusing on the West offers that "Hardin killed well over twenty men."[13] The truth probably lies closer to the still sobering figure of eleven, calculated by one writer who attempted to verify the obviously conflicting claims.[14] As is true with much about outlaws, the sources have become as important as the facts.

Part of the confusion results from the cult which has grown up around the legend of the fast-drawing, straight-shooting heroes and villains of the American frontier.[15] Much of this myth developed during the time Hardin spent in prison. Those years coincided with the appearance of another word often used to describe the American outlaw: gunman. North American Indians who carried firearms in the seventeenth and eighteenth centuries were probably the first to be described as gun-men, but the term remained hyphenated until the 1880s. After that, it became a single word, and by the early twentieth century, at least in the United States, it clearly and negatively implied one who robbed and killed.

John Wesley Hardin was obviously a gunman, whether his correct total of victims stands at eleven or forty-four, a range which indicates the extent of exaggeration often found in connection with noted brigands. Perhaps a quarter of the total in the typical story is true. Hardin was one of the most lethal gunfighters of the day, but not the West's most effective killer. Jim Miller, a hired assassin based in Fort Worth, probably committed a dozen homicides between 1884 and 1909. Harry Orchard (Albert E.

Horsley), a dynamiter for the Western Federation of Miners, apparently murdered twenty-six in a single bombing incident. Augustin Chacón, desperado of the Arizona-Mexico border, admitted killing fifty-two. But their personalities and activities did not fit the developing image of the cowboy-gunman. The foremost example of that variety appeared in New Mexico Territory and became a legend equaling that of Jesse James, with added elements of mystery.

After more than a century of investigation, no one can be certain of his exact name, the details of his birth, his motives, or all the facts surrounding his death, but he is known throughout the world as the colorful young bandit of the American Southwest who died at the age of twenty-one, having killed a man for every year of his life. He was Billy the Kid. Endless research on the story of this noted outlaw has only served to produce an enigma. "The whole history of Billy the Kid's life, as it has come down through the years, has been false," writes Ramon F. Adams. "It has been made up of misstatements of fact, some more consequential than others, but all contributing to the tissue of lies."[16]

The information which can be confirmed indicates that Henry McCarty, aged about fifteen, was arrested for theft in Silver City, New Mexico, soon after the death of his mother (the wife of William Antrim) in 1874. He escaped from jail and fled to Arizona. In 1877, by then known as "Henry Antrim alias Kid," he killed a man in a saloon fight near Camp Grant. Shortly thereafter he returned to New Mexico and entered the dispute usually referred to in western lore as the Lincoln County War. The legend of Billy the Kid was about to begin.

In 1878, Lincoln County was enormous, several times its present size. Larger than many eastern states, it extended over most of southeast New Mexico from the Llano Estacado on the Texas border to a snow-capped mountain peak called Sierra Blanca. It should be best known today not for an outlaw, but for skiing, quarter-horse racing, and a wonderful symbol for forest fire prevention: Smokey the Bear. A modern traveler will pass through wondering what could possibly have caused bloody battles to erupt in such a quiet setting a century ago. Explanations abound.

It was a struggle between small and large ranchers, between sheep and cattle raisers, between Anglos and Mexicans, between good and evil, between Indians and whites, between rich and poor, between rustlers and stockmen. None of these story lines is correct. It had to do, as so much still does, with greed and corruption. There were no real heroes, but villains abounded. As Robert Mullin has written:

> The Lincoln County War was essentially a struggle for economic power. In a land where hard cash was scarce, federal government contracts for the supply of provisions, principally beef, for the military posts and for the Indian reservations, were the grand prize. The competition for these contracts was bitter and frequently ruthless. Since the early 1870's Lawrence Gustave Murphy . . . and the political clique at Santa Fe . . . enjoyed a near monopoly.[17]

The "Santa Fe Ring" had close ties to Washington; its most obvious leader was an enormously influential attorney named Thomas Benton Catron, who obtained appointments as a federal prosecutor and then territorial attorney general. He eventually served as mayor of Santa Fe and in the United States Senate.

The ring had one serious competitor in Lincoln County, a calculating, aging, cow-rich rancher named John Simpson Chisum, who should not be confused with the trader who blazed the world's most famous cattle trail, Jesse Chisholm. The secretive Chisum owned vast herds in New Mexico, preempted government land, enjoyed strong Texas backing, and was prepared to do battle with the Santa Fe Ring, or at least to let others do so. Like Catron, he worked through intermediaries, controlling judges, sheriffs, and perhaps governors. Chisum had two principal agents in Lincoln County: Alexander McSween and John Tunstall. The Santa Fe Ring also had direct representatives on the scene, including Lawrence Murphy and James Dolan.

Both sides may well have sensed the possibility of violent conflict and may have taken precautions. These included the hiring of hoodlums willing and able to use force in defense of person and property. Those enlisted did not command high wages; there were better gunfighters in the West. Still, McSween and Tunstall acquired the services of one, as their opponent James Dolan duly noted, "Wm. H. Antrim, alias the kid, a renegade from Arizona where he killed a man in cold blood."[18]

It is simple and incorrect to portray the West as a lawless land where violence occurred without reason. The Lincoln County War erupted quite differently—over the mishandling of an estate. McSween, a lawyer of rather questionable repute, became embroiled in a dispute with Dolan concerning debts and insurance. Early in 1878, estate administrators secured a writ of attachment against property belonging to McSween's partner, Tunstall. A deputy of Sheriff William Brady and possemen attempted to seize livestock in question. An argument followed and, whether by accident or design, John Tunstall, age twenty-four, was killed.

A series of legal battles ensued, after which McSween's "regulators" obtained warrants and arrested two possemen involved in Tunstall's death. Both prisoners were killed on the trail.[19] Less than a month later "the kid" and several other gunmen ambushed and murdered Sheriff Brady and a deputy in the town of Lincoln. A grand jury promptly returned several indictments, including one against Dolan for the Tunstall killing, as well as those suspected of the sheriff's murder, not omitting the "kid" McSween quite incidentally referred to as "W. Bony."[20] Meanwhile, Santa Fe's *Weekly New Mexican* grimly reported:

Several bodies of armed men were at last accounts said to be in the woods looking for each other with the avowed purpose of killing upon sight; other parties are trying to prevent this and to have the parties disband and go home; what the end will be no one can tell, but it is the opinion of those best informed that if one gun is fired there will be bloodier work in Lincoln in the next few weeks than has ever been in the past.[21]

And so it came to pass. Several gunfights followed, culminating in the "five-day battle," or siege, of the McSween home in Lincoln by a large force of Dolan supporters. When a bibulous army officer declined to intervene, the house was set afire. Five of the defenders, including McSween, died in the fighting, but others escaped into a nearby riverbed, among them the young man who subsequently identified himself as William H. Bonney, becoming far better known as Billy the Kid.

The brief war in Lincoln County had ended, although its ramifications lasted for years. Both Tunstall and McSween were dead by gunfire; Murphy drank himself to death in that fateful year of 1878. Dolan lived on, a man of considerable prominence in the region, for nearly two decades. John Chisum gradually lost his health and some of his wealth; he died of cancer in 1884. And Thomas Benton Catron remained a dominant figure in New Mexican politics for another generation.

The pawns used in the Lincoln County War still remained to cause trouble. Furthermore, a new character rode into play by stagecoach. Lew Wallace, a retired general soon to become the author of the novel *Ben-Hur,* arrived to serve as the newly appointed governor of the New Mexico Territory. Lincoln County had become a national disgrace, and he soon attempted to restore order. Wallace asked President Rutherford B. Hayes to declare the region in a state of general insurrection, permitting wider use of federal troops. The governor also issued a broad amnesty to contestants in the war, covering the period from February through November 1878.[22]

Such dramatic steps were not inappropriate. Wallace reported to the secretary of the interior that grand jurymen "found nearly 200 indictments in the county of a voting population 150 total."[23] In order to facilitate a measure of justice, he visited Lincoln in March 1879 and held a secret meeting with a critical potential witness. The two soon made a deal, with Billy the Kid agreeing to be arrested (supposedly against his will) to testify in pending cases and eventually to receive a pardon for prior misdeeds. During the next several months, most of the terms of this agreement were fulfilled, but Billy eventually lost faith in the governor's promise (or got a better offer) and simply rode away from his place of supposed confinement.

In January 1880 he appeared in the town of Fort Sumner, killing yet another man in a saloon fight. He also had a confrontation with John Chisum. Billy clearly felt that the rancher had not paid him for previous work, so he threatened Chisum with a leveled revolver and demanded five hundred dollars in back wages. The rancher calmly lighted his pipe and replied, "Billy, you couldn't shoot an honest man, could you, while he was looking you square in the eye? You have killed several men, I know, but they needed killing."[24] However misguided or misinterpreted they may have been, westerners did not lack courage.

Billy the Kid did not shoot Chisum, but he apparently did begin to steal cattle and horses on a rather wide scale. As reports of such activity filtered in, the outlaw sent various notes to the governor protesting his innocence. Eventually the frustrated Wallace announced a five hundred dollar reward for "persons who capture William Bonny, alias The Kid,"[25] That sum, incidentally, was indicative of the relatively low status still accorded Billy; members of the fugitive James gang had individual bounties ten times such a promised amount.

Matters took another turn in the fall of 1880 with the election of Patrick Floyd Garrett as sheriff. "His coming into New Mexico from the buffalo grounds of West Texas had coincided almost exactly with the beginning of open warfare in Lincoln County."[26] Garrett enjoyed the support of powerful cattle ranchers and was personally acquainted with Billy the Kid. The new sheriff raised the stakes by a considerable margin, bringing in agents of Texas stockmen. These were experienced lawmen, and they quickly brought an end to more obvious aspects of bandit activity.

After a series of gunfights, Billy and two companions were captured at their hideout near appropriately named Stinking Springs. All three of the prisoners eventually escaped from custody. Dave Rudabaugh fled to Old Mexico, resumed his rustling activities, and was killed in a gambling dispute. Pleased citizens paraded his head through the streets of Parral in 1886. Billy Wilson went to Texas, assumed his true name of David L. Anderson, and became a rancher. Pat Garrett later helped him secure a pardon for past crimes, and the reformed rustler was finally elected sheriff of Terrell County, Texas, only to be killed by a drunken cowboy in 1918. Residents of Sanderson promptly lynched his assassin.[27]

After surrendering at Stinking Springs, Billy the Kid was taken to the town of Mesilla for trial, convicted of the murder of Sheriff Brady, then sent back to Lincoln to await execution. He continued to bombard Wallace with demands for a pardon, by now signing his name as "W. Bonney." The governor obviously felt no sympathy and signed the death warrant; he was waiting for an opportunity to leave the territory and clearly expressed his views in a sad note to his wife: "I am getting very tired of this office. There is nobody here who cares for me, and nobody I care for."[28] Within weeks the *Las Vegas Optic* noted his departure by stating, with possible accuracy, "We believe Gov. Wallace to be the only respectable and worthy gentleman who was ever appointed to a federal office in New Mexico."[29] By that time, Billy had broken out of jail.

Somehow (there are several plausible explanations) the outlaw obtained a revolver, killed two guards, and calmly rode away from Lincoln on April 28, 1881, precisely three years after his indictment for Brady's murder.

The spectacular feat of regaining his freedom accomplished the apotheosis of Billy the Kid. To some he had been a hero, to many others a desperate character, but now the dramatic story of his escape caught the popular imagination and won a kind of grudging admiration from those who decried the fact that two more names were added to the long list of those who had lost their lives in both factions of the Lincoln County War.[30]

Pat Garrett, who had been in White Oaks during the escape, had another manhunt to conduct. Again he wisely accepted assistance from Texas. One of the great mysteries of Billy the Kid concerns his reason for remaining in the area. He surely knew that by simply going a few hundred miles in any direction, the chances of his recapture would virtually vanish. Staying in the territory under a sentence of death probably related to a clear reason. Did the Kid still want revenge, had something been promised to him, or was he involved in another plot? Whatever his motivations, Billy remained in the area, and Garrett's operatives soon provided a tip that the desperado might be found at the Peter Maxwell home at Fort Sumner.

The sheriff and two agents promptly proceeded to that location. On the night of July 14, 1881, Garrett entered Maxwell's darkened bedroom, followed a short time later by another intruder. According to the sheriff's report:

Maxwell whispered to me. "That's him!" Simultaneously the Kid must have seen, or felt, the presence of a third person at the head of the bed. He raised quickly his pistol, a self-cocker, within a foot of my breast. Retreating rapidly across the room he cried: "Quien es? Quien es?" ("Who's that? Who's that?") All this occurred in a moment. Quickly as possible I drew my revolver and fired, threw my body aside, and fired again. The second shot was useless; the Kid fell dead. He never spoke.[31]

The following morning the local alcalde held an inquest, ruling that William H. Bonney died as a result of a gunshot fired by Sheriff Garrett in the discharge of his official duty. Billy was immediately buried in Fort Sumner's military cemetery. Some months later Garrett, responding to the exhibition of bones throughout the country, wrote: "the Kid's body lies undisturbed in the grave—and I speak of what I know."[32]

The initial reaction to news of the desperado's death was clearly that of relief. Few at the time considered him anything other than a dangerous rustler with an unusual ability to escape custody, but within a short time questions developed, rumors circulated, and two widely divergent views appeared, apart from that simply accepting Garrett's version of the final encounter. Some suspected that the sheriff had acted under instructions not to bring the fugitive back alive and that the outlaw's death amounted to deliberate murder. Fred E. Sutton writes: "One account which had wide circulation, was that Garrett killed the Kid as he lay in bed, asleep. A variation of that account was that the Kid was in a drunken sleep, and helpless, when Garrett sneaked into his room and murdered him in his bed."[33]

The sheriff's own version of the shooting raised a question. If Billy could not recognize Garrett in Maxwell's bedroom, how did the lawman see him raise his double-action "self-cocker" revolver? It was no secret that powerful men in New Mexico remained uneasy until word of the outlaw's end reached them, and it took little imagination to transform such knowledge into the belief that Pat Garrett had something more than recapture in mind. Thus Billy could be made a victim in death if not in life.

On the other hand, a totally different rumor also spread. "Many people in New Mexico could not believe that the desperado was dead, so strong was the legend of his invincibility."[34] It seemed possible that somehow Billy had escaped even his reported demise in keeping with ancient outlaw legend: "Old desperadoes never die, they do not even fade away. . . . John Wilkes Booth died in Texas long after he should have been mouldering in his grave. Jesse James passed on at one hundred seven."[35]

The theory that Billy did not die at Fort Sumner usually hinged upon his presumed previous friendship with Pat Garrett, but another, darker variation exists. The fiction was part of a greater conspiracy that extended back to his escape in Lincoln and explained his illogical behavior in remaining in the territory. The speed of the inquest and burial (even given the climate in July) did seem peculiar. Lawmen of the era normally went to considerable effort to verify the deaths of fugitives for two good reasons: to foreclose a later charge of killing an innocent party and to facilitate the collection of rewards. Garrett, in fact, had to resort to legal action to collect the promised bounty on the Kid. Furthermore, only three witnesses identified the body, and one of them later said that another person had really been killed.[36]

Those who wished to believe in Billy's survival found considerable support, although convincing evidence of such remained lacking. Two generations after his death, Eugene Cunningham noted that "occasionally, we hear it whispered down here that the 'killing' was merely 'a put up job,' that the Kid still lives in Mexico. I heard that tale only yesterday on an El Paso street. I cannot credit it."[37]

And of course there is the strange story of William Henry ("Brushy Bill") Roberts. He surfaced in 1948 through reports from a Lincoln County War survivor. Roberts eventually "admitted" being the Kid, and he most certainly possessed remarkably detailed knowledge about the outlaw's life. Although the old man did not convince experts, he raised serious doubts before his death in 1950. The yet unanswered nagging question remained: "If Brushy Bill Roberts wasn't Billy the Kid, then who was he?"[38]

Those willing to accept the outlaw's death and burial may still wonder about the authenticity of his grave, upon which, incidentally, flowers are reported not to grow (almost nothing grows in Fort Sumner, without irrigation). The original wooden marker, used by drunks for target practice, disappeared. Half a century after burial, the grave's location could no longer be determined.[39] Some years later, in response to repeated requests from tourists, a stone monument was erected and subsequently surrounded by a fence to discourage vandals. If the present marker stands at some distance from the actual grave, it matters very little; most of what is believed about outlaws has nothing to do with the facts.

Even the gun used to kill Billy the Kid has a false legend: it had been carried by Wild Bill Hickok when he was murdered.[40] The facts indicate otherwise. James Butler Hickok was presumably carrying his pair of converted .38-caliber Navy Colt revolvers at the time of his death.[41] Garrett used a far more modern and powerful .44–40 Frontier Colt, but the weapon did have a history. Shipped from the factory in early 1880, years after Hickok's murder, it belonged to the outlaw Billy Wilson; Garrett obtained the gun from him as a result of the capture at Stinking Springs. The sheriff carried the Frontier Colt for some twenty years, then allowed it to be placed on display at the Coney Island Saloon in El Paso. Shortly before Garrett's death in 1908, he came to examine his illustrious revolver and brought along a friend, Billy Wilson. The gun eventually was returned to the sheriff's family and safely preserved in an El Paso bank vault.[42] There are at least a dozen Garrett or Billy weapons now on display throughout the Southwest, and a few of them are authentic as to ownership, but they are not the one used to kill the Kid.

Many of the stories later accepted as facts surrounding Billy first surfaced in newspapers shortly before or just after his death. These include the supposed boast of killing a man for each year of his life, the promised murder of one Chisum cowboy for every five dollars owed him, and his birth in New York City. Several sensational dime novels quickly appeared, presenting grotesquely garbled versions of real events. Such popular books, combined with the success of those dealing with other outlaws of the period, encouraged creation of a notable early landmark in the legend of Billy the Kid.

Pat Garrett combined forces with Ash Upson, a journalist, clerk, schoolteacher, and postmaster, to write the flamboyantly titled *The Authentic Life of Billy, the Kid: The Noted Desperado of the Southwest, Whose Deeds of Daring and Blood Made His Name a Terror in New Mexico, Arizona and Northern Mexico*. The book, first published in Santa Fe less than a year after the outlaw's demise (and within days of Jesse James's death) was filled with errors and became the foundation for hundreds of subsequent versions. It underwent a complete and abrupt change of style with chapter 16, when "the author . . . first became personally and actively engaged in the task of pursuing and assisting to bring to justice the Kid, and others of his ilk, in an official capacity."[43] The previous portions, presumably created by Upson, are incredible tales with almost no relation to the truth. Those which follow, probably written by Garrett, are far more realistic and accurate accounts of the sheriff's efforts.

Ash Upson apparently made no effort to discover or relate facts but simply made up such events as the Kid's rescue of a wagon train, his eighty-one-mile ride in six hours (partly in rhyme), and the killing of countless numbers of evil Indians (eight with an ax). In reality, the Mescalero Apaches would have made short work of the youthful gunfighter. Upson may have used certain

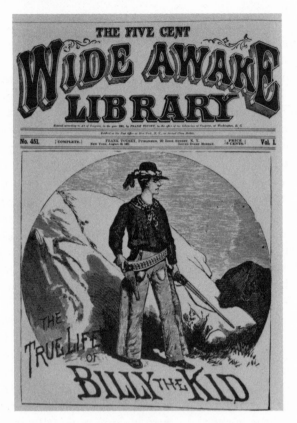

The noted desperado of the Southwest, 1881.

rumors then current about the Kid's early years, but he also copied episodes from stories of other outlaws, including the obvious
parallel of Dick Turpin's epic ride to York.

The Authentic Life fixed the date of William H. Bonney's birth
(assigning him the name adopted in his final years and accepting
New York City for the site) as November 23, 1859. Upson happened to have been born on the same day of the same month in
1828. The book was probably intended, in part, to rebut whis-
pers that Garrett had killed a mere boy in Fort Sumner by purposely creating the image of a remarkable bad man. *The Authentic
Life* actually provided a basis for two conflicting images. It soft-

ened the earlier portrayals, assigning good qualities as well as bad and magnifying both far beyond fact.[44] According to Garrett:

"The Kid's" career in crime was not the outgrowth of an evil disposition, nor was it caused by unchecked youthful indiscretions; it was the result of untoward, unfortunate circumstances acting upon a bold, reckless, ungoverned, and ungovernable spirit, which no physical restraint could check, no danger appall, and no power less potent than death could conquer.[45]

The Authentic Life, copied to the degree of continuing misspelled names, began a long succession of publications piling layer upon layer of apparently realistic portrayals on a foundation of fiction. The book also marked another development in outlaw literature: a key lawman seemingly revealed the true story of a fugitive. *The Authentic Life* created many myths, even through its illustrations. A line drawing taken from a photograph showed the kid with a revolver on his left hip and holding the muzzle of a carbine in his right hand. The photograph (which may not even show the actual outlaw) has since been used in countless publications, but the original image was, and usually still is, reversed in printing. The carbine, which most experts believe to be a model M-1873 Winchester, shows the loading port on the wrong side. When corrected by double reversal, it is properly illustrated and Billy the Kid emerges as right handed. Legend, however, conquers truth. William H. Bonney is now known as a "left-handed gun."[46]

Reflective images of the kid's personality also appeared. In one extreme, "he was a human tiger, the most pitiless killer of that period. In his short life of twenty-one years he killed twenty-one men, and the most of those killings were murders done in cold blood."[47] This psychotic monster, distinguished by his extreme evil, contrasted with portrayals of a brave and likable youth driven to crime by forces beyond his control. Both aspects were illustrated by mythic outlaw figures ranging from America's murderous Harpes to the romantic English highwayman Claude Duval.

Billy the Kid, image reversed, from Pat F. Garrett, *The
Authentic Life of Billy, the Kid,* 1882.

The far more appealing character took on much greater significance in 1926 with the publication of Walter Noble Burns's
popular and well-titled book *The Saga of Billy the Kid.* In this inaccurate but beautifully written volume, the bandit's story is

transformed into a southwestern tragedy ready for the Greek stage. In Burns's own words:

A boy is its hero; a boy when the tale begins, a boy when it ends; a boy born to battle and vendetta, to hatred and to murder, to tragic victory and tragic defeat, and who took it all with a smile.

Fate set a stage. Out of nowhere into the drama stepped this unknown boy. Opposite him played death . . . forever clutching at him with skeleton hands. . . . But the boy was not to be trapped. . . . He laughed at death. Death was a joke. . . . But again the inexorable circle closed. Now life seemed sweet. It beckoned to love and happiness. A golden vista opened before him. . . . Perhaps for a minute the boy dreamed this drama was destined to a happy ending. But no, Fate prompted from the wings. The moment of climax was at hand. The boy had had his hour. It was Death's turn. And so the curtain.[48]

Despite abundant factual error, *The Saga of Billy the Kid* remains the best telling of the tale, and it had enormous impact on later portrayals. Out of the bloody encounters of the Lincoln County War leaped the imaginary legacy of a carefree youth who became a deadly gunfighter, a tale suitable for an endless variety of vehicles.

Billy the Kid naturally became the subject of a folk ballad (see the appendix), although it never achieved the enduring popularity of those about Jesse James and Sam Bass. After 1903, Walter Wood's play *Billy the Kid* brought the heroic outlaw to cities throughout the nation, to be followed by dozens of motion pictures relying on similar themes. And then, in 1938, New Mexico's famous fugitive received a true distinction. At the suggestion of Lincoln Kirstein, composer Aaron Copland wrote the episodic score for the ballet *Billy the Kid*.[49] He then arranged a lovely orchestral suite from the same music. The southwestern outlaw had entered the world of art while also providing the name for a line of children's clothing.

Nevertheless, writers continued to increase Billy's special reputation. Putting selected "authentic" bits of information together, one may draw the following conclusions, none of which contains a single element of truth. The Kid was born in Ireland, the son of a peasant (whom the outlaw eventually killed) and an American Indian woman from New Orleans. His mother married Mr. Antrim, a wealthy New York mechanic, in Canada. Billy began his career in crime to avenge a Civil War raid on his parents' home. By the age of eight he had become a skilled monte dealer and soon thereafter killed his first man defending his mother (by then a pretty dance-hall singer) from a drunken bum. Although an adept pianist and female impersonator, he also found time to attend college in the East. Billy killed a total of forty-five, although he failed to keep track of Indians and Mexicans, whom he shot "to see them kick." The latter trait is particularly notable as he became a great folk hero to surviving Hispanics. His gang of ninety bank and stage robbers terrorized the entire Southwest. Billy shot the judge who sentenced him to death, and escaped from prison through the use of a knife smuggled to him in a *tortita*. His secret wife, Peter Maxwell's daughter, had him buried in Illinois.[50]

Beneath this cloud of lunacy may still be found the rich growth of legend. There remains an abundance of stories which may or may not be true. After all, Billy the Kid *might* have developed a friendship for Tunstall and embarked on a crusade of vengeance after his murder. He *could* have met Jesse James to discuss the possibility of joining forces. He *may* have been betrayed and refused to shoot an old acquaintance. We will never know; perhaps we do not want to know.

When reduced to proven facts, very little is certain about the Kid's actual life before his arrival in Lincoln County. And much of that which occurred afterward remains controversial and incomplete. He surely did not occupy a leading role in that struggle, but he undoubtedly emerged from it as a figure infinitely larger than life. The cowboy-outlaw and the pursuing lawman joined in forming an epic struggle as certainly as a forest archer and an English sheriff had done centuries before.

Today the fugitive and his hunter are both essential symbols of freedom and order, representing anew what each generation requires. "The Kid and Garrett together are America. . . . [T]heir

violent skirmish in the last century will always provide acknowl-
edge the desperado with festivals and pageants, while monu-
ments are dedicated to his memory."[51] Don't bother to look for
the chamber of commerce in modern Fort Sumner; it is called the
"Billy the Kid Outlaw Gang."[52] As Frederick W. Nolan, biographer of John Tunstall, has eloquently noted:

> Curious tourists flock to see the old places and hear the old stories
> of a time already as far removed from today as the time of Robin
> Hood. . . . Heroes have been made of yesterday's criminals, and names
> today command respect which in their time merited none. . . . Time,
> filtering a gentle layer of legend upon the harsh and cruel realities of
> the past, has obscured Truth, and history has not brought about
> Justice.[53]

History has, in fact, played tricks. By selecting the unusual,
romantic, and violent, it produces distorted and disjointed
visions of the past. The western frontier becomes a place of savagery and innocence frequently illustrated by extremes of right
and wrong. To this wondrous time and place comes the cowboy-
gunman, a character of daring, deadly purpose and rare skill with
firearms. The revolver and lever-action carbine are his icons.
Guns, to him, are life. In the presence of his steady nerve, fast
draw, and superb marksmanship, ordinary boundaries separating
hero and villain blur.[54]

Billy the Kid clearly occupies such a role, but it is largely a
myth. He did not kill twenty-one men, even counting Mexicans
and Indians. In fact, "a total of six or seven would be more realistic. . . . There is no real evidence that the Kid killed even one
Mexican or Indian."[55] None of the probable deaths involved great
skill or speed; most occurred through either surprise or in bar
quarrels. In the West, as Joseph G. Rosa states, "the gunfight
was a fact; the fast draw, a fantasy."[56] Frontiersmen were not
cowards, but neither were they fools.

Western gunfighters felt and acted as human beings, not killing machines. When rumors circulated that a frightened Pat
Garrett shot Billy the Kid, without giving him a chance, while

hiding under Maxwell's bed, the lawman replied honestly and in full:

I would have utilized any safe place of concealment which might have presented itself—under the bed, or under any article which I might have found. . . . Scared? . . . Wouldn't you have been scared? . . . Well, I should say so. I started out on that expedition with the expectation of getting scared. I went out contemplating the probability of being . . . killed; but not if any precaution on my part would prevent such a catastrophe. The Kid got a very much better show than I had intended to give him.

•••

I had a hope—a very faint hope—of catching the Kid. . . . I believed, that he would make good his threat to "die fighting with a revolver at each ear"; so with the drop, I would have been forced to kill him anyhow. I, at no time, contemplated taking any chances which I could avoid by caution or cunning. The only circumstances under which we could have met on equal terms, would have been accidental, and to which I would have been an unwilling party. Had we met unexpectedly, face to face, I have no idea that either one of us would have run away, and there is where the "square fight" would, doubtless, have come off.[57]

The Code of the West was in part an invention of easterners and Europeans.[58] A society relying upon the immediate use of deadly force to redress presumed transgressions while giving opponents a fair chance would promptly destroy itself rather than subdue a wilderness. The frontier was indeed a place of danger, but the principal causes included disease, hostile Indians, extremes of temperature, and drought rather than violent crime. Any peculiarly western code for expected behavior probably encompassed self-reliance, suspicion of authority, and a need for expedience. In addition the frontier reflected the value of respectable women and considerable tolerance, at least with regard to public morality.

Others portrayed westerners as uncivilized savages always ready to resort to the law of the gun. "Avenge insult or wrong, real or imagined, the code decreed. Never retreat before an aggressor. Any degree of violence is permissible, including death. 'I'll die before I'll run,' vowed practitioners of the code.''[59] On the surface, Billy the Kid and other western gunmen might appear to personify such an attitude, but those familiar with events and individuals often had a conflicting view. Lily Klasner, who as a young lady lived on the Chisum ranch and grew up "among outlaws," recalled the Kid not as a hero but a "harum-scarum" willing to take desperate chances only when no other means existed. She quotes him as expressing the far more likely view of a real gunmen: "He who fights and runs away will live to fight another day."[60]

In the game of survival life had ultimate value and westerners, good and bad, avoided needless risk. They attached their own definitions to both need and risk, of course, but they did the same with good and bad. The flexible images of Billy the Kid and Pat Garrett exemplify such cultural pliancy.

Although the Lincoln County War and the personalities associated with it are used very widely to illustrate the role of the gunfighter-desperado, many other events and individuals contributed to the outlaw myth. In his own time Billy the Kid occupied no great national significance. A host of brigands from throughout the nation shared in the attention devoted to deeds of deadly daring. These included Oliver Curtis Perry in New York, Fred Whittrock in Missouri, Marion Hedgepeth in Nebraska, Eugene Bunch in Mississippi, Bill Miner in Colorado, the Marlow and Burrows brothers in Texas, Jefferson ("Soapy") Smith in Alaska, and many others.

Still, in retrospect, popular interest in outlawry focused on the Southwest as the end of the nineteenth century approached. The region certainly offered a variety of interesting subjects. Immediately to the west of New Mexico lay Arizona (the two territories had been divided as a consequence of the Civil War), which provided its own distinguished desperadoes. The southeastern portion, bordering Mexico, attracted special attention.

In an era when *cowboy* carried connotations quite different from those of today, Arizona faced major problems in the form of organized bandits. At times working with strong economic and political factions, organized criminals plagued the territory for years. Informal agencies of justice, such as the Outlaw Exterminators, had limited success establishing control. By 1881 the situation had become alarming, as is indicated by Tombstone's famous "gunfight at the O.K. Corral."[61] The acting governor, John J. Gosper, reported:

We have within our borders a small army of outlaws well armed and fully able to cope with the ordinary civil power of our several counties. . . . [T]hreatening combinations of men . . . go upon raids of theft and common plunder. . . . Something must be done . . . to quell these constant raids upon the property of peaceful citizens and the occasional taking the life of the innocent.[62]

President Chester A. Arthur responded by recommending an exception to the federal posse comitatus law, to permit federal troops to assist civil authorities in the territory.[63] His threat of military intervention, combined with such events as formation of an armed company of citizens from Cochise County and the execution of six killers for the "Bisbee massacre" of 1883, caused the crisis to ease. The governor's annual report noted:

Lawlessness and the depredations of "cowboys" and "rustlers," which at one time had portions of the Territory in a condition of terrorism have succumbed in a large degree to law and order. The active measures resorted to by the local authorities early in the spring of 1882, in connection with the proclamation of the President, resulted in much good, and since the 15th of May of last year fewer acts of violence have been committed.[64]

Crime continued, of course, as it always does. Furthermore, it did not conform to the stereotypes of fiction. Old Tucson's most notorious gunfight, for example, might well be imagined as the classic shootout. Two bronzed figures, one perhaps clad in black, face each other on the dusty street as children and dogs run for cover. Blue eyes narrow and in a blur guns roar; the evildoer falls as law and order triumph.

The reality is rather different. It did not involve barbed wire, water rights, or the introduction of sheep to cattle country. This 1891 street battle was between Francis J. Heney, a prominent attorney, and John C. Handy, chancellor of the newly created University of Arizona. The subject, as an experienced investigator might immediately suspect, was a woman. An argument developed over the interests of Handy's young and curvaceous wife. And in a period when some professional men still carried firearms, gunshots followed. The bar triumphed over academe. Although the expert Dr. George Goodfellow was rushed from Tombstone to render aid, Handy expired.[65] Heney moved to the West Coast.

Arizona attempted to deal with more mundane offenses, such as cattle rustling, by creating of a territorial police agency modeled to some extent on the Texas Rangers. Between 1901 and 1908 this small force tried to combat still widespread banditry.[66] The Arizona Rangers, while active and successful in many instances, encountered constant and growing opposition. "In every legislature following that of 1901 at least one bill was introduced providing for abolishment."[67] Local peace officers resented the territorial agents, and suspicions arose that the Rangers were really gunmen employed for political purposes. Another argument "was a belief—held in some degree in many counties— that the Ranger force advertised Arizona as an outlaw infested country and was therefore a deterrent to settlement and investment."[68] Proponents of the organization countered by noting the creation of the New Mexico Mounted Police, claiming, "It is obvious that if our ranger force should be discontinued this Territory would soon be an asylum for criminals that had been driven out of New Mexico."[69]

The Arizona Rangers enjoyed their brief existence in part because of the perception that the quality of local lawmen left something to be desired. William Henry Robinson tells us: "While as a whole the peace officers of the State have been capable, fearless and energetic men, in a few conspicuous instances they seem to have been chosen on the theory that it takes one desperado to capture another."[70] This view gained significant support from the activities of two of the Southwest's less publicized outlaws: Burt Alvord and Billy Stiles.

They were, in fact, peace officers while secretly part of a small gang of train robbers. With discovery of their criminal activity, the two escaped to Mexico, where they apparently helped capture the notorious Augustin Chacón. Alvord and Stiles later failed in a ruse to convince authorities of their death by sending coffins supposedly containing their bodies to Tombstone. In 1903, Arizona Rangers improperly entered Mexico in pursuit of the fugitives. Alvord was captured and sentenced to prison. Upon his release, legend has him retrieving buried loot and disappearing into Central America. Reports of his 1910 death in Panama filtered back but could never be verified. Stiles, who escaped the Ranger raid, went to the Orient and then returned to the United States under the name William Larkin. In 1908 he was killed in Nevada while working once again as a local peace officer.[71]

California also had its notorious train robbers in the last decade of the nineteenth century. George and John Sontag, together with Christopher Evans, successfully led the band until the Battle of Sampson's Flat in 1893. An accomplice of the outlaws, Ed Morrell, had meanwhile infiltrated the railroad police. Eventually caught and sentenced to life imprisonment, he underwent incredible tortures in both Folsom and San Quentin. After many years the "dungeon man" obtained a pardon and became a major exponent of prison reform, testifying before numerous investigating committees. Author Jack London made Morrell a supporting character in his disturbing 1915 exposé of penal conditions, *The Star Rover*. And nine years later the former outlaw wrote his autobiography, *The 25th Man*.[72]

Such books had little influence on the well-defined outlaw image. Public misperceptions were clearly defined before the close of the nineteenth century. Groundwork was laid before the Civil War through the efforts of such writers as Alfred W. Arrington. Under the pseudonym Charles Summerfield, he produced a variety of grossly fictionalized accounts of violence in Texas and Arkansas. His books *The Desperadoes of the Southwest, Illustrated*

Lives of the Desperadoes of the New World, and *The Rangers and Regulators of the Tanaha* (reprinted frequently with different titles and authors' names) established a florid pattern for romanticized gore.[73]

Western outlaws later became favorite subjects for pulp magazines and inexpensive paperback series. Frank Munsey's *Golden Argosy* and *Beadle's Half-Dime Library* were among the first publications to recognize, or perhaps create, this public demand, but a major factor in the enormous market was Richard K. Fox, owner and editor of the *National Police Gazette.* While covering much more than crime news, this magazine unquestionably had a significant effect on perceptions of American banditry in the last two decades of the nineteenth century.

The staff of the *National Police Gazette* followed a successful formula: they adhered closely to reported dates, names, and places while making up episodes and anecdotes to complete interesting tales. Since the stories carried the superficial appearance of being both current and accurate, all the contents tended to become accepted as facts. Peter Lyon succinctly identified the consequences: "Crime, when commercially exploited, does pay, and the more sadistic the better. The Wild, Wild West, as exploited by irresponsible men . . . has created for the world an enduring image of America. Over it hangs the stink of evil."[74]

Lyon's careful analysis of heroic bad men in the *National Police Gazette* revealed many common traits: they enjoy prodigious accuracy with weapons; they are brave and courageous; they are courteous to women; they are gentle and modest; they are handsome and attractive; they have blue eyes; they are driven into outlawry defending a loved one from an affront; they protect widows and children while robbing banks and railroads; they die through betrayal or treachery, but their death is inconclusive, permitting reappearance in the future.[75]

It should be clear that these patterns had an ancestry reaching back through the tales of English highwaymen to outlaws of medieval legend. Little of significance has changed, or is likely to change, this proven montage. Apart from the introduction of modern technology and occasional minor modifications of personality or appearance, the bandit continues to roam through time and space.

The basis for this enduring image has cultural as well as psychological elements. Its appeal, as Burton Rascoe delineated it half a century ago, involves several underlying themes. Civilized man has a hidden desire to rebel against the law. While he openly deplores outlaw depredations, he secretly admires them. The heroic bandit must be a superior man, driven by injustice to crime, serving as the representative of right. He must die, though never in a fair fight, as retribution for his sins.[76]

By the end of the nineteenth century, these enduring themes had been grafted to the image of the western gunman. If the facts lent little credence to the application of such characteristics, fiction provided the necessary support. Biographers of Jesse James or Billy the Kid turned robbers and killers into defenders of true justice and the oppressed. If their actual histories offered nothing to explain their choice of banditry, episodes could be easily created to fill the gap. When their deaths really appeared to result from reasonable law-enforcement efforts, betrayal of some kind might be inferred from rumor or simply invented. And, after all, just enough truth existed to allow the myth to flourish.

The United States had its legendary outlaws, selected from tens of thousands of actual criminals, but equaling those from any land. Given the romantic background of the West and the repeating handgun of Samuel Colt, these desperadoes could confront all opponents and flee to the wilderness. A flood of books and articles isolated such mystic figures from the ravages of academic history. These outlaws became self-perpetuating legends whose names alone represented things both good and bad about the American society. But their images would soon find even greater clarity and detail. The twentieth century offered new opportunities and dimensions for crime and its exploitation. The cowboy-gunman was about to move.

CHAPTER 9

The Gangster

> *The two most successful creations of American movies are*
> *the gangster and the Westerner: men with guns.*

> —ROBERT WARSHOW

AS the twentieth century dawned, America viewed crime and the
frontier in ways quite unlike those of today. This resulted, in
part, from the simple perspective of time. The frontier may have
formally closed in 1890, but it remained as a very clear memory
and really continued in Alaska for at least another generation.
The image of the West, however, applied almost entirely to the
vast region beyond the Mississippi. And however wild it was portrayed, fiction could still be separated from fact.

The reason for a degree of authenticity could scarcely be overlooked. Many prominent personages, including those concerned
with law and disorder, remained alive and active. Frank James,
Wyatt Earp, Cole Younger, Pat Garrett, Emmett Dalton, Bill
Tilghman, Charles Siringo, and a host of others lived well into
the twentieth century, along with Nelson Miles, Chief Joseph,
Benjamin Grierson, and Geronimo. Millions of Americans remembered the West not through books or plays, but as participants.

Theodore Roosevelt, former North Dakota rancher and cavalry
officer, served as the nation's president from 1901 to 1909. He
was, to many, an obvious example of the frontier spirit. And
their attitudes were supported by the literary efforts of Owen
Wister and the artistic contributions of Frederic Remington. The
West had not yet crystallized into a romantic complex dividing
civilization from savagery.

Those who depicted and analyzed this unique and short-lived phenomenon had in many cases witnessed its final phases, and most of the time they remained close to its basic themes, although they were willing to heighten and embroider. But exaggeration had long been a frontier trait. The humorous "boasting chants" illustrated such tendencies and left a false picture of incredibly bad men from such diverse locations as Bodie, Brazos, Carson City, Cripple Creek, Dodge, and Duck Pond.[1]

Historians of the era knew the truth behind the songs and stories. Crime was an inconvenience in the winning of the West. A perceptive academician in the field, Frederick Jackson Turner, paid it little attention. To him the solutions to any problems appeared as a matter of course:

If there were cattle thieves, lynch law was sudden and effective: the regulators of the Carolinas were the predecessors of the . . . vigilance committees of California. But the individual was not ready to submit to complex regulations. . . . If the thing was one proper to be done, then the most immediate, rough and ready, effective way was the best way.[2]

More popular historians also tended to stress the success of efforts to combat crime. As Hubert Howe Bancroft noted, "stages frequently carried a guard of soldiers, who, together with the armed passengers, generally succeeded in intimidating attack. Under such circumstances it required a larger force than was usually found in one company of marauders successfully to rob a stage."[3]

Less-scholarly writers painted a glowing, simplistic view. To novelist Emerson Hough, author of *The Covered Wagon,* "the life was large and careless, and bloodshed was but an incident."[4] He played loosely with factual details but nevertheless maintained a realistic perspective. For Hough the West offered settlers vistas of hope, not shadows of fear:

It was a wild, strange day. But withal it was the kindliest and most generous time, alike the most contented and the boldest time, in all the history of our frontiers. There never was a better life than that of the cowman who had a good range on the Plains and cattle enough to stock his range. There never will be found a better man's country in all the world.[5]

Hough found a twofold character in the frontier population. He portrayed not only the courageous and self-reliant but also the desperate and violent. Interest in the latter led to *The Story of the Outlaw* in 1907. It clothed many stories of frontier bandits with an air of authenticity and offered a peculiarly chauvinistic interpretation of brigandage: "There are bad Chinamen, bad Filipinos, bad Mexicans, and Indians, and negroes, and bad white men. The bad white man is the worst in the world, and the prize-taking bad man of the lot is the Western white bad man."[6] Such a view unquestionably reflected one aspect of the countless fictional representations which had been spewing forth for a generation.

Writers like Prentiss Ingraham, Clarence Ray, Leon Lewis (Julius Warren), Harry Hawkeye, and Ned Buntline (Edward Judson) produced endless successions of dime novels, with the western outlaw emerging as a favorite theme. In virtually every instance the desperado appeared as an extreme manifestation of good or bad. To be charitable, the authors of these cheap little volumes probably meant only to provide entertainment, particularly for weary train travelers. Most readers took them in the way intended, although some undoubtedly accepted the fiends and Robin Hoods of the West as historical representations.

One early writer of a few supposedly autobiographical dime novels deserves special notice. William F. ("Buffalo Bill") Cody eventually had a significant influence on America's perception of its frontier heritage. While still personally providing manuscripts, he commented to his publisher, "I am sorry to have to lie so outrageously in this yarn. My hero has killed more Indians on one war trail than I have killed all my life. But I understand this is what is expected of border tales. . . . cut out a fatal shot or stab whenever you deem it wise."[7]

The primary contribution of Buffalo Bill did not come through such books as *The Prairie Rover; or the Robin Hood of the Border* and *Prairie Prince, the Boy Outlaw,* however. As early as 1872 he was appearing on the stage as himself. In 1883, Cody took these performances a giant step forward. Inspired by his success with an 1882 outdoor exhibition in North Platte, Nebraska, he organized a traveling show, Buffalo Bill's Wild West and Congress of Rough Riders of the World. Its star remained a dominant figure in the rapidly developing entertainment business for the next thirty years.

Early tours of Buffalo Bill's Wild West show displayed no significant concern with crime or its control. This gradually changed with passing decades, perhaps in response to public expectation. By 1886 the show included appearances by David Cherry ("Doc") Middleton, a prominent Nebraska horse thief, as well as Gabriel Dumont, an exiled leader of Canada's Riel Rebellion. But Cody's creative imagination achieved greater heights a few years later.

Sioux Chief Sitting Bull briefly appeared in Buffalo Bill's Wild West, but, unfortunately, he returned to the reservation in South Dakota and became involved in the Ghost Dance tragedy. He was killed by Indian police in 1890, precipitating an uproar that led to the Wounded Knee Massacre on December 29 of that year. In a tragic but true incident, during the melee in which he was killed, Sitting Bull's show horse took the shooting as a cue and began its performance, pirouetting and sitting. The Indians quite reasonably assumed that the dead chief's spirit had entered his pony, as perhaps it had. Cody eventually regained the horse and returned it to the show, where it appeared once more, ridden in ceremonies by the bearer of the American flag.

During the Indian trouble that followed Wounded Knee, Buffalo Bill obtained a commission as brigadier general and provided about fifty of his show's Indian performers as scouts and intermediaries. When the army took more than a dozen Sioux warriors hostage, Cody managed to have them placed in his custody and took several to Europe as part of his show. Touring the Continent with Buffalo Bill was certainly better than languishing in a military prison.[8]

All of this might seem a self-serving publicity stunt and elements of such were probably present, but one should not be too quick to reach conclusions. Despite revisionist interpretation, Buffalo Bill and most of his performers were not fakes. Cody really was a Pony Express rider and noted scout. William Levi ("Buck") Taylor really was a champion cowboy, and Annie Oakley (Phoebe Moses), Little Sure Shot, really was an incredible shot. To a degree, the Wild West shows did represent some aspects of the West, and they most certainly served such a purpose for hundreds of thousands of customers season after season.

After the turn of the century Buffalo Bill's shows and those of his several competitors began paying more attention to law enforcement and less to Indian fighting. By 1907 the program included a scene entitled "The Great Train Hold-Up and Bandit Hunters of the Union Pacific." Wild West performers made every effort to keep up with events. Pancho Villa's attack on Columbus, New Mexico, became part of the spectacle in the year of the raid.[9]

Traveling exhibitions were an obvious example of public interest in western themes, but such themes appeared in many other forms, including several successful plays. The high point in stage entertainment occurred in 1910 with the premiere in New York of Giacomo Puccini's opera *La Fanciulla del West* (*The Girl of the Golden West*). Arturo Toscanini directed the orchestra and Enrico Caruso sang the male lead, the role of a highwayman saved from a mining camp lynching by a saloon girl. The American outlaw had very quickly reached the pinnacle of musical portrayal.

There were, of course, more pedestrian counterparts in reality and they existed in many parts of the country. According to Ray Allen Billington, "the image makers singled out Texas as the ultimate haven for scoundrels—a sanctuary for every outlaw and every cutthroat fleeing justice in other lands."[10] One reason for the choice was that Texas had a far larger percentage of the West's population than any other state or territory until the 1930s. But many places had been known as centers of American outlawry: the Carolinas, the Natchez Trace, the upper Mississippi Valley, Kentucky, the western Ozarks, the Dakota Badlands, New Mexico, and all of Arizona. The entire West still seems dotted with an incredible number of "Robbers Roosts," most of which endured far less crime than is now routine in any eastern city.

In the last decade of the nineteenth century, however, the area now occupied by Oklahoma held rather clear title as the nation's "outlaw country." In a sense, it had been created as such. The problem originated with the Indian Removal Act of 1830. Thousands of Cherokees, Choctaws, and Creeks were forcibly driven from their lands in the Southeast to the region west of Arkansas. During the next two generations, remnants of some three dozen other tribes followed tragic routes from many parts of the country. These removals, while technically by treaty, were in nearly all instances achieved through fraud, corruption, or coercion. It should be no wonder that there was disenchantment with the rule of law.

Several confusing areas developed. Indian Territory lay in the eastern portion of what is now the state of Oklahoma, and Oklahoma Territory lay to the west, but major portions of the region consisted of the Unassigned Lands, including a huge northern strip called the Cherokee Outlet. To confuse matters further, a section in the Southwest continued to be claimed by Texas (the Texans claimed land from Mexico to Wyoming), and as yet another element of disorder there remained a region of nearly six thousand square miles running from the Cherokee Outlet to New Mexico and extending from Texas to Kansas. This remained in legal limbo from 1850 to 1890 and became known as No Man's Land. The name referred to the impossibility of obtaining clear title rather than to any fear settlers might have of outlaws. No Man's Land eventually became the Oklahoma Panhandle.

To say that legal authority and means of law enforcement did not exist in these areas would be quite wrong technically. In a practical sense, however, there were occasions when such appeared to be true. Difficulties arose over the formal relations between the United States and the various Indian nations. The latter held, sometimes by treaty, a status closer to that of foreign countries than federal dependencies. Criminal jurisdiction was a legal quagmire. Tribal law did not apply to whites on Indian land, and federal enforcement reached only the most serious offenses.[11]

Fugitives in significant numbers made their way to Oklahoma and under certain circumstances found sanctuary. Those accepted into tribal membership enjoyed special protection. Although deputy federal marshals might have proper warrants of arrest, they often found these virtually impossible to execute. Boundaries were sometimes difficult to determine, and local officers did not always provide full assistance. The major tribes maintained their own police forces, but these dealt primarily with offenses committed by one Indian against another. Organization of counties and towns provided no simple solution; local officers had limited jurisdiction and often functioned under strong political domination. A degree of order resulted after 1885 from the Seven Major Crimes Act, which gave federal courts authority in serious offenses on reservations; still, many problems remained.[12] As one pioneer recalled: "A citizen of Arkansas or Kansas or some other state would commit a crime there and would flee into Indian Territory where he was safe as he could not be extradited by the federal government as he had violated no Federal law and there was no state law requiring him to be returned to the officers of his own state."[13]

Oklahoma still did not seethe with lawlessness and disorder. Peace officers usually cooperated with one another, whether white, red, or black, and they often overlooked procedural formalities to expedite justice. In particularly heinous circumstances, citizens handled offenders by lynching them, as the infamous Jim Miller and three colleagues discovered at Ada in 1909.[14]

Most crimes were minor, with illegal introduction of alcohol being one of the most frequent charges. Harry Sinclair Drago estimated quite reasonably that the entire Indian and Oklahoma territories suffered the depredations of fewer than two hundred "genuine horseback outlaws,"[15] but their number included several of special note.

They were by no means evenly dispersed. Activities of the more notorious "long riders" were concentrated in the northern half of Indian Territory and even more specifically within the Creek and Cherokee nations. From this area several bandit gangs operated in the early 1890s:

The long rider derived his name from the many hours he spent in the saddle between his place of work and his first night of peaceful sleep. In the early days, hastily formed posses made up of local volunteers were no impediment to a well-planned escape. But as the train robbery menace grew and railroad and express company detectives took up almost every chase, the train robber found distance to be his only salvation.[16]

Four brothers, born in Missouri but raised in Kansas and Indian Territory, are associated with such crimes. Their mother, Adeline Younger Dalton (an aunt of Frank and Jesse James's accomplices), attempted with considerable success to raise fifteen children. If Grattan, Robert, Emmett, and William became outlaws, their siblings did not. The first three Dalton brothers served as peace officers while stealing horses; by 1891 they had turned to robbery of trains and banks. Authorities in Indian Territory, together with private detectives, were unable to cope with the well-armed and mobile gang.[17] Then, in October 1892, the Daltons made a major error. They attempted to rob two banks in Coffeyville, Kansas, where they were well known. Thoughtful bandits made a point of avoiding crimes near their homes. Generally, "the outlaws were more law abiding than many of the citizens and were regarded as good for business because they nearly always had money to spend."[18] The three Daltons and their two companions were not welcome in Coffeyville, however.

Townsmen recognized the outlaws and a battle promptly ensued. In about twelve minutes and approximately two hundred shots, eight men died, including four of the five robbers. A quiet Bavarian liveryman named John Kloehr, a member of the Coffeyville gun club, proved most effective. Taking cover near the bandits' tethered horses, he decimated the Dalton gang with one careful shot after another.[19] Only Emmett survived to face conviction and a life sentence. Newspapers throughout the region reported the event with an encouraging note for readers:

The Dalton gang has been exterminated—wiped off the face of the earth. Caught like rats in a trap, they were to-day shot down, but not until four citizens . . . yielded up their lives in the work of extermination. . . . [The robbers] could not have spent all their ill gotten money even if they had lived within the luxuries of civilization; as it was they were hiding during the greater part of their criminal career and have had no opportunity to spend the money. The location of the treasure is therefore a matter of great interest.[20]

The Daltons' major legacy was not hidden wealth, however, but emulation by others. Brother Bill, after unsuccessful efforts in California politics and a bid to persuade Frank James to join him in opening a saloon at the Chicago World's Fair, turned to Oklahoma outlawry.[21] He survived the Battle of Ingalls in 1893 but died by gunfire near Ardmore two years later.

The king of Oklahoma outlaws during this period was William M. ("Bill") Doolin. He led surviving remnants of the Dalton gang for several years. His long riders, while poorly educated, were shrewd and cautious. "A few of them got away, but they always returned, and that was their undoing."[22] George ("Slaughter Kid" or "Bitter Creek") Newcomb and Charley Pierce were murdered for rewards.[23] The former's father immediately blamed his son's treacherous companions, adding that the boy had been attracted to crime by the "Dalton Gang's glorious representations of ease and plenty without the formality of manual labor."[24]

A combination of deals for information, undercover agents, and increasing rewards led to the gang's disintegration. In January 1896, Deputy U.S. Marshal Bill Tilghman walked quietly up to Doolin in the bathhouse of the Davy Hotel in Eureka Springs, Arkansas, and placed him under arrest. The lawman battled the bureaucracy for many months before collecting three hundred dollars of the five thousand dollars reward money.[25]

Doolin was taken to Guthrie, where a crowd of some five thousand assembled to greet him. The marshals drove him about town and then permitted citizens to file by and shake the desperado's hand. A blonde commented, "He doesn't even look very bad; I could capture him myself," to which the gallant Doolin responded, "Yes, ma'am, I believe you could!"[26] Six months later he escaped.

Bill Doolin remained at large about six weeks. He then determined to move his family from Lawson (later Quay), perhaps to New Mexico, where he had previously hidden on the ranch of Eugene Manlove Rhodes. But it was too late. Deputy Marshal Heck Thomas received a tip from a local blacksmith as to the outlaw's intentions, and Doolin was caught in an ambush near his home and killed.[27] Myth provides another version, with Doolin dying in his sleep and Thomas propping the body upright in bed and blasting it with buckshot. The purpose of such a morbid act supposedly was the collection of reward money to provide for the bandit's widow and young son.[28] In fact, Thomas had the usual difficulties, collecting $1,435, having to meet $1,016 worth of expenses, and dividing the remainder among members of his posse. Contributions were collected for the widow from the several thousand spectators who gathered at Guthrie to view Doolin's body. The following year she married Col. Samuel Meek; her son adopted his stepfather's name.[29]

Americans seemed fascinated by a variety of criminals, so western bandits held no special place of honor. In fact, they were often portrayed as boorish and crude. Oklahoma outlaws attracted attention for their violence and audacity, but they did not rank particularly high in the nation's criminal hierarchy. Urban centers had their own brigands of note, such as Max ("Kid Twist") Zwerbach in New York and James ("Big Jim") Colosimo in Chicago. Expert safecrackers and cat burglars enjoyed special acclaim. George Leonidas Leslie, whose skillful defense attorneys blocked every effort at prosecution, was widely admired as the mastermind for countless robberies throughout the nation. Legendary confidence men, such as Joseph ("Yellow Kid") Weil (his nickname came from the pioneer color-comic-strip character) and

Arnold Rothstein (later famous for fixing the 1919 World Series) received national attention. Their frauds far surpassed the money taken by any violent offender.

One famous criminal of the era, however, never existed. He appeared first in a 1903 short story, "A Retrieved Reformation," by O. Henry (William Sidney Porter), who may have based the character on actual gentlemen thieves the author met in jail. Seven years later the safecracker appeared as the title role in the play *Alias Jimmy Valentine*. Shortly after that, vaudevillian Gus Edwards wrote the popular song which made him a household name: "Look Out for Jimmy Valentine."

A real criminal of the same era, but one with a totally different image, also had a song, "Harry Orchard." His real name was Albert E. Horsley and he blew people up for the Western Federation of Miners. In an era of extreme conflict between labor and management, Harry Orchard became an ultimate union assassin. In 1903, almost certainly on orders, he murdered former Gov. Frank Steunenberg of Idaho. The killing resulted from the intervention of federal troops in the Coeur d'Alene area during a major labor dispute.[30]

Steunenberg's death led to an extended investigation by Pinkerton agents in several western states. Orchard was arrested and subjected to intense questioning and probably torture. On the basis of his statements and other information, William D. ("Big Bill") Haywood and two other union leaders were kidnapped in Colorado and illegally brought to Idaho. Their 1907 trial attracted worldwide attention. Harry Orchard received a death sentence, but the brilliant defense attorney Clarence Darrow secured acquittals for the three union officials.[31] The struggle for organization of western miners lasted another generation.

Big Bill Haywood emerged as a charismatic but doomed figure in the American labor movement. A victim of the Palmer Raids of 1920, he fled the country and went to the Soviet Union, dying there in 1928. Harry Orchard's death sentence was commuted to life imprisonment but, unlike nearly all other noted outlaws of the period, he never received a pardon or parole. The dynamiter died in prison in 1954.

The really great outlaws of the era gained their fame through neither vaudeville tune nor folksong. They had to be seen to be believed. Even before that they enjoyed considerable notoriety as the American West's most distinguished desperadoes. Frank and Jesse James, the Youngers, the Daltons, the mysterious Wild Bunch, and many others served in their ranks. They robbed trains.

By 1907 the attention focused upon these outlaws caused William A. Pinkerton, head of the famous private detective agency, to address the convention of the International Association of Chiefs of Police on the subject. His comments and privately published summaries not only revealed much about such criminals but provided a basis for hundreds of subsequent portrayals:

The "hold-up" robber originated among bad men of the gold mining camps. Unsuccessful as a prospector, too lazy to work, and with enough bravado and criminal instinct to commit desperate crimes, he first robbed prospectors and miners en route on foot to stage stations, of their gold dust and nuggets, becoming bolder, looting stages and eventually after the railroads were built, he "held-up" railway trains and robbed express cars.

We also find them from the "dare-devils" of the Civil War, those from the Southwest who engaged in guerrilla warfare, where, as the pride of the States which sent them to the front and, because of their ambuscades, raids and lawless acts during the war, they were received as heroes when they returned to their homes. . . .

In the early days of the plains, the cowboy, with criminal inclination, noted for deeds of daring, began his career by cattle "rustling" and horse stealing, and then became a "hold-up" of stages and trains, committing the most of these robberies since 1875.

Also certain sensational newspapers and publishers of "yellow" covered literature, by exploiting and extolling the cowardly crimes of these outlaws and filling the youthful mind with a desire for the same sort of notoriety and adventure are responsible for many imitators of the "hold-up" robber.

The "hold-up" man operated as the footpad does to-day concealed in ambush awaiting his victim, suddenly pouncing upon and commanding him to throw up his hands, "covering" him by thrusting a revolver in his face, then relieving him of his money and valuables. Usually the "hold-up" man to avoid identification and arrest, covers his face below the eyes with a triangular cloth or pocket handkerchief, tied back of the head, wore a soft hat well down over his eyes, although in many of the great train and bank robberies shortly after the war, no masks of any kind were worn.

The average train robbery band formerly consisted of from five to eight men, but in recent years successful robberies have been committed by from three to five men and in a few instances by a lone individual.

Usually in these train robberies, one member of the band, with red lantern or flag, at a lonely spot would signal the train to a standstill, or one or two would board the "blind end" of a baggage or express car and nearing the point selected for the robbery, would climb over the tender into the locomotive, "cover" the engineer and fireman while others of the bandits uncoupled the express or money car and forced the engineer to carry them a mile or two distant, where the cars and safes would be forced open with dynamite. Resistance usually resulted in the death of those who interfered. Our study of the murders committed by these desperadoes shows fully 90 per cent to be assassinations, those killed generally being defenseless, or outnumbering desperadoes . . . giving them no chance for their lives.

Escapes were usually made with horses in waiting, in charge of a confederate at the place of the robbery, and often with relays of horses previously arranged, for covering five or six hundred miles, until they arrived at their homes or hiding places.

There is no crime in America so hazardous as "hold-up" robbery. Over two-thirds of those who have been engaged in these crimes, were killed while operating, or in resisting arrest, or from their wounds, lynched by posses, or as is known "died with their boots on," while nearly all others were either captured or sentenced to long terms of imprisonment or driven from the United States, becoming exiles in distant foreign climes. Those at large are constantly in fear of arrest, living secluded lives, and risking no chances of discovery by communicating with friends.[32]

Pinkerton's reference to "exiles in distant foreign climes" indicated continuing concern with remnants of a criminal group prominent at the turn of the century:

One of the most notorious bands of train robbers and bank "hold-ups" who operated in the West and Southwest, from Wyoming to Texas from 1895 to 1902, was known as "the Wild Bunch." After each robbery they would hide in the "Hole in the Wall" country of Wyoming, and after the excitement had blown over would return to their headquarters in small cities in Texas.[33]

Sometimes called "the Train Robbers Syndicate," this association probably consisted of several loosely associated gangs which almost surely never functioned under centralized control. Various members came into contact with one another and adopted shifting allegiances to fit personal needs. They had a number of leaders and operated from several refuges now linked in myth by "the Outlaw Trail."[34]

Hole-in-the-Wall, a barren valley in central Wyoming about sixty miles northwest of Casper, was only one retreat. Brown's Hole, part of the Green River Valley near the juncture of Colorado, Utah, and Wyoming, provided another convenient refuge. Some two hundred miles farther south was Robbers Roost, an isolated plateau in southeastern Utah. And some four hundred miles still farther to the south lay the high valley of the San Francisco River in western New Mexico. Such regions were by no means lacking in law enforcement and criminal justice, but outlaws probably did find them sparsely populated by people quite willing to ignore questionable activities in other places for friendship or a fee.

The most likely leaders of these gangs included Thomas ("Black Jack") Ketcham in New Mexico and Harvey ("Kid Curry") Logan in Wyoming. Over a decade, perhaps as many as one hundred outlaws may have associated with their depredations, but never at one time or in close cooperation. Nevertheless, their number included such subsequently infamous personages as Butch Cassidy, the Sundance Kid, and Harry Tracy.

Black Jack Ketcham came from Texas and is best remembered for having robbed the same train, the Fort Worth express, on three occasions. The last effort, in 1899, proved his undoing. He was executed at Clayton, New Mexico, in 1901, but his hangman apparently proved somewhat less than skilled. Black Jack's head was torn from his body when the trap dropped. There are no reports of the outlaw's surviving that particular demise, although his face, carved in stone, mysteriously appeared in the mountains near Cimarron.[35]

Harvey Logan was probably born in Iowa and raised in Missouri. He became a rustler and killer in Montana and Wyoming before attaining prominence as a bank and train robber. By 1898, criminal depredations by his division of the Wild Bunch prompted the governors of Colorado, Wyoming, and Utah to join in a concerted action that allowed officers to ignore state boundaries.[36] Pinkerton detectives began infiltrating the gang, ready to continue for years if necessary.[37] Railroads began assigning armed guards to passenger trains and organized teams of rangers to patrol Wyoming's "bandit belt."[38] The cumulative effect of these efforts proved sufficient. The Wild Bunch (a nickname probably attached to members after their bibulous visits to saloons) fell apart.

Logan, a very prominent fugitive, was captured in 1901 after a poolroom brawl in Knoxville, Tennessee. Identified as Kid Curry, he still made a daring jail break and vanished. "Just what became of him is still something of a mystery."[39] The most widely accepted explanation involves his participation in a train robbery near Glenwood Springs, Colorado, in 1904. Trapped by a posse, one of the bandits committed suicide. James McParland, the well-known Pinkerton operative, subsequently identified the body as Kid Curry's, but William Canada, chief of detectives for the Union Pacific, refused to agree.[40] Many westerners suspected that the outlaw escaped, perhaps to South America, where Butch Cassidy and the Sundance Kid were believed to have fled. In 1907, William Pinkerton indicated that Logan remained at large, cryptically stating, "He has not been recaptured."[41] Reports and rumors of his appearances persisted for years from Montana and Nebraska to Argentina and Chile. A generation later, Eugene Cunningham, granting that no conclusive evidence of Kid Curry's death existed, added poetically that the most credible report "is that placing him on the Andean slope, beginning a climb that took him out of sight forever."[42]

Harry Tracy, a member of the Wild Bunch for a relatively short time, escaped from custody on several occasions. He was eventually convicted and sentenced in Oregon for robbery. Then, in June of 1902, he broke out of the state prison in Salem, precipitating one of the nation's biggest manhunts. For two months Tracy remained a fugitive wanted "dead or alive" in Oregon and Washington, leaving behind a trail of nine corpses. Finally, in August, a posse surrounded him in a field about fifty miles west of Spokane. Seriously wounded, he took his own life. Cautious pursuers found Tracy's body the next morning. The fugitive had by that time become a celebrity from coast to coast.[43]

As the disintegration of the Wild Bunch occurred, circumstances created opportunities for their glorification. Train robbery and the attention it received coincided with the genius of Thomas Alva Edison. As a consequence, the American outlaw suddenly underwent a remarkable technical transformation for commercial purposes. The key factors in this unprecedented enterprise were the Edison Company and its agent, Edwin S. Porter. In 1903 he went to Dover, New Jersey, on a risky business venture: the direction of a ten-minute film depicting a fictional crime. It became an epoch-opening motion picture: *The Great Train Robbery*. Nothing quite like it had ever been attempted before, but thousands would follow in its wake throughout the world.

The Great Train Robbery was not the first film to tell a story or even the first with a western motif; *Cripple Creek Bar-room* (1898) had preceded it by years. But the earlier motion pictures were very brief vignettes intended primarily to be viewed through machines. *The Great Train Robbery* would be projected in makeshift theaters called nickelodeons. Audiences had never seen anything like it. The outlaws moved, outdoors, and actually robbed a train! This was no historical piece, it appeared almost as a contemporary documentary. Criminals were shown tying up a telegraph operator, boarding a train, robbing the passengers, and retreating into the woods. This was followed by chase scenes and a climactic gun battle. A closing shot presented one of the bandits (actor George Barnes) firing his revolver directly at the audience—perhaps in an effort to drive them from the theater for the next seating!

Today it is impossible to imagine the impact of this film. Many viewers probably assumed that they were somehow actually watching a real train robbery. They could, for a few cents, undoubtedly see a miracle. *The Great Train Robbery,* while humorously primitive to modern audiences, was creative in many ways. It told a story without the need for captions, used double exposures, intercut scenes, and even included an astonishing pan shot. It also made enormous sums of money. After nearly a century, the film continues to be shown. *The Great Train Robbery* remains the feature attraction at the Main Street Cinema in both Disneyland and Disney World, logical parts of their nostalgic magic kingdoms.

The immediate commercial response to *The Great Train Robbery* was emulation and exploitation. One competitor actually attempted to duplicate the entire film, scene by scene. Others proved more imaginative: *A Race for Millions* (1906) included a remarkable chase sequence involving a train and an automobile. Usually, however, efforts focused on crime and the West. G. M. Anderson (Max Aronson), one of the actors in *The Great Train Robbery,* made a film entitled *Broncho Billy and the Baby* (1908). It featured a good badman who gives up his freedom to help an ailing child, a frequently repeated plot. Since the director needed an actor, he played the role himself; because the title named the leading character, Broncho Billy Anderson inadvertently became the first star in motion pictures. In scores of sequels he appeared as a rugged, colorful hero who created his own law as he roamed the West.[44]

At the same time, Oklahomans were striving to capitalize on an outlaw reputation, which apparently delayed statehood several years. Former lawman Bill Tilghman joined reformed bandit Al Jennings in the production *The Bank Robbery* (1908). Crudely made near Lawton, it attempted to arouse sympathy for the outlaw; in addition, there were scenes of bare-handed wolf catching.

Both Tilghman and Jennings continued their association with motion pictures for years.

The rapidly developing film industry had a voracious appetite for stories and America's fiction machine went into high gear. Previously a great deal of humor had been associated with frontier themes. This promptly diminished in the tide of action and romance. A Manhattan dentist led the way and continued to do so for decades. His name was Zane Grey, and with the possible exception of Louis L'Amour, no other writer left such a lasting impression on perceptions of the West. Within a short time, fiction overwhelmed anything resembling fact.

Zane Grey routinely wrote two novels a year and found time for numerous articles on outdoor life. He had marvelous descriptive gifts and a rare ability with titles. His transparent plots and shallow characterizations were anything but literary achievements. Half a century after Grey's death, about one hundred editions of his works remain in print. More respectable authors, such as Hamlin Garland and Bret Harte, could never compete.

In his first incredibly popular novel, Grey created stereotypes which have been copied thousands of times. *Riders of the Purple Sage,* previously serialized in *Field and Stream,* appeared as a book in 1912. It contained a good man so bad he was introduced as an italicized scream: *"Lassiter!"*[45] Clad entirely in black leather, he rode about Utah on a blind horse, killing Mormons (only the men, he liked the women). But Lassiter, unfazed by five bullet wounds in one episode, was saved by a lovely lady, an heiress trying to save her ranch (and body) from *real* evildoers. *Riders of the Purple Sage* had many other fascinating characters, including a mysterious masked rider, revealed to be a virginal young girl raised by an outlaw gang led by a giant black-bearded "honest thief." In addition, the book had valiant cowboys, devious rustlers, venal Mormons, a magic hidden valley, an enormous balanced rock, and even a secret tunnel behind a waterfall. The real West could never compete; Zane Grey made it the violent, romantic wonderland everyone wanted and provided an outlaw-gunfighter as a means of salvation.

Meanwhile, the motion picture industry was expanding at a bewildering pace with several types of embryonic genres: romances, comedies (satirical and slapstick), and spectacles. It also produced a surprising number of crime films focusing on various aspects of a still dimly perceived underworld. These began as simple adventures and vice exposés, such as *A Desperate Encounter* (1905) and *Traffic in Souls* (1913), made in New York, where most of the early studios were located. In several instances slum violence could be re-created within days and blocks of actual occurrences.

David Wark Griffith emerged as a leading director of urban crime movies. He contributed such features as *The Fatal Hour* (1908), in which Chinese white-slavers kidnap innocent girls; *The Lonely Villa* (1909), in which a mother and daughter are menaced by burglars; and *The Lonedale Operator* (1911), in which payroll robbers terrorize a telegrapher. These motion pictures reinforced popular views of eastern cities as seething centers of sin and danger. Griffith's key contribution to crime films is generally conceded to be *The Musketeers of Pig Alley* (1912), which featured a young tough, "The Snapper Kid," who served for decades as a prototype for depictions of appealing urban hoodlums.[46] Griffith, of course, would subsequently transform motion pictures from simple entertainment to sophisticated art in *The Birth of a Nation* (1915) and *Intolerance* (1916).

Crime movies of the period created their own descriptive word: gangster. It was based on the ancient English word for a group of workers and Americans began associating it with criminals in the nineteenth century. It even became a verb, to gang, indicating a mass attack on a victim. By the 1890s *gangster* was appearing in print and received prompt acceptance in England as well as the United States. It applied to membership in any type of violent criminal association, including those of the closing frontier, but the early motion-picture producers seized and consistently used it in reference to urban hoodlums. It appeared in several film titles, including Griffith's *The Gangster and the Girl* (1914), in which the plot focused on a detective masquerading as a criminal, a theme since employed on countless occasions.

A lawman's adventures infiltrating a gang, perhaps to save the lovely leading lady, was also a convenient story line for westerns. In fact, the two developing film genres (often with interchangeable plots) were interwoven from the first decade of motion pictures,[47] but their relationship remained difficult to ascertain for at least a generation, partly because of the western's clear dominance in the market. Within that popular segment the frontier bandit expanded to astonishing stature.

The motion-picture industry quickly made dramatic transformations. Regular features became much longer; the center of production shifted to the southern California area called Hollywood. The success of films with frontier backgrounds served as both a cause and effect of this change. "The West was dying as the movies were coming to life, but for a while, at least, they overlapped."[48] opportunities to film the final days of the frontier were sadly lost. A few wily participants attempted to provide a kind of record, however, at a profit. Buffalo Bill himself appeared in several features made at the Pine Ridge Reservation in South Dakota.[49] Once again, however, outlaws had more success than Indian fighters.

Emmett Dalton, sole survivor of the Coffeyville raid, emerged from prison in 1907, having obtained a pardon after serving fourteen years of a life sentence for murder. He held several jobs in Oklahoma, became a movie fan, and then embarked on a film venture of his own, *The Last Stand of the Dalton Boys* (1912). It proved very successful, and Emmett toured with the production, admonishing audiences on the mistaken route of crime. Copies of the feature soon followed; more than a dozen rival films based on the Daltons appeared. Emmett subsequently wrote the book and produced the film version of *Beyond the Law* (1918). He eventually moved to southern California and became a builder.[50] Many years later the reformed outlaw commented that after his release from prison no one ever so much as "referred to my trouble or incarceration."[51] After all, they could see it at the movies.

Others were quick to follow Emmett Dalton's path. Former outlaw and convict Ed Morell toured with *The Folly of a Life of Crime* (1914), which dealt with exploits of California's Sontag gang. Oklahomans Al Jennings and Bill Tilghman also got back into the act; outlaw and lawman displayed much renewed interest in film careers. Jennings proved a far more successful showman than he had been a bandit. His well-received articles in the *Saturday Evening Post* of 1913 led to a book entitled *Beating Back* the following year. This he turned into a New Jersey–made film, playing himself. *Beating Back* (1914) proved both controversial and popular. It showed a criminal (albeit reformed) in a favorable light. Jennings then attempted to transfer his film success into politics. He ran for the governorship of Oklahoma, finishing a strong third.

Jennings made two more films, *Bond of Blood* (1918) and *Lady of the Dugout* (1918). Sordid and tragic, they may have been sincere efforts at realism, but they failed to attract receptive audiences. Al Jennings then became an evangelist (he always seemed ahead of his time) and continued to produce autobiographies of dubious accuracy. The self-proclaimed "last of the Western outlaws" died in California in 1961 at the age of 98.[52]

Disturbed by Jennings's success with *Beating Back,* former peace officers Bill Tilghman, Chris Madsen, and E. D. Nix organized the Eagle Film Company. Their immediate objective was production of a semidocumentary made primarily in the Chandler area, about sixty miles east of Oklahoma City. The result was the plotless but influential film *The Passing of the Oklahoma Outlaws* (1915). Some indication of its reliability can be detected between the lines of later comments from Tilghman's widow:

Every incident used was staged with historical accuracy. Bill used records where necessary. But his own mind was a storehouse of western history. He had a remarkable memory for events and dates and could relate instantly the story of any notable outlaw, or any bank or train robbery that occurred during his official days, whether he had any part in it or not.[53]

In fact, *The Passing of the Oklahoma Outlaws* was a major source of popular misinformation. Widely assumed to be authentic, it represented a clear effort to fictionalize events or simply make them up. Tilghman played himself; a former convict and outlaw named Arkansas Tom Jones (Roy Daugherty) assumed the role of Bill Doolin. The bandit-actor was actually killed by police in Joplin, Missouri, in 1924. Ten weeks later the lawman-actor was killed by a prohibition agent in Cromwell, Oklahoma.

Meanwhile, Tilghman did rather well by *The Passing of the Oklahoma Outlaws*. Its appearance coincided with that of a publicity intended book entitled *Oklahoma Outlaws* by Richard S. Graves (L. P. Stover), who provided aid with the film script. Both contained scenes, such as an incident in a dugout when Doolin saves Tilghman's life, which had no basis in fact but became accepted outlaw lore.[54]

Publicity efforts also involved a faked picture of a young woman, identified as "Rose of the Cimarron," who has subsequently received several identifications and has been transformed into a mythical heroine of the gunfight at Ingalls.[55] Like so many other people and events of outlaw legend, a basis of fact is lacking. Nevertheless, Tilghman made fiction pay. He spent much of his remaining life touring the country (the producers having failed to secure proper distribution) with *The Passing of the Oklahoma Outlaws,* complete with a collection of "authentic" rifles and revolvers, and explaining how law was finally brought to the West. Thousands of customers unquestionably accepted every word and every silent scene as the absolute truth.[56]

The Passing of the Oklahoma Outlaws was advertised as containing actual scenes of criminal activity. During production, supposedly, the Henry Starr gang robbed the bank at nearby Stroud, Oklahoma, and Tilghman (conveniently accompanied by a camera crew) raced to the site and participated in the successful manhunt which followed.[57] In reality, the feature had been completed some weeks earlier. Tilghman arrived after all the excitement had ended and most certainly did not rescue Starr from a lynch mob. He did shoot some footage outside a jail, but the action sequences were staged.[58]

Henry ("Bearcat") Starr had his own interesting role to play. Part Cherokee and a relative of Belle Starr, he was born in Indian Territory in 1873. Henry drifted into horse theft, robbery, and homicide before the age of twenty. In and out of prison repeat-

Henry Starr (Photograph by J. L. Rivkin, Tulsa, courtesy of
Western History Collections, University of Oklahoma)

edly, he developed a reputation as an intelligent and personable
young man unfairly victimized because of his Indian heritage.
While in the Colorado penitentiary he wrote *Thrilling Events: Life
of Henry Starr,* denouncing his unfair treatment and court corrup-

tion. Released as a model prisoner, he returned to Oklahoma and participated in a remarkable series of bank robberies (fourteen in five months), culminating in his capture at Stroud in 1915.

Henry spent less than four years of a twenty-five-year sentence in the Oklahoma State Penitentiary. Paroled, he determined to enter the film business, portraying himself in *A Debtor to the Law* (1919) for Tulsa's Pan American Picture Company. The production was a success, and Henry had the opportunity of going to California as an adviser. He declined the offer, probably in fear that his departure from Oklahoma would permit other states to pursue his extradition on earlier criminal charges. And so Henry Starr once more turned to bank robbery—with dire consequences. He died in 1921 after being shot and paralyzed at Harrison, Arkansas. "In the thirty years he had followed the bandit trade he had more holdups to his credit than the James-Younger, Dalton-Doolin gangs combined."[59] And during that time, crime changed. Henry Starr had bridged the narrow gap between bandit and gangster; the bank robbers at Harrison used an automobile, not horses.

Western outlaws continued to ride with ever increasing frequency in films. Someone identified as Scout Younger appeared in *The Younger Brothers* (1915), although the star's relationship to the actual bandits remained unclear. Jesse James, Jr., came to California and appeared as his father in *Jesse James Under the Black Flag* (1921) and *Jesse James as the Outlaw* (1921).[60] Billy the Kid apparently made his initial appearance in *Billy the Bandit* (1916), although no relatives were available as actors. This deluge of motion pictures glorifying bandits raised questions about their influence; Congress considered bills to ban the interstate shipment of such films.[61]

Proposals to outlaw the outlaws failed, however; a New York–born Shakespearean actor made the contemplation of such suggestions an absurdity. He reduced the rather pathetic images of real bandits to near irrelevance and became the incomparably best badman of the silent screen.

Despite his eastern birth, William Surrey Hart was raised in the Dakotas, played as a child with Sioux Indians, and worked briefly as a cowboy before becoming an actor. He appeared on Broadway and portrayed Messala in *Ben-Hur*. Hart's considerable stage success led to roles as villains in films. Then Thomas Ince gambled on him in western features. William S. Hart, at the age of forty-four, suddenly became a symbol of the American frontier identified around the world. From the first film imports to Europe, he was identified as Rio Jim, an ultimate "hell-for-leather hero."[62]

On the Night Stage (1914) set a pattern which saw relatively little alteration for a decade. Hart played the badman Texas, who battled a preacher until he was reformed by love for the beautiful heroine. A long succession of similar vehicles followed. Hart wrote and directed many of his later films, with considerable realism and attention to detail. The costumes and sets appeared as remarkably authentic, although characters and stories remained completely erroneous. Most of his films included a considerable amount of comedy; the star usually survived, and he seldom failed to kiss the girl. Comely leading ladies in Hart's films were a key to their success. Opposite actresses such as the winsome and versatile Bessie Love, audiences could easily believe that Hart's bandit really might abandon a life of crime:

He might be playing a ruthless outlaw, but the plot ensured he would be accepted as the unmistakable hero by having his misdeeds occur before the action began: on screen Hart's characters were almost invariably irreproachable. As films and audiences increased in sophistication, such precautions became unnecessary. Like the gangster, who for the average American incarnated his impatience with the Prohibition or his rebellion against the frustrations of the Depression, the outlaw once more came to represent the spirit of independence. And on the screen he was free to rob, cheat and kill, and still remain the hero.[63]

Hart's many films were sentimental and austere. He disdained overt fakery and seldom used stuntmen while relying heavily on close-ups and overhead shots. Hart sometimes appeared as a gambler but consistently returned to his established good bad-man image. It was indicated quite clearly in a subtitle in one of his most popular features, *Hell's Hinges* (1916): "Blaze Tracey, the embodiment of the best and worst of the early West. A man-killer whose philosophy of life is summed up in the creed, 'shoot first and do your disputin' afterwards!' "[64]

In that particular film, Blaze Tracey is redeemed by a minister's sister. When drunks burn the town's church and kill the preacher, the outlaw destroys everything in sight, turning the entire community into a raging inferno. A similar climax appears in Clint Eastwood's *High Plains Drifter* (1973). Other similarities in the actor's work exists. On several occasions Hart used the theme of a westerner in a big city applying frontier virtues to urban corruption. In *Branding Broadway* (1918) he pursued the villain through New York's Central Park. Half a century later, Eastwood did much the same in *Coogan's Bluff* (1968).

William S. Hart remained a dominant force in westerns for more than a decade. He established many patterns which remain deeply etched in the popular mind, and in real life he reflected elements of his solid, sentimental, courtly image. As one illustration, Hart's affection for horses was much more than public-ity. It created a relationship which subsequent western stars and mounts maintained for a generation. On one occasion in an in-volved contractual dispute, Hart delivered a unique blow to the studio: he "retired" his beloved pony, Fritz, placing notices in trade papers in the pinto's name.[65]

Hart's popularity declined during the 1920s, but he endured as a film embodiment of the western outlaw, reflecting the ex-tremes of America's frontier related character. In various guises his character has been played perhaps more frequently than any other in screen history. Hart died in 1946, leaving most of his substantial estate for the maintenance of his Los Angeles ranch as a living museum. Fritz's carefully tended grave is located there.

Hart was buried in a family plot in New York, but in the mythic world of film the old outlaw and his horse remain to-gether. Their joint role may be best expressed as an echo to

Hart's own emotion-filled words describing the making of early motion pictures. As the dangerous riding scene ends, the faint voice of the director comes through the clouds of acrid dust: "Okay, Bill, okay. Glad you made it. Great stuff, Bill, great stuff. And say, Bill, give old Fritz a pat on the nose for me, will you?"[66]

CHAPTER 10

The Renegade

When a Kiowa is placed in a pen he dies.

—SATANTA

THE legendary American outlaw is white. He is, moreover, very likely of British (particularly Irish) ancestry. This racial and ethnic stereotype has at best a very limited historical basis. As with so many aspects of outlaw legend, perceptions rely on false and fictional images rather than truth. Reality provides a poorly defined backdrop; the players reflect audiences' perceived desires. In nearly all instances, portrayals are not of fact but of myth.

American outlaws were of course from all races. On the frontier they came in various shades of white, red, brown, black, and yellow. Such distinctions probably meant far less to those directly involved than they may be made to represent today. Any outlaw then represented a threat requiring and usually receiving, prompt eradication. Today, fashion frequently dictates that bandits from minority groups represent the oppressed, a direct parallel to outlaws of medieval origin. In the American West, such was not always the case.

Subjected to careful scrutiny, most criminals found victims throughout a cross section of society. If the powerful and wealthy lost property more frequently than others, it was usually because they were appealing targets. The presence of bank and train robbery in the West, together with livestock theft, simply reflected apparent wealth. What else was worth stealing?

Popular portrayals of minority outlaws reveal a remarkable degree of perhaps unintended bigotry. The white bandit routinely appears as the only variety worth attention. Counterparts from

194

other groups attract little concern, and when they do occupy significant roles, they often resemble devils and demons intended as a contrast to the good (or at least better) bad man. White outlaws are sometimes placed (usually in error) in an aura of social banditry, but those of other hues seldom receive this accolade, although they frequently seem more likely choices.

Behind the surface of glowing legend lies a sobering prospect. The white bad man could be good, or at least recognized for special distinction, such as "first," or "worst," or "greatest," or "last." Desperadoes of other races seem either to be evil almost beyond description or presumably ignored because of their unimportance. This peculiar kind of perverse prejudice (our criminals are better than yours) is perhaps found in all cultures, but it found clear expression in the United States.

At an ultimate level, such views reflect an ugly attitude. Minority outlaws, unlike those of the majority, are considered subhuman, unworthy of either fear or admiration; they are monsters, deserving only contempt and elimination. In fact, these creatures may resemble the ancient outlaws rather than those surrounded by a century of contrived myth.

More than a thousand years ago, brigands lost all protection of the law and the church. They became rovers of the wilderness, subject to being hunted and killed like beasts. These outlaws enjoyed the blessings of neither God nor man. They were complete social outcasts who had so violated the rules of expected conduct as to lose any kind of status. Much the same may be said of many outlaws who came from minorities.

There were exceptions, of course. A degree of humanity did attach to some of the Mexican desperadoes. Less often, such could be said of Indian marauders, but it applied in virtually no instances to black brigands. Such removals from grace were, of course, partly the product of popular and later writers. Contemporary local accounts indicated more equality of attitude than those which followed or were geographically removed. Ranchers were not particularly interested in a rustler's color.

Anyone offering tales of minority outlaws faced a dilemma. Resort to obvious explanations based on traditional themes turned the bandit into a representative, or at least a reflection, of the oppressed. That technique fit the good-badman image admirably well, but brigands from lesser groups could rarely match such a mold; it might, after all, alienate a prospective majority audience by making them oppressors.

An approach along typical lines risked another hazard: the minority outlaw, if revealed as one eliciting support or even sympathy from among his people, indicated major dissatisfaction with the rules of behavior imposed by the majority. And that raised the unacceptable specter of rebellion. It might even prompt accusations of fomentation. The typical solution involved presentation of the minority outlaw not as a social bandit or even an ordinary criminal, but as an outcast from his own group. A popular term for such an offender was *renegade.* Applied frequently to Indians, it also found use in reference to whites, blacks, and others. The word came from the Spanish as early as the sixteenth century and perhaps originally meant one who renounces Christianity for Islam, but it eventually included any blasphemer, turncoat, or deserter. In America *renegar* took on special implications in Spanish, signifying hatred and protest. Thus *renegade* fit well some of those involved with frontier outlawry.

Americans routinely applied the term to people who abandoned white society to join and fight alongside the Indians rather than against them. For nearly three centuries those who renounced civilization for savagery received special vilification. Outlaws by choice, their status probably represented suppressed fears and perhaps secret desires. In fact, few fugitives found homes or protection among the Indians. Those who did usually died by violence, sharing in the defeat of their chosen culture. But a small number still left a significant legacy of apprehension and a threat of imagined evil lurking in the wilderness. The foremost of these came from Pennsylvania to join the Senecas and Wyandots in support of the British during the Revolutionary War. We are told that "no renegade—perhaps no individual in American frontier history enjoyed such adverse publicity as did

Simon Girty."[1] He found his way into countless works of fiction
as the frightful white leader of bestial Indians. Rumored to have
been killed on numerous occasions, "the Great Renegade" actually went to Canada, obtained a British pension, and died in
1818.

The concept of sending an offender into exile was not a unique
concept of European civilization. American Indians had their
own versions of outlawry, revealing different interpretations. To
the Cheyenne, for example, banishment seemed suitable only for
the crime of murder, and even then the punishment might be
commuted or limited in duration. Outlawry proceeded directly
from the forbidden act rather than judicial formalities. The criminal had, in a sense, declared himself to be "out of tribe," and a
renegade, by taking another's life. A Cheyenne decree of banishment followed the finding of guilt; it constituted a penalty while
simultaneously lessening the problem of revenge. No direct parallel with the European notion of outlawry existed.[2]

Conceptions of frontier criminals were perpetually confused by
the status of Indians. From colonial times they posed difficult
legal as well as social and political problems. England dealt with
the natives on a piecemeal basis, relying on concepts of theoretical tribal autonomy. A multitude of routinely ignored treaties
resulted. Unlike the Spanish Law of the Indies, no coherent set of
governing regulations applied. England even lacked the theory of
racial equality expressed by Spain's distinguished jurist and theo-
logian Francisco de Vitoria as early as 1532.[3] Fraud and force,
founded on religious principles, developed as obvious solutions to
problems posed by native Americans:

Puritan divines and colonial governors sought to justify claims to
Indian lands by arguing that European farmers had a right to settle in
areas that were incompletely possessed by nomadic hunters. . . . [T]his
claim was grounded in divine sanction. In later years, stripped of
its theoretical overtones, it would reappear in Theodore Roosevelt's
[1889] assertion: "This great continent could not have been kept as
nothing but a game preserve for squalid savages."[4]

By the eighteenth century, New England colonies routinely offered bounties for Indian scalps. In some instances, captured hostiles were sold into slavery. The clearest indication of official attitudes came from Lord Jeffrey Amherst, the English military commander in chief in 1763: "You will do well to try to inoculate the Indians [with smallpox] by means of blankets, as well as to try every other method that can serve to extirpate this execrable race. I should be very glad your scheme for hunting them down with dogs could take effect."[5]

At times, Indians were almost regarded as an outlaw race. White scalp hunters operated against them until the late nineteenth century. Certain groups and leaders obviously enjoyed no legal protection. Black Hawk of the Sauks and Osceola of the Seminoles were not technically considered outlaws, but they received comparable treatment. In fact, the entire Seminole tribe can be regarded as a fugitive group. *Seminole* means "wild" or "those who camp apart." They separated from the Creeks early in the eighteenth century and fled to Spanish Florida to escape British oppression. When the United States demanded their removal to the Indian Territory, the Seminoles resisted, retreating into their protective swamps to be hunted and killed like animals. They fought the longest war in the history of the nation, extending from 1835 to 1962.[6]

The Whitman Massacre of 1847 in southeast Washington led to another instance of Indian outlawry. After a military expedition against the responsible Cayuses (the tribe which furnished a western name for mustangs) and two years of pursuit, five leaders surrendered. Before their hanging, one of them reportedly explained why they had given themselves up to face execution. "Did not your missionaries teach us that Christ died to save his people? So we did it to save our people."[7]

Whites often declined to view reds as participants in wars. They frequently resorted to imposition of criminal law as a means of punishment. This took its most extreme form in the 1862 Santee Sioux uprising in southern Minnesota. Perhaps enraged by nefarious traders, bands led by Chief Little Crow struck a wide area by surprise. The number of victims remains unknown, but hundreds of pioneers were indeed cruelly massacred. With the Civil War already under way, the duty of response fell to local militia units. These put the Sioux to rout, forcing thousands to flee to Canada and Dakota. Primarily through the intervention of the friendly Chief Wabasha, 269 white and half-blood captives were rescued at a spot promptly named Camp Release.

Detachments scoured the region and eventually collected some two thousand prisoners. Plans for Santee Sioux annihilation were averted, in part through efforts of missionaries. But, nearly four hundred went to trial, with about three hundred convicted and sentenced to die. Any evidence of presence at a battle was regarded as sufficient; individual hearings lasted as little as five minutes. President Abraham Lincoln subsequently decreed that the Sioux should be considered as participants in a war but that those committing crimes, such as murder and rape, apart from an actual battle deserved death. This compromise substantially reduced the number for execution. Further appeals to the president met a prompt rejection. Lincoln responded, "Say to them that they have so sinned against their fellowman that there is no hope for clemency except in the mercy of God; I earnestly exhort them to apply to that as their only remaining source of comfort and consolation."[8]

On the day after Christmas 1862, thirty-eight Sioux (at least one through error) were hanged simultaneously on a huge scaffold at Mankato, Minnesota. William Duley, who had lost his wife and five children in the uprising, acted as executioner. The Indians were buried in a mass shallow grave, but local doctors promptly dug them up for use as skeletons. Soldiers held hundreds of the remaining prisoners at Rock Island, Illinois, for the duration of the Civil War. Most inmates became Christians and eventually were sent on to a Sioux reservation in Dakota.

In 1863 a farmer near Hutchinson, Minnesota, caught and killed an Indian picking berries. The body subsequently was identified as that of Little Crow, leader of the tragic uprising.[9] Hatred between Sioux and whites lasted in the region for two generations, followed by open dislike for two generations more; suspicion still lingers.

Indians were tried and punished as criminals on many other occasions. These included the four Modocs hanged for the treacherous murder of Gen. E. R. S. Canby and another peace commissioner in 1873. Although the whites in most instances placed no special significance on the means of execution, it meant more to red men. Angie Debo explained that "hanging was a terrible fate for an Indian, shutting him out forever from a warrior's hereafter."[10] Among those who narrowly escaped such an ignoble end were several leaders of the Kiowas on the Southern Plains.

The best known of these, Satanta, proved a particularly belligerent adversary. Born about 1820, perhaps of a Mexican mother, he became famous as a warrior and an orator. Wild Bill Hickok said of him, at the Medicine Lodge Council in 1867: "That man has killed more white men than any other Indian on the plains, and he boasts of it."[11] The Kiowa war chief reportedly spoke several languages and also could play U.S. Army bugle calls used to direct troops in combat. Satanta engaged in many battles over a period of several years. That which led directly to his criminal status occurred in 1871 at Salt Creek in northern Texas. The Kiowas waited in ambush, allowing a small wagon train to pass, to attack a larger one which followed. Several teamsters were killed and their corpses mutilated. The small wagon train which had not been attacked, incidentally, carried William Tecumseh Sherman, then the army's general-in-chief. Satanta and other Kiowa leaders were arrested later at Fort Sill, Indian Territory, and sent to Jacksboro, Texas, for trial. Along the way an older chief, Satank, attacked a guard and was killed.[12]

In Jacksboro, Satanta was tried and convicted of murder and sentenced to death, but political pressure by philanthropists caused the Texas governor to commute the penalty to life imprisonment. That, too, was revised; he was paroled in 1873.

In September of the following year, Satanta is believed to have led yet another attack on a wagon train, initiating one of the least-appreciated battles in the Indian Wars. A small mixed detachment of soldiers fought desperately against a large and efficient force four times their number at the almost forgotten site of Buffalo Wallow in the Texas Panhandle. Equipped with modern firearms, the Indians also used entrenchments. The soldiers distinguished themselves to a degree unique in American history; thirteen of the defenders at Buffalo Wallow received the Medal of Honor (one of them soon deserted).[13] It was a display of valor similar to that of South Wales Borderers against the Zulus at Rorke's Drift, Natal, in 1879, resulting in the award of eleven Victoria Crosses.

The Kiowas lost the bitter fight at Buffalo Wallow, and Satanta appeared some time later at the Southern Cheyennes' Darlington Agency, Oklahoma Territory, looking for food. He was placed under arrest and returned to Texas's Huntsville Prison for violating parole. Satanta then aged rapidly, spent hours gazing out of windows, and rather pathetically fashioned toy bows and arrows for souvenirs. No record of his ever being subjected to the almost routine whippings then practiced at Huntsville exists. Then, in 1878, he presumably dived from a dispensary window and died of a broken neck. A Houston woman provided a stone marker in the prison graveyard; it read: "Satanta, Chief of the Kiowas," and was stolen some forty years later. Various groups continued to agitate, however, and in 1963 Satanta's remains were exhumed, transferred, and reburied in the post cemetery at Fort Sill, Oklahoma.[14]

The issue of whether certain Indians should be regarded as renegades and outlaws or as combatants in wars occurred frequently. It determined not only the applicability of criminal penalties, but also tribal and possible federal liability. Questions concerning the legal status of Indians considered responsible for depredations arose in regard to the Nez Percés, the Utes, the Northern Cheyennes, and the Oglala Sioux, among others.[15]

Enforcement of the laws in cases involving Indians also posed significant problems. Causes extended from questions of jurisdiction to fundamental social conflicts. Texas Rangers at one time refused to arrest whites accused of murdering Indians.[16] Tribal police forces faced their own difficulties. Members were sometimes viewed as agents for oppression, particularly when violations conformed to customs. A Navajo officer committed suicide rather than arrest a suspect in such a situation.[17]

Very real problems occurred when significant numbers of Indians, sometimes from different tribes or bands, struck in unison. Then civil and military forces on the frontier faced what seemed to constitute a war. At the same time, a majority of Indians and tribal leaders might remain peacefully on their reservations. Those committing acts of extreme violence and cruelty were among the most likely to be considered renegades and criminals rather than warriors. But such groups often consisted of families and clans which had never agreed to treaties or quite reasonably considered such agreements to have been violated by federal agents.[18]

The legal outcome depended on a variety of factors, including attitudes of officers in the field, publicity, and extent of depredations. In practice the law was sometimes secondary to public opinion. The most feared Indians in all of North America, at times regarded collectively as outlaws, lived from western Texas to central Arizona: the Apaches. The very name comes from the Zuñi word for enemy. It is actually misleading to describe them as one nation. Apaches recognized no central leadership and consisted of six distinct but widely scattered divisions with many subdivisions and clans. Their separate disputes with Europeans began with Spanish slave hunters and lasted for three centuries.

Cunning, ruthlessness, endurance, and mastery of desert conditions made the Apaches legends of the Southwest. In one 1865 instance the Mescalero Apaches had been placed on a reservation at Bosque Redondo in what is now New Mexico. Disappointed with the land and living conditions, they complained without success to authorities. "Then on the night of November 3, they vanished. Even to this day no white man knows where they spent the following years. No doubt they raided; with so many wild Apaches and white outlaws about, it was hard to pin down the raids."[19] How an entire tribe could simply disappear, without leaving a trace, has never been explained. By 1873 the Mescaleros had returned, presumably from refuges in Mexico, and secured a far better reservation in the mountains, where they still live.

Hatred of the Apaches reached a zenith one night in 1871 when a powerful mixed force of Hispanics, Anglos, and Papago Indians conducted the Camp Grant Massacre, in which they slaughtered 125 members (nearly all women and children) of Eskiminzin's Arivaipa band living under the supposed protection of the United States Army about forty miles northwest of Tucson, Arizona. The raiders took as captives nearly thirty children, only six of whom were ever returned. A few months later about 100 perpetrators were put on trial for murder. The jury returned a verdict of not guilty in nineteen minutes.[20]

Among the many well-known Apache leaders, one name reverberates like a drum roll: Geronimo. His name was the jumping cry of army paratroopers in World War II. A Chiricahua medicine man whose family had been killed by Mexican soldiers in 1858, he became noted as a warrior and enemy of whites on both sides of the border. Although wanted for murder and robbery, Geronimo would never be tried. As Angie Debo, a supporter of Indian causes, noted, "Apaches did not leave living witnesses."[21] But Geronimo was certainly no ordinary criminal or renegade.

On and off reservations on several occasions, he achieved his greatest fame leading fewer than fifty Chiricahuas. This group of men, women, and children once moved 120 miles across the Arizona desert without stopping for food or rest. In 1886, Geronimo's tiny band occupied the best efforts of one-fourth of the United States Army and some four thousand Mexican troops. In the end, San Carlos Apache scouts located the Chiricahuas in Mexico's Sierra Madre Oriental and made the tentative agreements which led to ultimate surrender:

In our military history this Indian army will be known as "Geronimo and his band." If the narrative of this Indian's exploits had come down to us in tradition from a former age, it is safe to say that scientific criticism would condemn it as a myth, as an instance of the love of the exaggerated and superstitious and impossible which dwells in the unscientific mind. But the costly record of Geronimo is one which never can be questioned: His campaign taxed the powers of two great civilized governments; it involved a treaty which allowed the forces of the one to cross the frontier of the other; it received the energy and experience and ability of our two greatest masters of Indian warfare, General Crook and General Miles. The war was waged, on the part of the United States at least, with the best military appliances of modern warfare, including steam, electricity, and the heliostat; and, more valuable than any other element in the military case, it was an instance of Apache against Apache, for our troops were led by Apache scouts, who faithfully and heroically served the Government. Yet Geronimo armed his band with the best of modern breechloaders and ammunition, and even equipped them with field glasses taken from us, and drew his supplies from wherever he would, and inflicted incalculable damage on the country of both of his enemies, and carried on his last campaign successfully for five months. There is not, probably, in the history or traditions or myths of the human race another instance of such prolonged resistance against such tremendous odds.

Moreover, the Indian soldier was successful even in the ending of his campaign; for the surrender of this paltry band involved more prolonged negotiation than the army of Burgoyne at Saratoga or of Lee at Appomattox, and concluded by the granting of terms that the surrender be "as prisoners of war to an army in the field"—terms which effectually removed the sagacious savage and his followers beyond the jurisdiction of the civil authorities.[22]

Public demand for the execution of the renegade Apaches lasted for many weeks. Only Gen. Nelson A. Miles's insistence upon his commitment to treat Geronimo's band as prisoners of war rather than criminals finally convinced President Grover Cleveland to reject demands for prosecution.[23] Nevertheless, the Chiricahuas were confined in Florida, Alabama, and finally Oklahoma, where Geronimo died in 1909. His surviving followers remained in captivity four more years.

One of Geronimo's men escaped from the train taking the Chiricahuas to military prison. Somehow he made his way back, a distance of one thousand miles, kidnapped a young Apache woman for a wife, and disappeared. He became a legend of freedom and independence: Massai.[24] A quarter of a century later, his wife and four children returned to her family, bringing word of

Geronimo, Chiricahua Apache medicine man, from *Outing Magazine,* 1886.

the fugitive's death in Mexico. In myth, of course, the "last real Apache" remains forever beyond the white man's world: as an eagle soaring high through southwestern skies.

The scouts who succeeded in finding Geronimo were part of the first regular Indian agency police in the nation. Established in 1874, the San Carlos Apache force captured or killed 159 renegades during the first three years of its existence and served as a model for law enforcement on dozens of other reservations.[25]

However, a later member also became a very notable Indian outlaw. Has-kay-bay-nay-ntayl was born about 1867 and served with considerable distinction, rising to the rank of sergeant. He then abruptly took revenge against his father's killer and began a career of outlawry; white men called him the Apache Kid. After some two years as a fugitive, he surrendered and received a presidential pardon. Authorities then tried him for the murder of a whiskey peddler and gave him a seven-year prison sentence. On the way to prison the Apache Kid and several other convicts broke free, killing Sheriff Glen Reynolds and a deputy. For the next five years he remained at large, striking lonely ranch families and prospectors without warning. Numerous rapes and murders were attributed to the Apache Kid during this period, but the combined efforts of civil, military, and Indian authorities proved unsuccessful in the hunt for the dreaded fugitive.[26]

The Apache Kid's rampages stopped abruptly in 1894. A prospector named Ed Clark shot at and possibly killed a horse thief outside Tucson, but there was no proof that it had been the Apache Kid. Most of Arizona's settlers apparently believed the renegade left for Mexico, where he ceased his criminal activities. Rumors of his death floated in on various occasions for decades. Thus the Apache Kid died, of different causes, in 1901, 1907, and 1923. As late as 1935 he was reported living in Hot Springs, Arkansas, having attended college in Europe and become a doctor![27] To confuse matters a bit more, the state of New Mexico indicates that the Apache Kid's grave is in Cibola National Forest in the San Mateo Mountains.[28] Legend has many ends.

Through misconception, the Apaches emerged as unique symbols of American crime. Total destruction and extreme violence were associated with them; an "Apache Indian Job" indicated firebombing by urban gangsters. In Europe, similar usages developed. Members of the Parisian underworld were identified by the term, leading to an even more bizarre twist: the apache became a dramatic and stylized French dance depicting rather sadistically inclined love affairs.[29]

As might be expected, American Indian outlaws flourished

west of Arkansas in Indian Territory, partly because of the peculiar and confused legal status of the various tribes that had been forced into the region and their efforts to defend their shrinking sovereignties. As early as 1832, Cherokee law provided that "those selling National [tribal] Lands are declared to be outlaws and any person . . . may kill him . . . within the limits of the Cherokee Nation."[30] Choctaws gave their sheriffs and light horsemen vast powers in an effort to control crime.[31]

Indian Territory experienced internal political disturbances that were virtual civil wars.[32] In addition, it suffered depredations from numerous desperadoes. Ned Christie, a member of the Cherokees' executive council, became enmeshed in a bootlegging controversy and built a fortress which eventually required attack by artillery.[33] A gang led by Bill and Bob Christian operated extensively among the Chickasaws.[34] Chitto Harjo, a leader of the Creeks' Snake band, provoked political protests and various manhunts until his mysterious disappearance in the Kiamichi Mountains in 1911.[35] Rampages of a small gang led by Rufus Buck, a Euchee, proved particularly alarming. Although the gang's criminal career lasted only thirteen days in 1895, it included a multitude of robberies, murders, and rapes. Captured by Creek light horsemen, the gang was executed en masse the following year at Fort Smith. Rufus Buck left behind a poem that was discovered in his cell:

> MY, dream. — 1896
> i, dremp'T, i, was, in, heAven,
> Among, THe, AngeLs, Fair;
> i'd, neAr, seen, none, so HAndsome,
> THAT, TWine, in golden, HAir,
> THey, looked, so, neAT, And; sAng, so, sweeT,
> And, PLAY'd, THe, THe, goLden, HArp,
> i, wAs, ABout, To, Pick An, ANgeL, ouT,
> And, TAke, Her, To, mY, HeArT,
> BuT, THe, momenT, i, BegAn, To, PLeA,
> i, THougHT, oF, You, mY, Love,

THere, wAs, none, i'd, seen, so, BeAuTiFuLL,
On, eArTH, or, HeAven, ABove,
gooD, By, My. Dear. Wife, AnD. MoTHer
                            all. so, My, sisTers
                            RUFUS, BUCK
                        youse. Truley
1 DAy. of. JUly
Tu, THe, Yeore
off 1896.[36]

Rufus Buck's gang included members of diverse racial mixtures; any combination tended to place outlaws in a particularly
detestable status. Brigands of this stripe in Indian Territory
included Bill Cook, part Cherokee, who eventually was captured
and imprisoned in New Mexico.[37] But the worst of all racial mixtures was considered to be that of red and black, as it supposedly
combined the worst features of both races. Cherokee Bill (Craw-
ford Goldsby), a member of Cook's gang, fell into this scorned
category. Like Rufus Buck, he died on the gallows at Fort Smith
in 1896.

A combination of Indian and black ancestry appeared in the
myths of many fearsome bandits. It was rumored of the dreaded
Harpes, who roamed the Ohio Valley in the late eighteenth century, and there were similar stories concerning the Lowry (also
spelled Lowery) band in North Carolina. This group of desperadoes pillaged Robeson and other counties for a decade after the
Civil War. They represented more than crime.[38]

Under the leadership of Henry Berry, the Lowry gang reflected
political and social conditions affecting people of old, diverse
ancestry (red, white, black) along the Lumber River in North
Carolina. From their swamp refuges, fewer than a dozen outlaws
struck repeatedly in communities, looting and pillaging. Although authorities eventually managed to kill or capture most of
the brigands, Berry escaped—to a long life in California, according to legend. W. McKee Evans wrote of him: "Henry Berry . . .
gave the Indians, with all their diverse origins, the sense of being
a people. From just what tribal origin one was not quite sure,

whether Lumbee, Cherokee, Croatan, or descended from the survivors of the unsuccessful English colony on Roanoke Island during the 1580's."[39]

Some of the conditions which contributed to exploits of the Lowry band have continued for more than a century. In 1988, armed Lumbees seized hostages and occupied newspaper offices at Lumberton, North Carolina. They meant to protest and focus attention on the death of several Indian and black hostages in police custody. In a sense, the struggles of the Lowry gang go on.[40]

Blacks routinely received an extreme position in the spectrum of American outlawry. Alternately ignored or described as monsters, they represented the deepest suppressed fears of whites. As a result, "from the beginning some dark people abandoned any effort to live by the law, even their own peoples' sense of justice. Called outlaws, they took up the sword and musket and became outlaws. It would be strange indeed if a brutal system produced only gracious victims."[41]

For more than two centuries many white Americans lived in fear of slave uprisings. This concern, of course, had a logical basis because in much of the South a very large portion of the population lived in subjugation. About four hundred thousand people were slaves in the United States by 1860; they were a clear majority in South Carolina and Mississippi. Southern whites' fear of a black revolt extended even to freedmen. Emancipated slaves were, by law, required to leave the jurisdiction.[42]

Runaway slaves posed a significant problem for whites from colonial times. Most attempted, rather pathetically, to pass as freedmen or return to former masters, following predictable routes along rivers to older settled areas. Smaller numbers tried to escape east by sea or west to Indian country, although chances of success in any direction were slim:[43] whites maintained military patrols on boats and horseback. A few runaways managed to form alliances with other wilderness renegades, but these usually ran afoul of unfriendly forces. In 1737, for example, "seven Upper Creeks had come upon an outlaw band composed of a Spaniard, an Indian, a Negro, and a mulatto, known to have made forays against whites and Indians alike. The Creeks promptly killed the brigands and sold their stolen Spanish horses to the English."[44]

"Outlawing a slave was a legal action, placing the runaway beyond the law, making him a public liability, and encouraging his destruction by any citizen," says Gerald W. Mullin. "Those who killed outlaws . . . also collected a fee from the public treasury and a reward from the slave's owner."[45] Such bounties sometimes went beyond those for fugitives sought "dead or alive." One Virginia master offered forty shillings for an outlawed runaway returned alive or five pounds if destroyed.[46]

For nearly a century the Spanish in Florida welcomed escaped slaves and even formed a black regiment from their number. It was stationed at Fort Moosa, just outside Saint Augustine. Promises of freedom, calculated to foment rebellion, probably contributed to the Stono Revolt in 1739. Futilely, slaves rose in arms near Charleston, South Carolina, seeking escape to Spanish Florida.[47]

On the eve of the American Revolution, garbled rumors of liberty spread throughout the South and increased the number of runaways. A British court had accepted the wisdom of Lord Chancellor Henley: "As soon as a man sets foot on English ground he is free."[48] Somerset, a slave taken to England from America, was thus emancipated by common law; the decision did not apply to the colonies.[49]

The American Revolution brought no end to tensions. Risings associated with Denmark Vesey in 1822 and Nat Turner in 1831 showed quite clearly that major slave rebellions remained a continuing likelihood. Black leaders of these attempted revolts were routinely treated as outlaws and hanged as a consequence of their presumed misdeeds. Horror of a truly massive slave rebellion provided the explanation for extreme reactions against the activities of whites John Murrell and John Brown.

Noteworthy black outlaws may be distinguished primarily by the remarkable extent to which they have been deliberately ignored. White writers demonstrated an almost complete lack of interest. Blacks naturally sought a positive focus featuring representatives from law-abiding elements, but a lack of specific and reliable information resulted. America's legendary black brigands survived not through history, but in oral and musical myth, for "the Negro balladist, like the white folksinger, heroized the desperado."[50]

As with so much of outlaw myth, fact has little significance. Blacks were unquestionably major contributors to crime in the nineteenth century, yet they went largely unrecognized by the general public. Thomas Byrnes, New York City's chief of detectives, surveying 204 offenders in *Professional Criminals of America* in 1886, included 17 women but not a single black. Yet he identified 8 of the 33 men executed from 1851 to 1886 at the Tombs as "negro" or "colored."[51] In 1880 reports from state penitentiaries indicated that blacks made up 29 percent of inmates, having increased from 25 percent in 1870; the proportion in 1980 was 44 percent, increasing from 41 percent in 1970. Such figures hid extreme geographic differences a century ago. In 1880 blacks made up more than 85 percent of prison population in Mississippi, Georgia, Florida, and Alabama; Arizona and Dakota reported none.[52]

There most certainly were notable black fugitives. Railroad Bill (Morris Slater) roamed through parts of Florida and Alabama robbing trains from 1893 until his death in 1896.[53] In the West, Isom Dart (Ned Huddleston) operated successfully as a rustler for decades; Tom Horn, working as a detective for cattlemen, killed him near Brown's Hole, Colorado, in 1900.[54]

The truly legendary black bandits remain subjects of myth rather than figures of reality. Bras Coupe (Squier) certainly ranks high among these. He was, apparently, a slave in New Orleans who escaped and organized a group of similar fugitives in the Louisiana swamps. Blacks ascribed superhuman powers and abilities to him. Bras Coupe deflected flying bullets, lived on the flesh of men, paralyzed pursuers with mere glances, and disappeared in puffs of smoke and mist. In 1837, however, the brigand of the bayous was murdered in his sleep by a fisherman and his body was displayed for two days in New Orleans's Place d'Armes.[55]

A later black outlaw perhaps surpassed the deeds of Bras

Coupe. He is known entirely through a ballad combining extraordinary detail with complete fantasy. Stackalee (Stagolee, Stakerlee, or Stagerlee) appears in countless variants throughout the South. The ballad, as a pulsating blues, may have been heard first among black inmates of Mississippi's penitentiary early in the twentieth century. Most accounts establish the details of his birth as Market Street in Saint Louis in 1861 (with a veil over his face). He possessed a magic ox blood–colored hat made from the fur of a man-eating panther.

Stackalee had many adventures, allegedly selling the devil his soul and battling Jesse James. He could change himself into a horse and perform other wondrous acts as he traveled throughout the West. In 1906, Stackalee became angry over the poor service in a San Francisco bar and blew the entire city down, causing an earthquake and a devastating fire. A few years later the bad man had a terrible fight in Memphis (over the magic hat) and killed Billy Lyons. This led to his conviction and sentence of seventy-five years. A major variant of the legend has Stackalee electrocuted (hanging would not suffice) and going to hell, which he promptly took over and thereby reclaimed his soul.

Whether these exploits refer to a real or completely fanciful character remains unknown. In some versions, Stackalee appears as the mulatto son of a dashing Confederate cavalry officer (Stack Lee); in others he consorts with a remarkable girlfriend (Stackodollars) or has a love affair with a New Orleans voodoo queen. His name also has been associated with a famous Mississippi River steamboat, the *Stack-O-Lee,* which found its way into Edna Ferber's *Showboat.*[56] And Stackalee goes on, as a versatile big bad black man who represented masculinity and magic power to an oppressed people in need of hope. Such has been the mythic outlaw's common mission for those of many races suffering injustice at all times. He does what we cannot.

Minority status was attached to outlaws from groups not as obvious as blacks and Indians. The West had some Chinese bad men. The infamous mining camp of Bodie contended with the likes of Ye Park, who successfully escaped from jail to disappear in the mountains, and Sam Chung, who was tried three times for murder but never convicted.[57] Later, attention to Chinese brigands focused on the reputed leaders in San Francisco's Tong Wars, such as Fung Jing Toy (Little Pete). The greatest alarm, however, concerned the involvement of these villains in white slavery and the opium trade. The Chinese were perhaps the first American minority group closely associated in court and the popular mind with organized urban vice.[58]

Others quickly followed. As early as 1881, Italians and Sicilians in eastern cities were believed to have powerful criminal organizations that preyed on members of their own ethnic groups. Victims in New Orleans attempted "to protect themselves against the depredations of the renegadoes and desperadoes who infest the city and disgrace the name of their native land."[59] By 1890 conditions in New Orleans caused a lynch mob, containing many blacks, to kill eleven Mafia suspects.

The United States has for many generations linked crime with minority status, whether it be ascribed through nationality, ethnic association, or race. Prison records reveal a remarkable consistency during the past century. Roughly half of the inmates represent minority groups, although their nature has changed considerably. Although the percentages of "foreign born" have declined sharply among those in prison during the last century, the proportions of blacks and Hispanics have increased dramatically.[60]

And of course minority outlawry has included followers of suspect religions. In the American West this applied primarily to Mormons. Antagonism between Latter-day Saints and Gentiles was long, bitter, and violent. In 1838, Missourians slaughtered some twenty Mormons at Haun's Mill near Independence. Nineteen years later, at Mountain Meadows in southwestern Utah, about 120 Gentile pioneers died in a massacre. Although Indians were blamed initially, it soon became clear that Mormons directed the attack. The hunt for responsible parties lasted two decades as federal investigators found their efforts repeatedly frustrated. Finally, in 1874, John Lee was arrested by deputy marshals at Panguitch, Utah. Church officials apparently had decided to sacrifice him as a scapegoat. Lee was tried and convicted of the killings and executed at Mountain Meadows in 1877.[61]

Mormon polygamists came into frequent conflict with federal law. Some two hundred leaders of the church were imprisoned in 1887 alone, with many others remaining as fugitives. The government made prosecution much simpler, excluding all those sympathetic to polygamy from juries. Overt controversy subsided after the Manifesto of 1890 denied church support for multiple wives, but thousands of fundamentalist Mormons, rejecting the interpretation and thereby their membership in the church, have continued the practice polygamy in secret throughout the Southwest and Mexico.[62]

Individuals along the frontier unquestionably suffered because of their faith. Attitudes spawned the usual stereotypes, including appearance. In a remarkable early case from Ohio which recognized the influence of prejudicial publicity in 1853, the judge wrote of the defendant: "In person, she is Mormon, remarkably ugly. The eyes encroach on the space proper to the brain. Her head, in shape rather than size, is unfavorable to the usual presumption of sound mind and full capacity."[63]

Special condemnation applied to Mormons suspected of belonging to the Danites, or "Destroying Angels," that mysterious band of assassins believed to act on orders from high church officials. Such associations were rumored of various desperadoes, including Porter Rockwell and Long Haired Sam Brown, who was killed near Carson City, Nevada, in 1861.[64] The designation also applied to Teton Jackson, leader of a gang of horse thieves which operated extensively throughout the northern Rockies:

He was a Mormon and a member of a gang of Mormon outlaws whom they called Destroying Angels. John D. Lee, who was executed for the Mountain Meadows Massacre, was his uncle. Jackson was a most dangerous and vicious character. He had killed several Deputy United States Marshals in Utah and Idaho, who had followed him into the mountains . . . as he could always get assistance from one of the Mormons in any of their settlements along the borders of Idaho and Utah, it was almost impossible to get an even break with him.[65]

Teton Jackson did not provide the name for Jackson Hole, Wyoming (the name comes from David Jackson, an early trapper), but the horse thief remained a prominent fugitive in the region for many years.[66] In 1885, Frank Canton (Joe Horner) captured the desperado at a cabin near Hyattville and left the following description: "He was not a pleasant companion. I have never seen a man of his description before or since. He was about forty-five, over six feet in height, weight a hundred and ninety, stubby beard, raw-boned, coarse features, flaming red hair, and eyes as black as a snake's."[67] Transported to prison at Boise City, Idaho, he escaped a few weeks later, leaving behind a list of those he planned to kill. Instead he vanished into the mountains, to be seen no more.

A clear but almost never expressed theme links the common but special fear of most minority outlaws: sex. This factor may exist as a hidden cause for much of bandit legend, but it has a much sharper expression in relation to those regarded as inferior. In fiction, lecherous old Mormons sought young Gentile women for additional wives. Chinese villains, and later Mafiosi, supposedly engaged in the enslavement of innocent white girls for purposes of prostitution.

As early as the seventeenth century Americans were reading tales of women taken into captivity by Indians, a literary device which has been extended with increasingly prurient design to the present. And fear of rape played a major role in concert with the dangers of slave revolts and, later, rampages by black criminals.[68]

A studiously unstated terror in such expressions was, of course, the desire these brigands manifested for not just women but *white* women. Furthermore, in most fictional representations the proposed victims almost invariably seemed young, virginal, and attractive. To some degree, carefully crafted accounts avoided accurate but appalling aspects while concentrating on the unlikely and titillating. Still, the basic fears underlying extreme views associated with minority outlaws remained. These creatures wanted white women for their pleasure. And what was even less often implied, some of the victims might be *willing!*

CHAPTER 11

The Moll

Thou shalt not suffer a witche to live.

—EXODUS 22:18

UNDER early English common law, women technically could not be outlawed. This probably resulted not from a desire to protect females, but from their inability to enter a plea in court. The law devised ways around the impediment, however, allowing wives to be "waived" as their husbands became outlawed.[1] Originally implying repudiation of privilege, the waiver process enjoyed no particular rarity. In time the word *waive*, to lawyers, came to indicate a female outlaw, but whatever the term employed, she remained something of a conceptual enigma.

If the gap between fact and fiction is great in regard to male brigands, it is enormous in regard to their female colleagues:

In our male-dominated culture, women have always been considered as strange, secretive, and sometimes as dangerous. Men . . . have attempted to deny women the ability to do things men do and have either idealized them into a sweetness and purity which made them appear docile and harmless, or they have maligned them in order to be able to condemn them. Both types of behavior help men to feel better about their denial of equality to women.[2]

Contradiction and self-deception reached extremes with respect to views of female criminality. Women convicted of serious offenses posed a direct threat not only to peace and order, they rejected their femininity. Still, men found them strangely fascinating and even provocative. Their defiance of the law, together with rules of basic social behavior, seemed appalling, mysterious, and enticing.

Women held special and extreme places in outlaw legend. They could be the charming helpmate of the brigand or the source of treachery and deceit, causing his ultimate downfall. Both characterizations were well established with regard to Robin Hood as early as the sixteenth century. The forest outlaw enjoyed the aid and comfort of the lovely Maid Marian, but he died through the perfidy of the prioress of Kirklees Nunnery, his cousin by some accounts.

The peculiar combination of attitudes toward women probably contributed to the attention given a special variety of crime with which they were particularly and insidiously associated: witchcraft. It is difficult to grasp the significance accorded these deeds of darkness in our cultural heritage. "The Middle Ages toppled woman from Earth Mother to witch. The process was a slow one, taking at least a thousand years, from around 500 to 1500 A.D."[3]

In Britain, Christians denounced witchcraft and its commonly related evils, sorcery and heresy. By the early tenth century, condemnation had appeared in written law. According to a treaty between Edward of Anglia and Guthrum of the Danes, "if wizards or sorcerers . . . be met with anywhere in the country, they shall be driven from the land and the nation shall be purified, otherwise they shall be utterly destroyed."[4]

Those practicing sorcery in Anglo-Saxon times simultaneously violated laws of church and state; they might be "cast out for ever from the fellowship of God" and also burned alive. After the Norman conquest, procedures changed somewhat. Separation of church and state led to variations from the Continental pattern. After some dispute, the king's courts acquired jurisdiction over witchcraft, with hanging accepted as the correct means of execution. In Europe the offense remained subject to ecclesiastical jurisdiction, with burning at the stake the approved method of eradication.

Witchcraft cases were unusual until the fourteenth century. A combination of factors, including the Black Death, then led to a rapid increase, with women (almost always selected from those surviving beyond childbearing years) serving as suspects in most instances. The celebrated investigation of Ireland's Lady Alice Kyteler in 1324 and the publication of *Malleus Maleficarnum (Hammer of Witches)* by Dominican inquisitors Jakob Sprenger and Heinrich Kramer in 1486 set the stage for a great hunt which lasted centuries and in which "hundreds of thousands . . . were marched to the stake or forced to the gallows. Executions, almost always in groups, numbered five or six women for every one man."[5]

England's first statute, Act Against Conjurations, made witchcraft a felony in 1542; previous trials had been conducted under general principles of common law.[6] There were, however, relatively few cases in the British Isles until the seventeenth century. James I (Scotland's James VI) had a sincere interest in and fear of witchcraft. In 1597 he wrote a booklet, *Daemonologie,* exploring the subject in detail. The first year of his reign in England produced the important "Act agaynst Conjuracions Inchantments and Witchecraftes"; it remained an integral part of the legal system transported to the American colonies until its repeal in 1736.[7]

England's most serious outbreak of cases occurred from 1644 to 1660, particularly through the efforts of "Witchfinder General" Matthew Hopkins.[8] Trials typically followed a pattern: old women were accused and thoroughly examined for signs of evil; young girls, identified by public fits of hysteria, appeared as witnesses. At least one of the suspects was then revealed to be the daughter of a witch previously executed. Extended interrogation produced some necessary confessions. As noted generations ago, "where there is no torture there can be little witchcraft."[9] Still, many resisted, refused to admit their guilt, and died. "Perversely, those who confessed to witchcraft, the presumed downfall of any society, went free; whereas the accused who denied they were witches were usually executed."[10] It was yet another pattern destined for frequent repetition.

These elements naturally appeared in America, although at a somewhat later date. The English colonies recorded only twenty-three cases of witchcraft before 1660. Less than half of those accused were hanged, and a few others were banished. The early colonial witchcraft suspects included three men, all of whom were acquitted.[11] Only the trials at Salem, Massachusetts, in 1692 made a lasting imprint on history. The colony had a frightful record of persecution. Anne Hutchinson had been suspected of witchcraft, excommunicated for heresy, and banished "as a leper" in 1638.[12] Twenty years later, Massachusetts outlawed Quakers.

The ugly inquiries at Salem lasted only a few months. A complex set of underlying causes, including disputes over land, seem likely.[13] Altogether, 141 individuals were accused of being witches; 14 women and 6 men were put to death. Ten others, although convicted, were released or died in jail; 1 escaped from custody.[14] The vast majority of the accused were discharged. After that, concern with American witches declined sharply, although sporadic investigations continued in various colonies throughout the first two decades of the eighteenth century. Time and imagination then began the process of reversing the image of the enchantress. By the twentieth century, a bewitching girl bore little resemblance to the frightful crones of the Middle Ages. The young and attractive witches of recent fantasy have lost connection with crime, with titillation substituting for terror.

Whatever the enduring legacy of the ancient British *wicce,* its era of greatest attention unquestionably coincided with publicity accorded a number of female offenders in England. The seventeenth century marked the age of the dashing highwaymen, and tales of these colorful road inspectors included a number of fascinating women. Joan Bracey, for example, often dressed as a man while performing her robberies. She was finally captured and executed in 1685 at the age of twenty-nine.[15] The escapades of the famous Jack Sheppard relied in part on assistance from his agreeable companion, Edgeworth Bess (Elizabeth Lyon).

The most enduring contribution to stories of female offenders came from a tough London woman named Mary Firth. Born near the Barbican in 1584, she drifted into crime, specializing in street theft requiring the deft removal of attached purses from unknowing victims. This practice contributed her nickname, Cut-purse Moll, the latter portion consisting of an abbreviation of Molly, the popular variant of Mary. Reputedly the consort of highwaymen and a participant in their robberies, she emerged as a truly notable figure.

In 1610, John Day made her the principal character in a book, *Madde Pranckes of Merry Moll,* and the following year she became famous through a London play, *The Roaring Girle.* Moll eventually became a fence, operating from a house on Fleet Street. She died in 1659, having left instructions that she should be buried facing down. By that time her nickname was accepted as indicating any female criminal or companion of outlaws. Daniel Defoe fixed it forever through his novel *The Fortunes and Misfortunes of the Famous Moll Flanders* in 1722.

The most exciting of all the renowned female brigands of the era, however, were neither witches nor thieves. They were pirates! Legendary lady sea rovers have a thin foundation in fact. The most famous actual pirate queen was surely Ireland's Grace O'Malley (Gráinne Uí Mháille), who swept the Atlantic outside her stronghold on beautiful Clew Bay in the closing decades of the sixteenth century.[16]

America also had a basis for the legend of female buccaneers. It appeared through the exceptional exploits of Anne Bonny and Mary Read. They were captured with the pirate crew of the colorful Calico Jack Rackham off Jamaica in 1720. Anne was born in Ireland, the illegitimate daughter of a lawyer, William Cormac. He then took the young girl with him to a new home in Carolina. Rumored to have killed a serving girl, Anne ran away with a sailor named James Bonny. He took her to the Bahamas, where she eventually met and became Calico Jack's paramour. Among the pirates she discovered the equally remarkable Mary Read. The latter young lady was probably born out of wedlock in London. She served in both the English army and navy, pretending to be a boy. Mary was working on a ship seized by the pirates and apparently decided to join the sea rovers. Rackham did not know her sex until Anne Bonny arrived. The girls became friends and were active members of raiding crews until their capture.

Carolina piratess Anne Bonny, from *Historie der
englische Zee-Roovers,* 1725.

Tried with the other pirates, the young women were convicted
and sentenced to death, but both promptly pleaded pregnancy,
which effectively prevented their execution. Mary died in prison
before the birth of her child. Anne's later history remains a mystery. One plausible version has her prosperous father eventually
buying her freedom, followed by her return to Carolina.[17]

The United States had a relatively high regard for women,
including those associated with certain criminal activities. This
attitude quite possibly developed because of the frontier, where

comparative rarity and unquestioned courage of females produced special consideration. One and a half centuries ago a most perceptive foreign observer detected and described their unique status. Alexis de Tocqueville wrote:

It is true that the Americans rarely lavish upon women those eager attentions which are commonly paid them in Europe, but their conduct to women always implies that they suppose them to be virtuous and refined; and such is the respect entertained for the moral freedom of the sex, that in the presence of a woman the most guarded language is used, lest her ear should be offended by an expression. In America, a young unmarried woman may, alone and without fear, undertake a long journey. The legislators of the United States, who have mitigated almost all the penalties of criminal law, still make rape a capital offense, and no crime is visited with more inexorable severity by public opinion. This may be accounted for; as the Americans can conceive nothing more precious than a woman's honor, and nothing which ought so much to be respected as her independence, they hold no punishment is too severe for the man who deprives her of them against her will.[18]

These attitudes continued in the West throughout the nineteenth century. The statute against rape in Texas, for example, allowed conviction upon uncorroborated testimony from the victim, thus placing the burden of proof on the defendant.[19] In the same penal code, the state made a particular variety of simple verbal impropriety a serious crime: "If any person shall, orally or otherwise, falsely . . . impute to any female of this State, married or unmarried, a want of chastity, he shall be deemed guilty of slander and shall be fined . . . and in addition thereto imprisoned in jail not exceeding one year."[20]

American jurisdictions continued old rules of English common law and even extended them to protect women. The ancient doctrine of coverture, for example, made prosecution of wives difficult for crimes committed in their husbands' presence. The women could claim they acted as dutiful spouses upon command.[21] Theory and practice also made it virtually impossible to convict relatives of harboring fugitives. Nevada declared that "husband or wife, brother or sister, parent or grandparent, child or grandchild" could not be tried as subsequent accessories.[22] While such provisions are now rare, it has only been in recent decades that local prosecutors in the West began charging wives along with their husbands. The change may result from disintegration of the American family. Today wives are a primary source of information for criminal investigators throughout the nation.

The protection accorded frontier women clearly extended to known associates and accomplices of noted outlaws. The female consorts of the much feared Harpes (Sally Rice, Susan and Betsey Roberts) were released after their capture. Katherine King, William Clarke Quantrill's mistress and probable companion in crime, was never charged. Complicity by the ladies meant comparatively little to the pioneers; a wilderness awaited.

It would, however, be wrong to assume that female crime was rare or routinely ignored in the nineteenth century. Women enjoyed an unusual status on the frontier, but elsewhere they served as major targets of penal law. Figures from England in 1805 illustrate the extent of recognized female crime. During that year, 28 percent of the people convicted of serious offenses were women; they constituted 23 percent of the offenders transported (primarily to Australia) and 9 percent of those executed.[23] Such large proportions did not apply in the United States and most certainly not on the frontier, but comparison still reveals a significant degree of crime by and punishment of females.

In the American West there were two categories of women, although the line of demarcation probably remained a bit more difficult to discern than in most of the nation. A lady, such as Isabella Bird, traveled alone and without fear through some of the wildest parts of the frontier in the 1870s. She found in Colorado that "the settlers are steady, there are few flagrant breaches of morals, industry is the rule, life and property are far safer than in England or Scotland, and the law of universal respect to women is still in full force."[24]

Some females did not enjoy the same degree of respect, however, and they furnished a constant supply of criminals as well as victims. Most prostitutes were young, poor, and uneducated. A few managed to pass into respectability, but most suffered lives of degradation and violence.[25] Considered a necessary vice, they gave many communities a steady source of income through routine fines or licenses. Images of women, even on the frontier, reflected extreme views of refinement or debauchery.

Most pioneer females undoubtedly became hard-working homemakers who dreamed of but never achieved the trappings of cultivated living. Neither, however, did their number include "the bad woman, found outside the boundaries of society and in association with sex and sin."[26] America's frontier may have contained a larger proportion of such women than the rest of the nation, and it may also have been more tolerant and accepting of those who, through their very misdeeds, represented a degree of independence, born perhaps of desperation, which westerners always seemed ready to appreciate.

Such appears to be indicated by available statistics. A most obvious conclusion from crime data of the past century indicates the role of women has changed relatively little. Beneath the surface, however, lay hidden currents. "Ever since the 1870's, criminologists have predicted that the progressing social equalization between the sexes . . . would lead to an increase in the volume of female crime and thereby to a decrease, if not a disappearance, of the sex differential apparent in criminal statistics."[27] To date, at least in the United States, such has not occurred. In 1880 women were 9 percent of the nation's prison inmates; by 1980 their number represented only 4 percent, having reached lows of 3 percent in 1935 and 1970.[28] Total numbers of men and women confined had, of course, increased about tenfold throughout the nation—far in excess of general population growth. The percentages of females of all people held in the country's jails also fell: from 9 percent in 1890 to 7 percent in 1983.[29] In short, the emancipation of American women correlated not with an increase in their relative likelihood of penal confinement, but a decline. The major effect may really have been more victimization.

A century ago, there were marked regional differences in the rate of apparent female crime. In 1880, when women made up 9 percent of prison inmates throughout the nation, they accounted for about 2 percent of those held in the West. There were, of course, relatively fewer females on the frontier, but their comparative rarity does not explain such a pronounced regional variation. And within the West, even bigger differences existed. In 1880 only Texas and California reported significant numbers of female convicts. Oregon, Utah, and Idaho had none, while New Mexico, Nevada, Arizona, Dakota, Montana, and Wyoming held a combined total of only nine.[30] Very high percentages of the confined women were black.[31] Similar although less pronounced patterns also existed in jails.[32] The West had its full share of prison and jail inmates, but this did not apply to females. No such regional distinction exists today.

It would be incorrect to assume that women remained truly unusual in terms of arrests in the West. They made up a small but steady stream of persons apprehended and charged with crimes.[33] In reference to women, throughout the nation at the time these typically concerned prostitution and minor offenses against property. Cases of this variety did occur along the American frontier, but their handling was probably affected by prevailing attitudes toward women. Serious charges against them remained rare until well into the twentieth century. Perhaps because of this infrequency, a few cases attracted much attention.

Despite later misrepresentations, the major female offenders of the era did not come from the West. The most notable American female criminal during the last decades of the nineteenth century was Fredericka ("Marm") Mandelbaum, a leading fence in New York City. The most notorious murderess, who may have escaped, was Indiana's Belle Gunness. Farther west, the women best known for crime did not participate in rustling and robbery but vice. The great madams of the day included Ada and Minna Everleigh in Chicago, Josie Arlington in New Orleans, Mattie Silks in Denver, and Tessie Wall in San Francisco. But myth would make other western ladies into outlaw legend and they would be incorporated into both academic and popular works:

The frontier of the pioneer often created conditions favorable to the entrance of women into criminal gangs. Women were usually attached to the bandit gangs that created terror in the early days of Illinois. Then there was Kitty Kelly, as hard boiled as any member of the notorious gang of bushrangers; and Texas had its Belle Star, who has been compared and contrasted with the modern Brooklyn gun-girl.

Cases of this type indicate how a woman, abandoning what are conventionally regarded as feminine traits, may play the role of a man in a gang and be accepted on terms of equality with the other members. It is quite possible in some of these cases that she may play the dual role of gangster and sweetheart, but ordinarily one part or the other seems to dominate.[34]

Dime novels originated many misconceptions concerning female outlaws. Writers like Maturin Ballou and Frederick Whittaker prepared a foundation for the ferocious fictional females who appeared after the Civil War. These included Edward Willett's half-blood Dove-Eye, who attacked her enemies with a battle ax, and Joseph Badger's Mountain Kate, the fast-shooting daughter of a desperado. "Toward the end of the 1870's," writes Henry Nash Smith, "the Amazons and heroines in male attire took a distinct turn for the worse, no doubt corrupted by the general increase of sensationalism. One can even think of fixing the date 1880 as a critical point in the transformation of the genteel heroine."[35] Edward Wheeler invented a number of fascinating frontier females, including Hurricane Nell, Wild Edna, and Phantom Moll. He also created many of the false tales surrounding the real Calamity Jane (Martha Canary).

As is often the case, fact provided some basis for hopelessly distorted representations. The West did have some female criminals of passing note, most of whom were minor accomplices of male outlaws. Wyoming vigilantes hanged Cattle Kate (Ella Watson) in 1889. Little Breeches (Jennie Stevens) and Cattle Annie McDougal tried to join Oklahoma's Bill Doolin gang in 1894 and Pearl Hart helped rob an Arizona stagecoach in 1899. Ann Bassett ran a rustling operation as Colorado's "Queen of Brown's Park" at the turn of the century. And infamous desperadoes were almost routinely rumored, but seldom proved, to have female followers.

The frontier's best-known female bandit remains Myra Belle Shirley. She was born near Carthage, Missouri, in 1848; her family subsequently settled outside Dallas, Texas. Soon after the Civil War, Belle became involved with Cole Younger and presumably bore his daughter, Pearl. She soon also had a son, Edward, fathered by a lesser outlaw named Jim Reed. When the latter was killed in 1874, Belle reportedly refused to identify his body to prevent collection of a reward. The hawk-faced widow then moved to Indian Territory and began an affair with a peculiar individual of uncertain ancestry using the name of Blue Duck. By the time he went to prison, Belle had apparently become an active rustler.

In 1880 she married a Cherokee outlaw named Sam Starr, thereby acquiring her subsequently famous name, and settled near the Canadian River at a location she significantly identified as Younger's Bend. The troublesome couple was convicted of horse theft and sent to prison for several months.[36] Belle Starr had emerged as a rather widely known annoyance suspected of various criminal activities. Her difficulties with keeping a husband continued, for in 1886 an Indian police officer killed Sam Starr at a dance. Belle stayed on at Younger's Bend and next married a young Creek named Jim July. A few months later, in 1889, someone ambushed her with a shotgun on a nearby road.

Who killed Belle Starr? There are several theories. A neighbor who had attempted to lease land from her was an obvious suspect. Some believed the culprit to be her son, Edward, with whom she fought and may have had an incestuous relationship. Then, too, the murderer could have been the jealous husband, Jim July. And still others cast suspicion on the brother of a previously ambushed outlaw. Most citizens in the area probably had little interest in seeing anyone brought to justice. Belle Starr had gone somewhat beyond even the flexible boundaries westerners accorded women.

She was buried at Younger's Bend, although someone soon robbed the grave. Jim July died in jail at nearby Fort Smith, Arkansas, three years after his wife's demise. Her son, Edward, served briefly as a deputy federal marshal after a conviction for bootlegging but was killed in a saloon fight in 1896. Belle's daughter, Pearl, became a prostitute of some note in Fort Smith; she retired in 1915 and died ten years later.

Belle Starr's false place in history was assured within a few months of her death through the publication by New York's Richard Fox of a sensational supposed biography entitled *Bella Starr, the Bandit Queen, or the Female Jesse James: A Full and Authentic History of the Dashing Female Highwayman*. Filled with completely fabricated "extracts from her journal," it provided a unique source of misinformation. As a later biographer commented, "this narrative does not have a single fact correct."[37] Nevertheless, it created an absurd but enduring image: "Of all women . . . the universe produced none more remarkable than Bella Starr, the Bandit Queen. Her character was a combination of the very worst as well as some of the very best traits of her sex. She was more amorous than Anthony's mistress, more relentless than Pharaoh's daughter, and braver than Joan of Arc."[38]

Belle Starr was actually a rather plain, lewd thief, quite undeserving of fame, who undoubtedly contributed to and presumably enjoyed her distressing reputation. "She turned herself out gloriously in flowing black velvet . . . adding several innovations . . . a man's white and black Stetson hat, with . . . an ostrich plume attached. . . . She might even wear a necklace of rattlesnake rattlers. . . . [P]eople began calling her the 'Bandit Queen.' This pleased Belle."[39]

If so, she should have been delighted with the reputation created for her in later years.[40] Belle Starr became, with Calamity Jane, almost automatically associated with women on the American frontier. Probably no more grotesque a misrepresentation has transpired in American history. Of the millions of brave females who made homes in the early West, none was perhaps a less suitable example than Belle Starr. But the power of myth is inexorable.

In 1941, Burton Rascoe's *Belle Starr "The Bandit Queen"* appeared in print, making its subject well known to another generation. The book served, very loosely, as the basis for a popular film, in glowing color, of the same title. But, that was quite a different story. The motion picture *Belle Starr* (1941) transformed the heroine, played by the glamorous Gene Tierney, into a vision of feminine grace in voluminous antebellum white dresses far closer to Scarlett O'Hara than Calamity Jane. The Cherokee outlaw Sam Starr became a dashing Confederate cavalry captain, portrayed by Randolph Scott, fighting valiantly on after the Civil War. The couple led a band of 250 in battles against ruthless scalawags and carpetbaggers. In the end, Belle is killed saving the handsome Sam from an ambush. He then reverses the story of the refused identification. Despite its rampant historical errors, the film proved successful and in odd ways rather perceptive. In an introductory scene a black farmer explains to his little granddaughter, "Miss Belle is what white folks call a legend . . . the prettiest part of the truth."

Belle Starr came in the wake of several popular western outlaw films, and it led to succession of less expensive and worse progeny. Both *Belle Starr's Daughter* (1948) and *Son of Belle Starr* (1953) appeared on the screen. It even gave illegitimate birth to *Montana Belle* (1952), with several bits of presumably unintended humor. Jane Russell played the major role, incredibly ill disguised as a man in one scene. The story is set at Guthrie, Oklahoma, in mountains about a day's ride from Mexico! After the death of Sam, Belle is rescued by the Dalton brothers from a lynch mob. She then pretends to be from Montana while working as a saloon singer and leading the secret life of a "lady outlaw." The film also includes an Indian named Ringo (one of Hollywood's favorite names in westerns) given to such lines as "Pain in the face" and "Only trouble come with squaw."[41] At the end, Belle survives a great gunfight and the Daltons are captured. None of this, of course, has the slightest relation to fact. Belle Starr died in the same year of Guthrie's founding, neither in mountains nor near Mexico, and before the Daltons began their brief criminal careers.

Montana Belle may also be distinguished as containing "The Gilded Lily," perhaps the worst musical number to appear in any wild western film. The best, incidentally, appeared only one year later—"The Deadwood Stage," which enabled Doris Day to introduce joyfully and ingeniously the leading characters in *Calamity Jane* (1953). "Atchison, Topeka and the Santa Fe," from *The Harvey Girls* (1946), elevated its principals to quite a different class.

By this time the female outlaw had become well established in motion pictures and was by no means limited to westerns, where good-hearted saloon girls and civilized ladies predominated. While misogyny may indeed be a common theme in films, it took strange turns in reference to female criminals. In direct terms, movie women are frequently placed in the two categories which have long led to extended confusion: virgins and whores. From the feminist viewpoint, time has brought little change. "The closer women come to claiming their rights and achieving independence in real life, the more loudly and stridently films tell us its a man's world,"[42] says Molly Haskell.

Portrayals of the female criminal sometimes contradicted this pattern, although the outcome usually reinforced the theme. In early silent films, women rarely appeared as significant villainesses. That changed radically with the appearance of Theda Bara (Theodosia Goodman) in *A Fool There Was* (1915). Her name, supposedly an anagram of "Arab death," offered a clue that she was not intended as the essence of female purity and restraint:

> Enticingly gowned in macabre costumes decorated with spider webs and bat wings, the better to suggest the predatory beast of prey . . . and with a sullen smile that betrayed her utter contempt for her male victims, Theda was a literal man-killer. . . . [H]er victims, disgraced, degraded, financially ruined, took suicide as the only way out. Nobody took Theda too seriously. . . . Her films were warnings of hellfire and brimstone—with showmanship. Moviegoers were able to watch some lavish helpings of forbidden fruit for an hour or so, and talk themselves into believing they had learned a moral lesson.[43]

However grotesque it now appears, the female vampire character of Theda Bara hid some deep desires and fears. "The temptress . . . was a sexually devouring woman who consumed men but in doing so eased his burdens of guilt and responsibility.

Whether the woman was virginal or impure, she . . . bore the onus of man's incapacity or unwillingness to deal with his sexuality."[44] The pattern, in less obvious form, would reappear again and again.

This image of a devouring temptress was by no means restricted to films. It found its way into the law, as reflected in a 1923 decision by the supreme court of Missouri reversing a conviction for carnal knowledge of a female under the age of fifteen: "A lecherous woman is a social menace; she is more dangerous than T.N.T.; more deadly than the 'pestilence that walketh in darkness or the destruction that wasteth at noonday.' "[45]

The phenomenon of Theda Bara lasted only a few years. The vampire was then replaced by the vamp, a derivation immediately and widely adopted to indicate any unscrupulous flirt. Hear Sumiko Higashi: "The sensual woman still posed a dangerous temptation for man, however, and she had to be anesthetized to prevent the collapse of male ethics, if not supremacy. . . . The bad woman divorced from her supernatural powers ceased to act as evil incarnate and became subject to redemption through love."[46]

If sex appeared as the key to portrayals of bad women in motion pictures, such a driving force was rarely disguised. Female offenders usually gained their place in plots precisely because of sensuality and suppressed lust. In gangster films of the 1930s, molls typically fared rather poorly as rather incidental predators who ultimately paid for their crimes. The men sometimes got away.

During the transition to sound, American actresses somehow lost the best roles for good villainesses. Greta Garbo and Marlene Dietrich filled many parts for sophisticated vamps, with sinful backgrounds overcome through love for various handsome heroes. They were, of course, still white. In the history of American motion pictures, only one minority actress, Anna May Wong, enjoyed a consistent and successful career playing evil women. And then, suddenly, the role ascribed for female criminals changed markedly: American girls took over.

Perhaps because of their new importance and independence or

the simple fact that many leading men went to war, "the 1940's seem to have spawned more notable female villains than any period in film history."[47] Within a few years Hollywood furnished a dazzling array of gorgeous women luring ordinary men into doomed lives of crime. Such a lineup had never been seen before and probably never will be again: "In the dark melodramas of the forties woman came down from her pedestal and didn't stop when she reached the ground. She kept going down like Eurydice, to the depths of the criminal world . . . and then compelled her lover to glance back and betray himself."[48]

Ann Savage in *Detour* (1945), Rita Hayworth in *The Lady from Shanghai* (1948), Jane Greer in *Out of the Past* (1947), Barbara Stanwyck in *Double Indemnity* (1944), Lana Turner in *The Postman Always Rings Twice* (1946), Joan Bennett in *Scarlet Street* (1945), Ava Gardner in *The Killers* (1946), and Peggy Cummins in *Gun Crazy* (1949) represented an incomparable demimonde. But a steamy, petite former Miss Florida with a famous peekaboo hair style was really the quintessential bad girl of the 1940s. The meteoric career of Veronica Lake (Constance Ockelman) coincided almost precisely with the era of fascinating movie molls.[49] She even added new variations to old male fantasies in *I Married a Witch* (1942).

Beautiful but treacherous women tempting simple men to deeds of evil was an important element of the motion-picture genre now known as film noir. With its demise in the 1950s, the significance of devious females began a steady decline. There was, however, a short interlude featuring female pirates. Rhonda Fleming appeared as the privateer Rouge in *The Golden Hawk* (1952), while Maureen O'Hara became the swashbuckling Spitfire Stevens in *Against All Flags* (1952). In Hollywood, gun molls were usually dumb blondes and pirate queens voluptuous redheads.

Female outlaws with varying hair colors still occasionally found places in westerns, sometimes with great effect. Katharine Ross was superb as Etta Place in *Butch Cassidy and the Sundance Kid* (1969). Jane Fonda became a really distinguished female outlaw in a rare successful comedy western, *Cat Ballou* (1965).

Geena Davis and Susan Sarandon brought liberation, of a sort, to *Thelma and Louise* (1991).

Opportunities for actresses in strong criminal roles nevertheless diminished in later years. Actors dominated outlaw films throughout the 1970s and 1980s. There were, of course, exceptions; among these, the best of the later bad girls was certainly Kathleen Turner. In *Body Heat* (1981), *Crimes of Passion* (1984), and *Prizzi's Honor* (1985), she convincingly demonstrated that the American *femme fatale* remains an image of enduring fascination. Sex and sin still sizzle and sell, even in an age of liberated women.

CHAPTER 12

El Patrio

It is a good deal like hunting a needle in a hay stack this hunting for a man in the mountains.

—HARRY MORSE

OUTLAWS are known everywhere. Their number and significance, both in fact and legend, vary with social conditions and attitudes, but when one culture dominates another, the tendency for diverse interpretations of crime and justice increases. Then, one group's hero becomes another's villain. A brigand may be regarded as a patriot or an anarchist or a maniac or a savior, depending upon the point of view. Identical offenses can represent defiance of oppression or deviance from fundamental morality. This dichotomy has occurred many times for different groups throughout United States history. In outlaw legend, however, contrasts have been sharpest in regard to Mexican Americans. No other minority produced a comparable assortment of bandits. And, probably because of a convenient border separating not only sovereign nations but distinctive cultures with different languages, none other produced desperadoes so simultaneously admired and despised.

Roots of disorder routinely extend back for centuries. The Mexican American variety began with the Spanish conquest of the Aztecs, setting the stage for generations of class conflict. Some native warriors resisted long after Europeans established dominance in central Mexico. The Spanish called them *bandoleros,* to indicate those banned as outlaws. Centuries later the term became confused with bandoleer, for the cartridge belts worn by other desperate men and women struggling against a later Mexican tyranny.

Spanish settlement pushed slowly northward in America, carrying new legal formalities as well as criminal activities. Problems relating to the forbidden slave trade and conflicts between ecclesiastical and secular authorities were common. Within the small, isolated Spanish communities, however, ordinary violations against person and property rarely caused alarm. The Los Angeles region of California, even while used as a kind of penal colony, recorded only 127 criminal cases from 1830 to 1846, about one every two months. Assault, cattle theft, and robbery were the typical charges, with banishment serving as a routine punishment.[1] It may have been a necessity; all of California contained only six jails prior to 1849.[2]

War with Mexico brought significant changes in law, agencies of justice, and social structure. The United States expanded by more than a million square miles and acquired a new Hispanic facet to existing outlaw legend, beginning in California's fabled gold-rush region. The principal manifestation became known first as Joaquín, then by the last name Murieta, and finally through the appellation *El Patrio*. Although it is often translated as "patriot," the term really implies a paternalistic representative, not of a nation, but of a people. To some Mexican Americans of California, Joaquín Murieta, El Patrio, came to represent a Robin Hood, the brightest side of outlawry.

His (or their) depredations began about 1850 southeast of Sacramento. Within three years, widespread horse theft threatened the entire San Joaquin Valley, from the Coastal Range to the Sierras. In May 1853 the California legislature authorized a special company of rangers under Harry Love to destroy not one but five Joaquíns (Carrillo, Valenzuela, Bottilier, Ocomoreña, and Murieta) thought responsible for the banditry. The governor offered a reward of one thousand dollars.

Love's rangers had success in July. A detachment encountered a group of Mexicans at Panoche Pass between Monterey and Fresno on a trail used by horse thieves. A gunfight ensued, resulting in the death of two suspected bandits, including the apparent chief, and the capture of two others. Three members of the group escaped. One of the captives drowned on the way to jail; a mob lynched the survivor. The severed head of the Mexican leader subsequently was identified as that of Joaquín Murieta. Love received the promised reward in August, and the wave of banditry ended.[3]

The legend of El Patrio then began. Did California's rangers get the right man? Was there only one Joaquín? Where did he come from? Did he have good reasons for his depredations? Was he a hero? Did he escape? Did he ever really exist? Over the years, numerous authors have provided a multitude of conflicting answers to such questions, along with many others.

Californians showed much immediate interest in the celebrated bandit. Joaquín's head was preserved in a bottle of alcohol, auctioned, exhibited throughout the region, and put on display at Dr. Jordan's Pacific Museum of Anatomy in San Francisco. It eventually disappeared, perhaps as a consequence of the 1906 earthquake and fire. Claims of preservation still persist.[4]

A detailed biography appeared in 1854: *Joaquín Murieta* by Yellow Bird (John Rollin Ridge), a part-Cherokee who had come to California in 1850. Clearly following the pattern of journalistic efforts to capitalize on the deaths of noted fugitives, this volume established many questionable facts of the subject's supposed life. Ridge created a Robin Hood of the Sierras, driven to ferocious outlawry by brutal and greedy Anglos. The concept of a romantic California desperado was not, however, entirely original. A tale of the similar "Outlaw of the Sacramento" had appeared in 1847.[5]

According to the basic legend that was either followed or created by Yellow Bird, Murieta was born in Sonora, Mexico, and had come to California by 1850 (the year Ridge arrived). Generous and cordial, he suffered greatly from the prejudice and brutality of Anglo miners. They stole his property, ravished his lovely mistress, Rosita, falsely accused him of theft, whipped him without mercy, and lynched his half-brother. "It was then," Yellow Bird says "that the character of Joaquín changed, suddenly and irrevocably. Wanton cruelty and the tyranny of prejudice had reached their climax. . . . [H]e would live henceforth for revenge and . . . blood."[6]

Murieta became the leader of a gang of more than sixty rustlers who divided into several small bands for their raiding activities.[7] In many instances they were aided by large Mexican landowners who had lost much of their holdings to Anglo invaders. Joaquín ranged throughout central and southern California, "sometimes accompanied by three beautiful girls dressed as boys."[8] Says Yellow Bird:

Harry Love's rangers may have ended an outlaw's life in 1853, but they also initiated the legend of *El Patrio:* His career was short, for he died in his twenty-second year; but, in the few years which were allowed him, he displayed qualities of mind and heart which marked him as an extraordinary man. . . . He also leaves behind him the important lesson that there is nothing so dangerous in its consequences as *injustice to individuals.*[9]

John Rollin Ridge had many imitators and several blatant plagiarists in later generations. They added a multitude of twists and turns to the story:

An awful poet named Cincinnatus Heine Miller wrote a long and awful poem called "Joaquin" and . . . changed his name to Joaquin Miller. He asserted that Rosita was a direct descendant of Montezuma. Someone else, citing "new historical evidence" claimed that Murieta had been Santa Anna's bodyguard. Joaquin . . . had never died, but gone home to Sonora, in Mexico; no, to Chile; no, to Castile. His love's name was not Rosita, it was Carmela; no, it was Clarina. In 1932 there appeared a biography that laced all these lies into . . . *The Robin Hood of El Dorado.*[10]

Actually, Walter Noble Burns's 1932 book simply recapitulated many plausible bits of fact and fiction which had developed concerning Joaquín Murrieta (the passing years added a second *r* to the outlaw's name). It assumed the subject's existence, an issue of lingering controversy today. California's rangers killed someone, of course, but it could have been an innocent traveler or a minor criminal, simply to gain the reward.[11]

"Rumors persist today that he lived to die in his bed, in Sonora, at the age of ninety years. But nobody in California ever again saw Joaquin Murieta, *El Patrio,*"[12] Edwin L. Sabin writes. That could well be true because "most researchers today agree that the famous bandit Joaquin Murietta never existed," even while for others "there is no question that he did actually exist, but if he had a thousand men and a helicopter, he couldn't possibly have committed all the crimes and atrocities that have been blamed on '*El Patrio.*' "[13] There still remains a Carmelite priest's disturbing portrait of a bandit hiding in sanctuary from authorities.[14] It unquestionably created the enduring visual image of Joaquín.

No other outlaw in American history arouses such divergent opinion. To one he is "America's super bandit" and to another entirely fictional.[15] The absence of demonstrable facts simply contributes to the legacy of California's greatest bandit. According to Joseph Henry Jackson, "his cattle-thievery forgotten, his cold-blooded murders (if indeed he committed them) conveniently ignored, he remains the perfect gold-rush manifestation of man's age old compulsion to make a hero out of the best materials available, because The Hero is a creature men need."[16]

The Mexican American version brought him into very sharp contrast. As Murieta demonstrated, this outlaw could serve as bloodthirsty demon or justified savior simultaneously. A few years after the exploits of El Patrio in California, Texas suffered the depredations of another character subject to opposed opinion. Juan N. ("Cheno") Cortina raided Brownsville in 1859 and proclaimed the short-lived Republic of the Río Grande. When his little army dissolved, he retreated into Mexico. There, President Benito Juárez recruited him along with many local bandits, some of whom formed the famous—or infamous—*rurales.* Cortina later served in Mexico's government and its prisons prior to his death in 1892.[17]

By this time, America's image of Mexicans and their outlaws had been well established. Popular novels developed ugly themes, running back to the Texas Revolution and the war with Mexico. It mixed images of Catholics as venal idolators, associating *bandidos* with exceptional cruelty to animals and women. At the same time, ordinary Hispanic workers appeared as dirty, ignorant cowards.[18] Thus two common illusions developed. Contemptible Mexicans were either incredibly vicious desperadoes or pathetic and craven *campesinos*. Neither view, of course, was correct, although both have endured.

In fact, Mexican Americans had their full share of competent *pistoleros* on both sides of the law, as Elfego Baca, the Espinosa brothers, Francisco Griego, Juan Soto, Solomon Pico, Yginio Salazar, and many others illustrate. Like every other group in the West, they included some criminals and much larger numbers of brave and honest men. Legendary outlaws are almost entirely the product, not of reality, but of their fictional portrayals. The bandit is a desired creation molded to fit perceived demand. The Mexican desperado was most often portrayed as both pointlessly cruel and deceitful in comparison to the Anglo fugitive. An opposite and equally misinformed view held that "the difference between Hispanic and American outlaws was that the bandidos were impelled by revenge, whereas the Americanos went out for profit and gain."[19] Nearly all really had much in common, with personal greed routine and interest in social justice extremely rare.

There was, for example, little to admire in the career of Tiburcio Vásquez. Between 1856 and 1874 he rustled, robbed, and murdered along the California coast from San Francisco to Los Angeles. Vásquez, pursued by Sheriff Harry Morse, undoubtedly received a measure of support from local Mexican Americans, but it was probably because of fear more than sympathy.[20] The *bandido*, betrayed by a gang member angry over an affair between his wife and his leader, was ultimately captured in the Cahuenga Hills near Los Angeles and hanged in 1875.

An even more fearsome desperado appeared some two decades later in Arizona and Sonora. Augustin Chacón really was a character beyond redemption. Sentenced to hang, he escaped in 1896 to continue criminal activities which probably took the lives of scores of victims on both sides of the border. Captured by the Arizona Rangers, exercising questionable jurisdiction and with the help of fugitives Burt Alvord and Billy Stiles, Chacón was executed at Solomonville, northeast of Tucson, in 1902. He admitted killing fifty-two people (including thirty-seven Mexicans), although the actual total may have been substantially higher.[21]

Even Chacón became the subject of Robin Hood myth, described as a member of an oppressed minority who "robbed only the rich and gave to the poor peons."[22] These tales, even when entirely fictional, were the result of real prejudice and injustice. Amid widespread discrimination, any *bandido* managing to frustrate justice received a measure of respect from many Mexican Americans. When his escapades added real feats of daring and an original basis of sympathy, respect turned to widespread admiration. Such a pattern unquestionably occurred in the case of Texas's Gregorio Cortez. Born in Mexico in 1875, he came to the United States as a child. His life as a fugitive began in 1901 with an attempted arrest for horse theft and the shooting of his brother by police. During the next ten days, Cortez killed two sheriffs, walked 120 miles, rode another 400, and was pursued by hundreds of possemen, numerous local officers, and Texas Rangers. His capture near Laredo led to public outcry, numerous court appearances, and an eventual life sentence.[23]

In 1913, Cortez received a pardon, after which he spent a short time in Mexico, returned to Texas, and died at Anson in 1916. But Gregorio lived on in song. As the subject of several *corridos* (stylized ballads popular along the border), he became a famous hero (see the appendix). In legend he killed dozens and spent only a year in jail. Some variants have him released through intervention of Abraham Lincoln's daughter, or poisoned, or killed in the Mexican Revolution. It was even rumored that *El Corrido de Gregorio Cortez* had been banned throughout all of the United States.[24]

The injustice apparently imposed upon Cortez, who could properly use force to defend himself against illegal arrest under Texas law, served as an example of the discrimination suffered

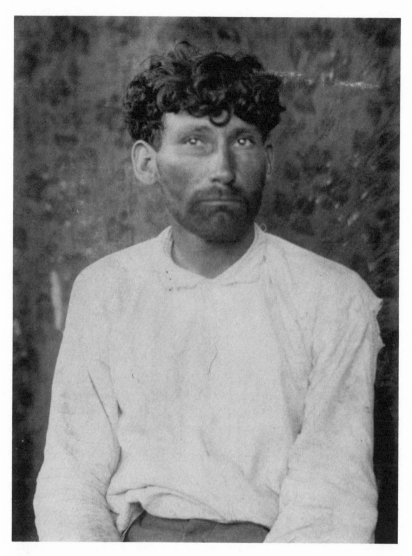

Gregorio Cortez ("You take me because I'm willing"), 1901. (Archives Division, Texas State Library, Austin)

by countless Mexican Americans. Ample evidence of prejudice exists, although victims included representatives of most minorities. Mexican suspects undoubtedly suffered abuse at the hands of citizens and peace officers alike. In Texas they were tortured, branded, earmarked, lost their tongues, and were lynched.[25] It is a brutal, ugly heritage, one which by no means ended by the turn of the century.

The tradition of law enforcement by "emergency forces" of untrained and partisan men recurs in the history of Mexican-American labor disputes. . . . Conflict between police and workers has been endemic in . . . agricultural strikes. These cases reflect the situation in small communities. Strikes represent a threat to the established social system; they vehemently call into question the rationales and the mutual myths by which local ethnic stratification is maintained . . . local law enforcement agencies know . . . "who put them there," and they know who are the "best" people and who are "trash."[26]

The degree to which such attitudes affect rates of crime, arrest, prosecution, and punishment can never be determined. Current statistics indicate that Hispanics are represented in United States prisons and jails in considerably higher proportions than may be found in the overall population.[27] Such rates of confinement are nearly always present among poor minorities throughout the world and history.

A century ago statistics were rarely kept according to ethnic classification, but prisons did report foreign-born inmate totals. These indicate that disproportionate numbers of Mexicans and Chinese were incarcerated. In 1870 and 1880, for example, the Far West had the country's highest percentages of foreign-born prison inmates. The proportions in Arizona, Nevada, California, and Washington were more than double the national average.[28]

Still, it would be incorrect to assume that overt discrimination was uniform throughout the West; there were vast differences in degree in time and place. In the infamous Sierra mining community of Bodie, home of the frontier's worst bad man, such bias never appeared:

Bodie's Mexicans . . . like the town's Chinese, saw no organized violence directed against them. Nor did any individual suffer from violence simply because he was a Mexican. The legal system seemed to treat Mexicans just like everyone else. . . . In the one instance in which a Mexican was implicated in the murder of a gringo, the Mexican was not even arrested, let alone prosecuted.[29]

In some areas Hispanic offenders made up significant elements in organized crime. These included Vicente Silva and his "gang of forty thieves," who operated in and around Las Vegas, New Mexico, in 1892 and 1893. Shortly after their destruction, journalist Manuel Cabeza de Baca, following a common literary path, reported the group's crimes and punishments in *Historia de Vicente Silva sus Cuarenta Bandidos*.

Even in contemporary and influential presentations frontier Hispanics sometimes received quite favorable treatment. William F. Cody clearly held them in high regard. Buffalo Bill's Wild West prominently featured *vaqueros* throughout its decades of operation. Antonio Esquival was the show's best rider and thus probably the finest horseman in North America. Cody selected him to ride in 1888's international ten-mile relay race. Esquival won; no one could match his consummate skill in transferring from one galloping mount to another; it had, after all, been honed by countless appearances in the Pony Express act. Buffalo Bill's Wild West also starred Vincent Orapeza for many years. He was the country's master roper and later taught the Ziegfeld Follies' great Will Rogers.[30]

Despite the existence of such distinguished caballeros, a distinctly negative image endured and was worsened by motion pictures during the first two decades of the twentieth century. Westerns needed a convenient villain; the movies found him in the Mexican *bandido*. They even popularized an ethnic slur, dating back to the war with Mexico, identifying the standardized character as a "greaser." Audiences learned to associate him automatically with cowardice, deceit, and greed. A title described the villain's character in *Hell's Hinges* (1916) as "mingling the oily craftiness of a Mexican with the deadly treachery of a rattler, no man's open enemy, and no man's friend." And then images darkened even more because of Mexican political events which threatened the United States.

There had been tension along the border for generations, but the outbreak of the twentieth century's first great social revolution brought new heights of concern. The departure of the dictator Porfirio Díaz marked the beginning of a long struggle toward greater freedom in Mexico. The United States expressed grave concern about the security of citizens and their properties in the nation to the south. There were other, deeper fears. The revolution might spread north; Mexico could become the staging ground for a foreign invasion. World War I in Europe and the Bolshevik Revolution made such fears seem both reasonable and immediate.

Evidence to excite concern abounded. Armed bands of rebels sometimes crossed the border. In 1915, discovery of a mysterious "Plan of San Diego" indicated an uprising of minority groups in Texas, New Mexico, Colorado, Arizona, and California. In 1917, the coded "Zimmermann note" apparently disclosed a German plot to enter into an alliance with Mexico, promising return of the territories lost to the United States seventy years earlier.[31]

Into this mixture of political violence and diplomatic intrigue rode an outlaw destined for unique places in the histories of two nations. Doroteo Arango was born in central Mexico in 1878, the son of peasants. He drifted into petty theft and soon advanced to cattle rustling. By the age of seventeen he was an outlaw, becoming chief of a gang formerly led by Ignacio Parra. Shortly after that, he adopted the name Francisco Villa. Mexicans often used the nickname Pancho in place of the formal Francisco, so Doroteo Arango disappeared from history, replaced by Pancho Villa.

For the next fifteen years he remained a prominent *bandido* with no apparent interest in politics. For reasons never made clear, but probably to justify previous crimes, this concern suddenly underwent a marked change. With the outbreak of revolution, Villa, who never abandoned his quest for personal gain, allied himself with the cause of reformist Francisco Madero. "Only with difficulty does the evidence demonstrate that Villa truly embraced the crusade for social justice,"[32] but he never abandoned Madero's cause and his influence on Mexico cannot be doubted. Villa began a new and strange career which involved mysterious dealings with the United States, near execution in Mexico City, and escape to El Paso. Early in 1913 he invaded Mexico with a total force of eight men. Less than two years later he entered the nation's capital as commanding general of the *División del Norte* to meet Emiliano Zapata and change the course of North American history.

John Reed, a reporter for *Metropolitan* magazine, accompanied the *villistas* during this period. To him the uneducated *bandolero* seemed "a mature man of extraordinary shrewdness, he encountered the twentieth century with the naive simplicity of a savage."[33] Pancho Villa was gifted and greedy, brave and ruthless, loyal and secretive: "He never seems to sleep. In the dead of night he will appear somewhere along the line of outposts to see if the sentries are on the job; and in the morning he returns from a totally different direction. No one, not even the most trusted officer of his staff, knows the least of his plans until he is ready for action."[34]

Throughout the early years of the Mexican Revolution, Villa received generally favorable reviews in the United States as a simple but colorful peasant fighting oppression. Attitudes began to change with the 1914 killing of William Benton, a wealthy American with vast land holdings in Mexico.[35] At the same time, questions arose concerning the peculiar relations between Pancho Villa and motion pictures. In his continuing quest for gain, he contracted with the Mutual Film Corporation to film the revolution and his own adventures. This received considerable and unfavorable comment in the United States; suspicion spread that people were literally dying for the motion pictures. A diplomat's wife in Mexico noted, "There are strange rumors of Villa's succumbing to temptation from the 'movie' men, and holding the attack {on Torreón} back till daybreak! It is terrible to contemplate the slaughter of unquestioning and innocent Pepes and Juans."[36]

Scenes—actual, arranged, and faked—appeared in newsreels

and a hurriedly made feature film.[37] Indeed, some fighting had occurred on the signal of cameramen between the sunlit hours of 9:00 A.M. and 4:00 P.M. Photographers also were furnished with executions, which they sometimes managed to delay if not prevent.[38] Pancho Villa's public-relations efforts preceded those of later world leaders by decades. *The Life of General Villa* (1914), released in several versions under different titles, told its own story:

Vivid fighting scenes photographed under fire by Mutual cameramen under special contract with General Villa are the features of this motion picture. . . . General Villa himself, with his generals, appear in many of the scenes. The famous Constitutionalist leader is seen to good advantage. . . . This tells the story of Villa's life. . . . At the last great and decisive battle he met face to face with the Federal officer who assisted in the abduction of his sister and helped to start him on the road to banditry and outlawry and kills him with his own hands on the battlefield. The Federals are defeated, and Villa is finally proclaimed president of the great Republic of Mexico, he who was once an outlaw with a price on his head.[39]

This fictional scenario affected perceptions of Villa's story considerably. It also marked the first time that public awareness of an actual outlaw was molded primarily by film rather than by the press. The pattern became routine in subsequent years. In fact, director Raoul Walsh played the part of Villa in many scenes, parts of which were actually shot in California after the crew returned from Mexico.[40] Even today some of the surviving footage occasionally appears as newsreels from the revolution. Illusion had already replaced reality.

Meanwhile, chaos continued in Mexico, and Pancho Villa remained a prominent figure on both sides of the border. He attracted attention testing motorcycles for his army.[41] He considered offers to tour with a Wild West show.[42] Once he halted an attack because of the World Series.[43] Slowly, however, the tide turned against the *bandido*. In 1915 the United States recognized the regime of Venustiano Carranza and moved troops into the

Pancho Villa, when illusion became reality (1915). (Archives Division, Texas State Library, Austin)

Southwest. Villa, who opposed the new developments, reacted in a remarkable way. On March 9, 1916, he attacked Columbus, New Mexico. It was the only armed incursion on United States territory between the War of 1812 and World War II, and it made Pancho Villa the most famous American outlaw of the era.

Today no one knows the reason for the invasion. The most obvious explanation is reprisal against the United States. Another theory has the raid staged for Pathé News cameramen who either missed the event or destroyed their film in fear of public reaction. One view holds that the United States government secretly requested the attack to permit subsequent troop exercises in preparation for involvement in World War I. A simpler analysis concludes that Villa needed money, arms, ammunition, and horses, which perhaps had been promised by American agents. Yet another variation rejects Pancho's participation, holding that Carranza forces made the attack in disguise to provoke United States military intervention in the Mexican Revolution.[44]

The attack on Columbus lasted two hours, appeared concentrated on stores and hotels, and took eighteen lives. There were no rapes or kidnappings and no evidence of Villa's own presence. The Thirteenth U.S. Cavalry, while poorly prepared and led, resisted with courage and initiative. Whatever the desired response, the United States's reaction proved swift and impressive.

Under General John J. ("Black Jack") Pershing, ten thousand U.S. troops crossed into Mexico in pursuit of the elusive Pancho Villa. Cavalry units penetrated 516 miles beyond the border, and elements of the Aero Squadron went farther. The Pershing Expedition lasted almost a year, provided the military with valuable experience in the field, and failed to accomplish its announced objective.[45] Villa remained at large.

He made a deal with emerging political powers in Mexico, accepting amnesty and a huge estate at Canutillo, in 1920. Villa remained there in peace for three years. He continued to pose a potential threat to the prevailing Mexican administration, however, and in 1923 a team of assassins, probably under Jesús Salas Barrazas, ambushed and killed him as he drove through the town of Parral. Legend has him dying of forty-seven wounds. Barrazas was briefly jailed, then released. Grave robbers stole Pancho's skull a few years later, perhaps for secret delivery to Yale University.

The raid on Columbus naturally caused a complete change in Villa's image: from controversial bandit to bestial savage. Dime novels, then costing a quarter, quickly crafted a frightful portrait. Grisly stories based partly on fact made Pancho a fiend. His men experimented to find out how many prisoners could be lined up and routinely murdered with a single rifle bullet (five). Villa would tie up husbands, have sham marriages performed, and then rape the wives.[46] He tortured women and young children for money. And he chopped people up alive with meat cleavers.[47] The new devil fit well into the mold of the movies' greaser.

For a time Mexicans invariably served as villains in motion pictures, prompting complaints and then demands. These efforts, combined with Hollywood's recognition of a significant and endangered Hispanic market, brought about a rapid transformation. Writes Allen L. Woll: "When official complaints to American film producers and the United States government appeared futile the Mexican government clamped an embargo on all films which presented Latins in a derogatory manner. Thus films like *Tony and the Greaser* (1911) and *The Greaser's Gauntlet* (1908) . . . were swiftly eliminated from production schedules."[48] Moreover, Hollywood displayed its special ability to turn a liability into an asset and a villain into a hero. In 1920 it transformed one variety of *bandido* into a romantic opponent of tyranny. He came galloping out of the night when the moon was bright, a horseman with a flashing sword and a devilish grin responding to desperate need. According to the opening title of his first film:

Oppression—by its very nature—creates the power that crushes it. A champion arises—a champion of the oppressed—whether it be a Cromwell or someone unrecorded, he will be there. He is born.

In California, nearly a hundred years ago, with its warmth, its romance, its peaceful beauties, this dread disease, oppression, had crept in.

Then—out of the mystery of the unknown—appeared a masked rider who rode up and down the great highway—punishing and protecting and leaving upon the vicious oppressor—THE MARK OF ZORRO.[49]

This quite remarkable figure was born in Denver in 1883, the son of a prominent attorney and a beautiful southern belle. Distinguished at an early age by a fine memory and unique athletic gifts, he drifted into acting, achieving considerable comedic success in New York and then in motion pictures. But when Douglas Fairbanks became Zorro, something very special happened.

The character first appeared in "The Curse of Capistrano," a short story by Johnston McCulley in the August 9, 1919, issue of *All Story Weekly*. This served as the basis for the film *The Mark of Zorro* (1920), in which Fairbanks created the prototype of the movies' charming superswashbuckler. The often retold story concerns the dissipated Don Diego, returning from Spain to find California under a tyrannical governor. The apparently idle playboy secretly becomes the masked avenger Zorro, Spanish for "fox" or "wily pretender." In retrospect, the tale may be seen as a skillful blend of the Murieta legend and Baroness Emnuska Orczy's popular novel *The Scarlet Pimpernel* of 1905.

Fairbanks played the parts of Don Diego and Zorro brilliantly. His carefully choreographed athletic stunts have never been surpassed, and these contrasted perfectly with comedic interludes. Fairbanks repeated the basic role many times in a dazzling succession of pioneering outlaw films. And while the star remained a quintessential American hero, he was also *Robin Hood* (1922), *The Thief of Bagdad* (1924), *The Black Pirate* (1926), and even *Don Q, Son of Zorro* (1925). Fairbanks's career faded with the advent of sound, but his impact on Hollywood was unquestionable.[50]

Zorro, of course, went on and on, in motion pictures, serials, and on television. He found followers throughout the world, appearing in Spanish, French, and Italian as well as American films. A historical foundation for him appeared,[51] and a perverse reality occurred: Zorro was the code name for illegal FBI efforts to defame and destroy Martin Luther King, Jr., in the 1960s.[52]

Another important Mexican good badman appeared *In Old Arizona* (1929). Warner Baxter played the Cisco Kid, based on a rather disreputable character in short stories by O. Henry (William Sidney Porter). *In Old Arizona* was the earliest western to incorporate sound successfully and also the first to include a popular song, "My Tonia." Warner Baxter won an Academy Award as best actor of the year and played similar roles on several later occasions. He subsequently appeared as Joaquín Murieta in *The Robin Hood of El Dorado* (1936), a rather dark and bitter film based on Walter Noble Burns's 1932 book.

A succession of competent Hispanic actors took over as the Cisco Kid, who, with his humorous companion, Pancho, rode on for decades. Gilbert Roland, Cesar Romero, and Duncan Renaldo made the *bandido* into a charming rogue, fighting truly bad men throughout the Southwest. The numerous Cisco Kid films made their romantic hero a quite distinctive and positive western figure. Unlike cowboy stars of the era, Cisco had clear interest in the ladies and did much to dispel previous images of Mexicans as brigands and cowards on the frontier.

Pancho Villa was resurrected. Edgcumb Pinchon's 1933 book *Viva Villa!* recognized the contradictory reputations the *bandido* enjoyed: the bestial bad man north of the border and the patriotic hero to the south. "Between these myths of the American reporter and the Mexican ballad-singer lurks . . . the man himself."[53] Efforts to develop these images came to fruition with the motion picture *Viva Villa!* in 1934. Filmed with considerable difficulty in Mexico and with a perceptive screenplay by Ben Hecht, it created a singularly enduring impression of Pancho Villa. Portrayed by Wallace Berry, he was a childlike, sadistic simpleton with good intentions clouded by greed. In the final scene, Villa lies dying from the assassins' bullets and is comforted by an American reporter. The great *bandido,* foreseeing the obituary soon to be written, asks:

"What were my last words?"
" 'Good by, my Mexico,' " said Pancho Villa, 'Forgive me for my crimes . . . I loved you too much.' "
"Forgive me? What I done wrong?"[54]

Pancho, of course, has appeared in numerous other films, but never with comparable force and depth. He enjoyed a return to considerable respectability in the United States. To a degree, and for no particular reason, the *bandido* benefited from a growing Hispanic movement. New Mexico created Pancho Villa State Park at Columbus ahead of a California effort to do the same for Joaquín Murieta and provided unique recognition for a foreign invader. In 1983, matters took another odd twist. Mexico offered the United States a gigantic statue of Pancho mounted on a horse. After considerable controversy, it found a home in Tucson, Arizona.[55]

Despite the improving depiction of *bandidos,* the greaser image endured. The filthy, vicious outlaws seeking *The Treasure of the Sierra Madre* (1948), who killed for shoes, and those fought by *The Magnificent Seven* (1960), who terrorized the poorest of *peones,* left indelible impressions. "Spaghetti westerns" of the 1960s kept the treacherous greaser in grim focus. Such portrayals bore striking similarities to those of previous generations. The Mexican desperado was consistently shown as extraordinarily violent, the subject of scorn, and unable to cope with a superior North American hero.[56]

This followed old techniques of making a bad man look good by contrasting him with someone worse. It was combined, of course, with obvious chauvinism. Such is the practice of legend rather than fact. Fanciful and colorful disguises apply to the myths of all peoples. Real criminals seldom manifest the slightest concern with the oppressed and in fact more often align themselves with tyrants. Minorities, and majorities, typically suffer as victims rather than serve as beneficiaries of outlaw exploits. Nevertheless, the romantic fugitive still offers an almost universal appeal to people sharing the widespread and frequently soundly based resentment of authority. El Patrio is a creature of dreams, not facts.

Mexican Americans maintain such common but contradictory views, occasionally in regard to a single figure. Such was true of Fred Gómez Carrasco, a notorious and cunning drug dealer of the Texas border in the 1970s. He had his own ballad, was rumored to have killed fifty men, and still held remarkable appeal for women. Finally captured and convicted, Carrasco died in a bloody prison break at Huntsville in 1974.

There is, nevertheless, little that is truly unique about the *bandido* of past or present. Every culture has some kind of desperado-hero, and they share common characteristics. The United States has no monopoly on the distinguished outlaw. Virtually every national heritage boasts of a bandit. In China he is the seventeenth-century pirate Koxinga (Kuo Hsing-yeh). In Japan he is Minamoto Yoshimoto, who kidnapped a twelfth-century emperor. In Canada he is the nineteenth-century leader of the Metís, Louis Riel. In Germany he is the eighteenth-century robber Schinderhannes (Johannes Pueckler). In central Asia he is the seventeenth-century Islamic bandit Kuroghli.

The parade continues. The twentieth century offers an abundance of notable outlaws, including Mao Tse-tung. South Africa has Nelson Mandela, North Africa has Raisouli, Ukraine has Nikolas Shuhaj, India has Phoolan Devi, Sicily has Salvatore Giuliano, Cyprus has George Grivas, Brazil has Lampião (Virgulino Ferreira da Silva), and England has Percy Toplis. Their significantly parallel stories reveal the consequences of interwoven concepts of social banditry. Their potentially legendary status, usually with scant basis in fact, reflects fundamental human emotions which defy international boundaries. As Paul F. Angiolillo has written:

The appearance of the outlaw seems to occur when living conditions among the larger mass of society are such that frustration, anger, fear, insecurity, poverty, discrimination, protest, and lack of hope are widespread among the people. It is then . . . that the mythologizing process begins. . . . Perhaps all but the extremely privileged in wealth and power in any civilized society yearn subconsciously for freedom from the constraints of civilization. . . . Closely allied to this unconscious thirst for unbridled personal freedom is a natural human admiration for heroic deeds . . . common to all men is the strong desire for fair treatment and justice.[57]

The simplest expression of this explanation for the apparently universal appreciation of the outlaw was perhaps that of Eric Hobsbawm: "Men can live without justice, and generally must, but they cannot live without hope."[58] Such fundamental desires have no clear connection with nationality, race, or ethnic classification. They permit the easy transition of myth from one country to another. Such flexibility resulted in the addition of the *bandido* to the cast of imagined desperadoes from the United States. But the joinder of nationalities is clearer in regard to those of similar ancestry and cultural heritage.

Within the collection of the great National Museum of Ireland in Dublin may be found a most peculiar flag. At first glance it may appear to be that of the United States in some sort of color negative. Rather than red, white, and blue, it is green, white, and orange. Closer inspection reveals that the numbers of stars and stripes do not resemble those of any American flag. This Irish emblem was an outlaw banner, the planned pennant of the Fenian Brotherhood. Based on the American flag, its stars represented counties and its stripes stood for ancient provinces. The colors had their own heritage and may be seen today in the banner of the Republic of Ireland.[59] The Fenians kept alive the dream of Irish independence for more than half a century, from the times of Daniel O'Connell to those of Charles Stewart Parnell.[60] They existed because of support from the United States, which was receiving as many as one hundred thousand emigrants a year from Ireland. Wherever they settled, including the most raucous of western mining towns, Irish freedom remained an issue of great concern.[61] American contributions of money and men were essential for survival of the Fenian Brotherhood.

While their one effort at rebellion (in 1867) proved a dismal failure, American involvement could not be denied. The "Acting Chief Executive of the Irish Republic" was Thomas J. Kelly, an American and one of many Union army veterans taking part in the aborted rising. Betrayal ended the effort. Kelly, awaiting trial in Manchester, England, was freed in a daring rescue by Fenian agents. Three men, still known in Ireland as "the Manchester Martyrs," were executed as participants in the escape. Kelly got away.

The Irish connection with American outlawry existed in other forms, some of which have seen strange twists. For example, the somber rebel song "The Rising of the Moon" became the sprightly jig "The Wearing of the Green" in the United States. A rising, of course, meant rebellion rather than earthly rotation; even in some American versions, happily sung on Saint Patrick's Day, may be found a haunting refrain: "They're hanging men and women for the wearing of the green." The forbidden green indicated sympathy for Catholic freedom as opposed to the Protestant orange.

Outlaw myth reveals many things while hiding many others. One bit of Irish whimsy, for example, "says that Ned Kelly's mother was a sister of Buffalo Bill's father."[62] This blarney neatly ties the American Wild West to Australia's renowned bushranger. It is not true, in a literal sense, but it tells something all the same. William F. Cody's ancestors left Ireland long before Kelly's. Buffalo Bill's father, Isaac Cody, actually came to the United States from Canada. Ned Kelly's mother was the daughter of an Irish born free settler to Australia; her maiden name was Quinn.

Ireland provided many of the often reluctant early settlers of Australia; it also furnished a multitude of famous figures on America's frontier. The Irish are proud of them all, sometimes naming pubs in their honor. Buffalo Bill would probably have featured Ned Kelly in his Wild West shows; unfortunately, the latter had been hanged before Cody began his tours.

Attitudes were very different a few decades earlier. The perception spread that large numbers of convicts transported to Australia managed to escape and make their nefarious ways to America. In 1834, prisoners on Norfolk Island did indeed revolt in a doomed scheme to seize a ship and sail across the Pacific.[63] The later gold rush to the Sierra Nevada served as a presumed attraction to heinous fugitives from British penal colonies. In California by 1851, *Australian* was virtually synonymous with *criminal*.[64] The San Francisco Vigilance Committee of that year made them a focus of attention, banishing many suspects.

An earlier Australian bushranger provides a different insight into the strange relations of international outlaw myth. One John Donohoe was convicted in Dublin and sentenced to transportation for life in 1823. Some two years later he bolted from captivity in Australia to become an outlaw. Until he was killed near Sydney by dragoons (hence the term *goons*) in 1830, he led a small band of marauders. The bandit then became quite famous through souvenirs (including smoking pipes modeled on his head, complete with bullet holes), the 1835 play *The Tragedy of Donohoe* by Charles Harpur, and most particularly a song. Somewhere along the fatal shore a popular ballad was created, eulogizing one Jack Doolan as "The Wild Colonial Boy."[65] It crossed the sea to the United States and circled half the world to Ireland. Names and places changed many times. To balladeers in Irish pubs he became Jack Duggan; to cowboys in the American West he was Jack Donahoo. Variants in other lands called him Donovan, Dowling, Dolan, Davis, or Dollard.

However named, the Wild Colonial Boy remained an idealized symbol of resistance, fleeing from injustice, to roam throughout the frontier. In that mythic wonderland, with outlaws such as Jesse James, Sam Bass, Black Bart, and the Sundance Kid, he found an imagined refuge with fugitives of diverse ancestry. The *bandidos,* with their own *corridos,* surely appeared. In reality, the brigands might have fought and killed one another. But it seems more likely that they joined with legendary desperadoes, pirates, and highwaymen of many nations in the chorus of "The Wild Colonial Boy." With sufficient libation, it could serve as their anthem:

> O come along, me hearties,
>   and we'll roam the mountains high
> Together we will plunder
>   together we will die.
> We'll wander over valleys
>   and we'll gallop over plains
> And we'll scorn to live in slavery
>   bound down by iron chains.

The story of one Wild Colonial Boy may illustrate yet another aspect of the unique Irish-Australian-American outlaw linkage.

Thomas Francis Meagher was born in County Waterford in 1823. He received a death sentence for involvement with the Young Irelanders and their doomed rising of 1848. The penalty was commuted to transportation, for life; four years later, Meagher bolted from captivity in Tasmania.[66] He soon made his way to the United States, where he became a lawyer and newspaper editor. When the Civil War began, the charismatic Meagher raised the Union army's famous Irish Brigade in New York, Pennsylvania, and Massachusetts and served as its commanding general during bloody battles from Bull Run to Chancellorsville. He subsequently was appointed governor of Montana Territory.

Democrat Meagher then became a controversial proponent of statehood. In 1867, preparing for a campaign against the Blackfeet, he fell (perhaps while intoxicated) from a Missouri River steamboat and drowned.[67] The Irish know him as Meagher of the Sword, a transported rebel, escaped convict, and opponent of slavery who died in the winning of the American West. He lived an outlaw's dream and so participated in the mythical transformation of wilderness into a land of freedom.

CHAPTER 13

The Mobster

The best hiding place in the world for a man with money
is some big city.

——FRANK JAMES

BETWEEN World Wars I and II the image of the American outlaw changed considerably. As writers familiar with the frontier
passed away, less realistic portrayals became dominant and the
setting for outlawry shifted from cattle ranges to city streets. The
West, while still a land of hope, increasingly represented lawlessness; placed in contrast with contemporary criminals, its famous fugitives gained new status. Such modifications of image
involved a host of contributors.

Walter Prescott Webb, acknowledging that reputation outran
fact, still found ample disorder on the plains: "The West was a
lawless place. It was turbulent in the early days because there was
no law. It was lawless in the later period because the laws were
unsuited to the needs and conditions. Men could not abide by
them and survive."[1] As a substitute for ordinary agencies of justice, vigilantes supposedly enforced the Code of the West, which
insisted on fair play and personal honor.

Such concepts emerged as hallmarks of legend, so the image of
the western outlaw crystallized as an appealing yet dangerous
bandit matched only by the bravest of peace officers. This found
expression in the myth of the fast draw, exemplified by lawman
Bill Tilghman's remarkable revelation to Theodore Roosevelt
that a man in the right has an advantage of one-sixteenth of a second over evildoers![2] The appearance of bandits also was accorded
incorrect retrospective observation: "Virtually all the noted out-

laws . . . had blue eyes. The eyes of most of them were of a steel-blue tint."[3]

Relentless popular depictions of peace through violence demanded a setting seething with crime. Western historians created a firm foundation:

> Little effort was made . . . to banish lawlessness. Their saloons and gambling halls were generally filled with disreputable characters of all classes. . . . [I]t was difficult to find men who would assume the burdens of office of sheriff or deputy, since they had to be men of iron nerve, quick on the draw, and fearless in tight places.[4]

Such an environment found clear expression on the screen through hundreds of motion pictures displaying heroics of the West. A prominent example of the era was *Billy the Kid* (1930). Apparent realism mixed with typical romanticism in a long and primitive sound film very loosely based on Walter Noble Burns's 1926 book *The Saga of Billy the Kid*. All-American football player Johnny Mack Brown appeared as the famous bandit, purposely missed and allowed to escape by an amiable Pat Garrett, portrayed by Wallace Beery.[5] An experimental Realife seventy-millimeter film format restricted the market for *Billy the Kid* and led major studios to approach western outlaws with trepidation for nearly a decade. They were, after all, discovering even more fascinating rivals.

For a time, motion pictures devoted particular attention to odious white frontier outlaws who either led hostile Indians (usually portrayed as barbaric simpletons) or supplied them with liquor and guns. A collection of notably wicked renegades helped the savages attack the pioneers in such well-directed films as *America* (1924), *Drums Along the Mohawk* (1939), *Allegheny Uprising* (1939), and *North West Mounted Police* (1940).

The frontier endured, of course, as a great favorite of popular fiction. Academicians delved, with varying success, into studied explanations of America's "lawless heritage."[6] In 1927 a pioneering criminologist, Frederic M. Thrasher, identified the criminal organization flourishing in the wilderness:

That the conception of the gang as a symptom of an economic, moral, and cultural frontier is not merely fanciful and figurative is indicated by the operation of similar groups on other than urban frontiers. The advance of civilization into a wild country is heralded by marauding bands which result both from relaxed social controls and attempts to escape authority. The period before and following the Civil War has been called the "era of banditry," so numerous and so desperate were the outlaw gangs.[7]

Ample support for such views came from aging participants. Lawman Frank Canton believed that the "loose element in New York, Chicago, and other cities" took the railroads west to become rustlers.[8] A former cowboy recalled his early days in West Texas:

Around the campfires I heard of the brave deeds of John Wesley Hardin, King Fisher, Ben Thompson, and other great gun-fighters who were at that time apparently enjoying their lives. Well-dressed and equipped strangers who rode into our camps were shown all sorts of favors if they needed them. A man on a good horse, wearing a Mexican sash about his waist and packing a pair of ivory-handled six-shooters would have no trouble getting something to eat in anybody's cow camp. He was welcomed without question—and if Rangers were known to be near, he would soon be warned of the fact.[9]

Reformed outlaw Al Jennings agreed: "Nearly every range on the prairies sheltered and winked at outlaw gangs."[10]

When fugitives committed local crimes, however, attitudes changed abruptly. Likely victims then willingly joined in the hunt. James H. Cook remembered that captured outlaws could never explain the reasons for their crimes; he looked upon them with a measure of pity, prudently adding that "the enmity of such characters was a most dangerous thing."[11]

Nevertheless, realistic observations were swept away in the tide of distorted remembrance. Western outlaws came to be viewed through a glowing haze associated with dreams of a vanished frontier rather than reality. They were placed in sharp contrast with contemporary criminals. Frontier brigands, their exploits exalted by a long succession of magazines, plays, books, and films, were seen as bold and resourceful rather than cunning and murderous:

When we compare the red-blooded desperadoes, who did things in an open way like Sam Bass and Jesse James, with the thugs and hijackers of the present day, we can hardly help admiring the former. They took a chance, and were brave; the present day bandits don't purposely take a chance, and they are cowardly, killing innocent people.[12]

Former lawmen, supported by a host of popular writers, looked back on frontier killers as pleasant, likable characters attracted to crime because of difficult economic conditions.[13] A retired federal officer from Oklahoma expressed scant respect for criminals of the later day:

They're cheapskates. . . . Just tin-horn robbers who sneak through dark alleys for a chance stick-up that may net only a dollar or two. . . . [I]n the early nineties when bad men were really bad . . . no outlaw thought he'd done a good day's work unless he had relieved a bank or a train of $50,000 or so. Back in those days . . . outlaws had a code of honor all their own, and did things in a big way scorning petty thievery.[14]

Not everyone recalled frontier brigands in the same light, however. The imaginative Bill Tilghman decried "the 'sob-stuff' . . . written about the old bandits and the false romance . . . woven into stories of their careers."[15]

A well-known fugitive dispelled some of the gathering cloud of confused memory in 1931. Emmett Dalton, with the assistance of Jack Jungmeyer, provided considerable distortion of his own, but he also offered insight into American outlaw myth:

One thing puzzled me profoundly . . . in prison: the curiously inconsistent attitude of the American public toward its malefactors. In his dealing with the reprobate, the American truly does not let the left hand know what the right is doing. With the one hand the recreant is subtly incited, with the other he is ruthlessly crushed. With one breath he is all but venerated, with another cried to his death. It is as if some bilingual, imbecilic monster were alternately blowing him hot and cold.

To-day as never before the scapegrace is the demi-hero of countless fictions, in book, on stage and screen; a picaresque fellow of song and story at whose clever outwitting of the law great audiences laugh and thrill sympathetically. The so called good bad man. The cult of the rogue!

But let him not be jailed, for then the iridescent bubble is pricked. Once call him convict, and the rogue becomes merely a shabby, despicable creature. Strange anomaly!

Why has the free-running reprobate always been so extolled? Is it because he symbolizes the undying anarchy in the heart of almost every man? Because he has the rude courage of his desires? Represent the rogue as a man fighting against odds—even against the police—and we tacitly encourage him. Give him the slightest pretext of a "cause," and we follow in his train—in spirit, at least. He becomes our fighting vicar against aristocracy, against power, against law, against the upstart, the pretender, the smugly virtuous, and the pompously successful person or corporation whom we envy. He becomes a hero of democracy.

The kid-glove bandit . . . is the current fashion in outlaws. He is almost enshrined in our national gallery of hero types. With scarce secret complaisance we thrill at his maraudings—until he sticks a gun under our own nose. Then he becomes a dastardly villain.

It is enough to make the old-time outlaw, rough and tough and sailing under no false colors, turn over in his unhallowed grave. Even Robin Hood of Sherwood Forest wouldn't recognize himself in the idolatrous cloak posterity has flung across his phantom shoulders.

And so it is with the fictions of the old West—the vanished West of grim, glamorous figures, many of them pseudo-heroes, sung by many a facile Tom, Dick, and Harry in addition to a few authentic chroniclers. How much of romantic nonsense woven in with the fact![16]

Dalton knew frontier killers as quiet and deliberate, with reputations based upon hearsay and embellishment. He recognized the effect of a death through treachery on the development of the outlaw-martyr myth. Furthermore, Emmett Dalton accepted and adhered to the unwritten code of silence so important to criminals of all ages. It cost him a sentence of life imprisonment:

This, then, is the folk way with lawbreakers. Inciting, condoning, and condemning with incalculable whim; the secret sanction, the open flattery, and the insensate recoil. Even the general repugnance against treachery knows no code or consistency. At one moment half the populace may applaud a spectacular crook, in the next moment they are ready to betray him for a dollar. Explain that as you like.

In my time the lawless frontier was along the edge of the wilderness. To-day the crime frontier is in the shadow of the skyscraper.

The old model outlaw was already becoming pass[é] at the time I went to the penitentiary at Lansing [Kansas], in March, 1893. I was one of the last of this old-fashioned gentry of the road. . . . As the years dragged on a new kind of freebooter began to drift into prison. More and more of him began to hail from the larger cities. Not so frequently were his legs bowed from much riding. His lingo smacked less of the range. His technique was different. He took his loot from new sources. His armament changed. There was more of the prowler about him. He was beginning to be hunted by finger prints . . . rather than by . . . his horse's imprints in the soil.

By the time of my release from prison in 1907 he had become a decidedly new variant. One of the inducements to crime in the West was the presumed ease of escape into untrammeled lands. This supposed easy refuge was a fallacy, for in a sparsely settled land every stranger was a bid for curiosity. The color of his horse was noted, the cut of his beard was marked, the directions he asked were remembered. A thousand-mile ride for the Western outlaw might harbor more pitfalls than a city block for the modern gangster.

To-day the country-bred outlaw is practically extinct. Crowded places, city canyons, night clubs, and public amusement places are his cradle and his habitat. Naturally he clings to his environment. He takes his spoil close to where he spends it. And amid the millions of jostling but incurious strangers in a Chicago, New York, or Detroit he is as safe or safer than was the plains outlaw in his remote brush camp.[17]

These new criminals did not, however, prove to be skulking, characterless villains in all instances. Some, such as Florida's "Phantom of the Everglades," John Ashley, demonstrated remarkable potential for public attention. The favorite western outlaw faced a very serious contender: "Waiting in the wings, ready to take over, was a new crop of bandits of a deadlier breed, mad dogs who killed without compunction. Armed with automatics, submachine guns and bombs, using speeding automobiles to make their getaways."[18]

Two words crept into popular usage between World Wars I and II to describe these organized brigands. *Racketeer* indicated a member of an urban gang practicing extortion and intimidation. It may well have first, and suitably, appeared in Chicago. The term probably derived from a noisy French dance and associated illicit activities. *Mobster* came from the old English word *mobb,* which in the seventeenth century referred to disorderly, moving rabble. As a verb, it meant "to attack in a group." By the nineteenth century, *mobsman* indicated a member of a riotous crowd. *Mobster* developed in the American Midwest and signified a gangster or member of any violent criminal group. The United States provided numerous examples in both fact and in fiction.

America's cities replaced the frontier as the perceived breeding ground of crime, with an abundance of grisly participants. Chicago's "Shotgun Man," thought to be an assassin for the Black Hand, operated for years but could never be identified. New York's dreadful Albert Fish fared less well. Resulting in hundreds of instances of child molestation, kidnapping, murder, and cannibalism, his career lasted two decades. Police finally managed to trace a letter Fish sent to the mother of one of his young victims. The nation's worst serial killer died in the electric chair in 1936.

But the type of crime attracting the most publicity soon after World War I brought back clear echoes of the frontier. A remarkable upsurge in train robbery swept the country. An increase in the value of registered mail (including payrolls, currency, gold, silver, and unregistered bonds) created temptations that mobsters could not resist.[19] Hundreds of marines were assigned as guards, and the federal government authorized construction of 3,000 bullet-proof railway express cars.[20]

The wave of robbery lasted into the Great Depression, but the foremost instance occurred on June 12, 1924, at Roundout, Illinois. A disciplined gang stopped an express train with a flashing red light, overcame guards with tear gas, seized forty-two sacks of registered mail, quickly fled in four cars, and quite possibly escaped on an airplane.[21] Numerous arrests followed, including that of noted racketeer Charles ("Deanie") O'Banion. Eventually a postal inspector named William J. Fahy went to prison in connection with the case, but most of the robbers and their loot, more than two million dollars, disappeared.

Various names were connected with America's great train robbery. Terrible Tommy O'Connor seemed a plausible candidate,[22] for during the 1920s he was the nation's foremost outlaw. The notable Chicago gunman made a daring escape from the Criminal Courts Building in 1921 only four days before his scheduled execution for murder. Chicago kept his scaffold waiting while rumors of Tommy's continuing exploits circulated for decades. Frustrating all efforts to bring him to justice, he vanished.

Tommy O'Connor went on, however, to serve as a model for the emerging movie mobster. His story became the basis for *Underworld* (1927), the most important silent film dealing with urban gangsters. Six years later, Spencer Tracy played convict Tommy Connors in *20,000 Years in Sing Sing* (1933), in which the hero honors his pledge to return to prison and execution. The real Terrible Tommy probably found humor in that version.

But far more fascinating movie gangsters had appeared. Three of them had a major influence on perceptions of American outlaws. Enrico Bandello, Tom Powers, and Tony Camonte may not seem familiar, but when Edward G. Robinson, James Cagney, and Paul Muni played them as *Little Caesar* (1930), *The Public Enemy* (1931), and *Scarface* (1932), something quite significant happened: these films quickly established a new movie genre.

The distinguished gangster movie emerged with the advent of sound and the end of Prohibition. It had precedents in earlier motion pictures and the literary mobsters and private detectives of the 1920s. Linkages were remarkably close. For example, Ernest Hemingway's short story "The Killers" was published in 1927; its staccato, affective dialogue promptly made an appearance in the silent film *Walking Back* (1928), and so abrupt, rhythmic conversations became hallmarks of countless gangster movies.

With *Little Caesar,* Edward G. Robinson became a star at the age of thirty-seven. His swarthy Rico Bandello was the first antihero of note in American films. Retribution finally wins, of course, and Bandello glimpses his fate dying with the famous line, "Mother of God, is this the end of Rico?" In response to complaints, the sound track on many prints was edited to a more acceptable, "Mother of mercy, is this the end of Rico?" Whatever, it did not mean an end to Edward G. Robinson. He replayed his gangster role on many occasions, even as a Chinese-American assassin in *The Hatchet Man* (1932), and with increasing elements of deliberate humor.

James Cagney made an even bigger impression as Tom Powers, *The Public Enemy.* Selected in 1967 by Bosley Crowther as one of the world's fifty greatest films, it established the pattern of change in character used so frequently in gangster movies. In the early portion Cagney's "tough little guy . . . is an image of fierce determination and tightly controlled energy . . . impertinence, impatience, and brusque command"; by the end "he is a vicious little monster, still fascinating to watch, but as erratic, unreliable and dangerous as a fer-de-lance."[23]

Cagney became the country's favorite gangster. As Lincoln Kirstein perceived, "no one expresses more clearly in terms of pictorial action the delights of violence, the overtones of a semiconscious sadism, the tendency toward destruction, toward anarchy, which is the base of American sex appeal."[24] He would do so numerous times, culminating with *White Heat* (1949).

Paul Muni brought dark insight into *Scarface,* the nickname of Chicago's already renowned Al Capone. The film, originally intended as a tragicomedy, spawned much controversy before its release, so it concluded with a modified ending, deletion of several scenes, and addition of the subtitle *Shame of the Nation.* Muni appeared the same year in *I Am a Fugitive from a Chain Gang* (1932). Openly based upon the experiences of Robert E. Burns, trapped in the inhuman southern penal systems of the day, the movie proved a powerful indictment and contributed to eventual reforms. Muni then drifted away from gangster roles, concentrating on major biographical features and stage appearances. But his whispered final line in *I Am a Fugitive* remained to haunt the nation. When asked how he can live as an escaped convict, he replies from the shadows, "I steal."

The ties between illusion and reality in these early gangster films were very close. Al Capone sent emissaries to the set of *Scarface* to ensure that his reputation would not be sullied; they expressed satisfaction.[25] The same movie incorporated a real event of 1931, New York's "Siege of West 90th Street." Many motion pictures capitalized on well-publicized events. The murder of Chicago reporter Alfred Lingle in 1930 promptly led to *The Finger Points* (1931). *G-Men* (1935) included scenes based on the Kansas City Massacre of 1933 and the 1934 battle at Wisconsin's Little Bohemia Lodge. Several movies depicted Chicago's infamous Saint Valentine's Day Massacre of 1929. In fact, the motion-picture industry openly attracted audiences by blurring the distinction between shadow and substance. *Doorway to Hell* (1930) featured the character Legs Ricano in an obvious parallel to the real racketeer, Jack ("Legs") Diamond. The studio solemnly announced: "Every event shown in this film is based on an actual occurrence. All characters are portraits of actual persons, living or dead."[26]

None of the fictional portrayals approached fact, of course. Movie outlaws routinely appeared as more mature, violent, and handsome than their counterparts in life. But this was nothing new. Journalists and novelists for generations had avoided portraying youthful fugitives in their typically short, lonely, miserable careers. Still, the movie mobster brought the issue of crime causation into particularly sharp focus.

It was not, of course, a new question. Retrospective musings on the frontier had already attributed violence to portrayals of colorful gunfighters and desperadoes.[27] However, contemporary crime movies, consciously linked to reality, caused alarm. In 1933 appeared two books which related modern violence and a deterioration of public morals to the film industry. Herbert Blummer's *Movies and Conduct* and H. M. Forman's *Our Movie Made Children* insisted that America's young people were emulating images on the screen.

Hollywood responded to the crusade for decency by strengthening the Motion Picture Producers and Directors Association's code of self-regulation. The new rules applied primarily to sex and did not impinge to any marked degree on gangster films. Prostitution and drug abuse were not to be shown, nor was blood in killings, and of course sin of all kinds had to receive ultimate punishment.

Obviously, considerable latitude still existed and the gangster quickly evolved into America's tragic hero. Analysis of this film genre began and ended with an essay written for the February 1948 issue of *Partisan Review* by Robert Warshow. He recognized the gangster as a man of the city and the imagination who is, at the same time, "what we want to be and what we are afraid we may become."[28] The mythic mobster engages in rational, criminal activities marked by steady advancement and a sudden fall. He gives us two vicariously sadistic opportunities: that delivered and that received. And because routines of vice are seldom portrayed, force represents the means of the gangster's success. Action proceeds relentlessly to the criminal's fearsome end: "There is really only one possibility—failure. The final meaning of the city is anonymity and death."[29] The aggressive gangster dies because he strives to succeed, not because of his crimes. His film image embodies our dilemma and resolves it through another's violence; his punishment is our temporary redemption: "Failure is a kind of death and success is evil and dangerous, is— ultimately—impossible. . . . We are safe; for the moment, we can acquiesce in our failure, we can choose to fail."[30]

Perceptive critics added elements to this analysis, comparing the mobster movie to an ironic Greek tragedy: "Living out his life in public with a newspaper chorus commenting on his actions, the gangster also arrogates to himself a freedom of action possessed by no other citizen. . . . [T]he gangster's spontaneous, lawless acts bring about his ultimate capture and destruction."[31]

Critics also contrasted two American film genres: the gangster and the western. Movie outlaws appeared to represent either the old frontier or the contemporary city with some similar traits: "The bootlegger seemed heir to the American spirit."[32] In different eras, each illustrated national characteristics: ambition, independence, aggression, and violent death: "The Western and the gangster film have a special relationship with American society. Both deal with critical phases of American history. . . . [T]hey represent America talking to itself about, in the case of the Western, its agrarian past, and in the case of the gangster film, thriller, its urban technological present."[33]

Perhaps they reflected evolving views of social change. In the western, violence nearly always appears as a climactic end to crime. The hero rides away into the sunset, having brought law and order. Civilization triumphs and the frontier has been pushed ever farther into the wilderness. The era of tolerated lawlessness concludes with that of a natural society. The gangster film offers no such optimism. Violence appears as a matter of daily, institutionalized routine. The ultimate villains are part of the artificial, enduring, established, and corrupt power structure. Garbed in authority, lawlessness has triumphed. The anti-hero dies; his efforts to surmount or change the system have failed.

There were, of course, more subtle distinctions. Warshow again provided definitive comparisons in a somewhat more detailed article for the March–April 1954 issue of *Partisan Review*. In a memorable sentence he summarized the mobster mystique: "The gangster is the 'no' to that great American 'yes' which is stamped so big over our official culture and yet has so little to do with the way we really feel about our lives."[34]

Warshow recognized that the westerner imposes himself, reluctantly, through unshakable self-control, while the gangster's influence relies precisely upon the likelihood that he will resort, without warning, to violence. Of course the two characters have apparently opposite interests in law and order, but Warshow saw something deeper. While the gangster represents personal ambition gone wild, the lonely westerner simply does what he has to do.

What he defends . . . is the purity of his own image—in fact his honor. . . . When the gangster is killed, his whole life is shown to have been a mistake, but the image the Westerner seeks to maintain can be presented as clearly in defeat as in victory: he fights . . . to state what he is, and he must live in a world that permits that statement. The Westerner is the last gentleman, and the movies which over and over again tell his story are probably the last art form in which the concept of honor retains its strength.[35]

Hollywood had little interest in such erudite analyses. It saw both types of film as offering parallel paths to potential profit. Rather than contemplating distinctions, it acted on similarities. A viable plot could fit the requirements of either variety. Thus W. R. Burnett's 1930 western novel *Saint Johnson* became the contemporary urban vigilante film *Beast of the City* (1931). Months later the plot appeared again, moved to the Arizona frontier in *Law and Order* (1932). Many other examples of interchangeability exist. *Show Them No Mercy* (1935), a gangster film, reappeared as *Rawhide* (1951). Raoul Walsh directed another outstanding Burnett story, first as the mobster movie *High Sierra* (1941) and then as the western *Colorado Territory* (1949); it was brought back to the present as *I Died a Thousand Times* (1955). *The Asphalt Jungle* (1950), based upon yet another Burnett book, became *The Badlanders* (1958).

Perhaps the most distinguished gangster film of the Depression years also reveals the close ties between fugitives of the Old and New West. Robert E. Sherwood's play *The Petrified Forest* was a notable success in New York. However, actor Leslie Howard agreed to make the movie only if his costar on Broadway also appeared. Thus Humphrey Bogart entered the pantheon of movie outlaws as the Oklahoma fugitive Duke Mantee. *The Petrified Forest* (1936) dealt with a group of fugitives at Black Mesa, two hundred miles from Phoenix, with Bogart as a scowling, shuffling "last great apostle of rugged individualism." The film, complete with references to Billy the Kid, presented the emotionless Mantee as a creature apart from ethnic racketeers of the day. An aging character says of Duke: "He's an American. Gangsters is foreign."

Bogart's superbly menacing performance was matched by

those of Howard and a youthful Bette Davis. *The Petrified Forest* firmly established Warner Brothers as *the* studio for gangster films. It had an astonishing stable of actors, fulfilling a host of mobster roles. Bogart joined Cagney, Robinson, and Muni, along with John Garfield and George Raft, to form what subsequently but suitably was called "the Warner Mob."[36]

The studio also had another star as unsuited to the role of a western bandit or an urban gangster as could be imagined. Errol Flynn nevertheless became a memorable film outlaw. Born in Tasmania and serving as an inept constable in New Guinea, he drifted into motion pictures on Tahiti. His career skyrocketed in Hollywood when he starred as a dashing pirate in *Captain Blood* (1935). This venture proved so successful that Warner Brothers reassembled much of the same cast and crew for *The Adventures of Robin Hood* (1938). The colorful, chivalrous, roguish Flynn emerged as the only swashbuckler to rival Douglas Fairbanks. But accusations of statutory rape and general dissipation led to a gradual, persistent decline. Flynn's last film was *Cuban Rebel Girls* (1959). He had failed to complete a project dealing with William Tell.[37]

The Warner Brothers dominance of outlaw films continued throughout the 1930s, an era marked by attention to criminals, imagined and real. The degree to which this joint notoriety served as cause and effect will never be known, but parallels in fact and fiction, whether by design, influence, or coincidence, are undeniable. With half a century of hindsight, it is clear that nearly all legendary gangster activities of the Depression years occurred within a remarkably brief period: from June 1933 to January 1935. This concentration of famous fugitives and their infamous crimes has no equal in the nation's history. It did not transpire through simple coincidence.

A number of circumstances and designs made possible the apparent crest of outlawry. The motion pictures and the popular press had roles. Very difficult economic conditions contributed to social stress and created a public receptive to news and portrayals of noted fugitives warring against a system naturally associated with inequity and injustice. And agencies of the federal government contributed to, if they did not consciously create, the concept of a fearful crime wave.

It was a matter of publicity rather than reality. Crime rates in the United States rose gradually during the first three decades of the twentieth century. The 1930s witnessed the only sustained period in which numbers of violent and serious property offenses actually fell. Crime rates then resumed their consistent rise. Victimization in the 1980s was more likely than it was in the 1930s, just as that in the 1930s was more likely than that of the 1880s:

Urban Homicide Rates, 1880–1980
(reported, per 100,000 city population)

City[a]	1880[b]	1930[c]	1980[d]
Chicago, Illinois	2.8	10.4	28.9
Boston, Massachusetts	1.9	2.4	16.4
Cincinnati, Ohio	7.2	14.6	12.6
New Orleans, Louisiana	9.3	13.1	38.9
Newark, New Jersey	1.5	10.4	49.4
Milwaukee, Wisconsin	0.9	2.2	11.7
Oakland, California	2.9	4.6	38.8
Omaha, Nebraska	0	5.6	12.1
Galveston, Texas	9.1	4.0	27.4
Norfolk, Virginia	0	17.7	13.6
Salt Lake City, Utah	0	2.1	10.0
San Antonio, Texas	0	29.3	20.7
Elmira, New York	0	0	2.8
Portland, Oregon	0	0	12.6
Houston, Texas	6.1	18.2	39.1
Chester, Pennsylvania	0	6.7	34.8
Leadville, Colorado	0	0	0
Los Angeles, California	0	5.1	34.2
Dallas, Texas	0	7.7	35.4
Jackson, Mississippi	0	2.1	21.0
U.S. cities, average	2.3	6.0	10.3

[a]In descending order of size, 1880.

[b]"Report on the Defective, Dependent, and Delinquent Classes [1880]," Serial No. 2151 (1888), 566–74.

[c]*Uniform Crime Reports* [1930], 1–52.

[d]*Uniform Crime Reports* [1980], 87–136, 266–371.

But exploits of mythic bandits from the past loom far larger than those of the present. Today there are about thirty bank robberies in the United States every business day.[38] Bandits of the frontier and mobsters of the Depression never approached such figures. Crime to others remains more a matter of popular misconception than one of objective analysis.

Mobsters of the 1930s and their deeds were real. Murders, kidnappings, and robberies certainly occurred, as they always have. Still, the era is perceived with the end of Prohibition driving bootleggers to desperate measures. The Depression added to the problem, throwing millions out of work and toward lives of crime. Little evidence supports such relationships, but they nevertheless provide a persuasive setting.

Whatever the reasons and the facts may have been, late 1933 and 1934 were—and still are—viewed with particular relish and rejection. Rather than endangered by a single outlaw or gang in some isolated corner of the nation, the entire country appeared to swarm with marauding bands of criminals. All parts of the United States seemed threatened, although a remarkable number of the brigands came from the nation's heartland. These mobsters tended to have familiar-sounding names, rural backgrounds, and attitudes marked by desperation, fearlessness, and malice. Their foremost opponent described them in words as suited to a director of casting as of investigation:

[The] typical desperate criminal must not be of foreign country, but of American stock with a highly patriotic American name. He must not come from the slum of a great city . . . but from a small town. . . . He must not be hounded by the police or suffer any of the terrible afflictions with which our sob-sister patent-medicine criminologists immediately endow any foul murderer.[39]

Such characteristics, shared by virtually all notorious mobsters of the day, had several likely causes. The marauders could not be dismissed as insignificant or impotent; they represented a large portion of middle-class white society. And, like the bandits of the frontier, they posed a grave danger, thereby creating the need for straight-shooting and courageous heroes.

Still, these ascribed traits attracted public appreciation. In the worst of the Depression, banks seldom appeared as friends to farmers and the poor. Gunmen who stole from mercenary financial institutions posed no direct threat to most people. The gangster enjoyed celebrity status and some of the benefits of the good life when such remained beyond the dreams of ordinary mortals: "Because they were characterized as simultaneously glamorous and brutal, the criminal lords gained a respect that ordinary tycoons could never have. They were Faustian heroes who had achieved the American dream through an explicit contract with the devil."[40]

Exploits destined for lasting notoriety began with the relatively obscure arrest of Frank ("Jelly") Nash at the White Front Pool Hall in Hot Springs, Arkansas. Federal agents escorted the escaped train robber on his return journey to prison at Leavenworth, Kansas. But word of the trip reached those with nefarious interests, and at the Union Station parking lot in Kansas City, Missouri, three men waited in ambush. The machine-gun battle which followed resulted in the death of four officers and their prisoner, Nash.[41]

The June 17, 1933, Kansas City Massacre produced a multitude of theories and suspects. While the most obvious explanation was that of a failed escape attempt, another concerned deliberate assassination. Nash had connections with powerful and corrupt political organizations in the Midwest; his elimination removed a threat. An even more insidious conspiracy theory exists: some secretly welcomed the spectacle to promote expansion of authority.

One of the leading early suspects came to an end within less than six months. Wilbur Underhill, called the Tri-State Terror for his escapades in Oklahoma, Kansas, and Missouri, had been located through surveillance of his wife. On New Year's Day 1934, officers fired more than one thousand rounds of ammunition into the couple's bungalow at Shawnee, Oklahoma. The dying outlaw confessed to many crimes but denied any connection with the Kansas City Massacre.[42]

Federal investigators then turned their attention to a trio identified through a combination of descriptions, fingerprints, and associations. The primary suspects included one of the nation's leading getaway drivers, Verne C. Miller; a farm boy with an unlikely name, Adam Richetti; and a young man who ultimately received outlaw deification, Charles Arthur Floyd.

Although he was born in Georgia, Floyd had been raised in Oklahoma, at Akins, in an area already known as a refuge for bandits, the Cookson Hills. He and the region had connections and relations extending back to some very well-known families: the Starrs, the Youngers, the Daltons, and the Jameses.[43] They shared a special heritage in a land where authority and respect had nothing in common. Writes J. Edgar Hoover: "In Oklahoma bandit history there is a tradition that a desperate gang is never completely eliminated. While the rest may go to prison or death, some one member always remains free to make contacts, teach new disciples, build new outlaw crews."[44]

Criminal tendencies did not appear in the youth of Charles Arthur Floyd; he went to barber college in Wichita, a background which may well have contributed to his nickname, Pretty Boy. Hard times may well have pushed him into bootlegging, robbery, and killing, but he never earned the enmity of old friends and neighbors. To them he was the last of the nation's social bandits: "To this day, in the Cookson Hills . . . Pretty Boy Floyd remains a hero to some of the inhabitants. Legends are told, in which the old, almost outworn Robin Hood pattern appears, picturing him as one who robbed the rich to give to the poor."[45]

Countless apocryphal tales apply to Pretty Boy. He would, for example, warn sheriffs of his intentions to visit in the area or rob local banks so they could avoid confrontations. When word spread that lawmen were resorting to bulletproof vests, Floyd sent his thanks for the information and promised to shoot only at heads in the future.[46]

Pretty Boy eventually became the most wanted fugitive in the nation, but his claim on that dubious title was brief. In October of 1934 he and Richetti were recognized near East Liverpool, Ohio. Police arrested Floyd's companion, but Pretty Boy became the object of a manhunt. Trapped in a cornfield, he fell under a hail of machine-gun fire. Newspapers dutifully reported that the "infamous outlaw whose bullets blazed a crimson path over a dozen Midwestern states is dead."[47]

The people who knew Floyd best never accepted his fearsome reputation. Ten thousand attended his funeral at Akins; for months people stole dirt from his grave, and his younger brother was elected sheriff of Sequoyah County, Oklahoma.[48] Woody Guthrie wrote a ballad about Pretty Boy, leaving a musical portrait of a man who became an outlaw defending his wife from an aggressive deputy sheriff. In it the fugitive provided the poor with food and money. Unlike those funny men who rob with fountain pens, Pretty Boy never drove a family from their home.[49]

The killers at Kansas City's Union Station remained a question. Even at death, Pretty Boy denied any association with that particular crime. Richetti died in Missouri's new gas chamber in 1938, refusing to confess involvement.[50] Decades later another plausible theory appeared: Floyd and Richetti had been framed. The real killers were hired, and eliminated, to protect politicians. Verne Miller's nude body was discovered, his head crushed, near Detroit in late 1934. That of another supposed participant, William ("Solly") Weismann, appeared in Chicago in similar condition two weeks later. The third rumored killer, Maurice Denning, was never seen after the Kansas City Massacre.[51]

Meanwhile, the country had other outlaws to consider. George ("Machine Gun") Kelly gained notoriety. Legend has him creating a well-known epithet when arrested by federal agents in Memphis by shouting, "Don't shoot, G-Men." Kelly, who spent the rest of his life in prison, insisted the story was false. He had been taken into custody by local officers and said simply, "I've been waiting for you."[52]

The fame of Machine Gun Kelly and even that of Pretty Boy Floyd did not approach the notoriety of the most charismatic mobster of the time, however. His name became synonymous with the new outlaw era: Dillinger. In ten months John Dillinger's men reputedly killed sixteen, wounded seven, plundered three police arsenals, raided three jails, robbed more than one hundred banks, and made fools of law-enforcement officers throughout the United States.[53]

John Herbert Dillinger was born in Indianapolis in 1903. His mother died soon thereafter. John's father eventually remarried and the new family settled near Mooresville, about twenty miles southwest of Indianapolis. The first decades of Dillinger's life indicated little of the adventures to come. He went to school, played baseball, worked in his father's store, and attended the local Quaker meeting. After an aborted tour with the U.S. Navy, Dillinger became involved in serious crime. Convicted of participation in attempted robbery, he received a remarkably severe sentence and served in prison from 1924 to 1933. During the next year, John Dillinger would become Public Enemy No. 1 and make his name perhaps the second best known in the country, rivaling Franklin D. Roosevelt in publicity.[54]

His fabled career has two parts, both associated with independent gangs. The first of the Dillinger mobs came to an unexpected and quiet end in Tucson, Arizona, in late January 1934. Firemen answering a call became suspicious of faces resembling those appearing in a detective magazine. Local police arrested Dillinger by simply waiting at a rented house a short walk from the University of Arizona. A fingerprint technician made the critical comparison. They had the nation's most wanted fugitive, "for whom all America has searched," in custody.[55]

After a dispute over jurisdiction, Dillinger was flown back to Chicago and transported by motorcade to a specially selected and heavily guarded jail at Crown Point in the far northwest corner of Indiana. It did not hold him long. On March 3, 1934, John Dillinger made the most remarkable escape in the history of American outlawry. There is still doubt about the precise method he employed. The most probable, and colorful, version is that he carved a small wooden gun, colored it with shoe polish, and bluffed twenty guards on his way to the arms room. With the assistance of another prisoner, Herbert Youngblood, he seized two machine guns and calmly drove away in the lady sheriff's car.[56]

With the incredible escape from Crown Point, Dillinger secured his status as a legendary American outlaw. His reputation as a cool, affable, dangerous man had no equal in the era. He posed for photographs with unknowing police officers. *Time* magazine published a "Dillinger Land" manhunt map of the country for use as a party game. His picture and that of Pretty Boy Floyd appeared on gum cards,[57] and his bank-robbery style was a hallmark: Dillinger's considerable athletic ability allowed him to vault over the high partitions commonly separating tellers from their customers. Astonished bank employees would discover the smiling fugitive behind them armed with the mobsters' icon, a .45-caliber Thompson submachine gun. The robbers would escape by taking hostages, driving them to the edge of town, and setting them free. Dillinger provided carfare for the return trip. Once, when a pretty bank employee became distraught, the outlaw detoured the caravan of cars and deposited her safely at home. Hostages often commented on the calm, pleasant demeanor shown by the nation's favorite fugitive. Some noticed that he hummed a popular and catchy cowboy tune of the day, "I'm Heading for the Last Roundup." Newspapers compared his exploits with those of Wild West heroes.

One tale has Dillinger personally delivering a package to the office of a prominent Indiana State Police investigator. It contained a booklet entitled *How to Be a Detective*. Meanwhile, citizens of Mooresville circulated a petition requesting that he be granted a pardon. There was no evidence that Dillinger personally killed anyone; he was a hero who robbed banks, not people.[58]

This attitude naturally infuriated officials, including J. Edgar Hoover. Bureau of Investigation agents were concentrated at Chicago under the command of Melvin Purvis. In April they had their chance to get the second Dillinger mob; they bungled the job. The owner of the Little Bohemia Lodge outside Rhine-

John Dillinger, "Public
Enemy Number One,"
with his notorious
wooden gun, 1934.
(Indiana State Library,
Indianapolis)

lander, Wisconsin, conveyed his suspicions concerning several odd guests. Dozens of officers swept down on the resort. Barking dogs alerted the fugitives; Dillinger and the other gang members slipped away. A man destined for his own infamy, George ("Baby Face") Nelson (Lester Gillis) stayed behind long enough to kill a special agent and steal a federal car to escape.

Although it launched the disintegration of the second Dillinger mob, the raid at Little Bohemia was correctly perceived as a debacle. Federal agents allowed all of the gangsters to escape while killing an innocent bar customer and wounding two others. Humorist Will Rogers expressed a popular view: "They had Dillinger surrounded and was all ready to shoot him when he come out, but another bunch of folks come out ahead, so they just shot them instead. Dillinger is going to accidentally get with some innocent bystanders some time, then he will get shot."[59]

Rogers's comment proved prophetic. According to the accepted scenario, a madam named Anna Sage, facing deportation as an undesirable alien, contacted Martin Zarcovich, an East Chicago detective. The officer relayed word to Melvin Purvis: Dillinger would be attending a movie with her and a waitress named Polly Hamilton. The trap was sprung on July 22, 1934, at Chicago's Biograph Theater. Sage wore a red dress for easy identification. At about 10:40 in the evening, with the temperature still close to one hundred degrees, *Manhattan Melodrama* (1934) ended with Clark Gable going to the electric chair.

When Dillinger and the two women exited the theater, three men closed in from behind. A series of handgun shots followed, and Public Enemy No. 1 was dead. The three officers, all of whom have been credited with the killing, are believed to have been Purvis, Zarcovich, and federal agent Sam Crowley. They also wounded two innocent female bystanders.[60]

Federal Bureau of Investigation press releases indicated that Dillinger had resisted arrest and tried to draw a pistol. J. Edgar Hoover later insisted that the fugitive, "living true to his real character of a sneak and a coward, had attempted to throw a woman in front of him to act as a barricade as he attempted to draw his gun."[61] Witnesses reported no such occurrences. Dillinger's father expressed the opinion of many, one routinely associated with the deaths of legendary outlaws: "They shot him down in cold blood."[62]

At the scene of the killing, women soaked the hems of their skirts in blood; a promoter offered to buy the pavement bricks for twenty-five dollars each.[63] Questions promptly arose, in typical fashion, concerning the identification of the deceased. Doubt grew when photographs and autopsy descriptions did not appear to match those previously available. The explanation involved plastic surgery, supposedly conducted on the fugitive to disguise his features.

Dillinger was quickly buried on July 24 on the edge of Indianapolis; five thousand people attended his funeral.[64] His father had the grave covered with reinforced concrete to prevent disinterment. The following day, the primary witness to the reported plastic surgery fell from the nineteenth floor of a federal office building in Chicago. Surviving gang members were hunted down and killed.

Myron J. Quimby has noted that "over the long, bloody trail followed by Desperado John Dillinger, Indiana arch-criminal, who finally met his end before a volley of federal bullets in Chicago, numerous women, some of them unusually attractive, have appeared in the limelight."[65] Anna Sage was deported to Europe, where she died in 1947, but the public's fascination with the mysterious female informant continued. Hollywood took prompt action, putting Barbara Stanwyck in *The Woman in Red* (1935). Enduring fame came through a song "In Caliente" (1935) that immortalized the Lady in Red.

Dillinger's father toured with the Crime Does Not Pay show and appeared at a museum established at Little Bohemia. He died in 1943 and was buried next to his son. Baby Face Nelson, the most lethal of the Dillinger mob, became Public Enemy No. 1 briefly. Federal agents spotted him in a car a few miles northwest of Chicago in November 1934 and he died in the gun battle that followed, but not before he killed Sam Crowley. Martin Zarcovich never received his promised reward. Polly Hamilton was promptly released. Melvin Purvis resigned in 1936 to organize the Junior G-Men for Post Toasties cereal. He later ran a South Carolina radio station and committed suicide in 1960. Dillinger reportedly was seen for decades visiting the Midwest. As John Toland wrote, "the myth was not mere fiction, for the man himself was possessed by it. . . . [H]e even exceeded it. . . . John Dillinger . . . has remained—understandably—the symbol of the modern outlaw."[66]

Attention quickly turned to one of the strangest families in American outlaw history. Ma Barker was the assumed center of a group of midwestern robbers and kidnappers. Her real function remains an enigma. She attracted, more than any other, the wrath of J. Edgar Hoover, who found her a cold-blooded creature of evil,

[the] most vicious, dangerous, and resourceful criminal brain of the last decade. . . . The eyes of Arizona Clark Barker always fascinated me. They were queerly direct, penetrating, hot with some strangely smouldering flame, yet withal as hypnotically cold as the muzzle of a gun. That same dark, mysterious brilliance was in the eyes of her four sons.[67]

Yet the most notable associate of these boys, Alvin ("Creepy") Karpis (Albin Karpowicz), insisted on an opposite view: "The most ridiculous story in the annals of crime is that Ma Barker was the mastermind behind the Karpis-Barker gang. . . . She wasn't a leader of criminals or even a criminal herself. . . . It's probably too late to rewrite the legend. . . . She was just an old-fashioned homebody."[68]

Arizona ("Kate") Clark was born in 1872 and raised near Springfield, Missouri. She married a poor farmer named George Barker at the age of twenty. They had four sons, each of whom turned to crime and eventually met a violent end. No evidence ever appeared to connect their father with their offenses, and remarkably little involved their mother. Ma and the boys nevertheless became subjects of national attention. Federal agents eventually traced the girlfriend of the youngest son to a rented house at Oklawaha, Florida, about fifty miles northwest of

Orlando. On the morning of January 16, 1935, they poured fifteen hundred rounds of ammunition into the cottage and then sent a black cook in to investigate. Ma Barker and her boy were dead.[69]

The remaining members of the gang were found and sent to prison. George Barker lived on at Welch, Oklahoma, for many years. He gradually saved enough money to have the bodies of his family brought back and buried near his little gas station. Alvin Karpis, the last man officially designated Public Enemy No. 1, remained a fugitive until he was arrested on New Orleans's Canal Street in 1936.[70] He stayed in prison until 1969 and died quietly in Europe a decade later.

Referring to false stories that Hoover had personally taken him into custody, Karpis said simply: "I made that son of a bitch."[71] As with so many others in outlaw mythology, that claim contains a bit of truth. Much of the unique publicity focused on fugitives of the era was related directly to the director of the formally renamed *Federal* Bureau of Investigation. In 1933, few in the country knew of the man or his agency. By 1935 he and the FBI were national institutions. At the height of the mobster hysteria, Congress, without so much as a recorded vote, greatly expanded the federal government's role in restoring order to a lawless land. Attorney General Homer Cummings promised action to save a nation groggy with crime.[72] New laws gave Hoover's FBI powers associated with those of a police agency.[73] Among created offenses were those of robbing a federally insured bank and interstate flight to avoid prosecution for a felony.[74] Buried deep within the labyrinth of the Internal Revenue Code appeared a statute regulating automatic weapons, silencers, and short-barreled firearms.[75]

The orchestrated program almost went awry, however: "There was at one time actual agitation in Congress to invoke martial law throughout the nation. This was opposed by Hoover, who insisted that, given proper powers, the Federal Bureau of Investigation could cope with any wave of outlawry."[76] As a direct consequence of superb public relations and mastery of political realities, the number of FBI agents increased from about seven hundred in 1934 to more than four thousand by 1941. This had little effect on crime, of course. The federal prison population grew slightly, but then it had nearly tripled during the 1920s because of Prohibition. Then, as now, state institutions held the overwhelming majority of people confined for serious crimes.[77]

In 1932, Hoover's still small division of the Justice Department began publication of a periodical, *Fugitives: Wanted By Police,* which became the *FBI Law Enforcement Bulletin* three years later.[78] With the notoriety accorded Dillinger, Floyd, Nelson, and Karpis, the public enemy had been permanently established. In 1935 the film *G-Men* was released, depicting events similar to those reported in the newspapers. The FBI and its newly prominent director cooperated in publication of a book by journalist Courtney Riley Cooper. *Ten Thousand Public Enemies* told the story of how federal justice came to the mobster and the nation. Hoover prepared the foreword, denouncing the "innate urge of human nature to picture the widely publicized criminal in the role of a Robin Hood when the facts reveal him as exactly the opposite."[79]

In dozens of articles Cooper proceeded to explain how, from the millions of villainous Americans with police records, the FBI identified particularly dangerous gangs of five to eight members and selected ten thousand "men and women whose capture must be made by armed men. . . . These are America's Public Enemies."[80] Their persistent appearance had a purpose: "As one gangster succeeded another in the No. 1 spot, Hoover was able to propagate the notion that America was filled with a never ending supply of vicious criminals. . . . [H]e glorified both the gangsters and his own invincible G-Men."[81]

The FBI director was intrigued by the impact of motion pictures and created opportunities for suitable depiction. He appeared in the documentary *You Can't Get Away With It* (1936) and was rumored to be joining the film industry as an executive. Instead he endorsed a series of productions by Paramount Studios showing ferocious villains hunted down by relentless and courageous federal agents. The FBI even assisted in production of the "War on Crime" comic strip.[82]

Portrayals in films, books, and articles left an indelible imprint on the public mind; they had subtle, not always intended, effects. In order to create the image of a heroic law enforcer, one must have a formidable criminal. The simplest dramatic technique is to focus on the character of the offender, but such a method turns the criminal into a protagonist, creating a bond between spectator and outlaw. Revelations of increasingly sophisticated police technology might appear to bring an end to lawlessness, but they also led to indications of ever increasing desperado power.

And there was perhaps another contrived consequence in an era when the nation seemed on the verge of economic and social collapse: "A successful campaign against . . . outlaws vividly demonstrated the government's strength. Hoover's cleverness in devising the revolving public enemy file was undeniable: men who rob banks . . . are enemies of the people and of America herself. Men who catch the men who rob banks are therefore protectors of the people."[83]

Thus the era of the spectacular mobster drew to a close. The FBI found new villains: spies, saboteurs, and subversives. In 1941, Hollywood brought down the curtain with the death of Humphrey Bogart in *High Sierra*. His character of Mad Dog Roy Earle was that of the last gangster, an existential hero fleeing to the wilderness. Trapped in the mountains and shot by a marksman, he seems destroyed by a modern society, but the outlaw never dies. Earle's delicious moll (Ida Lupino) has the film's last word, expressing spiritual survival of the fallen mobster: "Free." Mad Dog heralded equally formidable fugitives already on the horizon.

CHAPTER 14

The Badman

The world has changed, but the bad man of old West has not and never will.

—GEORGE D. HENDRICKS

DIRECTOR John Ford (Sean O'Feeney) wanted to make another western. He had done so in the days of silent films, but then he moved on to achieve considerable distinction, particularly with *The Informer* (1935). Studio executives were, however, reluctant to give Ford funds for a project on location and without real stars. He finally obtained backing, but only to a maximum of $230,000. This sum ordinarily would have meant sound stages and lesser players, but the producers had not reckoned with the genius of John Ford. He assembled a remarkable cast and crew and took them to Monument Valley in southern Utah. In *four days* they were finished, having written into the script an unexpected snowfall. A few additional scenes remained to be completed back in California. *Stagecoach* (1939), a western by which all others are still measured, came in $8,000 under budget.

Eight people set out on that stage to Lordsburg: Claire Trevor, Thomas Mitchell, John Carradine, Andy Devine, Donald Meek, George Bancroft, Louise Platt, and Berton Churchill. "For every one of them, the role in *Stagecoach* was to prove the most memorable of his career."[1] Along the way they stopped to pick up a fugitive, the Ringo Kid, and so transformed the image of the western outlaw. J. A. Place tells what happened: "Ford rapidly tracks in on his face. He appears like a God out of the desert. John Wayne immediately registers his star quality in the close-up, and we are drawn to him irresistibly."[2] Wayne (Marion

Morrison) and Ford would make many more westerns, together and apart. They molded a generation's vision of the frontier and left a deep imprint on the national psyche. The most popular actor and perhaps the best director in American motion-picture history were a powerful combination for a quarter of a century. Those portions of their work concerning outlaws formed, as never before, the visual image of the West's good badman.

Indirectly, Wayne gave popular language the very word. His film *The Angel and the Badman* (1946) fixed the compound in vernacular English with a contradictory meaning. A badman is not necessarily bad; *goodman* has no meaning. Films issued before 1946 consistently divided the term; those made later routinely adopted the compound. For the original it was of no significance; whenever John Wayne played a badman, as he did with some frequency, something was clearly wrong with the law.[3] His mere appearance in the role of a criminal made justification for illegality pointless; it could be assumed.

For John Ford, outlaws appeared in two opposite visions. They were either very good or very bad. In *Grapes of Wrath* (1940), *Three Godfathers* (1948), and *The Searchers* (1956), outlaws were heroic figures. In *Wagonmaster* (1950), *My Darling Clementine* (1946), and *The Man Who Shot Liberty Valance* (1962), they were creatures of evil, tainted with hints of perversion and sadism. The frontier bandits of Ford and Wayne remained creatures of myth, however. Hollywood had somewhat different views of supposed reality.

In terms of specific focus, few outlaw films had an impact comparable to that of *Jesse James* (1939), directed by Henry King. It glorified the dashing Jesse while presenting his brother Frank as calm and dependable. A glowing Technicolor production made on location in Missouri, starring Tyrone Power and Henry Fonda, *Jesse James* proved enormously popular. The real Jesse's granddaughter provided an accurate measure of authenticity, commenting after a preview that "about the only connection it had with fact was that there was a man named James and he did ride a horse."[4]

The great success of *Jesse James* led Hollywood to seize upon

American pride in its outlaws and promptly spawned a multitude of similar projects. *The Return of Frank James* (1940) brought Henry Fonda back for a pardon after the treacherous Bob Ford conveniently committed suicide. Gene Tierney made a lovely *Belle Starr* (1940). No man could say where facts end and fantasies began *When the Daltons Rode* (1940). The Younger brothers emerged again as *Bad Men of Missouri* (1941). Then matters got out of hand.

Metro-Goldwyn-Mayer cast Robert Taylor as *Billy the Kid* (1941). Dark, mature, incredibly handsome, dressed entirely in black, and mounted on a black horse, he first appeared riding through a particularly gaudy impression of Monument Valley as the prologue scrolled by:

The history of the West was written with the blood of men both good and bad. In 1880 the last frontier was being won to the music of six-shooters on the cattle ranges. At the time, and into this stirring scene, there rode a young outlaw who lived his violent hour in defiance of advancing civilization. His name has gone down in legend as "Billy the Kid."[5]

Taylor's pianist version was soon in the shadow of another Billy from the most controversial western film in history, Howard Hughes's *The Outlaw* (1943). Crude and blatant, it resulted in a remarkable and precedent-setting publicity campaign that used censorship as titillation and Jane Russell's magnificence in low-cut blouses. *The Outlaw* concluded with Pat Garrett killing Doc Holliday to allow Billy to escape! Modified versions appeared in 1943, 1946, and 1951, edited to satisfy vigilant censors and secure widening audiences.

The effect such major outlaw films had on those of scholarly inclination can never be determined. While rejecting obvious romanticized portrayals of individual bandits, academicians generally accepted conditions of lawlessness and crime already associated with the frontier. Decades of misrepresentation, from dime novels to epic motion pictures, had created the Wild West. While revisionist writers painted increasingly negative portrayals of many gunmen, learned inquiries concluded that the frontier served as a haven for social misfits fleeing from the normal evolution of civilization. Thus enduring lawlessness became part of the violent, criminal American culture.[6]

One scholar determined that western outlaws had red hair (overlooking Indians, blacks, Asians, and Hispanics), presumably combined with the blue eyes identified by earlier generations. It appeared that survival on the frontier, at least for whites, required a fast draw because "life in those days and in those surroundings depended largely on the rapidity with which a Colt or a Derringer was used. It seems that red-headedness is often combined with accelerated motor innervation."[7]

George D. Hendricks tried to take a serious look at the frontier bandit. His 1941 book *The Bad Man of the West* attempted to analyze the backgrounds and careers of several dozen prominent desperadoes. While accepting many of the old simplistic stories and concentrating on a small number of notorious white gunmen, he nevertheless reached some interesting conclusions. Echoing views of the 1920s, Hendricks expressed the opinion that the frontier bandit could not be compared with the city gangster: "The typical Western bad man . . . came out in open daylight to meet his foe face to face. . . . [I]t was a gunfight of one armed man with another."[8] *The Bad Man of the West* also determined that much frontier lawlessness resulted from the Civil War:

The youthful Southerner, resenting the defeat and invasion of his beloved South and the evil effects of the reconstruction period with impudent newly-freed Negroes, carpetbaggers and scalawags, became a potential bad man and went West. He was the same typical Southern youth who had been taught to revere all womankind, to be courteous, gentle, polite. No, it was not an accident. At no other time and at no other place could there ever have been another typical bad man like that of the West.[9]

However restricted in view, Hendricks was attempting to conduct an objective study, and he presented a memorable, graphic composite of the frontier badman:

He isn't so bad to look at. He's sun-tanned; a cold, steel-blue gray eye seems to read your mind. He's blond, square-jawed, mustachioed, rough-skinned. He's five feet, nine and half inches, and he weighs 169 pounds. His hands and feet are small. His body is compact, muscular. He walks quietly and he talks quietly. He's well dressed, except when on the range. He's a youth, possibly between twenty and twenty-five.[10]

Portrayals of this nature left the movies with a problem. This western figure looked so heroic he could not always be bad. The solution involved distinction between the outlaw and the gunfighter. The latter could be both dangerous and very good. This expression reached its apogee in the purest and most beautiful western ever made, *Shane* (1953). In it the transient killer becomes the struggling farmers' savior. Robert Warshow provided the clearest interpretation: "The hero (Alan Ladd) is hardly a man at all, but something like the Spirit of the West . . . breathing sweetness and a melancholy . . . and destroying in the black figure of Jack Palance a Spirit of Evil."[11]

There were, in fact, relatively few outlaws with significant reputations as gunfighters. And despite rather common assumptions, the line between lawman and desperado was probably no more blurred on the frontier than in modern urbanized America. But respected historians, making increasingly negative interpretations of western bandits, routinely disagreed on such issues. Paul I. Wellman held that "the outlaws of the West, after the first post–Civil War period, were almost without exception cowboys."[12] Harry Sinclair Drago, on the other hand, concluded that "very few of them were cowboys."[13] Edward Everett Dale probably came closest to the truth: "That there were bad men and worthless men among the range riders cannot be denied, but their number was not large and even the worst were not as black as they have been painted, or as they at times sought to paint themselves."[14]

The divergence of even expert opinion probably contributed to an incredible range of fictional outlaw representations. One found expression in popular music through an odd sequence of events. Westerner Bob Fletcher wrote a simple poem, which

Cole Porter purchased. He revised the lyrics and wrote the music for a song intended for use in a film that was never produced. The studio allowed it to sit unused for a decade. As an afterthought, it was put into the wartime revue *Hollywood Canteen* (1944). "Don't Fence Me In" became a great hit and promptly served as the theme for the Roy Rogers film *Don't Fence Me In* (1945), with George ("Gabby") Hayes as the old outlaw Wildcat Kelly, thought dead and buried. Meanwhile, in a sad irony, Porter had been left crippled by a riding accident.

Another twist took the outlaw into a different realm of fantasy with remarkable results. It began in 1933 on Detroit radio station WXYZ and turned into an enduring symbol of a truly imaginary West. The mysterious masked rider of the plains had come to a generation of devoted followers. For two decades on radio, in movie serials, and then on television, the Lone Ranger was a champion of justice who never shot to kill and used bullets made of solid silver. And if not really an outlaw, he seemed automatically presumed to be such.

The Lone Ranger's great-nephew appeared three years and two generations later. He lived in a modern city and used a gas gun instead of silver bullets. The Green Hornet drove a sleek automobile (the Black Beauty) rather than riding a descendant of his great-uncle's famous stallion, Silver. He was, however, always hunted by the police despite his success in catching real criminals in a far more complex urban America.[15] Still, the Green Hornet and his Asian helper (whose nationality changed with political winds) never matched the enduring popularity of the Lone Ranger and his loyal Indian companion Tonto. What seemed believable on the frontier could not fit into city life, however much fans might wish it to be so. The Hornet was always imaginary; the Ranger was already part of frontier legend.

Motion pictures faced a similar dilemma with their western bandits and city gangsters. The end of the Depression marked a decline in the popularity of established movie mobsters. Hollywood needed something different. Paramount found it in Alan Ladd. Soft spoken, small, almost angelic in appearance, he seemed the antithesis of an outlaw, but the camera does strange things and sometimes provides an unpredictable link with audiences. In *This Gun for Hire* (1942) Ladd created a new kind of outlaw: lonely, cold, emotionless, a psychopath who killed on order without remorse.[16] And yet he merely had to feed a cat and attract Veronica Lake to establish an immediate and lasting appeal. In the character of Philip Raven, Alan Ladd lived in a frightening world of deceit and violence we all must fear; his fugitive served as a model for hundreds of successors in a grim contemporary setting.

This modern outlaw fit well in a short-lived variety of motion pictures the French called *film noir*. Developed during and immediately after World War II, these movies tended to have strong, complex stories, competent casts, and very limited production budgets. Imaginative directors solved many of their problems by using confined sets and minimal lighting. The resulting films were dark, in image as well as meaning. Heroes had serious flaws, fell victim to the wiles of beautiful women, and found themselves trapped in complex webs of evil. They and their audiences were purposely misled by plots in which good became bad and wrong became right.[17]

Film noir indicated that something fundamental was wrong with American life. These movies revealed an underside of a society marked by ambiguity and violence. Fugitives of many types attempted to escape, usually without success, in such motion pictures as *Swamp Water* (1941), *Detour* (1945), *The Killers* (1946), *Kiss of Death* (1947), *The Gangster* (1947), *Out of the Past* (1947), *White Heat* (1949), *D.O.A.* (1949), and *The Asphalt Jungle* (1950).

Real gangsters would have been ideal subjects for *film noir*, but there was an obstacle: A decade-old informal understanding between the motion-picture industry and the Federal Bureau of Investigation forbade portrayals of actual mobsters, presumably to prevent possible idealization by a naïve American public. In World War II, however, such a restriction had little significance. Ambitious producers quietly crossed the line with inexpensive and forgettable portrayals of *Roger Touhy, Gangster* (1944) and *Dillinger* (1945).

These opened the door to later films on notables of the 1930s, such as *Pretty Boy Floyd* (1960), *Machine Gun Kelly* (1958), and *Baby Face Nelson* (1957). Meanwhile, contemporary fugitives received relatively little publicity. There were occasional exceptions, such as escaped Illinois convict Roger Touhy, Canadian bank robber Eddie Boyd, New York assassin Louis ("Lepke") Buchalter, and southern murderer William Cook. It required an unlikely pair of teenagers from Nebraska to attract sustained attention, however. Charles Starkweather and his fourteen-year-old companion, Caril Ann Fugate, conducted a week-long rampage in 1958, with twelve hundred police officers and national guardsmen in pursuit. Starkweather was executed in 1959; Fugate received a parole in 1976.[18] Two years earlier, they had been well played in *Badlands* (1974).

Many important criminals did gain lasting fame in the 1940s and 1950s, but they cannot be considered hunted outlaws. Another kind of mobster had developed, one who managed vast organizations with limited need for personal violence. Minions and corrupt officials did such work. Americans knew well the names of Frank Costello, Carlo Gambino, Albert Anastasia, Vito Genovese, and Charles ("Lucky") Luciano. They fought the law with skilled attorneys instead of guns and found their significant opposition within the ranks of related associations in struggles over the control of illegal goods and services. These purveyors of vice eventually received their own unique niches in the annals of American crime, but never as simple fugitives. They provided gambling, drugs, and prostitutes while ordinarily viewing robbery with disdain.

Growing prominence of organized criminals reflected changing social conditions. While scarcely new, corruption was becoming accepted as routine. At the very least a growing recognition of suspects with clear ethnic and racial identification occurred. These included organized criminals of Sicilian and Italian heritage. Richard Wright's 1940 novel *Native Son* was a landmark. Through Bigger Thomas, a young black fugitive from the Chicago slums, Americans found a graphic portrayal of prejudice, crime, and punishment far closer to reality than could be routinely viewed at the movies. It should also be recalled that during

World War II some 120,000 loyal and quite innocent Japanese Americans were arbitrarily banished to "internment" camps.[19]

Popular outlaws require identification of a special magnetic personality, however. The movies found one of these on a motorcycle racing toward the audience on a lonely road. Marlon Brando, *The Wild One* (1953), had arrived. He played the sleazy leader of a motorcycle gang which briefly took over a small town. While mild by later standards, *The Wild One* stirred much controversy and attracted huge audiences. Supposedly based on actual incidents at Hollister and Riverside, California, in 1947 and 1948, it became a favorite of the world's youth. Young men adopted Brando's leather jacket and organized their own motorcycle gangs. British censors banned the film for twelve years. Naturally, Hollywood attempted to duplicate such success.

Agencies of law enforcement saw sinister consequences and denounced films they deemed to glorify such deplorable hoodlums: "Probably the most publicized of the movies was 'The Wild Ones [*sic*],' in which bikers were portrayed as modern-day Robin Hoods seeking revenge on a world that did them wrong. This and several other similar movies romanticized motorcycle club behavior and sparked an interest, drawing others to motorcycle clubs."[20]

The Wild One and the very successful western *High Noon* (1952), both produced by Stanley Kramer, probably brought about an odd phenomenon in outlaw films. Instead of bandits threatening individuals, they terrorized entire frontier communities. Although such incidents never occurred in American history, they seemed routine after *Day of the Bad Man* (1958), *Day of the Outlaw* (1959), *The Plunderers* (1960) and *Firecreek* (1968). One particularly objectionable version, *Welcome to Hard Times* (1971), had the pitiful town of Hard Times destroyed by a single brigand so odious that he broke liquor bottles open rather than remove the corks and, in a particularly perverse mood, shot his own horse!

Real outlaws were known for the attention and care they lavished upon their essential mounts. They also favored fashionable "cocktails" over broken bottles. But the movies offered a wide variety of fiction and fact. Between 1948 and 1960, almost every brigand of prominence became the focus of a motion picture. Black Bart, Bill Doolin, John Wesley Hardin, Al Jennings, Cole Younger, Sam Bass, Captain Kidd, Blackbeard, Jean Lafitte, and Jack Slade serve as examples.

Hollywood acted in predictable fashion, however. If one outlaw was good, several would be better. Pretense of accuracy became of no interest in a numbing succession of incredible distortions. What began with *Badman's Territory* (1946) went through *Return of the Bad Men* (1948) and *Best of the Badmen* (1951), with ever growing numbers of familiar names massed in conditions that never occurred. The ploy for *Badman's Country* (1958) is representative; it has Pat Garrett coming out of retirement to join Wyatt Earp and Buffalo Bill in the hunt for Butch Cassidy. Sadly, this was not a comedy.

Imaginary congregations of outlaws (Bill Doolin led a gang including the Younger brothers, Billy the Kid, and a murderous Sundance Kid in *Return of the Badmen*) made use of the importance such names had acquired. Moreover, the cumulative effects of such portrayals cannot be denied; people remember what they see, even as flickering images. All the learned articles and thoughtful books cannot dispel a simple, sobering fact: Jesse James and Billy the Kid are the most frequently portrayed figures of American history.[21] They surpass in appearances their nearest domestic rival (Abraham Lincoln) and approach the world's leader (Napoleon Bonaparte). Jesse and Billy may not equal in number the portrayals of favorite fictional characters (Count Dracula, Sherlock Holmes, Tarzan), but to the world they unquestionably constitute a critical part of American heritage.

For two decades and in many films the nation had a very special and unusual hero-outlaw to observe. Like no other, he represented the confused images associated with the good badman. This particular actor was a true warrior hero, although his appearance completely belied fact. Audie Murphy, a Texas farm boy born in 1924, was the most decorated American serviceman of World War II. Later he drifted into motion pictures, often playing western outlaws in modest features which returned consistent profits. Murphy first starred as Jesse James in *Kansas Raiders* (1950) and Billy the Kid in *The Kid from Texas* (1950). In one year he played both of America's favorite frontier bandits, a distinction achieved in the careers of only two others: Roy Rogers and Kris Kristofferson.

Audie Murphy made a restrained, unpretentious Billy; his first line in *The Kid from Texas* symbolized a subsequent screen career: "Nobody takes my guns." In the film he died trying to fight a sympathetic Pat Garrett, to be mourned only by Mexicans, "who called him the Kid and left his final judgment to God." Although Murphy was never highly regarded as an actor, he displayed flashes of considerable talent, particularly in rare villainous roles. *No Name on the Bullet* (1959) presented him as a chillingly effective assassin. Murphy produced his own final brief screen appearance as a mature Jesse James in *A Time for Dying* (1969), a dark and dispiriting film far different from his earlier efforts. Two years later the legitimate hero, all-American boy, proficient executioner, and doomed victim of the nation's greatest war died in a plane crash.[22]

Murphy's quiet, reflective Billy the Kid had several notable competitors during the same period. Paul Newman played the famous New Mexican outlaw in *The Left-Handed Gun* (1958). Its dubious conclusion had Billy commit an act of suicide by drawing against Pat Garrett from an empty holster.

The outlaw film was, nevertheless, losing public interest. For many years no notable gangster movies appeared, and the western bandit suffered an even worse fate: he became a caricature and the subject of humor both intended and accidental. Director William ("One-Shot") Beaudine, so called for his acceptance of first takes, was responsible for two truly incredible efforts: *Jesse James Meets Frankenstein's Daughter* (1966) and *Billy the Kid vs Dracula* (1966). These were actually meant as serious films, combining horror with the desperado; the results proved lamentable beyond fantasy.

Intentional comedies found far greater success. *Cat Ballou* (1965) put a fine cast in a funny western. Actor Lee Marvin won an Academy Award, which he attributed to his swaybacked horse, for a dual role allowing one badman to kill his worse self. The gang even managed to save the buxom Cat Ballou (Jane Fonda) from the gallows. In an equally rare western slapstick comedy, the Three Stooges struck with *The Outlaws Is Coming* (1965). The Sunstroke Kid, Rance Roden, and Trigger Mortis were trying to exterminate the buffalo to cause an Indian uprising. The Stooges, with help from Annie Oakley, managed to defeat a gang of virtually every outlaw from the frontier by pouring glue on their guns.

With such parodies and the decline in popularity of gangster movies after 1960, it appeared that the outlaw film was finished. Open ridicule and grotesque combination would seem to mark the end. Then, suddenly, things changed. The American outlaw returned to the screen, in nostalgically pure versions of old dreams. The dramatic comeback began with a couple from the Southwest a generation past. "They are young, they are in love, they kill people." They are called Bonnie and Clyde.

Their story began in 1930. Clyde Barrow was twenty and Bonnie Parker eighteen when they met near Dallas. Both came from small Texas villages. Clyde had served time in reform school; Bonnie had married a man subsequently sent to prison for life, and then found work as a waitress. Both were quite small: Clyde Barrow stood only five feet four inches tall and Bonnie Parker but four feet ten.

The couple lived together until Clyde went to jail for burglary. Bonnie helped him escape, but he was soon recaptured and sent to a brutal Texas penal farm. Released after serving 20 months, he swore he'd never go to prison again. In the fall of 1932, Bonnie and Clyde, with a renegade named Ray Hamilton who served as a lover to both, took to the open road, robbing small banks and stores and killing lawmen and others. Hamilton soon left the pair, who were then joined by Buck [Barrow, Clyde's brother] and his wife, Blanche, and a gas-station-attendant-turned robber named William Daniel Jones.[23]

The motley gang cruised about the country from Texas to Iowa, becoming prominent regional outlaws but never approaching the

Clyde Barrow and Bonnie Parker, when their troubles
were small, 1933. (Texas Ranger Museum Library,
Waco)

notoriety given John Dillinger and Pretty Boy Floyd. Nevertheless, they were among the objects of a futile search by hundreds
of lawmen and four companies of the Oklahoma National Guard
through the Cookson Hills.[24]

In January 1934, Bonnie and Clyde engineered a prison break

to free their former companion, Raymond Hamilton. This led to creation of a special team of investigators led by former Texas Ranger Frank Hamer. His mission was the elimination of Bonnie and Clyde; it required 102 days.[25]

On Easter Sunday, May 23, 1934, on a road near Arcadia in northern Louisiana, Frank Hamer and five men caught up with Bonnie and Clyde. Henry Methvin had betrayed the fugitives in return for a pardon for his son. The ambush worked as planned: the concealed officers simply blasted the murderous pair out of existence with an extended fusillade of shots. A large, fascinated crowd quickly gathered at the death scene. "They swarmed across the car; cutting locks of Bonnie's hair, tearing at their clothing and prying off hubcaps. . . . They snatched up bits of broken glass. . . . They chopped down trees to remove the bullets. . . . Such was the adulation of many misguided souls who looked upon . . . banditry as something romantic."[26]

Journalists raced with the news to relatives and acquaintances of the notorious couple. Bonnie's mother, Mrs. Emma Parker, fainted when she was told; Clyde's mother, Mrs. Henry Barrow, replied quietly, "Mister, is my boy really dead?"[27] Bonnie's aunt responded bluntly, "I am glad she is dead. . . . [S]he is surely in hell." The previously captured Blanche Barrow said: "I'm glad they were both killed; it was the easiest way out." And when asked if he had any regrets, Frank Hamer answered, "I hated to bust a cap on a woman, especially when she was sitting down."[28] Such was the real Code of the West.

But the best-remembered commentary on the pair reportedly came from Bonnie herself. On the day of the shootings the front page of the Dallas *Daily Times Herald* carried, in large type, a poem which mysteriously "came into the hands of *The Times Herald* several months ago with the understanding that it was not to be released until the death of the Parker girl."[29] Whatever the source of the piece, it has been accepted as authentic and, perhaps, the last of America's great outlaw ballads (see the appendix).

The bodies were taken to Dallas, where twenty thousand people gathered in front of the funeral home, eating hot dogs purchased from vendors and donating money for wreaths. At the insistence of Bonnie's mother, the two were buried in separate cemeteries. However, Mrs. Emma Parker quickly joined Clyde's sister, Nell Barrow Cowan, in writing a book entitled *Fugitives: The Story of Bonnie and Clyde*. It left glowing portraits of tragic figures and served as a primary basis for dozens of subsequent accounts: "Clyde and Bonnie had a love which bound them together in life and went with them to their graves. We believe that no two people ever loved more devotedly, more sincerely, and more lastingly than Clyde Barrow and Bonnie Parker."[30]

Hamer's men found three automatic rifles, two shotguns, twelve handguns, and three thousand rounds of ammunition in the death car, a stolen Ford V-8. That particular model had been a favorite of Clyde, whose complimentary note to the manufacturer served as a convenient item for advertising. The riddled Ford toured the Southwest for decades. In 1973 it was auctioned for $175,000—more than the price of Adolf Hitler's Mercedes.[31] The little couple had gone a long way down.

Bonnie and Clyde added the obvious element of romance to the outlaw story. Theirs became an enduring and popular story for the movies, although names other than Parker and Barrow were used in earlier versions. *You Only Live Once* (1937) reeked of social commentary and impending doom. *They Live by Night* (1948) and *Gun Crazy* (1949) proved imaginative and impressive in spite of limited budgets. *The Bonnie Parker Story* (1958) attracted only moderate attention in a flood of routine gangster movies then flowing out of Hollywood. None of these films attempted to parallel the truth closely. Some presented the girl as a complete innocent who could therefore be spared at the end. The boy usually appeared as a simple victim of fate rather than a murderous offender. It still required that magic confluence of money, imagination, talent, and effort to make the story of Bonnie and Clyde into a really significant motion picture.

Writers David Newman and Robert Benton were intrigued with brief mention of the fugitive couple in John Toland's fine 1963 book *The Dillinger Days*. They visited Texas, took a multitude of pictures, got some suggestions from French director

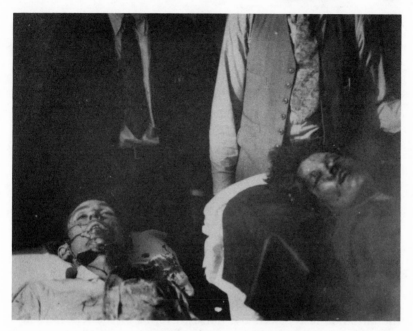

"To the law it's relief, but it's death to Bonnie and Clyde," 1934. (Texas Ranger Museum Library, Waco)

François Truffaut, and prepared a seventy-page shooting script while playing bluegrass records for inspiration. Warren Beatty agreed to produce and star in the film, although director Arthur Penn took almost complete control during location shooting in Texas.[32]

The story altered many facts, from providing the imaginary C. W. Moss (Michael J. Pollard) as a composite of several henchmen to dispensing with the real husband of Bonnie Parker (Faye Dunaway). Writers turned Clyde's rumored sexual perversions into impotence and allowed the gang to capture the pursuing Texas Ranger when such an event never occurred. The script still included many actual events placed in a nostalgic re-creation of the Depression. Many in the cast gave their characters rare depth; Beatty and Dunaway struck a special theme when they separately introduced themselves with shy smiles, adding slyly, "We rob banks." Arthur Penn took a great risk in combining elements of obvious humor with a controversial slow-motion conclusion of carnage, while "authentic Southwest locations added up to a magic heartland where the last American outlaws could lose their pursuers by simply driving their flivvers around a turn of the road."[33]

Bonnie and Clyde (1967) premiered at the World's Fair film festival in Montreal and promptly encountered critical wrath. Most reviewers found it immoral, irresponsible, and disgusting. But Pauline Kael of the *New Yorker* came to its defense, and millions of America's youths flocked to its showings. Within a year, *Bonnie and Clyde* had grossed more than twenty million dollars and had changed the course of outlaw movies.

Director Penn, while not regarding Barrow and Parker as social bandits fighting oppression, considered the couple as symbolic products of their era: "I don't think the original Bonnie and Clyde are very important. In American Western mythology, the automobile replaced the horse in terms of the renegade figure. . . . Bonnie and Clyde found themselves . . . folk heroes— violators of the status quo. Retaliators for the people."[34]

Many critics have attempted to analyze the extraordinary power of *Bonnie and Clyde*. John Cawelti found three major sources: "First, the compelling drama of its story, second, the highly effective cinematography, and finally, the relation of a traditional American fantasy of violence and outlawry to the . . . clash between the belief in social order and the ideal of the totally liberated individual."[35]

The success of *Bonnie and Clyde* naturally led to a rash of imitations. Producers brought back a host of noted mobsters from the Depression. *Dillinger* (1973) was a particularly well-done recreation, although filled with the usual alteration and simplification of fact. But the depiction of a nymphomaniacal Ma Barker in *Bloody Mama* (1970) left everything to be desired. Repugnant and gratuitously violent, it ranged from incestuous rape through drug abuse to pig drowning, all in the first thirty minutes!

Exploitation efforts of this nature were merely homage to the international phenomenon of *Bonnie and Clyde:* "For millions of people in the Western world the film image of the slim young woman in the beret, jumper, and the knee length skirt had become almost as familiar as that of the outlaw in Lincoln Green."[36] The real Bonnie's skirts were a once-fashionable ankle length, but they could go much higher. *Bonnie e Clyde all' Italiana* (Italy, 1983) raised Bonnie's skirts to midthigh in a film showing the "two fugitives as incompetent clowns, accidentally trapped into violent crime—a Latin parody of the tough-guy image of the Hollywood outlaw hero."[37]

Such films, while funny, also had a serious side. The world sees a country through its movies. John Wayne, Henry Fonda and his daughter Jane, Marlon Brando, Faye Dunaway, and Paul Newman are not mere players on an international stage, but enormous, two-dimensional, moving manifestations of myth. Fact fades into insignificance with the passage of time and sufficient well-crafted illusion.

Outlaws have a large part in this continuing scenario. They are representatives of a lawless, violent nation still striving to attain personal liberty despite ever increasing social demand. In the twentieth century, the mobile visual image clearly replaced similar written versions. The power of Hollywood deserves careful consideration; it propelled the principal villain of *The Killers* (1964) to the presidency of the United States.

Perhaps one of every twenty motion pictures has a clear outlaw theme, and the pattern also runs through another medium, constantly reinforcing an international view. " 'Gunsmoke' was syndicated in nineteen countries and seen by an estimated one-fourth of the world's population."[38] It had many rivals. Steve McQueen hunted outlaws of the Old West around television's globe on "Wanted—Dead or Alive." The infamous Chicago mobsters blasted "The Untouchables." A mysterious man named Paladin advertised "Have Gun—Will Travel." Jack Webb's "Dragnet" swept on through oceans of crime. They were all part of the American dream, and of the American nightmare.

CHAPTER 15

The Fugitive

Not that it matters, but most of what follows is true.

—BUTCH CASSIDY AND THE SUNDANCE KID (1969)

"DR. Richard Kimble, an innocent victim of blind justice, falsely convicted for the murder of his wife, reprieved by fate . . . to hide in lonely desperation . . . freed to run before relentless pursuit."[1] Every week for four years, tens of millions of anxious Americans listened to these somber words at the beginning of each weekly episode of one of television's most successful serials. "The Fugitive" consistently opened with a sequence of rapid shots showing Dr. Kimble driving to his home and seeing a one-armed man fleeing. He finds his house in disorder, his wife murdered. Convicted on circumstantial evidence, he escapes when the train taking him to prison is wrecked. Kimble flees in panic from the scene; he cannot be caught, nor can he cease to run.[2]

Episodes followed a standard pattern: the fugitive is desperately seeking the mysterious one-armed man with relentless police lieutenant Gerard (Barry Morse) in close pursuit. Kimble (David Janssen) routinely found ordinary jobs, became attached to a lovely girl, fell under suspicion, and once again had to resume his life as an innocent outlaw. In retrospect the series, sold to network executives as an afterthought and without a single working script, appears to have been an ingenious combination of themes. Victor Hugo's *Les Miserables* was transported to modern America, supplemented with elements of the story of Ohio's very real Dr. Sam Sheppard, convicted, imprisoned, and subsequently acquitted of killing his wife.

"The Fugitive" remained a tense, well-produced, and skillfully acted series kept two years in the past. The plot allowed stories to be set throughout the country, using a host of fine character actors. But it had one major problem: responsibilities could not be distributed among several cast members. "Gunsmoke" naturally relied on Marshal Dillon, for example, but many scenes could be assigned to Chester, Festus, Doc, or Miss Kitty. "The Fugitive" focused almost entirely on Kimble. David Janssen had to appear throughout the equivalent of fifteen feature motion pictures every year. That, in 120 hour-long episodes, eventually proved an almost literally killing pace. If David Janssen seemed exhausted, aging, and worn, he was.

After four years he could no longer sustain the pace. "The Fugitive" was brought to a climax in a deserted Indiana amusement park. The ingenious conclusion was kept secret from all but essential members of the cast and crew. The final hour, "which aired on August 29, 1967, was seen by more people than any single episode of a regular series in the history of television . . . and its 72 percent share of all television viewers that night set a regular series record."[3]

"The Fugitive," which spawned several imitations, had an unusual hero. Kimble was lonely, frightened, and desperate: "David Janssen was the supreme TV martyr . . . the question of whether Kimble should have turned himself in was never even broached. The reason? 'We've received no complaints . . . not even from police departments.' . . . [T]he show vicariously put 'us' in a race for our lives."[4]

The success of "The Fugitive" had many sources. It touched a familiar fear and allowed an audience to see an innocent victim escaping from a system gone mad. During his long flight, Kimble made many friends all over the country, frequently among the poor and powerless; most of them were not on television. Raymond W. Stedman tells us why:

The attractions of the series were many. The natural curiosity and suspense factor of the serial genre, of course, was one. But that aspect was enhanced by sympathy for a good man hounded for a crime that was not his, yet willing to risk his life or his vindication to help others. Then, too, there was the attraction for males of a hero who could kiss and run with complete justification—or at least comfortable rationalization.[5]

"The Fugitive" may have contributed, in some small way, to a still developing trend in the American outlaw legend. It concerned a loss of innocence and heightened skepticism in a period marked by the assassination of a president, the war in Vietnam, and revelations about misconduct in high offices in government. Reality provided ample explanation for pervasive deviation from expected behavior. For the first time, in a general pattern, the very institutions of power appeared unreliable, unreasonable, corrupt, even evil. Doubt in old values, beliefs, and interpretations crept into American life. It was no longer easy to discern good from bad.

New questioning attitudes even applied to the Old West. A few scholars investigated previous assumptions of rampant violence and disorder and found them doubtful. Philip D. Jordan recognized that frontiersmen simply reflected conditions common throughout the entire nation and all of Western civilization. "A few were criminals all of the time, some were lawless some of the time, and most were law abiding all of the time."[6] Vice and violence had long been part of American life:

Nothing in the evidence indicates that the national crime pattern was anything else than monotonous repetition the length and breadth of the nation. . . . The crimes of the wild Far West were no more abundant than were the shootings and stabbings and murders and lynchings and riots which occurred elsewhere. . . . Indeed, the crime rate of the land of the rustler and the cowboy possibly was lower than in regions . . . considered as settled down, civilized, and law-abiding.[7]

Bill O'Neal surveyed the lives of hundreds of the West's famous gunfighters, concluding that with few exceptions they rarely engaged in battles and seldom killed.[8] A handful of outlaws (Jim Miller, John Wesley Hardin, Bill Longley, Harvey Logan) probably deserved their notorious reputations, but the majority did not.

Joseph G. Rosa's exploration of the gunfighter myth put a realistic light on the romanticized exploits of famous desperadoes:

The gunfighter who followed the outlaw trail saw his family but rarely, and the hasty visit, usually one jump ahead of a posse, was marred by fear as he listened for a knock at the door. . . . As his notoriety grew and a price was placed on his head, there was the added fear that an informer would turn him in for the reward. Some fugitives changed their names, moved to new locations . . . and managed to live in peace. Others . . . spent their lives on the run. . . . [T]here was always the risk that sometime, somehow, their past would be discovered.[9]

These analyses fought a hopeless struggle against the tide of popular history. Even Wayne Gard included some common exaggerations: "The frontiersman always had to be prepared to defend his life with his six-shooter. A ready gun, nimble fingers, and a steady hand were the first requisites for longevity. He never knew when he might be ambushed by an Indian scalper, a Mexican brigand, or a white desperado."[10]

Scholarly studies continued to incorporate general impressions perhaps closer to myth than history: "Cattle rustling was so common as to be looked upon by many as no offense at all. Horse theft . . . was almost as routine. Homicide and attempted homicide occurred with bloody regularity. Assault, drunkenness, and general rowdyism were rampant, although almost never prosecuted."[11]

In some instances such reflections might be defended in regard to isolated and brief situations, but others had no valid excuse. Elmer Keith, a true authority on revolvers and ammunition, provided the following commentary on frontier life:

The law was confined to small communities backed by a gun fighting marshal, or was nonexistent. . . . [T]he law was a sixgun. . . . The old law of nature, the survival of the fittest, ruled. Many outlaws and peace officers became very fast and deadly with a gun; they had to in order to survive. . . . Those on the side of the law, backed by honest citizenry, gradually shot some semblance of decency and order into each community. Many a Western town had a dead man to bury every morning.[12]

If so, they died of disease, not gunfire.

As had long been true, the American frontier could still represent whatever might be desired, imagined, or created. That certainly applied to its outlaws. The best recent example of the phenomenon transpired in connection with two Wyoming fugitives at the turn of the century, now known throughout the world as Butch Cassidy and the Sundance Kid.

They were members of the Wild Bunch, a gang of bank and train robbers active in Wyoming, Colorado, and Utah between 1895 and 1902. Butch Cassidy (Robert LeRoy Parker) came from a large Mormon family in western Utah. He was born in 1866 and apparently borrowed the name Cassidy from a local hoodlum, while Butch derived from work in a butcher shop. He became a cowboy and served a prison term for rustling from 1894 until 1896.

The Sundance Kid (Harry Longabaugh) was probably born about 1863 in Pennsylvania. As a teenager he drifted west to Wyoming, picking up his nickname from an extended jail term for horse theft at the town of Sundance. He then joined the Wild Bunch and became acquainted with Cassidy. Whether either of the two ever occupied a position of real leadership in the gang remains doubtful. The murderous Kid Curry (Harvey Logan) probably exercised more authority.

The Wild Bunch struck various banks and trains in the northern Rockies, with frequent vacation trips to cities throughout the nation. In 1900, five members of the gang (Sundance Kid, Will Carver, Ben Kilpatrick, Kid Curry, and Butch Cassidy) made the mistake of posing for a formal photograph in Fort Worth, Texas. Subsequently identified individually by a prostitute, the outlaws had inadvertently provided Pinkerton detectives with an invaluable aid.[13]

Within two years the Wild Bunch had disintegrated. Cassidy and the Sundance Kid determined to reach a goal common to many bandits of the era: escape to South America. They were in

Members of the Wild Bunch, Fort Worth, Texas, 1900. *Left to right,* Harry Longabaugh (the Sundance Kid), Will Carver (Bill Odell), Ben Kilpatrick (the Tall Texan), Harvey Logan (Kid Curry), Robert Parker (Butch Cassidy). (Western History Collections, University of Oklahoma)

New York City by February 1901 with a special girl. She and Longabaugh boarded as Mr. and Mrs. Harry Place, and so in legend the two had become three. Etta Place was forever linked to Butch Cassidy and the Sundance Kid. She remains a mystery with diverse proposed backgrounds. One makes her a common prostitute from Texas, the other a teacher from Colorado. No convincing evidence to support the former theory has appeared.

A music teacher named Gertrude E. Place did, however, disappear from Denver about 1900.[14] There is another possible clue. The prosperous Mr. and Mrs. Place posed for a formal photograph in New York City, probably to display the lady's newly purchased lapel watch from Tiffany. The well-groomed, slender young woman in the picture would have made the most winsome whore on the fading frontier.

Whatever her moral status, Etta Place soon embarked with the Sundance Kid on a voyage to Argentina. Butch Cassidy apparently went first to England, then joined the couple within a matter of months. Pinkerton detectives were close behind. Agent Joe LeFors did indeed go to Buenos Aires in pursuit; his wife filed for divorce on grounds of cruel treatment during his absence from the United States.[15]

Still, Pinkerton's operatives failed to follow the trail. The trio of fugitives, possessing ample funds, had moved some eight hundred miles southwest to establish a ranch at Cholila near the Chilean border. They lived there peacefully for several years, openly using the names George Parker and Mr. and Mrs. Harry Longabaugh. They were considered respectable, friendly ranchers. Parker had the reputation of a gentleman. Longabaugh's remarkable skill with firearms and his comely wife's ability as an equestrian attracted no great attention.[16]

Then, in 1906, they left abruptly, and the record becomes quite vague. In 1907, William A. Pinkerton, whose detectives never gave up the hunt, reported that " 'Butch' Cassidy with Harry Longabaugh and Etta Place, a clever horsewoman and rifle shot . . . fled from the Argentine Republic and were last heard from on the Southwest Coast of Chile, living in the wild open country."[17] And that, for decades, was the end of the story. The Pinkerton agency recorded a number of confusing and conflicting rumors impossible to verify: Cassidy had returned to the United States in 1905 and soon died, he was in a Chilean prison in 1913, he and Longabaugh had been killed in an Argentine bank robbery attempt in 1911.[18]

The remnants of the Wild Bunch occupied positions of some continuing regional interest, never approaching the national acclaim accorded the Jameses, the Youngers, or the Daltons. It was usually assumed that they had managed what their more famous counterparts had failed to accomplish: to get away. Colorado's *Steamboat* (Springs) *Pilot* reported in 1910:

Butch Cassidy Busy in Argentine Republic. Three of the most noted train robbers in the history of the West are masters of a great cattle ranch and at the same time the leaders of a gang of brigands . . . according to a dispatch to the State Department in Washington. The bandits are George LeRoy Parker, alias Butch Cassidy, Harry Longabaugh, alias The Sundance Kid, and . . . Harvey Logan, who was the leader of the Wild Bunch.[19]

No one—or very few—really knew. The few who might did not talk.

In 1930 the legend began to grow. Germination occurred through a rather modest article on Butch Cassidy by Arthur Chapman in the April issue of *Elks Magazine*. The author made a number of interesting revelations based on information from one Percy Seibert, who had worked at Bolivia's Concordia Tin Mines early in the century and had known the fugitives. Etta Place had returned to the United States for an operation about 1907; Cassidy and the Sundance Kid went back to their outlaw ways, only to be killed in a gun battle with Bolivian military forces at San Vicente. That became the accepted conclusion.

Charles Kelly followed Chapman's version in *The Outlaw Trail*, a privately printed history of the Wild Bunch in 1938. He left a very favorable and enduring image of Butch. Chapman found that unlike the "mad dogs in human form," such as Jesse James, Harry Tracey, Cole Younger, and John Dillinger, Cassidy was a cheerful adventurer seeking excitement, demonstrating fair play, making many friends and few enemies, and performing many generous acts: "By ancestry he was as English as Robin Hood; by environment a typical American cowboy."[20]

George D. Hendricks apparently was next to determine that the fugitives deserved a more colorful death than a simple gunfight with authorities. With no clear basis, a murder and suicide became the consequences of an attack by soldiers: "They killed Longabaugh in his sleep, but Butch fought a day-long battle like a wildcat from a rocky corral. With his last bullet he shot his brains out with his unnotched gun, as the soldados made a rush at his shelter."[21]

Raconteur Seibert then reappeared, providing additional details for the benefit of writer James D. Horan. With a barrage of popular, entertaining, and less than entirely reliable books, he re-created the images of Butch, Sundance, and Etta in South America. These began in 1949 with *Desperate Men* (greatly enlarged in 1962) and continued with *Pictorial History of the Wild West* in 1954, *The Wild Bunch* in 1958, and *The Outlaws* in 1977. Along the way he made numerous assumptions and some corrections. One apparently minor error turned into an institution. In *Desperate Men,* "Butch Cassidy, the most wanted outlaw in America [*sic*], rode a bicycle up and down outside the cribs while the girls [of Fannie Porter's Sporting House] leaned from windows shrilling their encouragement."[22] Horan subsequently volunteered his mistake: the exhibitionist had actually been another member of the Wild Bunch, Ben Kilpatrick.[23] By then it was too late. The American West had acquired a new icon, Butch Cassidy in a derby hat on a bicycle, giving a ride to a young lady who would never have glanced at Fannie Porter's bordello.

During all this development, the movies paid little attention to the trio of bandits. Butch Cassidy and the Sundance Kid first appeared separately as supporting characters in 1951.[24] They also surfaced in several short television documentaries. In 1969, however, Hollywood's failure to recognize this particular story's potential came to a dramatic end. William Goldman wrote a screenplay masterpiece, obviously based on Horan-Kelly-Chapman-Seibert ancestry, which became the most popular western film ever made: *Butch Cassidy and the Sundance Kid* (1969).

In 112 minutes that motion picture projected three once lesser fugitives into the American outlaw firmament. With Paul Newman, Robert Redford, and Katharine Ross as Butch, Sundance, and Etta, the world fell under a magic spell of bandits so ingratiating as to dispel any fear or reservation. The film abounded with distinguishing touches, with dazzling montage effects combined with delightful musical interludes. In perhaps the most memorable of these, audiences know that it is really Katharine Ross (in negligee) riding on Paul Newman's bicycle, rather than Butch and Etta, cavorting to "Raindrops Keep Fallin' on My Head." It does not matter, for we have been transported through time and space to something beyond reality.

Originally, *Butch Cassidy and the Sundance Kid* included a key scene, filmed but edited out in the interests of time, which illustrated something of that magic. It has its own odd heritage. The aging Percy Seibert had recalled seeing a silent film on the Wild Bunch (no record of such exists) in New York just before going to Bolivia.[25] William Goldman's screenplay transported the antique movie to South America and created a sequence in which an amazed Butch and Sundance watch themselves killed while Etta walks away from the theater on her way back to the United States.[26] As originally written, it brought back an incisive comment she had made to the bandits earlier in the film: "I'm twenty-six, and I'm single, and I teach school, and that's the bottom of the pit. And the only excitement I've ever known is sitting in the room with me now. . . . [E]verything you ask of me I'll do, except one thing: I won't watch you die."[27]

The movie within a movie was salvaged and used as a prologue. *Butch Cassidy and the Sundance Kid* concluded with a famous frozen image of the outlaws in a hopeless charge against Bolivian soldiers, adhering generally to the accepted story of their dramatic demise. There is, however, no convincing evidence that such an event actually transpired: "The shooting at San Vicente was investigated by the late [Bolivian] President Rene Barrientos. . . . He put a team on to solving the mystery, grilled the villagers personally, exhumed corpses in the cemetery, checked the army and police files, and concluded that the whole thing was a fabrication."[28] Barrientos was probably correct. The climatic battle reportedly occurred not only in Bolivia, but Uruguay, Argentina, and Chile as well, and at a variety of times extending from 1908 to 1911.

Such confusion naturally contributed to a wealth of rumors

concerning the survival of one or both of the bandits. It was an old tradition of outlaw folklore occupying "the credibility gap between official governmental pronouncements and possible reality."[29] Many authors accept the suggestion that the Sundance Kid brought Etta Place back to Colorado for medical treatment and returned to face death with Butch in South America. When she recovered, she checked herself out of the hospital and vanished. Some Texans believe she went to Fort Worth under the name Eunice Gray, where she ran the Waco Hotel for decades, dying in a fire in 1962. When Leonard Sanders noted the story in a review of *Butch Cassidy and the Sundance Kid* for the Fort Worth *Star-Telegram,* an odd event transpired. The journalist had a visit from a Pinkerton detective who wanted to verify the facts. When asked the reason for the inquiry, the agent replied simply, "The file has never been closed on Etta Place."[30]

One of the strongest cases for outlaw survival is that of Robert LeRoy Parker's reincarnation as William Phillips of Spokane, Washington. If so, Butch lived until 1937. Larry Pointer's exhaustive inquiry *In Search of Butch Cassidy* includes much evidence for such a conclusion.[31] However, the outlaw's sister, Lula Parker Betenson, provided a different version. She insisted that Butch returned to his family in 1925, but not as William Phillips, while Etta Place and the Sundance Kid escaped to a happy life in Mexico City.[32] Yet another local variation has the latter returning to Wyoming, where he died in 1957. But as William Goldman indicated, the truth now matters little. On screens throughout the world, close to a *billion* people have seen *Butch Cassidy and the Sundance Kid;* they know the bandits simply stopped in a blaze of gunfire, forever bonded within a single, gilded, imploding moment.

The pattern of development for these particular outlaw figures is unusual only in having been compressed within a fairly short and recent period. Nevertheless, it should be clear that many people contributed to the myth, with the established facts ever diminishing in significance. No one probably meant to lie deliberately about what may have occurred, but many added colorful touches in order to add appeal. Over the years, fiction became accepted first as legend, then as reality. Precisely the same may be said of almost any notable outlaw from any land.

Butch Cassidy and the Sundance Kid brought the western into the twentieth century in a conceptual as well as a temporal way. It marked an end to the long celebration of frontier innocence. Butch and Sundance, through Newman and Redford, attracted audiences with personal magnetism; they were obviously criminals by choice, although more mischievous than malicious. Future portrayals of western desperadoes could not duplicate such seduction. They relied instead on something quite different. Violence and depravity emerged as new hallmarks. *The Great Northfield Minnesota Raid* (1972) even gave a vicious twist to the ancient tale of the bandit and the widow. The degenerate Jesse James (Robert Duvall) not only murders the landlord but frames the poor woman!

Presaged by the spaghetti westerns of Sergio Leone, the trend was toward grim reality, vengeance, and despair. *The Wild Bunch* (1969) put the bandits in the harsh, hot light of a new day. Not based on the actual Wild Bunch of the northern Rockies, it dealt with a gang of robbers on the Texas border in 1914 and achieved an almost lyric romanticism amid extreme violence. Director Sam Peckinpah thus began a remarkable succession of motion pictures with outlaw themes in different eras, including *The Getaway* (1972), *Pat Garrett and Billy the Kid* (1973), *Bring Me the Head of Alfredo Garcia* (1974), *Killer Elite* (1975), and *Convoy* (1978). In most of these he featured highly individualistic characters, emotionally and spiritually crippled, fighting nearly hopeless battles against outside forces.[33]

Westerns tended to become studies in melancholy and moral ambiguity, with "emphasis not upon victory and success but upon losing—the suggestion that to remain true to oneself will almost invariably result in defeat."[34] In an ineffective society, heroes were professional fighters whose deep sense of loyalty to a bloody vocation and each other usually led to multiple deaths, including their own.[35] John Cawelti detected in recent westerns themes of human depravity, corruption, fantasies of vengeance, disbelief in agencies of justice, and "the view that violence has been the underlying force in the development of American society."[36]

The frontier desperado naturally played a role in these scenarios. On occasion, his myth received remarkable insight. Such was the case *From Noon til Three* (1976), an obscure film written and directed by Frank Gilroy and starring Charles Bronson and Jill Ireland. A slow and unusual tragicomedy, it related the consequence of a brief dalliance between an outlaw and a wealthy widow which grew into a false legend which eventually destroyed them both. The story began with a dream and concluded with a nightmare: she commits suicide and he is trapped in a mental institution.

As has been true for more than a century, the western could do many things. The general decline in popularity of the motion-picture genre did not prevent serious efforts to reach younger audiences. Financial rewards even came to *Young Guns* (1988), a loathsome film in which Billy the Kid's gang, apparently having inexhaustible supplies of ammunition, slaughters numbers beyond counting.

There were other rockabilly efforts to transport the western into formats acceptable to a modern generation. An obvious example came in the form of the short-lived television series "Outlaws." Whatever the intended merits, it revealed something about perceptions of past and present. A thunderbolt transported the outlaws from the frontier to contemporary urban America, where they found society apparently so corrupt and crime ridden that their code of honor required them to fight modern evil. According to national advertising: "Time was, you fought for what you believed in. Five men have come from that time. And they're bringing justice to today's city streets. Outlaws."[37]

During their brief season they may have crossed paths with a somewhat similar contemporary though ancient (and far more successful) gang of television fugitives, "The A Team." They were, quite simply, transplanted from the dens of Sherwood Forest to the streets of Los Angeles with scarcely a change of character. This falsely accused special-forces unit used assault rifles instead of longbows, but it still helped the poor and mistreated.

With Hannibal as Robin Hood, B.A. as Little John, Mad Murdock as Friar Tuck, Colonel Decker as the sheriff of Nottingham, and (in the first season) Amy Allen as Maid Marian, they became symbols of yet another outlaw age.

Television's more serious outlaws tended to be lost in a sea of detectives, private and public.[38] But there was a gradual trend toward presenting selected organized criminals as figures of incredible power and stature. Leaders of mobs with fascinating characters attained almost heroic proportions, particularly when contrasted with ineffective and unethical systems of government. New mythic criminals personified American ethics of individualism and ambition while creating alternate systems of corruption rivaling or even superior to those of accepted legality.

The appeal of such disreputable mobsters represents a deepening suspicion that modern society has failed to fulfill its needs.[39] Through the screen, we avoid facing our denied despair: "The use of crime . . . enables the public to give some expression to its latent hostility and frustration while still maintaining . . . conventional morality . . . but the facade of morality and legality often appears to be so shaky and rotten that one becomes . . . aware . . . that America is a society of criminals."[40] Amid general corruption, greed, and hypocrisy, the outlaw looms as a final representative of common sense and justice.

This dark vision runs throughout what Stuart Kaminsky called the white-hot films of the 1970s. After abandonment of the formal production code, these bloody, starkly lighted motion pictures depicted the imperfect "explosive individual—the alienated American conformist," who defines himself by welcoming violence, denying sex, and going beyond the law "as the only salvation for society, the last hope in the face of a creeping chaos."[41]

Every major male motion-picture star of recent years has portrayed such characters and established them as American institutions. Two leading examples are Clint Eastwood and Charles Bronson. While lacking reputations as serious actors, they certainly succeeded at levels of commercial success and almost subconscious reality. How many critics would care to fight a duel with the created images of Clint Eastwood or Charles Bronson? Their mere appearance, in apparent anger, would cause most reviewers to flee in understandable terror.

In westerns, Eastwood almost invariably appeared as some kind of desperado. In contemporary settings, he is closely identified with one of the most significant characters in motion picture history, Inspector Harry Callahan, known throughout the world as *Dirty Harry* (1971). As such, Eastwood becomes society's avenging outlaw imported from the frontier, provided with a badge of convenience and routinely operating out of any agency's control.

Charles Bronson's most enduring (if not endearing) portrayal has even clearer and darker significance: Paul Kersey is urban America's darker version of a frontier vigilante, an architect driven to homicide by the violence which follows him from coast to coast and back again. *Death Wish* (1974) and its profitable, clocklike numbered sequels should dispel any doubts about perceptions of true values.

The basis for and influence of these great commercial successes cannot be denied. They represent the degree to which the motion picture has replaced literature in the creation of myth. Clint Eastwood's Harry and Charles Bronson's Kersey are immediately recognized figures on every continent on earth. How many people know who wrote the original stories for *Dirty Harry* (husband and wife Harry and R. M. Fink) or *Death Wish* (Brian Garfield, who sued for distortion of his novel)? In all the world only a few thousand people have actually read those works, but hundreds of millions have a fundamental faith that Dirty Harry is, at this moment, cruising the picturesque streets of San Francisco while the fearsome Kersey rides the dreaded subways of New York City.

As has been true for generations, there are serious questions about the possible consequences of these depictions of crime and violence. Little doubt of some effect exists, but its nature and degree remain elusive. Cathartic impact on viewers may equal or surpass possible harm. Of course, certain depictions may trigger unpredictable responses among the predisposed and emotionally unstable. These may also result from the antics of cartoon figures as easily as the deeds of Harry or Kersey. Moreover, the carnage of any war documentary may easily surpass the pasteurized violence of the most graphic of outlaw movies.

There was another message in later films about contemporary fugitives. Rather than appearing as simply ineffective, government emerged as a dominant force of actual evil. This fit the outlaw theme quite well, of course, but such diverse movies as *Three Days of the Condor* (1975), *First Blood* (1982), and *F/X* (1985) may also be viewed as containing a hidden political message. Rather than robbers or gangsters, the enemy now had a badge. He could even be successfully ridiculed, as *Smokey and the Bandit* (1977) hilariously proved.

Whatever their psychological consequences, white-hot films did correspond to renewed interest in actual fugitives. They extended over a wide spectrum and represented a variety of motives. In 1971 the nation gained a completely new kind of fugitive hero as daring and imaginative as any in fiction. In November a "cool, middle-aged man in a business suit" on a Northwest Airlines flight hijacked the first plane for ransom. He demanded and received two hundred thousand dollars and then, somewhere between Reno, Nevada, and Seattle, Washington, parachuted into immortality.[42] He is known to this day only by the alias used for ticketing, D. B. Cooper. Apart from some bills, possibly planted later to mislead persistent pursuers, no trace of the robber has ever been found.[43]

Gene Leroy Hart brought outlawry back to Oklahoma's Cookson Hills. A Cherokee hunted for the 1977 sexual assault and murder of three Girl Scouts, he had previously escaped from a 140-year sentence for rape and kidnapping. For ten months, Hart, certainly helped by some local people, remained a fugitive. Finally captured and tried, he was acquitted. The prosecution relied on obviously falsified evidence. Hart died in prison, supposedly of a heart attack, in 1979.[44] Outlawry remains a subject open to personal interpretation in the Cookson Hills.

Claude Dallas probably came closest to the traditional concept of the American badman, however. He had been accused of killing two Idaho game wardens in 1981. After a lengthy manhunt in several states, Dallas was convicted of manslaughter on the basis of a limited right to self-defense. Shortly thereafter he broke out of prison.[45] His story then became the television movie *Manhunt for Claude Dallas* (1986), with prospective audiences advised to, "watch it, Claude Dallas will be. Still at large, some people want him to stay that way." He was, in fact, captured in southern California a few months later. An Idaho jury then had no problem *acquitting* him of the prison escape! People in the West still hold the right of self-defense in high regard.

For sixty-five days in 1968 the most wanted man in America and the world was James Earl Ray. Identified by the tracing of a Remington 30–06 rifle and fingerprints, he became the paramount suspect in the assassination of Martin Luther King, Jr. Ray apparently drove from Memphis to Atlanta, took a bus to Detroit, crossed into Canada by cab, and took a train to Toronto, all within two days. He later flew to London and was captured by alert British police on his way to Belgium. The Royal Canadian Mounted Police had traced his passport through the examination and tedious comparison of 230,000 photographs.[46] Ray plead guilty and received a ninety-nine-year sentence. He soon denied his involvement, however, implicating a mysterious man named Raoul. Much about the case and its investigation raises doubts, not necessarily about Ray's conduct, but about the improbability of his acting alone. With the passage of time, "80% of Americans have joined Coretta King and Ralph Abernathy and Jesse Jackson in thinking King fell to a conspiracy."[47]

The foremost fugitive in recent decades was someone *really* unusual: a kidnapped heiress. For nineteen months Patty Hearst remained missing despite massive investigative effort. Seized and brutalized by the Symbionese Liberation Army in 1974, she eventually joined the radical band. After being photographed and recognized in a bank robbery, official attitudes toward Patty Hearst, alias Tania, underwent a complete reversal.[48] In her own words: "Once I had been a kidnap victim, but now I was a hunted criminal."[49] After traveling throughout the country, she

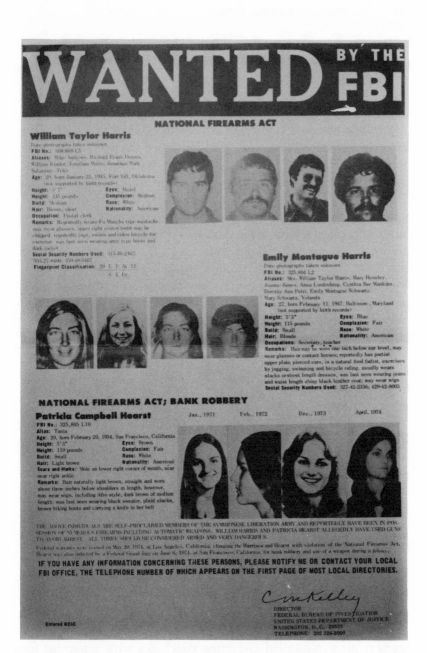

"Urban guerrillas" from 1974 (William and Emily Harris, Patty Hearst). (FBI)

was finally captured (or rescued) in 1975. A controversial trial concluded with a sentence of seven years; President Jimmy Carter granted clemency after twenty-eight months. Patty Hearst then resumed the life from which she had been so abruptly taken and forced to reject.

Exploits of noted fugitives, at least in popular portrayal, had little in common with the mass of lesser outlaws, and these existed in great abundance. It may seem that the era of the desperado has ended, but nothing could be further from the truth. There are, in fact, more outlaws among us than ever before, and they come in a multitude of varieties. Every month, many thousands of accused felons released on bail do not appear for trial and become fugitives. Numerous others are identified and made the subject of arrest warrants but never placed in custody. The nation contains more than two million convicted felons on probation or parole; approximately 1 percent of these abscond every year. The proportion may be small, but the total number could populate a city annually.

Close to ten thousand inmates escape from prison each year in the United States. Most are back in custody within twelve months, but many evade capture indefinitely.[50] A few of the more notorious contemporary outlaws are placed on the FBI's "Ten Most Wanted Fugitives" list. Started in 1950, the list's history indicates that the average time for apprehension is about five months, but significant numbers of the wanted manage to make their flight permanent.[51]

In 1967 the Federal Bureau of Investigation inaugurated its National Crime Information Center, which quickly grew to a vast computer network containing millions of active records. A primary component consists of hundreds of thousands of files on currently wanted persons, but even this does not provide a complete picture. The United States had approximately one hundred thousand draft evaders, deserters, and personnel absent without official leave during the Vietnam War; decades later, many still remain at large. About one in every three court orders for child support goes unfulfilled and often concludes with a warrant for arrest. Perhaps one thousand inmates escape from jail each month. And one should not forget the millions of illegal aliens now in the United States.

A total of all those currently sought by authorities would populate several states. Anyone thinking America enjoys a shortage of modern outlaws is quite mistaken. Walk down any busy street in a poor section of any large city and several can be seen. Inquiries, however, are not advised. The great American outlaw may be largely a product of fiction, but he is also a present and tangible factor of reality. Loss of innocence represents more than a concept; it has become our way of life.

Epilogue

That's the way it really happened. . . . Give or take a lie or two.

—*SUNSET* (1988)

THE great American outlaw is a legendary figure shrouded in myth. His stories are legends passed from generation to generation, retold as truth, and reflecting people's needs and hopes. These tales have suppressed meanings and long-forgotten origins. Of course the pattern is not unique to the United States; every culture includes countless assertions, endlessly recounted until they become accepted versions of reality, which are actually constructions of miscommunication. Myths may thus emerge as substantive parts of social history capable of influencing present concepts and courses of action, with consequences both good and bad.

Throughout the world, outlaw tales are most suitable to this process, since the lives of fugitives abound with gaps and confusion. Imaginative contributions or bits taken from other stories may then conveniently complete a desired picture. Contradictions and even easily detected errors can coexist with a few leading facts. When compounded by popular novels and motion pictures, these legends may be further transformed into cultural institutions.

In typical form, the outlaw's tale fits into a mythic formula: a hero answers a call to adventure and crosses into a world of mystery and darkness. He travels a road of trials, frequently including temptation or betrayal by a woman, but may nevertheless

324

win a decisive victory. The hero can then rejoin ordinary society as a master of two worlds.[1]

The fundamental plot has countless variations determined by heritage, happenstance, and design. Outlaws probably reflect another ancient mythic pattern, one that is particularly significant in America. The desperado is usually a variation of the violent hunter-herdsman (cowboy) image rather than that of the passive gatherer-farmer. From a psychological viewpoint, the outlaw is an expression of masculine violence, resisting the nurturing, restrictive, feminine culture. He is an independent killer, not a communal grower. When the bandit becomes the hunted, he reflects characteristics long associated with the frontier and American literary tradition.[2]

Fascination with outlaws has baffled investigators of many lands: "Why has the criminal held such an important place in the hearts of . . . peaceful and law-abiding citizens throughout the ages? Is it an expression of man's original sin, or some basic instinct toward destruction, or the result of an innate aggressiveness?"[3] Paul F. Angiolillo suggests that answers lie in three intrinsic human emotions: a subconscious yearning for escape from the constraints of civilization, a natural admiration for deeds of heroism, and a wish for fair treatment and simple justice.[4]

History need not record robbers dedicated to helping the poor, correcting wrongs, challenging the rich and powerful, or displaying extraordinary bravery; "Robin Hood . . . is invented even when he does not really exist."[5] "One might choose to see in the heart of the occasional exceptionally strong-willed leader (or rebel) the imperious compulsion to make ordinary people's lives a little better and a little happier."[6]

Anyone who attempts to dispel such concepts acts in peril. For example, in 1988 England's Nottingham tourist office prepared a modest brochure containing facts about "the real Robin Hood." A storm of protest erupted. British newspapers denounced the little publication; local residents, some claiming outlaw ancestry, demanded retraction; the modern sheriff of Nottingham expressed a desire to throw the blasphemers in the dungeon.

Within weeks the city issued an acceptable substitute citing a simple and indisputable fact: "It's a question of public demand."[7] As with the frontier, "in the long run it is the legend that wins."[8]

In the beginning it may be purposefully created. As a journalist reporting on Wyoming's Tom Horn, hanged for murder in 1903, advised: "In case a crime has been committed which incenses the public mind, if the accused is able to divide the public sentiment, then take the sympathetic side of the case; but if the accused has few or no friends, then jump onto him with both feet and stamp him out of existence, for in so doing you will satisfy the mind of the public and close the incident."[9]

For generations stories associated with American outlaws resulted from conscious journalistic efforts. Writers of fictional-fact selected anecdotes and adopted views intended to promote images of sympathy and daring. They frequently incorporated myths of ancient lineage to simplify their task and guarantee popularity for their descriptions.

As portrayed for centuries, certain outlaws opposed unfair authority. Forced to crime, romanticized fugitives enjoyed support from common people. They robbed the rich and helped the poor, killed only in self-defense or revenge, met defeat through betrayal, and violated the law to support a higher form of justice.[10] "Their actions are seen as a form of . . . rebellion within peasant societies, and the bandits are considered by their people as heroes, champions of liberty, avengers, . . . or, perhaps, even leaders of liberation."[11]

Logic seems to bind these themes, so appealing to universal dreams of freedom and fair treatment. J. C. Holt properly observed that "at the lowest social level, among the poor and unprotected, guilt and innocence are beyond true assessment."[12] Danilo Dolci, considering Italy's renowned outlaws, stated the case even more succinctly: "The hungry become bandits."[13] Maurice Keen wisely commented, "Robin Hood's place in the affection of the common man . . . is the indictment of the . . . social system."[14] Such truths apparently apply with similar effect throughout the world.

Numerous American outlaws, particularly those of the West, are routinely regarded as social bandits aided by ordinary citizens. Their number includes Billy the Kid, the James-Younger gang, the Daltons, Bill Doolin, Sam Bass, and others.[15] Through folklore, written and oral, these desperadoes received heroic stature as outcasts forced to fight against powerful enemies; they distributed wealth among the needy and found defeat through vile treachery.[16] "The folk mind . . . liked to believe they were inspired by a noble rage against economic inequalities."[17]

Popular myth supports the image of bandits representing disadvantaged elements of society in the United States. Its frontier offered ample violence and disorder as a background. Opportunity for crime and exploitation by special interests enriched the myth that outlaws had valid reasons for their offenses. Nevertheless, prominent badmen took rather than gave, killed without cause, and seldom sought anything resembling justice.[18] Characteristics once routinely associated with English highwaymen rarely appeared outside imagination; the romanticized frontier desperado emerged as a popular creation rather than a figure of fact. But the myth could no longer be divorced from reality.[19] As Kent Ladd Steckmesser has written: "The historical situations recede, and we then know the outlaw only through folkloric statements . . . outlaws of history . . . are not out for social justice, but for a fast buck."[20]

Frank and Jesse James enjoyed a degree of local sympathy in their early criminal careers, but they then had to move hundreds of miles away to live under assumed names. Billy the Kid was a hired gun of minor note involved in a range war between rival cattle interests. The Daltons were local bank robbers destroyed by their own neighbors. In America, "the bandit converted to social radicalism . . . made the transition in jail."[21] Badmen were greedy, violent brigands transformed into heroes after death by journalists fulfilling roles once occupied by minstrels and balladeers.

The myth itself, however, has its own considerable significance and enjoys ignored manifestations. American history does contain noted fugitives from oppression, representative of continuing quests for justice. They include Indians, members of some ethnic minorities, anarchists, blacks, unionists, and followers of suspect religions. Recognition of these renegades nevertheless falls outside the scope of most investigations of American banditry.[22] The United States must appear as a land of life, liberty, and relentless pursuit of happiness rather than slavery, genocide, class warfare, and religious intolerance. Famous American fugitives remain criminals rather than revolutionaries; legends form their own myths.

Fabled outlaws of the frontier continue to attract an odd assortment of literary efforts. Perhaps in emulation of Stephen Vincent Benét's *John Brown's Body,* Charles Boer produced an epic poem *(Varmint Q)* on the life of William Clarke Quantrill. Will Henry attempted to lay Jesse James once more in his grave with *Death of a Legend.* Interest increased notably in regard to New Mexico's celebrated desperado. Novelist Larry McMurtry did *Anything for Billy,* preceded by Michael Ondaatje's bizarre "autobiographical" *Collected Works of Billy the Kid.*

For generations writers of widely diverse skill have perpetuated and embellished myths surrounding desperadoes. As Eric Hobsbawm noted, "one might say that the intellectuals have ensured the survival of the bandits."[23] Veneers of fiction placed on a core of fact are not unusual; the process has been common through centuries of outlaw lore. In typical fashion, "it is the legend and not the history which has gripped the American imagination."[24] There are, however, recognizable changes in the perceived targets for brigandage.

Within the last century, renowned American outlaws have had their sights altered. Instead of simply seeking redress against the wealthy and powerful, they began appearing as victims of a corrupt system or of the government itself. Society could thus become the portrayed cause, as well as the target, of banditry. In such instances the fugitive might reflect enduring themes of innocence, corruption, and violence in the American national character.[25]

United States desperadoes share much in common with their

colleagues from other nations, with myths easily modified to span cultural and geographic borders. Still, depictions of American outlaws tend to include characteristics associated with self-reliance, strength in a society grown weak, and personal courage surpassing common sense.[26] Maintenance of domestic popularity naturally demands avoidance of needlessly bloodthirsty, evil, or perverse traits. There are, moreover, a number of specific themes in portrayals of notable American outlaws during recent decades. Personal victims of those in power and authority, these desperadoes have no significant political or social motivation; their goals are openly mercenary or concerned with revenge. They kill frequently, efficiently, and without a tinge of remorse. Mature white males, they manifest little interest in women or remain faithful to only one. They are not particularly well educated or good humored, but they have mastered their native environment, be it city or wilderness. They stand alone or with one close companion who probably dies. They are smart and loyal to their personal code of honor, which may contrast sharply with that of organized society. They demonstrate incredible skill with handguns, kindness to animals, and occasional success in almost hopeless individual struggles.

Such apparently driven, destructive, and ultimately doomed men are hallmarks of our culture. Their image is, of course, unrealistic and an example of rampant stereotyping. Recent portrayals, while certainly more graphic, remain as inaccurate as those of past centuries. These frightening yet reassuring mythic figures are their own commentary on American culture.

Despite a dubious basis, desperadoes are also enduring icons of the frontier. Modern urban outlaws often are compared with bandits of the Old West and medieval England.[27] Like brigands of the past, they are commonly perceived as products of a frontier heritage, denounced for acts against public safety but still admired as daring adventurers.

It is unlikely that the West produced far more criminal fugitives than other regions of the country or that the generation following the Civil War had significantly more of them than those

Claude Dallas in a detail of the Idaho wanted
poster, 1981. (Owyhee County Sheriff's Office, Murphy, Idaho)

which followed. Still, the time and place most closely associated
with the American outlaw remains that of the fading frontier.[28]
Jesse James and Billy the Kid are not rivaled in fame, even by
Blackbeard and Dillinger.

The unique status of the frontier bandit can scarcely be denied.
It probably delayed statehood for several territories; New Mexicans had to embark on a campaign to erase their badman image
in 1911.[29] This continuing significance contributed to—if it
did not cause—the attention devoted in the 1980s to Claude
Dallas, wanted for killing two Idaho game wardens, offenses
which would seem unlikely to elicit much sympathy in a time of
supposed support for law enforcement and environmental protection. T-shirts inscribed "Go Claude Go" proclaimed his importance while indirectly expressing lasting values.[30]

He was proof that the obsolete West was alive and vital. . . . People gave him money and food; they sheltered him, loaned him their trucks, celebrated his deed. Many who frowned on the murders, celebrated just the same, preferring to see (or hear of) him free. He was a benign spirit, the star-crossed picture book outlaw.[31]

The closing of the traditional frontier did not, either in fact or in illusion, mean an end for the fabled American bandit. He simply moved to the city to find continuing lawlessness and violence.[32] The urban setting provided changing opportunities for crime and for escape. The American city at night was the outlaw's new frontier.[33]

"There still exists in many people a sympathy and vicarious identification with the man with a gun,"[34] Joseph G. Rosa tells us. As a logical consequence, America's outlaws have become part of a cult of violence, the roots and results of which continue to defy comprehensive and practical analysis.[35] Their weapons are mythic symbols, capable of lending hints of character and morality while blurring the border separating villain and hero.[36]

In fact, a relationship between improved armament and outlaw popularity may exist. Eras noted for exploits of famous bandits correspond closely to periods when significant advances in weaponry began reaching ordinary people. English yeomen skilled as archers could drop a mounted knight, ending the nobility's obvious military advantage; Robin Hood appeared in the haunts of Sherwood. A few centuries later, Mediterranean sailors took small, maneuverable, two-masted ships (brigantines), heavily armed them with cannons, and began capturing enormous, slow merchantmen; the golden age of piracy had arrived (and *brig* became a nautical term for jail).

The reliable flintlock pistol crept into popular use after 1700; highwaymen armed with a pair were able to rob stagecoach passengers at will. In the next century Samuel Colt developed a powerful and dependable revolver; America's cowboy bandits became the equals of large numbers of victims and pursuers. After World War I, automatic weapons could be acquired with relative

"UNABOM"

VICAP (Violent Criminal Apprehension Program) Alert for a suspect wanted for a decade of
bombings in six states, 1987. (FBI)

ease; city gangsters armed themselves with submachine guns to
instill fear among train and bank guards.

Whether these parallels are the products of writers or actors,
fascination with the armed criminal endures. They produced
more folk ballads in America than any other subject.[37] "Unsolved
Mysteries" and "America's Most Wanted" revealed continuing

interest on television. A dark remaining issue is one of causation, or the degree to which real "outlaws might model their actions on legend."[38] The question goes beyond obvious attempts of disturbed individuals to copy exploits of particular noted fugitives; it involves possible contributions to subjective feelings of injustice, as well as perceptions of widespread social inequality.[39]

The fascinations of crime might, with different immediate consequences, apply to both offenders and observers. Constant depictions of American outlaws, far removed from reality and garbed in sympathetic legend, may create a subconscious foundation for violence and disorder of greater significance than indicated by studies of direct causation and effect. The allure of crime could well occur through a mirror, reflecting aspects of ourselves most do not wish to confront directly.[40] Representations may eventually conclude with manifestations of quite another variety. If others fall under a spell of myth, we can become their victims.

Results of this nature might be long delayed while images undergo constant alteration. Each generation views outlaws differently; the desperado's essential story goes on.[41] Blackbeard, Jesse and Frank, Billy, Butch and Sundance, Belle, Pretty Boy, Baby Face, Bonnie and Clyde—they are part of America's heritage. Outlaws of tomorrow will not be the same; they may not even observe national boundaries.

In recent years fugitives receiving the most publicity are truly of world note. They include many mysterious figures: Dr. Josef Mengele, the Nazi "Angel of Death," believed to have died in Brazil in 1979; Licio Gelli, alleged chief of Italy's mysterious P-2 Masonic lodge, who vanished from a Swiss prison in 1983; Robert ("Big Bobby") Vesco, a financier who defrauded international investors of some $250 million and escaped to the Caribbean on a yacht; and the most wanted man on earth, professional terrorist Ilich Ramirez Sanchez, alias Carlos, who kidnapped an entire congress of oil ministers from Vienna in 1975. These world outlaws are already subjects for new legends which dwarf those of ordinary national fugitives. However, it seems more likely that the brigand of old has already departed from the present; he is working in the future. Imaginary outlaws have found a refuge in the realms of science fiction, with most of their ancient traits still intact.

The heroic transgressor is scarcely new, even to this field. He was present at its very beginning in the form of the famous Captain Nemo (nobody), the enigmatic, marauding commander of the submarine *Nautilus* in Jules Verne's 1869 classic *20,000 Leagues Under the Sea*. Outlaws proved well suited to the literature of respected science fiction in such works as Aldous Huxley's *Brave New World* in 1932, Robert Heinlein's *They* in 1941, George Orwell's *1984* in 1949, Ray Bradbury's *Fahrenheit 451* in 1953, and Anthony Burgess's *A Clockwork Orange* in 1962.[42]

Imagination allows the fugitive to leap into space or the future with the greatest of ease. As an alien or a robot or the typical victim of injustice, outlaws thrived in science-fiction films. They appeared in quite different versions in such motion pictures as *The Day the Earth Stood Still* (1951), *Sleeper* (1973), and *The Terminator* (1984). These fantasy outlaws covered an incredible range. Mel Gibson's *Road Warrior* (1981) confronted an image of future society so degenerate that only an outcast from the wasteland retained elements of honor and valor. But the most memorable fugitive came from another world in a very different and uniquely endearing form: *E.T.* (1982).

The beloved extraterrestrial was neither an American nor an outlaw, of course, but his treatment as such nevertheless fit the classic mold and transformed the little visitor into a subject for limitless appeal. In every culture adoration of the fugitive is the consequence of perceived injustice. When those in authority increase their ability to deal with offenders, the latter only gain in public appeal. Efforts to crush them endanger the freedoms which facilitated their appearance. Even when desperadoes pose obvious but distant threats to personal safety and private property, they may enjoy a unique status resembling that of heroes. These avaricious, dishonest, violent, and deceitful dead (or vanished) underdogs receive popular nicknames with, in fiction if not in fact, reputations for generosity and service to the defenseless.[43]

Americans show little respect for great wealth and power.

Many still admire the few willing to fight, however hopelessly, against exhibitions of privilege. The outlaw's appeal, whether on the frontier or in a modern city, constitutes a hidden warning to those in authority. Fascination with fugitives cannot be divorced from dreams of suppressed liberty.[44] Endurance of that vision may ensure survival for the great American outlaw as it has for bandits from distant lands and long ago.

Appendix: The Ballads

QUANTRELL

Come all you bold robbers and open your ears;
Of Quantrell the lion heart you quickly shall hear.
With his band of bold raiders in double-quick time,
He came to lay Lawrence low, over the line.

All routing and shouting and giving yell,
Like so many demons just raised up from hell,
The boys they were drunken with powder and wine.
And came to burn Lawrence, just over the line.

They came to burn Lawrence; they came not to stay.
They rode in one morning at breaking of day
With guns all a-waving and horses all foam,
And Quantrell a-riding his famous big roan.

Oh, Quantrell's a fighter, a bold-hearted boy:
A brave man or woman he'd never annoy.
He'd take from the wealthy and give to the poor,
For brave men there's never a bolt to his door.

TOM DOOLEY

I met her on the mountain
And there I took her life;
I met her on the mountain
And stabbed her with my knife.

336

This time tomorrow,
Reckon where I'll be?—
If it hadn'-a been for Grayson
I'd-a been in Tennessee.

This time tomorrow,
Reckon where I'll be?—
Down in a lonesome valley
Hanging on a white oak tree.

Hang down your head, Tom Dooley,
Hang down your head and cry,
Hang down your head, Tom Dooley,
Poor boy, you're bound to die.

JESSE JAMES

It was on a Wednesday night, the moon was shining bright,
   They robbed the Glendale train.
And the people they did say, for many miles away,
   'Twas the outlaws Frank and Jesse James.

Jesse had a wife to mourn all her life,
   The children they are brave.
But that dirty little coward shot Mister Howard,
   And laid Jesse James in his grave.

It was Robert Ford, the dirty little coward,
   I wonder how he does feel,
For he ate of Jesse's bread and he slept in Jesse's bed,
   Then he laid Jesse James in his grave.

Jesse was a man, a friend to the poor,
   He'd never see a man suffer pain,
And with his brother Frank he robbed the Chicago bank,
   And stopped the Glendale train.

It was his brother Frank that robbed the Gallatin bank,
   And carried the money from the town.

It was in this very place that they had a little race,
  For they shot Captain Sheets to the ground.

They went to the crossing not very far from there,
  And there they did the same;
And the agent on his knees he delivered up the keys
  To the outlaws Frank and Jesse James.

It was on a Saturday night, Jesse was at home
  Talking to his family brave,
When the thief and the coward, little Robert Ford,
  Laid Jesse James in this grave.

How people held their breath when they heard of Jesse's death,
  And wondered how he ever came to die.
'Twas one of the gang, dirty Robert Ford,
  That shot Jesse James on the sly.

Jesse went to his rest with his hand on his breast.
  The devil will be upon his knee.
He was born one day in the county of Clay,
  And came from a solitary race.

This song was made by Bill Gashade,
  As soon as the news did arrive,
He said there was no man with the law in his hand
  Could take Jesse James when alive.

SAM BASS

Sam Bass was born in Indiana, it was his native home;
And at the age of seventeen young Sam began to roam.
Sam first came out to Texas, a cowboy for to be—
A kinder-hearted fellow you seldom ever see.

He made a deal in race-stock—one called the Denton mare.
He matched her in scrub races and took her to the fair.
Sam used to coin the money and spent it just as free;
He always drank good whiskey, wherever he might be.

Sam left the Collins ranch in the merry month of May
With a herd of Texas cattle, the Black Hills for to see.
Sold out at Custer City and then got on a spree—
A jollier set of cowboys you seldom ever see.

On their way back to Texas, they robbed the U. P. train,
And then split up in couples and started out again.
Joe Collins and his partner were overtaken soon;
With all their stolen money, they had to meet their doom.

Sam made it back to Texas, all right side up with care—
Rode into the town of Denton, with all his friends to share.
Sam's life was short in Texas—three robberies did he do;
He robbed all the passengers, mail and express cars too.

Sam had four companions, each a bold and daring lad—
Underwood and Jackson, Joe Collins and Old Dad.
Four of the boldest cowboys the ranges ever knew—
They whipped the Texas Rangers and ran the boys in blue.

Sam had another companion, called Arkansas for short;
He was shot by a Texas Ranger by the name of Thomas Floyd.
Tom is a big six-footer, and he thinks he's mighty sly.
But I can tell you his racket—he's a deadbeat on the sly.

Jim Murphy was arrested and then released on bail;
He jumped his bond at Tyler and took the train for Terrell.
But Major Jones had posted Jim and that was all a stall;
'Twas only a plan to capture Sam before the coming fall.

Sam met his fate at Round Rock, July the twenty-first;
They pierced poor Sam with rifle balls and emptied out his purse.
Poor Sam he is a corpse and six foot under clay;
And Jackson's in the bushes, trying to get away.

Jim had used Sam's money and didn't want to pay;
He thought his only chance was to give poor Sam away.
He sold out Sam and Barnes and left their friends to mourn—
Oh, what a scorching Jim will get when Gabriel blows his horn!

And so he sold out Sam and Barnes and left their friends to
mourn.

Oh, what a scorching Jim will get when Gabriel blows his horn!
Perhaps he's got to heaven, there's none of us can say;
But if I'm right in my surmise, he's gone the other way.

BILLY THE KID

I'll sing you a true song of Billy the Kid,
I'll sing of the desperate deeds that he did;
'Way out in New Mexico long, long ago,
When a man's only change was his old forty-four.

When Billy the Kid was a very young lad,
In old Silver City, he went to the bad;
Way out in the West with a gun in his hand,
At the age of twelve years he killed his first man.

Fair Mexican maidens play guitars and sing,
A song about Billy, their boy bandit king;
How, ere his young manhood had reached its sad end,
Had a notch on his pistol for twenty-one men.

'Twas on the same night that poor Billy died,
He said to his friends, "I'm not satisfied;
There are twenty-one men I've put bullets through,
And Sheriff Pat Garrett must make twenty-two."

Now this is how Billy the Kid met his fate,
The bright moon was shining, the hour was late;
Shot down by Pat Garrett who once was his friend,
The young outlaw's life had come to its end.

There's many a man with face fine and fair,
Who starts out in life with a chance to be square;
But just like poor Billy, he wanders astray,
And loses his life the very same way.

GREGORIO CORTEZ

In the county of El Carmen
Look what has happened;

The Major Sheriff has died,
Leaving Roman badly wounded.

The next day, in the morning,
When people arrived,
They said to one another,
"It is not known who killed him."

They went around asking questions,
About three hours afterward;
They found that the wrongdoer
Had been Gregorio Cortez.

Now they have outlawed Cortez,
Throughout the whole state;
Let him be taken, dead or alive;
He had killed several men.

Then said Gregorio Cortez,
With his pistol in his hand,
"I don't regret that I killed him;
I regret my brother's death."

Then said Gregorio Cortez,
And his soul was all aflame,
"I don't regret that I killed him;
A man must defend himself."

He struck out for Gonzales;
Several sheriffs saw him;
They decided not to follow
Because they were afraid of him.

The bloodhounds were coming,
They were coming on the trail,
But overtaking Cortez
Was like following a star.

Then said Gregorio Cortez,
"What is the use of your scheming?

You cannot catch me,
Even with those bloodhounds."

Then the Americans said,
"If we catch up with him, what shall we do?
If we fight him man to man,
Very few of us will return."

When the sheriffs arrive,
Gregorio gave himself up,
"You take me because I'm willing,
But not any other way."

Now they have taken Cortez,
Now matters are at an end;
His poor family
Are suffering in their hearts.

Now with this I say farewell,
In the shade of a cypress,
This is the end of the singing
Of the ballad about Cortez.

BONNIE AND CLYDE

You have heard the story of Jesse James,
Of how he lived and died.
If you still are in need
Of something to read,
Here is the story of Bonnie and Clyde.

Now Bonnie and Clyde are the Barrow gang.
I'm sure you all have read
How they rob and steal,
And how those who squeal,
Are usually found dying or dead.

There are lots of untruths to their write-ups,
They are not so merciless as that;

Their nature is raw;
They hate all the laws,
The stool pigeons, spotters and rats.

They class them as cold-blooded killers,
They say they are heartless and mean,
But I say with pride,
That I once knew Clyde
When he was honest and upright and clean.

But the law fooled around, kept tracking him down,
And locking him up in a cell,
Till he said to me,
"I will never be free,
"So I will meet a few of them in hell."

This road was so dimly lighted
There were no highway signs to guide,
But they made up their minds
If the roads were all blind
They wouldn't give up till they died.

The road gets dimmer and dimmer,
Sometimes you can hardly see,
Still it's fight, man to man,
And do all you can,
For they know they can never be free.

If they try to act like citizens,
And rent them a nice little flat,
About the third night,
They are invited to fight,
By a submachine gun rat-tat-rat.

If a policeman is killed in Dallas
And they have no clues to guide—
If they can't find a fiend,
They just wipe the slate clean,
And hang it on Bonnie and Clyde.

Two crimes have been done in America
Not accredited to the Barrow mob.
For they had no hand
In the kidnapping demand,
Or the Kansas City depot job.

A newsboy once said to his buddy;
"I wish old Clyde would get jumped;
"In these awful hard times,
"We'd make a few dimes
"If five or six cops would get bumped."

The police haven't got the report yet,
Clyde sent a wireless today
Saying, "We haven't a peace flag of white
"We stretch out at night,
"We have joined the NRA."

They don't think they're too tough or desperate,
They know the law always wins,
They have been shot at before,
But they do not ignore
That death is the wages of sin.

From heartbreaks some people have suffered,
From weariness some people have died,
But take it all in all,
Our troubles are small,
Till we get like Bonnie and Clyde.

Some day they will go down together,
And they will bury them side by side.
To a few it means grief,
To the law it's relief,
But it's death to Bonnie and Clyde.

Notes

CHAPTER 1. THE BANDIT

1. Carl Ludwig von Bar, *A History of Continental Criminal Law*, 62–66.
2. J. E. A. Jolliffe, *The Constitutional History of Medieval England*, 107–8.
3. Maurice Keen, *The Outlaws of Medieval Legend*, 10–13.
4. J. de Lange, *The Relation and Development of English and Icelandic Outlaw Traditions*, 127.
5. Case of Ralph Breton and Roger de Breteuil, 2 Ord. Vital. 262 (1075); The King v. Malet, 4 Ord. Vital. 6 (1102); The King v. Belisme, 4 Ord. Vital. 69 (1102).
6. Pipe Rolls, 7 Richard I (1196).
7. William Sharp McKechnie, *Magna Carta*, 384–85.
8. Pipe Rolls, 4 Henry III (1230).
9. William Vivian Butler, *The Durable Desperadoes*, 28.
10. J. C. Holt, *Robin Hood*, 159.
11. W. Carew Hazlitt, *Old English Plays*, 8:94–102.
12. Holt, *Robin Hood*, 42.
13. Anthony Wagner, *Heralds and Ancestors*, 42–43.
14. R. B. Dobson and J. Taylor, *Rymes of Robin Hood*, 59–60.
15. Kent L. Steckmesser, "Robin Hood and the American Outlaw," *Journal of American Folklore* 79 (April–June 1966): 349.
16. Evelyn Kendrick Wells, *The Ballad Tree*, 8.
17. Reginald Nettle, *Sing a Song of England*, 46.
18. W. E. Simeone, "Robin Hood and Some Other Outlaws," *Journal of American Folklore* 71 (January–March 1958): 32.
19. Holt, *Robin Hood*, 190.
20. Magna Carta, Clause 39 (Her Majesty's Stationery Office translation).
21. Henry de Bracton, *De Legibus et Consuetudinibus Angliae*, 353–78.
22. J. W. Jeudwine, *Tort, Crime and Police in Mediaeval England*, 39.
23. Edward James Watson, *Pleas of the Crown for Bristol: A.D. 1221*, 106.
24. Frederick Pollock and Frederic William Maitland, *The History of English Law*, 2:580–82.
25. W. S. Holdsworth, *A History of English Law*, 3:605.

26. John Milton Goodenow, *Historical Sketches of American Jurisprudence*, 116.

27. Keen, *The Outlaws of Medieval Legend*, 64–68.

28. John Bellamy, *Crime and Public Order in England in the Later Middle Ages*, 70–83.

29. Barbara A. Hanawalt, *Crime and Conflict in English Communities: 1300–1348*, 37, 201–16.

30. Civil Procedure Repeal Act, 42 & 43 Vict., c. 59, s. 3 (1879).

31. Bobby G. Deaver, "Outlawry," *North Carolina Law Review* 41 (Spring 1963): 639.

32. Pollock and Maitland, *The History of English Law*, 2:477–78.

33. Jeudwine, *Tort, Crime and Police in Mediaeval England*, 102–3.

34. Watson, *Pleas of the Crown for Bristol: A.D. 1221*, 109–10.

35. Proclamation 15, Ordering Keveston of Shropshire to Appear or Be Outlawed, 3 Henry VII (1478).

136. Ralph B. Pugh, "Early Registers of English Outlaws," *American Journal of Legal History* 27 (October 1983): 323–26.

CHAPTER 2. THE PIRATE

1. "Cinque Ports," Museum of Local History, Hastings, East Sussex, England.

2. "Smuggling," Museum of Local History, Hastings, East Sussex, England.

3. A. L. Lloyd, *Folk Song in England*, 275–76.

4. Neville Williams, *Captains Outrageous*, 78–80.

5. Anne Chambers, *Granuaile: The Life and Times of Grace O'Malley*, 127–52.

6. The Offences at Sea Act, 28 Henry VIII, c. 15 (1536).

7. United States v. Smith, 5 Wheat. (18 U.S.) 153, 181.

8. Alexander Winston, *No Man Knows My Grave*, 11–13.

9. George Wycherley, *Buccaneers of the Pacific*, 80–88.

10. C. H. Haring, *The Buccaneers in the West Indies in the XVII Century*, 66–79, 266–72.

11. E. O. Hoppe, *Pirates, Buccaneers, and Gentlemen Adventurers*, 38–39.

12. Alexander O. Exquemelin, *The Buccaneers of America*, 202.

13. Ibid., 20.

14. Howard Pyle, *The Buccaneers and Marooners of America*, 39.

15. An Act for the More Effectuall Suppression of Piracy, 11 William III, c. 7 (1698).

16. Williams, *Captains Outrageous*, 147.

17. Frank Browning and John Gerassi, *The American Way of Crime*, 56.

18. Philip Gosse, *The History of Piracy*, 178–80.

19. Douglas Botting, *The Pirates*, 100–122; Robert C. Ritchie, *Captain Kidd and the War Against the Pirates*, 52–109.

20. Trial of Captain William Kidd, 14 St. Tri. 147 (1701).

21. John S. C. Abbott, *Captain William Kidd*, 99.

22. Hugh F. Rankin, *The Golden Age of Piracy*, 106–16.

23. Shirley Carter Hughson, "The Carolina Pirates and Colonial Commerce: 1670–1740," *Johns Hopkins University Studies in Historical and Political Science* 12 (May–July 1894): 77–78.

24. Robert E. Lee, *Blackbeard the Pirate*, 124–25, 228–31.

25. Williams, *Captains Outrageous*, 158–60; Marcus Rediker, *Between the Devil and the Deep Blue Sea*, 278–83.

26. The Piracy Act, 8 George I, c. 24 (1721).

27. Rankin, *The Golden Age of Piracy*, 158.

28. Albert Cook Myers, ed., *Narratives of Early Pennsylvania West New Jersey and Delaware: 1603–1707*, 431.

29. Captain Charles Johnson, *A General History of the Robberies and Murders of the Most Notorious Pirates*, v.

30. J. Franklin Jameson, *Privateering and Piracy in the Colonial Period*, viii.

31. Gosse, *The History of Piracy*, 185.

32. Rankin, *The Golden Age of Piracy*, 122.

33. Pyle, *The Buccaneers and Marooners of America*, 15.

34. William Howard Bonner, *Pirate Laureate: The Life and Legends of Captain Kidd*, 103–12, 134–37, 151–75, 182–88.

CHAPTER 3. THE HIGHWAYMAN

1. John Coatman, *Police*, 24.

2. J. L. Rayner and G. T. Crook, *The Complete Newgate Calendar*, 1: 37–42.

3. Peter Newark, *The Crimson Book of Highwaymen*, 50–51.

4. W. L. Melville Lee, *A History of Police in England*, 139.

5. Eric Patridge, *Pirates, Highwaymen and Adventurers*, 68–77.

6. Colin Wilson, *A Criminal History of Mankind*, 407.

7. Lillian de la Torre, *Villainy Detected*, ix.

8. Thomas Wright, *The Life of Daniel Defoe*, 276.

9. Geoffrey M. Sill, "Defoe's Two Versions of the Outlaw," *English Studies* 64 (April 1983): 122–28.

10. Daniel Defoe, *The Fortunes and Misfortunes of the Famous Moll Flanders*, 3–4.

11. Stella Margetson, "Sweet-Tempered Satirist," *Country Life* 178 (19 September 1985): 832–33.

12. William Eben Schultz, *Gay's Beggar's Opera*, xxiii.

13. Stella Margetson, "Bold, Brave and Brilliant," *Country Life* 178 (5 December 1985): 1782.

14. Reginald Nettle, *Sing a Song of England*, 129; Lewis Winstock, *Songs & Music of the Redcoats*, 22–26.

15. Charles J. Finger, *Highwaymen*, 79–114.

16. Newark, *The Crimson Book of Highwaymen*, 95.

17. Christopher Hibbert, *Highwaymen*, 49–53.

18. Richard Blakeborough, *The Hand of Glory*, 212–52.

19. Barbara Allen, "The Heroic Ride," *Western Historical Quarterly* 19, no. 4 (November 1988): 397–412.

20. "My Bonny Black Bess," Louise Pound, ed., *American Ballads and Songs*, 157.

21. Philip Gosse, *The History of Piracy*, 170–71.

22. Pat F. Garrett, *The Authentic Life of Billy the Kid*, 31.

23. Ramon F. Adams, *A Fitting Death for Billy the Kid*, 138.

24. Sarah Helm, "Dick Turpin's Grave Mistake," *London Sunday Times*, 17 March 1985.

25. Rayner and Crook, *The Complete Newgate Calendar*, 1:v.

26. Melville Lee, *A History of Police in England*, 283.

27. Newark, *The Crimson Book of Highwaymen*, 35.

28. An Act for Punishment of Rogues, Vagabonds, and Sturdy Beggars, 39, Elizabeth I, c. 4 (1597).

29. An act for preventing theft and rapine, 18 Charles II, c. 3 (1666).

30. Habeas Corpus Act, 31 Charles II, c. 2 (1679).

31. Albert Cook Myers, ed., *Narratives of Early Pennsylvania West New Jersey and Delaware 1630–1707*, 106–7.

32. Abbot Emerson Smith, "The Transportation of Convicts," *American Historical Review* 39 (January 1934): 232–49.

33. Alan Frost, *Convicts and Empire*, 3.

34. "Transportation," Clare History Centre, Corofin, County Clare, Ireland.

35. K. S. Inglis, *The Australian Colonists*, 8.

36. P. F. Speed, *Police and Prisons*, 13–14.

37. Roger A. Ekirch, "Bound for America," *William and Mary Quarterly* 62 (April 1985): 186–93.

38. Wilkes v. Rex, 19 St. Tri. 1075 (1769).

39. "Long John Silver Collection," Maritime Trust, Greenwich, Greater London, England.

40. Administration of Justice Act, 1 & 2 George VI, c. 63, s. 12 (1938).

41. Criminal Justice (Scotland) Act, 12, 13 & 14 George VI, c. 94, s. 14, 15 (2) (1949).

CHAPTER 4. THE DESPERADO

1. Bradley Chapin, *Criminal Justice in Colonial America, 1606–1660,* 139.

2. Ibid., 140; *Sourcebook of Criminal Justice Statistics: 1984,* 456–57; Donna A. Spindel, "The Administration of Criminal Justice in North Carolina, 1720–1740," *American Journal of Legal History* 25 (April 1981): 141–62.

3. Kai T. Erikson, *Wayward Puritans,* 163–81.

4. Harold E. Davis, *The Fledgling Province,* 127–30.

5. Chapin, *Criminal Justice in Colonial America, 1606–1660,* 141–42.

6. Thomas J. Wertenbaker, *Virginia Under the Stuarts, 1607–1688,* 115–224; Wilcomb E. Washburn, *The Governor and the Rebel,* 136–66.

7. Chapin, *Criminal Justice in Colonial America, 1606–1660,* 35–36.

8. Douglas Greenberg, *Crime and Law Enforcement in the Colony of New York, 1691–1776,* 216.

9. Robert W. Weir, *Colonial South Carolina,* 192–94.

10. Ibid., 275–77.

11. William S. Powell, James K. Huhta, and Thomas J. Farnham, *The Regulators of North Carolina: 1759–1776,* xvi.

12. An Act for Restoring and Preserving the Public Peace of This Province, January 15, 1771, Colonial Assembly of North Carolina (Col. Rec. of N.C., III, 481–86).

13. Tryon's Order Book (Col. Rec. of N.C., VIII, 617).

14. William Edward Fitch, *Some Neglected History of North Carolina,* 244.

15. Catherine S. Crary, "Guerrilla Activities of James Delancey's Cowboys," *The Loyalist Americans,* 14–24.

16. Massachusetts Constitution, Part I, Sec. 13.

17. Respublica v. Doan, 1 U.S. (1 Dall.) 86 (Pa. Sup. Ct., 1784); G. S. Rowe, "Outlawry in Pennsylvania, 1782–1788," *American Journal of Legal History* 20 (July 1976): 227–44.

18. Richard Slotkin, *Regeneration Through Violence,* 62–63.

19. Ibid., 417.

20. Frederick Jackson Turner, *The Frontier in American History,* 212.

21. Paul I. Wellman, *Spawn of Evil,* 12.

22. Robert M. Coates, *The Outlaw Years,* 24.

23. Otto A. Rothert, *The Outlaws of Cave-In-Rock,* 61.

24. Ibid., 154–55.

25. Wellman, *Spawn of Evil,* 105–14.

26. Orlando [N. E. Paxton], *The Brigand, or, A Tale of the West Done into Rhyme,* 39.

27. Charles Gayarré, *Historical Sketch of Pierre and Jean Lafitte,* 1.

28. Jane Lucas de Grummond, *The Baratarians and the Battle of New Orleans*, 21.

29. Ibid., 104.

30. Gayarré, *Historical Sketch of Pierre and Jean Lafitte*, 22.

31. Grummond, *The Baratarians and the Battle of New Orleans*, 157–58.

32. Lyle Saxon, *Lafitte the Pirate*, 262–65.

33. United States Constitution, Art. I., sec. 10.

34. 18 U.S.C. 1651 (1790).

35. An Act to Protect the Commerce of the United States and Punish the Crime of Piracy, March 3, 1819, c. 76, sec. 5.

36. United States v. Smith, 5 Wheat. (18 U.S.) 153 (1820); United States v. Pirates, 5 Wheat. (18 U.S.) 184 (1820).

37. Commonwealth v. Hale, 2 Va. Cas. 241 (1821); Commonwealth v. Hagerman, 2 Va. Cas. 244 (1821); Commonwealth v. Anderson, 2 Va. Cas. 245 (1821).

38. Michael S. Hindus, "Black Justice Under White Law," *Journal of American History* 62 (December 1976): 576.

39. David J. Langum, "Pioneer Justice on the Overland Trails," *Western Historical Quarterly* 5 (October 1974): 439.

40. Roger Olmstead, "San Francisco and the Vigilante Style," *American West* 7 (January 1970): 10.

CHAPTER 5. THE REBEL

1. Paul I. Wellman, *Spawn of Evil*, 147.

2. Anthony Gish, *American Bandits*, 12.

3. Wellman, *Spawn of Evil*, 142.

4. Robert M. Coates, *The Outlaw Years*, 270.

5. James Lal Penick, Jr., *The Great Western Land Pirate*, 31.

6. Wellman, *Spawn of Evil*, 269.

7. Ross Phares, *Reverend Devil*, 241.

8. Ibid., 147–62.

9. Jonathan H. Green, *The Secret Band of Brothers*, 68–73.

10. Ibid., 147–62.

11. Emerson Hough, *The Story of the Outlaw*, 394.

12. Ramon F. Adams, *Western Words*, 128.

13. Edward Bonney, *The Banditti of the Prairies*, 5.

14. Ibid., xi–xiii.

15. Ibid., ix.

16. Ray Allen Billington, *Land of Savagery Land of Promise*, 152.

17. Charles Kelly and Hoffman Birney, *Holy Murder: The Story of Porter Rockwell*, 49.

18. Ibid., 272.
19. Helen Wilson, *The Treatment of the Misdemeanant in Indiana, 1816–1936*, 23.
20. Frank Richard Prassel, *The Western Peace Officer*, 128–31; Craig B. Little and Christopher P. Sheffield, "Frontiers and Criminal Justice," *American Sociological Review* 48 (December 1983): 804–8.
21. Hough, *The Story of the Outlaw*, 397.
22. Isabella Bird, *A Lady's Life in the Rocky Mountains*, 26.
23. Independent District, Gilpin County [Colorado], "Laws of Independent District [1861]," secs. 14–37 (University of Colorado Archives, Boulder).
24. Tom Tobin, Photo File (Colorado Historical Society, Denver).
25. Thomas J. Dimsdale, *The Vigilantes of Montana*, 25.
26. Ibid., 192.
27. Ibid., 205.
28. *Osawatomie, Kansas*, 9.
29. David Karsner, *John Brown: Terrible 'Saint,'* 3–4.
30. Stephen B. Oates, *To Purge This Land with Blood*, 351–52.
31. George D. Hendricks, *The Bad Man of the West*, 124.
32. Robertus Love, *The Rise and Fall of Jesse James*, 18.
33. John N. Edwards, *Noted Guerrillas*, 14.
34. Harry Sinclair Drago, *Outlaws on Horseback*, 3; Richard S. Brownlee, *Gray Ghosts of the Confederacy*, 53–75.
35. Hendricks, *The Bad Man of the West*, 171.
36. Albert Castel, *William Clarke Quantrill*, 120.
37. William Elsey Connelley, *Quantrill and the Border Wars*, 347.
38. Edwards, *Noted Guerrillas*, 191.
39. William A. Settle, Jr., *Jesse James Was His Name*, 24.
40. Carl W. Breihan, *Quantrill and His Civil War Guerrillas*, 136.
41. Paul I. Wellman, *A Dynasty of Western Outlaws*, 44–49.
42. Castel, *William Clarke Quantrill*, 149.
43. Ibid., 213.
44. Wellman, *A Dynasty of Western Outlaws*, 63.
45. "Is Quantrell Dead [1888]" (University of Colorado Archives, Boulder).
46. Castel, *William Clarke Quantrill*, 214.
47. Ibid., 215.
48. Connelley, *Quantrill and the Border Wars*, 41.
49. Perry Eberhart, *Colorado Ghost Towns and Mining Camps*, 122–23.
50. C. Arthur Hochmuth, "Reynolds' Rebel Raiders" (University of Colorado Archives, Boulder).
51. Christopher Morris, "An Event in Community Organization: The Mississippi Slave Insurrection Scare of 1835," *Journal of Social History* 22 (Fall 1988): 93–111.

CHAPTER 6. THE BUGHEWAY

1. A. S. Mercer, *The Banditti of the Plains*, 83–85.

2. Frank M. Canton, *Frontier Trails*, 152.

3. Charles Howard Shinn, *Mining Camps*, 170.

4. Mrs. Anna Dillon, Interviews Collected During 1933–34 (Colorado Historical Society Archives, Denver).

5. J. B. John Dunn, *Perilous Trails of Texas*, 87.

6. Hubert Howe Bancroft, *Popular Tribunals*, 1:131–32.

7. *Historical Corrections Statistics in the United States: 1850–1984*, 10–16.

8. Ramon F. Adams, *Western Words*. 11, 42.

9. Pearl Baker, *Robbers Roost Recollections*, 59.

10. John W. Caughey, *Their Majesties the Mob*, 13.

11. "Administration of Justice in California [1850]," *California Pamphlets* 26, no. 1 (n.d.): 355.

12. "On the Afternoon of the 3rd," *Weekly New Mexican* (Santa Fe), 12 July 1879.

13. "Gravette," "Comments on Chaining," *Arkansas Gazette* (Little Rock), 29 July 1987; Lamar House, "A Dark and Evil World," *Arkansas Times* 13, nos. 5–6 (January–February 1987): 26–88, 42–70; Holt v. Sarver, 300 F. Supp. 825 (E.D. Ark., 1969).

14. Oscar C. Mueller, "The Central Montana Vigilante Raids of 1884," *Montana Magazine of History* 1 (January 1951): 31–35; *Report of the Governor of Arizona to the Secretary of the Interior, 1885*, 19; Philip J. Ethington, "Vigilantes and the Police," *Journal of Social History* 21 (Winter 1987): 197–227.

15. Perry Eberhart, *Colorado Ghost Towns and Mining Camps*, 123–24.

16. Bancroft, *Popular Tribunals*, 1:129.

17. *Report of the Governor of Arizona to the Secretary of the Interior, 1905*, 69; *Report of the Governor of Arizona to the Secretary of the Interior, 1906*, 21; *Report of the Governor of Arizona to the Secretary of the Interior, 1907*, 13–14.

18. Albert D. Richardson, *Beyond the Mississippi*, 290.

19. Boulder Police Court Docket 1882–1885 (University of Colorado Archives, Boulder).

20. Grand Jury Docket, U.S. Court, Second Judicial District, Indian Territory, 1893 (Federal Records Center, Fort Worth, Texas).

21. "Report of the Grand Jury," *Weekly New Mexican* (Santa Fe), 7 August 1877.

22. William Ransom Hogan, *The Texas Republic*, 274.

23. Records of the U.S. District Court, Territory of New Mexico, First Judicial District, 1896–1899 (Federal Records Center, Denver, Colorado); U.S. Court Docket, Central District, Indian Territory, 1898–1904 [criminal cases] (Federal Records Center, Fort Worth, Texas); *Report to the Nation on Crime and Justice*, 55–56.

24. Bancroft, *Popular Tribunals,* 2:683.

25. Ibid., 650.

26. Charles F. Outland, "San Buenaventura Justice, 1870–1871," *Ventura County Historical Society Quarterly* 7 (November 1961): 12.

27. Rebecca Williamson Carter Bailey, "Wyoming Stock Inspectors and Detectives, 1873–1890" (M.A. thesis, University of Wyoming, 1948), 151.

28. Gragg v. State, 186 S.W.2d 234 (Texas, 1954); Jackson v. State, 34 Tex. Crim. 1, 28 S.W. 815 (1894); Northern v. State, 203 S.W.2d 206, 216 S.W.2d 192 (Texas, 1948).

29. *Historical Corrections Statistics in the United States, 1850–1894,* 13, 217–22.

30. "John Kinney," *Weekly New Mexican* (Santa Fe), 15 April 1879.

31. Constitution of Massachusetts (1780), Part I, sec. 13.

32. Constitution of Tennessee (1796), Art. I, sec. 8.

33. Green v. United States, 356 U.S. 165 (1958).

34. Virginia Code, sec. 19.1–15 (1887); Dale County v. Gunter, 46 Ala. 118 (1871); Texas Constitution (1876), Art. I, sec. 20.

35. Milliken v. City Council, 54 Tex. 388 (1881).

36. New York Code of Criminal Procedure, sec. 814–25 (1827).

37. Pennsylvania Statutes, Title 19, sec. 1321 (1791).

38. North Carolina General Statutes, sec. 15–48 (1868).

39. Bobby G. Deaver. "Outlawry," *North Carolina Law Review* 41 (Spring 1963): 645–46.

40. Autry v. Mitchell, 420 F. Supp. 976 (E.D.N.C., 1976).

41. "Reward for Murderers," *Weekly New Mexican* (Santa Fe), 2 October 1877.

42. Jack Schaefer, "Real Heroes of the West," *Holiday* 2 (December 1957): 77.

43. Joseph G. Rosa, *They Called Him Wild Bill,* 156–60; Box 368412, Records of the U.S. District Court, Western District, Arkansas, 1871 (Federal Records Center, Fort Worth, Texas); Frank Richard Prassel, *The Western Peace Officer,* 228; *Evening Review* (Albuquerque), 26 July 1882.

44. James H. Cook, *Fifty Years on the Old Frontier,* 246.

45. Territorial Secretary. Extradition papers for fugitives from New Mexico, 1900–1905 (University of New Mexico Archives, Albuquerque).

46. David J. Cook, *Hands Up,* 316.

47. Werner J. Einstadter, "Crime News in the Old West," *Urban Life* 8 (October 1979): 323–30; David Fridtjof Halaas, *Boom Town Newspapers: 1859–1881,* 77–82.

48. Wayne G. Broehl, *The Molly Maguires,* 228–29, 256–57, 317–18, 358.

49. William M. Kephart, *Extraordinary Groups,* 250–52.

50. Richard Patterson, *Train Robbery,* v.

51. Ibid., 68–63.

52. Stuart H. Traub, "Rewards, Bounty Hunting, and Criminal Justice in the West," *Western Historical Quarterly* 19 (August 1988): 287–301.

53. 18 U.S.C. 1991 (1902).

54. 18 U.S.C. 2116 (1903).

55. Roger Lane, *Policing the City*, 114–15; Eric H. Monkkonen, *Police in Urban America*, 70–85; David R. Johnson, "The Origins and Structure of Intercity Criminal Activity," *Journal of Social History* 15 (Summer 1982): 593–605.

56. Thomas Byrnes, *Professional Criminals of America*, 337–39.

57. Kent Ladd Steckmesser, *Western Outlaws*, 14–119; Paul Kooistra, *Criminals as Heroes*, 43–118.

58. Anton Block, "The Peasant and the Brigand," *Comparative Studies in Society and History* 14 (September 1972): 496–502; Eric Hobsbawm, *Primitive Rebels*, 19–25.

59. Robert Elman, *Badmen of the West*, 8–27; Robert G. Athearn, *The Mythic West in Twentieth Century America*, 257.

CHAPTER 7. THE HOODLUM

1. Lewis H. Garrard, *Wah-to-yah and the Taos Trail*, 63.

2. *Pioneer Days in the Southwest*, 65.

3. Isabella Bird, *A Lady's Life in the Rocky Mountains*, 79, 80, 126, 220.

4. Roger D. McGrath, *Gunfighters Highwaymen & Vigilantes*, 221–23.

5. William Carter, *Ghost Towns of the West*, 79.

6. Joseph G. Rosa, *The Gunfighter*, 40–41.

7. Alan Lomax, *The Folk Songs of North America*, 262.

8. Bruce Brigden, "The Bloody Benders" (Kansas State Historical Society Archives, Topeka).

9. C. W. Alexander, "The Five Families" (Kansas State Historical Society Archives, Topeka).

10. John Rolfe Burroughs, *Where the Old West Stayed Young*, 122.

11. Carl Sifakis, *The Encyclopedia of American Crime*, 64–65.

12. "Bender Mounds," *Kansas Historical Quarterly* 13 (Summer 1957): 146.

13. Sifakis, *The Encyclopedia of American Crime*, 551.

14. Perry Eberhart, *Colorado Ghost Towns and Mining Camps*, 384–95.

15. "Black Bart" File, Wells Fargo History Department Archives, San Francisco, California.

16. Ibid.

17. Charles Michelson, "Stage Robbers of the West," *Munsey's Magazine* 25 (July 1901): 457–59.

18. William M. Breakenridge, *Helldorado*, 238.

19. William A. Settle, Jr., *Jesse James Was His Name*, 6–9, 20–28.

20. Homer Croy, *Jesse James Was My Neighbor*, xii.

21. Ron Terrell, "The James/Younger Gang," *Guns and the Gunfighters*, 59.
22. Joseph G. Rosa, *They Called Him Wild Bill*, 220.
23. "The Chivalry of Crime," *Kansas City Times*, 29 September 1872.
24. Settle, *Jesse James Was His Name*, 46.
25. Croy, *Jesse James Was My Neighbor*, 62, 74, 301–2.
26. Burt Miller, "The Pinkertons," *Guns and the Gunfighters*, 70–71.
27. Croy, *Jesse James Was My Neighbor*, 131–32.
28. John N. Edwards, *Noted Guerrillas*, 196.
29. Ibid., 460.
30. "The Train Robbers," *New York Times*, 18 July 1881.
31. Duane Meyer, *The Heritage of Missouri*, 431–32.
32. "The Notorious Jesse James," *Weekly New Mexican* (Santa Fe), 15 November 1879.
33. "Jesse James Shot Down," *New York Times*, 4 April 1882.
34. Croy, *Jesse James Was My Neighbor*, 259.
35. Settle, *Jesse James Was His Name*, 118.
36. James William Buel, *The Border Outlaws*, 444–69.
37. Settle, *Jesse James Was His Name*, 166.
38. W. C. Bronaugh, *The Youngers' Fight for Freedom*, 9–12.
39. Don Russell, *The Wild West*, 67.
40. Jerry J. Gaddy, *Obituaries of the Gunfighters*, 150.
41. Robertus Love, *The Rise and Fall of Jesse James*, 446.
42. David Thelen, *Paths of Resistance*, 77.
43. R. B. Dobson and J. Taylor, *Rymes of Robin Hood*, 278.
44. Alan Lomax, *The Folk Songs of North America*, 346.
45. Settle, *Jesse James Was His Name*, 169–71.
46. Croy, *Jesse James Was My Neighbor*, 281.
47. Thelen, *Paths of Resistance*, 77.
48. Ramon F. Adams, *Six-Guns and Saddle Leather*, 77.

CHAPTER 8. THE GUNMAN

1. Charles L. Martin, *A Sketch of Sam Bass, the Bandit*, xviii.
2. *Life and Adventures of Sam Bass*, 3–4.
3. Walter Prescott Webb, *The Texas Rangers*, 375–90.
4. Martin, *A Sketch of Sam Bass, the Bandit*, xiii.
5. Wayne Gard, *Sam Bass*, 236.
6. Ibid., 247.
7. William A. Settle, Jr., *Jesse James Was His Name*, 55.
8. Gard, *Sam Bass*, 240.
9. John Wesley Hardin, *The Life of John Wesley Hardin*, 104.
10. Paul Trachtman, *The Gunfighters*, 175.
11. John Lachuk, "John Wesley Hardin," *Guns and the Gunfighters*, 80.

12. Carl Sifakis, *The Encyclopedia of American Crime*, 312.

13. Howard R. Lamar, ed., *The Reader's Encyclopedia of the American West*, 484.

14. Bill O'Neal, *Encyclopedia of Western Gunfighters*, 5, 126–31.

15. Joseph G. Rosa, *The Gunfighter*, 40–54; Robert M. Utley, *Billy the Kid*, 202–7.

16. Ramon F. Adams, *A Fitting Death for Billy the Kid*, 207.

17. Maurice Garland Fulton, *History of the Lincoln County War*, 8.

18. "The Troubles in Lincoln," *Weekly New Mexican* (Santa Fe), 25 May 1878.

19. "From Lincoln County," *Weekly New Mexican* (Santa Fe), 1 June 1878.

20. Fulton, *History of the Lincoln County War*, 205.

21. "Lincoln County," *Weekly New Mexican* (Santa Fe), 4 April 1878.

22. Calvin Horn, *New Mexico's Troubled Years*, 200–205.

23. Ibid., 207.

24. Fulton, *History of the Lincoln County War*, 379.

25. Trachtman, *The Gunfighters*, 190.

26. Fulton, *History of the Lincoln County War*, 381.

27. O'Neal, *Encyclopedia of Western Gunfighters*, 23–24, 269–71.

28. Horn, *New Mexico's Troubles Years*, 218.

29. Ibid.

30. Fulton, *History of the Lincoln County War*, 396.

31. Pat F. Garrett, *The Authentic Life of Billy the Kid*, 147.

32. Ibid., 149.

33. Fred E. Sutton, *Hands Up!* 48.

34. Kent Ladd Steckmesser, *The Western Hero*, 70.

35. C. L. Sonnichsen and William V. Morrison, *Alias Billy the Kid*, 11.

36. E. B. Mann, "Billy the Kid," *Guns and the Gunfighters*, 213; Robert M. Utley, *Billy the Kid*, 186–96.

37. Eugene Cunningham, *Triggernometry*, 170.

38. C. L. Sonnichsen and William V. Morrison, *Alias Billy the Kid*, 90.

39. Lee M. Price to Frank M. King, April 8, 1940, Frank Marion King Collection (Huntington Library, San Marino, California); Donald Cline, *Alias Billy the Kid*, 117.

40. Carl W. Breihan, *Outlaws of the Old West*, 169.

41. Joseph G. Rosa, *The West of Wild Bill Hickok*, 207.

42. Robert E. McNellis, "Pat Garrett," *Guns and the Gunfighters*, 164–65.

43. Garrett, *The Authentic Life of Billy the Kid*, 98.

44. Steckmesser, *The Western Hero*, 77–78.

45. Garrett, *The Authentic Life of Billy the Kid*, 5.

46. E. B. Mann, "Billy the Kid," *Guns and the Gunfighters*, 75.

47. Sutton, *Hands Up!*, 39.

48. Walter Noble Burns, *The Saga of Billy the Kid*, 53–54.

49. Stephen Tatum, *Inventing Billy the Kid*, 105; Jon Tuska, *Billy the Kid: A Handbook*, 163–87.

50. Adams, *A Fitting Death for Billy the Kid*, 35, 50, 56, 58, 60, 74–75, 116, 131, 137, 183, 194, 197, 200–201, 208–9, 257, 260.

51. Tatum, *Inventing Billy the Kid*, 202.

52. *New Mexico/1988*, 8, 15, 60.

53. Frederick W. Nolan, *The Life and Death of John Henry Tunstall*, 440.

54. Eric Mottram, "The Persuasive Lips," *Journal of American Studies* 10 (April 1976): 58–66; Utley, *Billy the Kid*, 203.

55. Garrett, *The Authentic Life of Billy the Kid*, xxiv.

56. Rosa, *The Gunfighter*, 198.

57. Garrett, *The Authentic Life of Billy the Kid*, 151–53.

58. Ray Allen Billington, *Land of Savagery Land of Promise*, 272–85; Bruce A. Rosenberg. *The Code of the West*, 159–74.

59. Robert M. Utley, *High Noon in Lincoln*, 176.

60. Lily Klasner, *My Girlhood Among Outlaws*, 174.

61. Tom Bailey to Eleanor B. Sloan, June 12 and 26, 1958, Tom (Seth) Bailey Manuscript File (Arizona Pioneers' Historical Society Archives, Tucson); Larry D. Ball, *The United States Marshals of New Mexico and Arizona Territories*, 107–27.

62. *Report of the Acting Governor of Arizona Made to the Secretary of the Interior for the Year 1881*, 9.

63. James D. Richardson, ed., *A Compilation of the Messages and Papers of the Presidents, 1789–1902*, 8:53–54; Odie B. Faulk, *Tombstone*, 132–57.

64. *Report of the Governor of Arizona Made to the Secretary of the Interior for the Year 1883*, xxx, 12.

65. C. L. Sonnichsen, *Tucson*, 130–32.

66. Frank Richard Prassel, *The Western Peace Officer*, 160–63.

67. Mulford Windsor, "The Arizona Rangers," *Our Sheriff and Police Journal* 31 (June 1936): 60.

68. Ibid.

69. *Report of the Governor of Arizona to the Secretary of the Interior, 1905*, 68.

70. William Henry Robinson, *The Story of Arizona*, 229.

71. O'Neal, *Encyclopedia of Western Gunfighters*, 22–23, 298–99.

72. Sifakis, *The Encyclopedia of American Crime*, 116–17, 234–35, 502–3, 675.

73. Ramon F. Adams, *Six-Guns and Saddle Leather*, 26–27.

74. Peter Lyon, *The Wild, Wild West*, 146.

75. Ibid., 35–36.

76. Burton Rascoe, *Belle Starr, "The Bandit Queen,"* 12–13.

CHAPTER 9. THE GANGSTER

1. B. A. Botkin, *A Treasury of American Folklore*, 50–76.

2. Frederick Jackson Turner, *The Frontier in American History*, 212.

3. Hubert Howe Bancroft, *Popular Tribunals* 1:720.

4. Emerson Hough, *The Passing of the Frontier*, 144.

5. Ibid., 142–43.

6. Emerson Hough, *The Story of the Outlaw*, 1–2.

7. Ramon F. Adams, *Six-Guns and Saddle Leather*, 98.

8. Don Russell, *The Lives and Legends of Buffalo Bill*, 356–69.

9. Ibid., 407–9, 445, 467.

10. Ray Allen Billington, *Land of Savagery Land of Promise*, 269.

11. C. Ross Hume, "Oklahoma History Embedded in the Law," *Chronicles of Oklahoma* 25 (Summer 1947): 96–97.

12. Frank Richard Prassel, *The Western Peace Officer*, 182–83; 18 U.S.C. 1153 (1885).

13. Indian-Pioneer History, 14:209 (Oklahoma Historical Society Archives, Oklahoma City).

14. "Four Men Charged with Murder Taken from Jail," *Daily Oklahoman* (Oklahoma City), 20 April 1909; Glenn Shirley, *Shotgun for Hire*, 92–116.

15. Harry Sinclair Drago, *Outlaws on Horseback*, xiv.

16. Richard Patterson, *Train Robbery*, 146.

17. *Sixty-first Annual Report of the Commissioner of Indian Affairs to the Secretary of the Interior, 1892*, 258; Glenn Shirley, *Law West of Fort Smith*, 99–105.

18. Bailey C. Hanes, *Bill Doolin, Outlaw, O.T.*, 102.

19. David Stewart Elliott, *Last Raid of the Daltons*, 65.

20. "Exit the Daltons," *Dallas Morning News*, 6 October 1892.

21. Richard White, "Outlaw Gangs of the Middle Border," *Western Historical Quarterly* 12 (October 1981): 405–6.

22. Harry Sinclair Drago, *Outlaws on Horseback*, xvii.

23. Hanes, *Bill Doolin, Outlaw, O.T.*, 160–62.

24. "Slaughter Kid's Father," *Daily Oklahoman* (Oklahoma City), 8 May 1895.

25. Zoe A. Tilghman, *Marshal of the Last Frontier*, 219–24.

26. Hanes, *Bill Doolin, Outlaw O.T.*, 170.

27. "Bill Doolin Killed," *Dallas Morning News*, 26 August 1896.

28. Carl W. Breihan, *Outlaws of the Old West*, 223–24.

29. Hanes, *Bill Doolin, Outlaw, O.T.*, 207–10.

30. In re Boyle, 6 Idaho 609, 57 P. 706 (1899); Stewart H. Holbrook, *Murder Out Yonder*, 42–68.

31. Louis Adamic, *Dynamite*, 124–56; James D. Horan and Howard Swiggett, *The Pinkerton Story*, 289–308; Stewart H. Holbrook, *The Rocky Mountain Revolution*, 216–34.

32. William A. Pinkerton, *Train Robberies and Train Robbers*, 4–6.

33. Ibid., 65.

34. James D. Horan, *Desperate Men*, 189–91; Robert Redford, *The Outlaw Trail*, 8–12.

35. Ed Bartholomew, *Black Jack Ketcham*, 5, 44–78.

36. Larry Pointer, *In Search of Butch Cassidy*, 141–48.

37. Charles A. Siringo, *Two Evil Isms*, 72–81; Frank Morn, *The Eye That Never Sleeps*, 151–63.

38. "Patrolling the Bandit Belt," T. F. Dawson Scrapbooks (Colorado Historical Society Archives, Denver).

39. Dorothy M. Johnson, *Western Badmen*, 234.

40. Patterson, *Train Robbery*, 185–89.

41. Pinkerton, *Train Robberies and Train Robbers*, 71.

42. Eugene Cunningham, *Triggernometry*, 349.

43. "Outlaw Tracy Bit the Dust," *Daily Oklahoman* (Oklahoma City), 7 August 1902.

44. William K. Everson, *A Pictorial History of the Western Film*, 14–19.

45. Zane Grey, *Riders of the Purple Sage*, 10.

46. Carlos Clarens, *Crime Movies*, 15–20.

47. William K. Everson, *American Silent Films*, 227–34.

48. Ibid., 222.

49. Don Russell, *The Lives and Legends of Buffalo Bill*, 457–58.

50. Kevin Brownlow, *The War, the West, and the Wilderness*, 287–88; Harold Preece, *The Dalton Gang*, 280–87.

51. Emmett Dalton, *When the Daltons Rode*, 312.

52. Brownlow, *The War, the West, and the Wilderness*, 281–87.

53. Tilghman, *Marshal of the Last Frontier*, 316.

54. Richard S. Graves, *Oklahoma Outlaws*, 87–92.

55. Drago, *Outlaws on Horseback*, 251–57.

56. Tilghman, *Marshal of the Last Frontier*, 324–30.

57. Ibid., 317–18.

58. Glenn Shirley, *Henry Starr*, 167–82.

59. Ibid., 191.

60. Allen Eyles, *The Western*, 90–91.

61. Brownlow, *The War, the West, and the Wilderness*, 287.

62. Billington, *Land of Savagery Land of Promise*, 321.

63. Tom Milne, "The Great American Myth," *They Went That-A-Way*, 50.

64. George N. Fenin and William K. Everson, *The Western*, 86.

65. Ibid., 93.

66. Sound prologue to *Tumbleweeds* (1925, 1939).

CHAPTER 10. THE RENEGADE

1. Colin G. Calloway, "Neither White nor Red: White Renegades on the American Indian Frontier," *Western Historical Quarterly* 17 (January 1986): 56.

2. Karl N. Llewellyn and E. Adamson Hoebel, *The Cheyenne Way*, 125–26, 137, 158, 166–68.

3. Felix S. Cohen, *The Legal Conscience*, 239–46.

4. Wilcomb E. Washburn, "The Historical Context of American Indian Legal Problems," *American Indians and the Law*, 14.

5. Cohen, *The Legal Conscience*, 235–36.

6. Angie Debo, *A History of the Indians of the United States*, 10, 76, 95, 117–26.

7. Ibid., 155.

8. John Peter Turner, *The North-West Mounted Police, 1873–1893*, 1:25–26.

9. Ralph K. Andrist, *The Long Death*, 27–68.

10. Debo, *A History of the Indians of the United States*, 167.

11. Joseph G. Rosa, *They Called Him Wild Bill*, 112.

12. Robert M. Utley, *The Indian Frontier of the American West 1846–1890*, 143–44.

13. F. Stanley, *Satanta and the Kiowas*, 314–22.

14. Ibid., 338–54.

15. Woolverton v. the Nez Perces, 29 Ct. Cl. 107 (1894); Herring v. the Utes, 32 Ct. Cl. 536 (1897); Salois v. United States, 33 Ct. Cl. 326 (1898).

16. William C. Holden, "Frontier Problems and Movements in West Texas, 1846–1900" (Ph.D. dissertation, University of Texas, 1928), 61–63; Walter Prescott Webb, *The Texas Rangers*, 270.

17. Ruth M. Underhill, *The Navajos*, 270.

18. Montoya v. the Mescaleros, 32 Ct. Cl. 349 (1898).

19. Debo, *A History of the Indians of the United States*, 199.

20. Don Schellie, *Vast Domain of Blood*, 213–47.

21. Debo, *A History of the Indians of the United States*, 276.

22. Scott v. United States, 33 Ct. Cl. 486 (1898).

23. Donald E. Worcester, *The Apaches*, 310.

24. Angie Debo, *Geronimo*, 300–301; Earle R. Forrest and Edwin B. Hill, *Lone War Trail of the Apache Kid*, 74–75.

25. William T. Hagan, *Indian Police and Judges*, 27–39; Irving McNeil, "Indian Justice," *New Mexico Historical Review* 19 (October 1944): 266–70; *Annual Report of the Commissioner of Indian Affairs, 1895*, 126.

26. *Report of the Acting Governor of Arizona to the Secretary of the Interior, 1890*, 29; Tom Horn, *Life of Tom Horn*, 214–17; William MacLeod Raine, *Famous Sheriffs and Western Outlaws*, 161–74; Forrest and Hill, *Lone War Trail of the Apache Kid*, 59–64.

27. Indians of North America—Apache Kid, Manuscript File (Arizona Pioneers' Historical Society Archives, Tucson); Frank M. Pool, "The Apache Kid," *The Sheriff* 6 (March 1947): 22–24.

28. *Travel Map of New Mexico*, H3.

29. Carl Sifakis, *The Encyclopedia of American Crime*, 27.

30. Rennard Strickland, *Fire and the Spirits*, 78.

31. Laws of the Choctaw Nation: Act of 1848 (s. 13), Act of 1849 (s. 8), Act of 1857 (s. 7–8) (Federal Records Center, Fort Worth, Texas).

32. Angie Debo, *The Road to Disappearance*, 328–31; "Assassins on Horseback," *Dallas Morning News*, 12 September 1892.

33. Clyde Good, "Ned Christie," *Guns and the Gunfighters*, 39–44.

34. "Jack Reeves Arrested," *Daily Oklahoman* (Oklahoma City), 24 August 1895.

35. Debo, *A History of the Indians of North America*, 310; Donald E. Green, *The Creek People*, 86–88.

36. Paul Trachtman, *The Gunfighters*, 165.

37. *Annual Report of the Commissioner of Indian Affairs, 1895*, 157–58.

38. Bobby G. Deaver, "Outlawry," *North Carolina Law Review* 41 (Spring 1963): 644.

39. W. McKee Evans, *To Die Game*, 252.

40. "Indians hold 17," *Arkansas Gazette* (Little Rock), 2 February 1988.

41. William Loren Katz, *Black Indians*, 155.

42. A. E. Keir Nash, "Fairness and Formalism in the Trials of Blacks in the State Supreme Courts of the Old South," *Virginia Law Review* 56 (February 1970): 98; Gerald Montgomery West, *The Status of the Negro in Virginia During the Colonial Period*, 49; H. M. Henry, *Police Control of the Slave in South Carolina*, 168.

43. Betty Wood, *Slavery in Colonial Georgia: 1730–1775*, 169–87.

44. Peter H. Wood, *Black Majority*, 263.

45. Gerald W. Mullin, *Flight and Rebellion*, 57.

46. Ibid.

47. W. Stitt Robinson, *The Southern Colonial Frontier, 1607–1763*, 190; Wood, *Black Majority*, 308–26.

48. Shanley v. Harvey, 2 Eden 126 (1762).

49. Somerset v. Stewart, Lofft 1, 20 How. St. Tr. 1 (1772).

50. John A. Lomax and Alan Lomax, *Best Loved American Folk Songs*, 288.

51. Thomas Byrnes, *Professional Criminals of America*, 368–71.

52. "Report on the Defective, Dependent, and Delinquent Classes [1880]," Serial No. 2151 (1888), 480–83; *Historical Corrections Statistics in the United States, 1850–1984*, 65.

53. Olive Woolley Burt, *American Murder Ballads*, 200–202; John W. Roberts, " 'Railroad Bill' and the American Outlaw Tradition," *Western Folklore* 40 (October 1981): 315–28.

54. John Rolfe Burroughs, *Where the Old West Stayed Young*, 24–30, 103–9, 206–13.

55. Sifakis, *The Encyclopedia of American Crime*, 95.

56. Charles J. Finger, *Frontier Ballads*, 91–93; Alan Lomax, *The Folk Songs of North America*, 559–71; B. A. Botkin, *A Treasury of American Folklore*, 122–30.

57. Roger D. McGrath, *Gunfighters Highwaymen & Vigilantes*, 132–37.

58. John R. Wunder, "The Chinese and Courts in the Pacific Northwest," *Pacific Historical Review* 52 (May 1983): 205–8.

59. "The Vendetta in New Orleans," *New York Times*, 20 July 1881.

60. Margaret Cahalan, "Trends in Incarceration in the United States since 1880," *Crime and Delinquency* 25 (January 1979): 9–41; *Historical Corrections Statistics in the United States, 1850–1984*, 65.

61. Juanita Brooks, *The Mountain Meadows Massacre*, 177–210; William Wise, *Massacre at Mountain Meadows*, 263–68.

62. William M. Kephart, *Extraordinary Groups*, 250–73.

63. Farrer v. State, 2 Ohio St. 54, 61 (1853).

64. James Otey Bradford Papers (Stanford University Archives, Stanford, California).

65. Frank M. Canton, *Frontier Trails*, 37.

66. Frank M. Canton, Manuscript File (Western History Research Center, University of Wyoming, Laramie); Richard Patterson, *Historical Atlas of the Outlaw West*, 207.

67. Canton, *Frontier Trails*, 39.

68. Raymond W. Stedman, *Shadows of the Indian*, 74–87; John E. O'Connor, *The Hollywood Indian*, 15–39; W. J. Cash, *The Mind of the South*, 115–20.

CHAPTER 11. THE MOLL

1. *The Laws Respecting Women*, 60–63.

2. Otto Pollack, *The Criminality of Women*, 149.

3. Selma R. Williams and Pamela J. Williams, *Riding the Nightmare*, 8.

4. "Treaties with the Danes," E. & G., 11 (c. A.D. 920).

5. Selma R. Williams and Pamela J. Williams, *Riding the Nightmare*, 60.

6. Act Against Conjurations, 33 Hen. VIII, c. 8 (1542); Ronald Holmes, *Witchcraft in British History*, 57–68.

7. "Act agaynst Conjuracions Inchantments and Witchecraftes," 1 Jac. I, c. 12 (1603); "The Witchcraft Act," 9 Geo. II, c. 5 (1736).

8. James Fitzjames Stephen, *A History of the Criminal Law of England*, 2:435–36.

9. Frederick Pollock and Frederic William Maitland, *The History of English Law*, 2:555.

10. Williams and Williams, *Riding the Nightmare*, 187.

11. Bradley Chapin, *Criminal Justice in Colonial America, 1606–1660*, 117–23.

12. Emery Battis, *Saints and Sectaries*, 235–47; Selma R. Williams, *Divine Rebel*, 199–200.

13. Paul Boyer and Stephen Nissenbaum, *Salem Possessed*, 1–21; John Putnam Demos, *Entertaining Satan*, 310–12.

14. Williams and Williams, *Riding the Nightmare,* 200–202.

15. J. L. Rayner and G. T. Crook, *The Complete Newgate Calendar,* 1:299–304.

16. Anne Chambers, "A Most Famous Feminine Sea Captain," *Ireland* 33 (May–June 1984): 38–42.

17. Rayner Thrower, *The Pirate Picture,* 85; Hugh F. Rankin, *The Golden Age of Piracy,* 143–45; E. O. Hoppe, *Pirates, Buccaneers, and Gentlemen Adventurers,* 73–82.

18. Alexis de Tocqueville, *Democracy in America,* 246.

19. Texas Penal Code, 1063 (1879).

20. Ibid., 645 (1879).

21. G. S. Rowe, "*Femes Covert* and Criminal Prosecution in Eighteenth Century Pennsylvania," *American Journal of Legal History* 32 (April 1988): 138–56.

22. Nevada Criminal Law, 10 (1885).

23. Hermann Mannheim, *Comparative Criminology,* 99–100.

24. Isabella Bird, *A Lady's Life in the Rocky Mountains,* 70.

25. Anne M. Butler, *Daughters of Joy, Sisters of Misery,* 1–16; Charles Caldwell Dobie, *San Francisco's Chinatown,* 177–214.

26. Beverly J. Stoeltje, "A Helpmate for the Man Indeed," *Journal of American Folklore* 88 (January–March 1975): 38–40.

27. Otto Pollack, *The Criminality of Women,* 58.

28. "Report on the Defective, Dependent, and Delinquent Classes [1880]," Serial No. 2151 (1888), 480; *State and Federal Prisoners 1925–85,* 2.

29. "Prisoners in County Jails [1890]," Serial No. 3028, Part 2 (1896), 25–27.

30. Anne M. Butler, "Still in Chains," *Western Historical Quarterly* 20 (February 1989): 22–34.

31. "Report on the Defective, Dependent, and Delinquent Classes [1880]," Serial No. 2151 (1888), 480–83.

32. "Prisoners in County Jails [1890]," Serial No. 3028, Part 2 (1896), 25–27.

33. Sam Howe Scrapbook, vol. 4, item 917 (Colorado Historical Society Archives, Denver).

34. Frederic M. Thrasher, *The Gang,* 168–69.

35. Henry Nash Smith, *Virgin Land,* 115.

36. Glenn Shirley, *Belle Starr and Her Times,* 167–68.

37. Burton Rascoe, *Belle Starr, "The Bandit Queen,"* 14.

38. *Bella Starr, the Bandit Queen,* 5.

39. Edwin P. Hicks, *Belle Starr and Her Pearl,* 27.

40. Shirley, *Belle Starr and Her Times,* 3–22.

41. Jack Burrows, "Ringo," *American West* 7 (January 1970): 17–21.

42. Molly Haskell, *From Reverence to Rape,* 363.

43. William K. Everson, *The Bad Guys,* 218–19.

44. Sumiko Higashi, *Virgins, Vamps, and Flappers,* 169.
45. State v. Snow, 252 S.W. 629, 632 (Mo., Div. 2, 1923).
46. Sumiko Higashi, *Virgins, Vamps, and Flappers,* 78.
47. Everson, *The Bad Guys,* 228.
48. Haskell, *From Reverence to Rape,* 189.
49. Ibid., 189–91; Foster Hirsch, *The Dark Side of the Screen,* 146–48.

CHAPTER 12. EL PATRIO

1. David J. Langum, *Law and Community on the Mexican California Frontier,* 60–77; Arthur L. Campa, *Hispanic Culture in the Southwest,* 90.
2. Michael N. Canlis, "The Evolution of Law Enforcement in California," *The Far-Westerner* 2 (July 1961): 10.
3. "Long Dispute Over Joaquin Murietta Slaying Settled," *Oakland Tribune,* 17 March 1941.
4. "The Pickled Head Puzzle," *San Francisco Chronicle,* 8 August 1980.
5. "The Outlaw of the Sacramento" (Huntington Library, San Marino, California).
6. John Rollin Ridge, *Joaquin Murieta,* 12–137.
7. Frank F. Latta, *Joaquin Murrieta and His Horse Gangs,* 77–143.
8. Jill L. Cossley-Batt, *The Last of the California Rangers,* 166.
9. Ridge, *Joaquin Murieta,* 158.
10. Peter Lyon, *The Wild, Wild West,* 4.
11. Walter Noble Burns, *The Robin Hood of El Dorado,* 292.
12. Edwin L. Sabin, *Wild Men of the Wild West,* 118.
13. Richard Patterson, *Historical Atlas of the Outlaw West,* 22; Lee Silva, "Joaquin Murietta," *Guns and the Gunfighters,* 17.
14. Pierce Collection (Huntington Library, San Marino, California).
15. Joseph Gollomb, *Master Highwaymen,* 211–312; James D. Horan, *The Outlaws,* 167–84.
16. Joseph Henry Jackson, *Anybody's Gold,* 120.
17. Paul J. Vanderwood, *Disorder and Progress,* xiv–xvii; Walter Prescott Webb, *The Texas Rangers,* 176–93.
18. Ray Allen Billington, *Land of Savagery Land of Promise,* 287–90.
19. Campa, *Hispanic Culture in the Southwest,* 103.
20. Robert Greenwood, *The California Outlaw Tiburcio Vásquez,* 26–27.
21. Burton C. Mossman File (Arizona Pioneers Historical Society Archives, Tucson); Jay J. Wagoner, *Arizona Territory 1863–1912,* 379.
22. George D. Hendricks, *The Bad Man of the West,* 91.
23. Cortez v. State, 43 Tex. Cr. R. 375, 66 S.W. 453 (1902); Cortez v. State, 44 Tex. Cr. R. 169, 69 S.W. 536 (1902).

24. Americo Paredes, *With His Pistol in His Hand,* 52–55, 79–83, 100–104, 114; John Oliver West, "To Die Like a Man" (Ph.D. dissertation, University of Texas, Austin, 1964), 174–90.

25. J. Frank Dobie, *A Vaquero of the Brush Country,* 47, 63, 71; John S. Ford, "Memoirs" (Texas State Archives, Austin).

26. Leo Grebler, Joan W. Moore, and Ralph C. Guzman, *The Mexican-American People,* 532.

27. *Jail Inmates 1983,* 2; *Historical Corrections Statistics in the United States, 1850–1984,* 65.

28. "Report on the Defective, Dependent, and Delinquent Classes [1880]," Serial No. 2151 (1888), 480–83.

29. Roger D. McGrath, *Gunfighters Highwaymen & Vigilantes,* 144.

30. Don Russell, *The Lives and Legends of Buffalo Bill,* 308, 317, 340, 371, 377.

31. Serrato v. State, 74 Tex. Cr. R. 413, 171 S.W. 1133 (1914); Webb, *The Texas Rangers,* 484–504.

32. Ramón Eduardo Ruíz, *The Great Rebellion,* 186.

33. John Reed, *Insurgent Mexico,* 117.

34. Ibid., 119.

35. Ernest Otto Schuster, *Pancho Villa's Shadow,* 142–43.

36. Edith O'Shaughnessy, *A Diplomat's Wife in Mexico,* 243.

37. Notice Catalog, Margaret Herrick Library (Academy of Motion Picture Arts and Sciences, Beverly Hills, California).

38. Francis A. Collins, *The Camera Man,* 23–37.

39. Moving Picture World File, Margaret Herrick Library (Academy of Motion Picture Arts and Sciences, Beverly Hills, California).

40. Kevin Brownlow, *The War, the West, and the Wilderness,* 87–105; Terry Ramsaye, *A Million and One Nights,* 2:670–73.

41. Mexico—Biography—Villa File, Southwest Reference Collection (El Paso Public Library, El Paso, Texas).

42. Jesse Ed Rascoe, *The Treasure Album of Pancho Villa,* 114.

43. Mexico—Juarez—Revolution File, Southwest Reference Collection (El Paso Public Library, El Paso, Texas).

44. John V. Young, *The State Parks of New Mexico,* 101–2; Haldeen Braddy, *Pancho Villa at Columbus,* 34–37; Stan Adler to Frank M. King, March 15, 1953, Frank Marion King Collection (Huntington Library, San Marino, California).

45. Herbert Molloy Mason, *The Great Pursuit,* 237–47.

46. *Francisco "Pancho" Villa,* 17–20.

47. Capt. Kennedy, U.S.A., *The Life and History of Francisco Villa,* 135–43.

48. Allen L. Woll, *The Latin Image in American Film,* 29.

49. Introductory title, *The Mark of Zorro* (1920).

50. James R. Parish and Don E. Stanke, *Swashbucklers*, 25–88; Kevin Brownlow, *The Parade's Gone By*, 248–57; Frank N. Magill, *Magill's Survey of Cinema*, 712–15.

51. George D. Hendricks, *The Bad Man of the West*, 141.

52. Mark Lane and Dick Gregory, *Code Name "Zorro,"* 94.

53. Edgcumb Pinchon, *Viva Villa!*, i.

54. Closing dialogue, *Viva Villa!* (1934).

55. Pancho Villa File (Arizona Pioneers Historical Society Archives, Tucson).

56. Woll, *The Latin Image in American Film*, 108.

57. Paul F. Angiolillo, *A Criminal as Hero*, 2–3.

58. Eric Hobsbawm, *Bandits*, 43.

59. Na Fíníní (National Museum, Dublin, Ireland).

60. Robert Kee, *Ireland: A History*, 103–17.

61. McGrath, *Gunfighters Highwaymen & Vigilantes*, 116–17.

62. *Fodor's Ireland*, 176.

63. Robert Hughes, *The Fatal Shore*, 470–79.

64. Robert M. Senkewicz, *Vigilantes in Gold Rush San Francisco*, 79.

65. K. S. Inglis, *The Australian Colonists*, 169–70, 263–65; Hughes, *The Fatal Shore*, 203–43.

66. Robert G. Athearn, *Thomas Francis Meagher*, 23–26.

67. Ibid., 164–66.

CHAPTER 13. THE MOBSTER

1. Walter Prescott Webb, *The Great Plains*, 500.

2. Fred E. Sutton, *Hands Up!*, 64–65.

3. Robertus Love, *The Rise and Fall of Jesse James*, 44.

4. Carl Coke Rister, "Outlaws and Vigilantes on the Southern Plains: 1865–1885," *Mississippi Valley Historical Review* 19 (March 1933): 546

5. Kent Ladd Steckmesser, *The Western Hero*, 89; Stephen Tatum, *Inventing Billy the Kid*, 183.

6. James Truslow Adams, "Our Lawless Heritage," *Atlantic Monthly* 142 (December 1928): 732–40.

7. Frederic M. Thrasher, *The Gang*, 33–34.

8. Frank M. Canton, *Frontier Trails*, 32.

9. James H. Cook, *Fifty Years on the Old Frontier*, 59–60

10. Al Jennings, *Through the Shadows with O. Henry*, 38.

11. Cook, *Fifty Years on the Old Frontier*, 13.

12. "Sam Bass, Famous Desperado Was Likable Outlaw," *Sheriffs' Association of Texas Magazine* 1 (July 1931): 14.

13. Austin Callan, "Sheriffing in the Old Days," *Sheriffs' Association of*

Texas Magazine 1, no. 1 (1930): 9; Gary L. Roberts, "The West's Gunmen," *The American West* 8 (January 1971): 13–64.

14. C. B. Rhodes, Manuscript File (University of Oklahoma Archives, Norman, Oklahoma).

15. "I Knew He'd Do It," *Daily Oklahoman* (Oklahoma City), 19 February 1924.

16. Emmett Dalton, *When the Daltons Rode*, 276–77.

17. Ibid., 285–87.

18. Henry Sinclair Drago, *Outlaws on Horseback*, 300.

19. Richard Patterson, *Train Robbery*, 203.

20. Thrasher, *The Gang*, 294–95.

21. "Train Bandits' Loot May Reach $3,000,000," *New York Times*, 14 June 1924; "Catch 5 Gas Bandits," *New York Times*, 15 June 1924; "Train Held Up Near Chicago," *Daily Oklahoman* (Oklahoma City), 13 June 1924.

22. "Tom O'Connor May Have Had Role in Theft," *Daily Oklahoman* (Oklahoma City), 15 June 1924; "Train Bandit Hunt Extends Over Country," ibid., 14 June 1924.

23. Bosley Crowther, *The Great Films*, 86–87.

24. Carlos Clarens, *Crime Movies*, 65.

25. Eugene Rosow, *Born to Lose*, 332.

26. Neil Hickey and Edward Sorel, "The Warner Mob," *American Heritage* 35 (December 1983): 34.

27. George W. Hansen, "True Story of Wild Bill–McCanles Affray," *Nebraska History* 10 (April–June 1927): 105; Cook, *Fifty Years on the Old Frontier*, 105.

28. Robert Warshow, *The Immediate Experience*, 131.

29. Ibid., 132.

30. Ibid., 133.

31. John Cawelti, *Focus on Bonnie and Clyde*, 42.

32. Clarens, *Crime Movies*, 24.

33. Colin McArthur, *Underworld U.S.A.*, 18.

34. Warshow, *The Immediate Experience*, 136.

35. Ibid., 140–41.

36. Hickey and Sorel, "The Warner Mob," 34.

37. James R. Parish and Don E. Stanke, *Swashbucklers*, 263–326.

38. *The Challenge of Crime in a Free Society*, 22–27; Edwin H. Sutherland and C. E. Gehlke, "Crime and Punishment," *Recent Social Trends in the United States*, 1114–67; *Sourcebook of Criminal Justice Statistics—1987*, 316, 346–47.

39. J. Edgar Hoover, *Persons in Hiding*, 93.

40. Frank Browning and John Gerassi, *The American Way of Crime*, 370.

41. "Five Killed in Kansas City Gun Battle," *Daily Times Herald* (Dallas, Texas), 17 June 1933; "5 Slain in Battle By Gang to Free Oklahoma Bandit: Massacre in Kansas City," *New York Times*, 18 June 1933.

42. "Dying Bandit Admits Series of Robberies," *Daily Times Herald* (Dal-

las, Texas), 1 January 1934; "Underhill Near Death," *New York Times*, 2 January 1934.

43. Paul I. Wellman, *A Dynasty of Western Outlaws*, 8–9.

44. Hoover, *Persons in Hiding*, 21.

45. Wellman, *A Dynasty of Western Outlaws*, 329.

46. B. A. Botkin, *A Treasury of American Folklore*, 72.

47. "Bad Man Floyd Dies," *Daily Times Herald* (Dallas, Texas), 23 October 1934.

48. Myron J. Quimby, *The Devil's Emissaries*, 62, 286.

49. *Songs of the American West*, 325.

50. Merle Clayton, *Union Station Massacre*, 200–203.

51. Jay Robert Nash, *Bloodletters and Badmen*, 294; "Pretty Boy Floyd Slain As He Flees By Federal Men," *New York Times*, 23 October 1934.

52. Carl Sifakis, *The Encyclopedia of American Crime*, 390.

53. Wellman, *A Dynasty of Western Outlaws*, 345.

54. Lisle Reedstrom, "John Dillinger," *Guns and the Gunfighters*, 94–101.

55. Dillinger, J., File (Arizona Pioneers Historical Society Archives, Tucson).

56. John Toland, *The Dillinger Days*, 209–11; "Dillinger Escapes Jail; Using a Wooden Gun He Locks Guards in Cell," *New York Times*, 4 March 1934.

57. Richard Gid Powers, *G-Men*, 122, 200–201.

58. Reedstrom, "John Dillinger," 98–99; Toland, *The Dillinger Days*, 72, 157, 258–60.

59. Sifakis, *The Encyclopedia of American Crime*, 210.

60. "Super-Bad Man Shot Down by U.S. Sleuths," "Girl Friend Led Dillinger to His Death," "Sixteen Fatalities Mark Hunt," *Daily Times Herald* (Dallas, Texas), 23 July 1934; "Dillinger, 'Broke,' Betrayed by Spies," "Dillinger Killing Arouses England," *New York Times*, 24 July 1934.

61. Hoover, *Persons in Hiding*, 98.

62. Browning and Gerrassi, *The American Way of Crime*, 390.

63. Dillinger, J., File (Arizona Pioneers Historical Society Archives, Tucson).

64. Quimby, *The Devil's Emissaries*, 256–60.

65. "A Woman Left Dillinger Behind," *Daily Times Herald* (Dallas, Texas), 27 July 1934.

66. Toland, *The Dillinger Days*, 331.

67. Hoover, *Persons in Hiding*, 7–8.

68. Alvin Karpis, *The Alvin Karpis Story*, 80–81.

69. "Mother and son, Kidnap suspects, Killed," *Dallas Morning News*, 17 January 1935; "Fred Barker and 'Ma' Die: Shoot to the Last When Trapped by Federal Agents in Florida, Machine Gun in Her Hand," *New York Times*, 17 January 1935.

70. "Karpis Trail of Crime Covers Map," "6 States Want to Try Karpis," "G-Men Whisk Karpis to St. Paul," *Dallas Morning News,* 2 May 1936.

71. Karpis, *The Alvin Karpis Story,* 11.

72. "Uncle Sam Lays Plans for War on Crime," *Daily Times Herald* (Dallas, Texas), 8 July 1934.

73. 18 U.S.C. 3052 (1934).

74. 18 U.S.C. 2113 (1934); 18 U.S.C. 1073 (1934).

75. 26 U.S.C. 1201 (1934).

76. Wellman, *A Dynasty of Western Outlaws,* 342.

77. *Historical Corrections Statistics in the United States, 1850–1984,* 29.

78. Thomas J. Deakin, "The FBI Law Enforcement Bulletin," *FBI Law Enforcement Bulletin* 54 (October 1985): 2–9.

79. Courtney Riley Cooper, *Ten Thousand Public Enemies,* vii.

80. Ibid., 5–6.

81. Browning and Gerassi, *The American Way of Crime,* 391.

82. Clarens, *Crime Movies,* 131–38; Tony Proveda, *Lawlessness and Reform,* 22–24.

83. Browning and Gerassi, *The American Way of Crime,* 393–94.

CHAPTER 14. THE BADMAN

1. *They Went That-A-Way,* 35.

2. J. A. Place, *The Western Films of John Ford,* 34.

3. Philip French, *Westerns: Aspects of a Movie Genre,* 60.

4. Dixon Wecter, *The Hero in America,* 352

5. Prologue to *Billy the Kid* (1941).

6. R. W. Mondy, "Analysis of Frontier Social Instability," *Southwestern Social Science Quarterly* 24 (September 1943): 172–73; Mabel A. Elliott, "Crime and the Frontier Mores," *American Sociological Review* 9 (April 1944): 192; William Seagle, *The Quest for Law,* 245; Wayne Gard, *Frontier Justice,* v–vi; Gary L. Roberts, "The West's Gunman," *The American West* 8 (March 1971): 20–23.

7. Hans von Hentig, "Redhead and Outlaw," *Journal of Criminal Law and Criminology* 38 (May–June 1947): 5.

8. George D. Hendricks, *The Bad Man of the West,* 156.

9. Ibid., 146–48.

10. Ibid., 120.

11. Robert Warshow, *The Immediate Experience,* 150.

12. Paul I. Wellman, *A Dynasty of Western Outlaws,* 188.

13. Harry Sinclair Drago, *Outlaws on Horseback,* xviii.

14. Edward Everett Dale, *Cow Country,* 115–16.

15. Raymond W. Stedman, *The Serials,* 110–15, 169–74.

16. Foster Hirsch, *The Dark Side of the Screen,* 147.

17. Carlos Clarens, *Crime Movies,* 191–233.

18. J. H. Gaute and Robin Odell, *The Murderer's Who's Who,* 218; Starkweather v. State, 167 Neb. 477, 93 N.W.2d 619 (1958). "Program Vindicates Her," *Arkansas Gazette* (Little Rock), 23 February 1983.

19. Hirabayashi v. U.S., 320 U.S. 81, 63 S. Ct. 1375 (1943); Korematsu v. U.S., 323 U.S. 214, 65 S. Ct. 193 (1944); Exparte Endo, 323 U.S. 246, 65 S. Ct. 208 (1944).

20. Roger H. Davis, "Outlaw Motorcyclists," *FBI Law Enforcement Bulletin* 51 (October 1982): 14.

21. Ray Pickard, *Who Played Who in the Movies,* 14–15, 113–14.

22. Don B. Graham, "Audie Murphy: Kid with a Gun," *Shooting Stars,* 143.

23. George C. Kohn, *Dictionary of Culprits and Criminals,* 24.

24. John Toland, *The Dillinger Days,* 250.

25. John H. Jenkins and Gordon H. Frost, *I'm Frank Hamer,* 209–48; Lee Simmons, *Assignment Huntsville,* 126–35; "Barrow and Woman are Slain by Police in Louisiana Trap," *New York Times,* 25 May 1934.

26. Myron J. Quimby, *The Devil's Emissaries,* 202.

27. "Two Mothers Grieve in West Dallas for Dead Bandit and Moll," *Daily Times Herald* (Dallas, Texas), 23 May 1934.

28. "Without Regrets," *Daily Times Herald* (Dallas, Texas), 24 May 1934.

29. "Here Is Story of Bonnie and Clyde," *Daily Times Herald* (Dallas, Texas), 23 May 1934.

30. Emma Parker and Nell Barrow Cowan, *Fugitives,* iv.

31. John Treherne, *The Strange History of Bonnie and Clyde,* 224.

32. Sandra Wake and Nicola Hayden, *The Bonnie and Clyde Book,* 14–26.

33. Clarens, *Crime Movies,* 262.

34. Wake and Hayden, *The Bonnie and Clyde Book,* 7.

35. John Cawelti, *Focus on Bonnie and Clyde,* 40.

36. Treherne, *The Strange History of Bonnie and Clyde,* 236.

37. Ibid., 255.

38. Ray Allen Billington, *Land of Savagery Land of Promise,* 322.

CHAPTER 15. THE FUGITIVE

1. Prologue to "The Fugitive" (1963–67).

2. Horace Newcomb, *TV: The Most Popular Art,* 144–51, 159.

3. Tim Brooks and Earle March, *The Complete Directory to Prime-Time Network TV Shows,* 303–4.

4. Jeff Rovin, *The Great Television Series,* 88.

5. Raymond W. Stedman, *The Serials,* 403.

6. Philip D. Jordan, *Frontier Law and Order,* 113.

7. Ibid., 114.

8. Bill O'Neal, *Encyclopedia of Western Gunfighters*, 3–12.

9. Joseph G. Rosa, *The Gunfighter: Man or Myth?* 160.

10. Wayne Gard, *Frontier Justice*, 62.

11. Robert M. Utley, *High Noon in Lincoln*, 173.

12. Elmer Keith, "Eyewitness to Six-Gun Law," *Guns and the Gunfighters*, 188.

13. Alan Swallow, *The Wild Bunch*, 2.

14. Larry Pointer, *In Search of Butch Cassidy*, 163.

15. Joe LeFors, Manuscript File (Western History Research Center, University of Wyoming, Laramie).

16. Pointer, *In Search of Butch Cassidy*, 198–99.

17. William A. Pinkerton, *Train Robberies and Train Robbers*, 74.

18. Pointer, *In Search of Butch Cassidy*, 15–16.

19. John Rolfe Burroughs, *Where the Old West Stayed Young*, 133.

20. Charles Kelly, *The Outlaw Trail*, 299.

21. George D. Hendricks, *The Bad Man of the West*, 180.

22. James D. Horan, *Desperate Men*, 283.

23. James D. Horan, *The Outlaws*, 3–4.

24. Allen Eyles, *The Western*, 39–40, 141.

25. James D. Horan and Paul Sann, *Pictorial History of the Wild West*, 235; James D. Horan, *The Wild Bunch*, 170.

26. William Goldman, *Butch Cassidy and the Sundance Kid*, 156–64.

27. Ibid., 115.

28. Bruce Chatwin, "In Patagonia," *American Way* 21 (15 May 1988): 94.

29. Janet L. Langlois, *Belle Gunness*, 134.

30. Leonard Sanders, *How Fort Worth Became the Texasmost City*, 85.

31. Pointer, *In Search of Butch Cassidy*, 215–50.

32. Lula Parker Betenson, *Butch Cassidy, My Brother*, 177–96.

33. Jim Kitses, *Horizons West*, 141.

34. Philip French, *Westerns: Aspects of a Movie Genre*, 52.

35. Will Wright, *Six Guns and Society*, 97–123.

36. John G. Cawelti, *Adventure, Mystery, and Romance*, 259.

37. "Outlaws," *TV Guide* 35, no. 2 (10 January 1987): A-27.

38. Newcomb, *TV: The Most Popular Art*, 83–109.

39. Jack Shadoian, *Dreams and Dead Ends*, 5–9.

40. Cawelti, *Adventure, Mystery, and Romance*, 79.

41. Stuart M. Kaminsky, *American Film Genres*, 91.

42. Earl Caldwell, "Hijacker Collects Ransom of $200,000," *New York Times*, 26 November 1971.

43. "Mysterious hijacker still stirs imagination," *Dallas Morning News*, 24 November 1983.

44. "Prisoner Acquitted in Sex Slayings Dies," *New York Times*, 5 June 1979.

45. "Manhunt is on for Idaho Killer," *USA Today*, 1 April 1986; Jeff Long, *Outlaw*, 195–237; Jack Olsen, *Give a Boy a Gun*, 92–97, 190–200.

46. William Bradford Huie, *He Slew the Dreamer*, 120–46; Gerold Frank, *An American Death*, 175–93.

47. James McKinley, *Assassination in America*, 199.

48. "Wanted by the FBI," *FBI Law Enforcement Bulletin* 43 (November 1974): 16–17.

49. Patricia Campbell Hearst, *Every Secret Thing*, 230.

50. *Correctional Populations in the United States*, 62; *Sourcebook of Criminal Justice Statistics, 1985*, 534–35; *Sourcebook of Criminal Justice Statistics, 1986*, 425; *Historical Corrections Statistics in the United States, 1850–1984*, 164–65.

51. "27 Years for 'Top Ten,'" *FBI Law Enforcement Bulletin* 46 (March 1977): 31.

EPILOGUE

1. Joseph Campbell, *The Hero with a Thousand Faces*, 30–40.

2. Richard Slotkin, *Regeneration Through Violence*, 550–65.

3. John G. Cawelti, *Adventure, Mystery, and Romance*, 52.

4. Paul F. Angiolillo, *A Criminal as Hero*, 3–4.

5. Eric Hobsbawm, *Bandits*, 4–8.

6. Angiolillo, *A Criminal as Hero*, 189.

7. Paul Hemp, "And We Suppose He Really Stole From the Poor to Give to the Rich," *Wall Street Journal*, 3 May 1988.

8. Don Russell, *The Lives and Legends of Buffalo Bill*, 480.

9. Tom Horn, *Life of Tom Horn*, 260–61.

10. Eric Hobsbawm, *Primitive Rebels*, 14–28; Paul Kooistra, *Criminals as Heroes*, 141–59.

11. James A. Inciardi, Alan A. Block, and Lyle A. Hollowell, *Historical Approaches to Crime*, 53.

12. J. C. Holt, *Robin Hood*, 154.

13. Danilo Dolci, *Outlaws*, 7.

14. Maurice Keen, *The Outlaws of Medieval Legend*, 218.

15. Richard White, "Outlaw Gangs of the Middle Border: American Social Bandits," *Western Historical Quarterly* 12 (October 1981): 387–408.

16. Jenni Calder, *There Must Be a Lone Ranger*, 25; Orrin E. Klapp, "The Folk Hero," *Journal of American Folklore* 62 (January–March 1949): 17–25; Kent Ladd Steckmesser, *Western Outlaws*, 3–15.

17. Dixon Wecter, *The Hero in America*, 350.

18. Billy James Chandler, *The Bandit King*, 240–47; Joseph G. Rosa, *The Gunfighter*, 49; Harry Sinclair Drago, *The Legend Makers*, vi.

19. Eric Hobsbawm, "Social Bandits," *Comparative Studies in Society and History* 14 (September 1972): 503–5.

20. Kent L. Steckmesser, "Robin Hood and the American Outlaw," *Journal of American Folklore* 79 (April–June 1966): 353.

21. Daniel Calhoun, "Studying American Violence," *Journal of Interdisciplinary History* 1 (Autumn 1970): 169.

22. Wayne Gard, *Frontier Justice*, vi; White, "Outlaw Gangs of the Middle Border," 387–408.

23. Hobsbawm, *Bandits*, 114.

24. Kent Ladd Steckmesser, *The Western Hero*, 102.

25. Jack Shadoian, *Dreams and Dead Ends*, 5–9; Richard Slotkin, *The Fatal Environment*, 126–37, 151–58.

26. Eric Mottram, "The Persuasive Lips: Men and Guns in America, the West," *Journal of American Studies* 10 (April 1976): 67.

27. Kooistra, *Criminals as Heroes*, 160–80.

28. Steckmesser, *Western Outlaws*, 141–45.

29. Porter A. Stratton, *The Territorial Press of New Mexico, 1834–1912*, 190.

30. Jack Olsen, *Give a Boy a Gun*, 153.

31. Jeff Long, *Outlaw*, 164.

32. Emerson Hough, *The Story of the Outlaw*, 393–401; Jon Tuska, *Dark Cinema*, xxi, 149–90.

33. Murray Melbin, "Night as Frontier," *American Sociological Review* 43 (February 1978): 10–12.

34. Rosa, *The Gunfighter*, 209.

35. James Wright, Peter H. Rossi, and Kathleen Daly, *Under the Gun*, 319–24; Philip D. Jordan, *Frontier Law and Order*, 174.

36. Mottram, "The Persuasive Lips," 60.

37. John A. Lomax and Alan Lomax, *Best Loved American Folk Songs*, 283.

38. Holt, *Robin Hood*, 73.

39. Hermann Mannheim, *Comparative Criminology*, 307, 582–83.

40. Jack Katz, *Seductions of Crime*, 310–24.

41. Holt, *Robin Hood*, 189–90.

42. Harold L. Berger, *Science Fiction and the New Dark Age*, 86–146.

43. Wecter, *The Hero in America*, 12–16, 482–86.

44. Hobsbawm, *Bandits*, 109–15.

Bibliography

ARCHIVAL MATERIALS

Academy of Motion Pictures Arts and Sciences, Margaret Herrick Library, Beverly Hills, California. Moving Picture World File. Notice Catalog.

Arizona Pioneers' Historical Society Archives—Arizona Heritage Center, Tucson, Arizona. Apache Kid, Indians of North America, manuscript file. Tom (Seth) Bailey manuscript file. J. Dillinger file. Burton C. Mossman manuscript file. Pancho Villa file.

Clare History Center, Corofin, County Clare, Ireland. Transportation.

Colorado Historical Society Archives, Denver, Colorado. T. F. Dawson scrapbooks. Mrs. Anna Dillon interviews. Sam Howe scrapbooks. Tom Tobin photo file.

El Paso Public Library—Southwest Reference Collection, El Paso, Texas. Mexico—Biography-Villa file. Mexico—Juarez-Revolution file.

Federal Records Center, Denver, Colorado. Records of the U.S. District Court, Territory of New Mexico, First Judicial District, 1896–1899.

Federal Records Center, Fort Worth, Texas. Grand Jury Docket, U.S. Court, Second Judicial District, Indian Territory, 1893. Laws of the Choctaw Nation. Records of the U.S. District Court, Western District, Arkansas, 1871. U.S. Court docket, Central District, Indian Territory, 1898–1904.

Huntington Library, San Marino, California. Frank Marion King collection. The Outlaw of the Sacramento. Pierce Collection.

Kansas State Historical Society Archives, Topeka. C. W. Alexander, "The Five Families." Bruce Brigden, "The Bloody Benders."

Maritime Trust, Greenwich, Greater London, England. Long John Silver Collection.

Museum of Local History, Hastings, East Sussex, England. Cinque Ports. Smuggling.

National Museum of Ireland, Dublin, Ireland. Na Fíníní.

Oklahoma Historical Society Archives, Oklahoma City. Indian-Pioneer History (WPA Project, 1937).

Stanford University Archives, Stanford, California. James Otey Bradford papers.
Texas State Archives, Austin. John S. Ford, "Memoirs."
University of Arizona Archives, Tucson. Joseph Thomas McKinney papers.
University of Colorado Archives, Boulder. Boulder Police Court Docket, 1882–1885. C. Arthur Hockmuth, "Reynolds' Rebel Raiders." Independent District, Gilpin County [Colorado], "Laws of Independent District [1861]." "Is Quantrell Dead? [1888]."
University of New Mexico Archives, Albuquerque. New Mexico Territorial Mounted Police Description Cards, 1906–1910. Territorial Secretary, extradition papers for fugitives from New Mexico, 1900–1905.
University of Oklahoma Archives, Norman. C. B. Rhodes manuscript file.
University of Texas, Austin. William C. Holden, "Frontier Problems and Movements in West Texas, 1846–1900," Ph.D. diss., 1928. John Oliver West, "To Die Like a Man: The 'Good' Outlaw Tradition in the American Southwest," Ph.D. diss., 1964.
University of Wyoming Archives, Laramie. Rebecca Williamson Carter Bailey, "Wyoming Stock Inspectors and Detectives, 1873–1890," M.A. thesis, 1948. Frank M. Canton manuscript file. Joe LeFors manuscript file.
Wells Fargo History Department, San Francisco, California. "Black Bart" File.

GOVERNMENT DOCUMENTS

Annual Report of the Commissioner of Indian Affairs, 1895. Washington: Government Printing Office, 1896.
The Challenge of Crime in a Free Society. Washington: Government Printing Office, 1967.
Correctional Populations in the United States 1985. Washington: U.S. Department of Justice, 1986.
Historical Corrections Statistics in the United States: 1850–1984. Washington: U.S. Department of Justice, 1986.
Jail Inmates 1983. Washington: Government Printing Office, 1985.
New Mexico/1988. Santa Fe: [New Mexico] Tourism and Travel Division, 1988.
"Prisoners in County Jails [1890]," Serial No. 3028, Part 2 (1896).
Report of the Acting Governor of Arizona Made to the Secretary of the Interior, 1890. Washington: Government Printing Office, 1890.
Report of the Governor of Arizona Made to the Secretary of Interior for the Year 1883. Washington: Government Printing Office, 1883.
Report of the Governor of Arizona to the Secretary of the Interior, 1885. Washington: Government Printing Office, 1885.

Report of the Governor of Arizona to the Secretary of the Interior, 1904. Washington: Government Printing Office, 1904.

Report of the Governor of Arizona to the Secretary of the Interior, 1905. Washington: Government Printing Office, 1905.

Report of the Governor of Arizona to the Secretary of the Interior, 1906. Washington: Government Printing Office, 1906.

Report of the Governor of Arizona to the Secretary of the Interior, 1907. Washington: Government Printing Office, 1907.

"Report on the Defective, Dependent, and Delinquent Classes [1880]," Serial No. 2151 (1888).

Report on the Mortality and Vital Statistics of the United States {1880}. 2 vols. Washington: Government Printing Office, 1885–1886.

Report to the Nation on Crime and Justice. Washington: U.S. Department of Justice, 1983.

Sixty-first Annual Report of the Commissioner of Indian Affairs to the Secretary of the Interior. 1892. Washington: Government Printing Office, 1892.

Sourcebook of Criminal Justice Statistics—1984. Washington: Government Printing Office, 1985.

Sourcebook of Criminal Justice Statistics—1985. Washington: Government Printing Office, 1986.

Sourcebook of Criminal Justice Statistics—1986. Washington: Government Printing Office, 1987.

Sourcebook of Criminal Justice Statistics—1987. Washington: Government Printing Office, 1988.

State and Federal Prisoners, 1925–85. Washington: U.S. Department of Justice, 1986.

Travel Map of New Mexico. Santa Fe: New Mexico State Highway Department, 1983.

Uniform Crime Reports for the United States {1930}. Washington: Government Printing Office, 1931.

Uniform Crime Reports for the United States {1980}. Washington: Government Printing Office, 1981.

CASES

Autry v. Mitchell, 420 F. Supp. 967 (E.D.N.C., 1976).

Case of Ralph Breton and Roger de Breteuil, 2 Ord. Vital. 262 (England, 1075).

Commonwealth v. Anderson, 2 Va. Cas. 245 (Virginia, 1821).

Commonwealth v. Hagerman, 2 Va. Cas. 244 (Virginia, 1821).

Commonwealth v. Hale, 2 Va. Cas. 241 (Virginia, 1821).

Cortez v. State, 43 Tex. Crim. 375, 66 S.W. 453 (Texas, 1902).

Cortez v. State, 44 Tex. Crim. 169, 69 S.W. 536 (Texas, 1902).

Dale County v. Gunter, 46 Ala. 118 (Alabama, 1871).
Earles v. State, 47 Tex. Crim. 559, 85 S.W. 1 (Texas, 1905).
Ex parte Endo, 323 U.S. 246, 65 S. Ct. 208 (1944).
Farrer v. State, 2 Ohio St. 54 (Ohio, 1853).
Gragg v. State 148 Tex. Crim. 267, 186 S.W.2d 243 (Texas, 1945).
Herring v. the Utes, 32 Ct. Cl. 536 (U.S., 1897).
Hirabayashi v. United States, 320 U.S. 81, 63 S. Ct. 632 (1958).
Holt v. Sarver, 300 F. Supp. 825 (E.D. Ark., 1969).
In re Boyle, 6 Idaho 609, 57 P. 707 (Idaho, 1899).
Jackson v. State, 34 Tex. Crim. 1, 28 S.W. 815 (Texas, 1894).
The King v. Belisme, 4 Ord. Vital. 169 (England, 1102).
The King v. Malet, 4 Ord. Vital 161 (England, 1102).
Korematsu v. United States, 323 U.S. 214, 65 S. Ct. 193 (1944).
Milliken v. City Council, 54 Tex. 388 (Texas, 1881).
Montoya v. the Mescaleros, 32 Ct. Cl. 349 (U.S., 1897).
Northern v. State, 150 Tex. Crim. 511, 203 S.W.2d 206 (Texas, 1947).
Northern v. State, 152 Tex. Crim. 569, 216 S.W.2d 192 (Texas, 1948).
Respublica v. Doan, 1 U.S. (1 Dall.) 86 (Pennsylvania, 1784).
Salois v. United States, 33 Ct. Cl. 326 (U.S., 1898).
Scott v. United States, 33 Ct. Cl. 486 (U.S., 1898).
Serrato v. State, 74 Tex. Crim. 413, 171 S.W. 1133 (Texas, 1914).
Shanley v. Harvey, 2 Eden 126 (England, 1762).
Somerset v. Stewart, Lofft 1, 20 How. St. Tr. 1 (England, 1762).
Starkweather v. State, 167 Neb. 477, 93 N.W.2d 619 (Nebraska, 1958).
State v. Hall, 115 N.C. 811, 20 S.E. 729 (North Carolina, 1894).
State v. Snow, 252 S.W. 629 (Missouri, 1923).
State v. Waddell, 289 N.C. 19, 220 S.E.2d 293 (North Carolina, 1975).
State v. Waddell, 428 U.S. 904, 96 S. Ct. 3211 (1976).
Trial of Captain William Kidd, 14 St. Tri. 147 (England, 1701).
United States v. Pirates, 18 U.S. (5 Wheat.) 184 (1820).
United States v. Smith, 18 U.S. (5 Wheat.) 153 (1820).
Wilkes v. Rex, 19 St. Tri. 1075 (1769).
Woolverton v. the Nez Perces, 29 Ct. Cl. 107 (U.S., 1894).

CONSTITUTIONS

Magna Carta, Clause 39 (England, 1215).
Massachusetts Constitution, Part I, Section 13 (1788).
Tennessee Constitution, Article I, Section 8 (1796).
Texas Constitution, Article I, Section 20 (1876).
United States Constitution, Article I, Section 10 (1789).

STATUTES

United States. 18 U.S.C. 1073 (Fugitive Felon Act, 1934), 1153 (Seven Major Crimes Act, 1885), 1651 (Piracy Act, 1790), 1991 (Train Robbery Act, 1902), 2113 (Bank Robbery Act, 1934), 2116 (Station Robbery Act, 1903), 3052 (FBI Act, 1934); 26 U.S.C. 5848 (Machine Gun Act, 1934).

Nevada. Criminal Law, Section 10 (1885).

New York. Code of Criminal Procedure, Section 814–25 (1827).

North Carolina. Act for Restoring and Preserving the Public Peace, Colonial Assembly, 1771 (Col. Rec. of N.C., III, 481–86). Tryon's Order Book, 1771 (Col. Rec. of N.C., III, 617). General Statutes, Section 15–48 (1868).

Pennsylvania. Title 19, Section 1321 (1791).

Texas. Penal Code, Article 645 (1879). Penal Code, Article 1063, (1879).

Virginia. Code, Section 19.1–15 (1887).

England. Treaties with the Danes, Edward and Guthram, 11 (c. A.D. 920). Pipe Rolls, 7 Richard I (1196). Pipe Rolls, 14 Henry III (1230). Proclamation 15, 3 Henry VII (1478). Offences at Sea Act, 28 Henry VIII, c. 15 (1536). Act Against Conjurations, 33 Henry VIII, c. 8 (1542). Act for Punishment of Rogues, Vagabonds, and Sturdy Beggars, 39 Elizabeth I, c. 4 (1597). Act Against Conjurations, Enchantments, and Witchcrafts, 1 Jac. I, c. 12 (1603). Act for Preventing Theft and Rapine, 18 Charles II, c. 3 (1666). Habeas Corpus Act, 31 Charles II, c. 2 (1679). Act for More Effectual Suppression of Piracy, 11 William III, c. 7 (1698). Piracy Act, 8 George I, c. 24 (1721). Witchcraft Act, 9 George II, c. 5 (1736). Civil Procedure Repeal Act, 42 & 43 Vict., c. 59, s. 3 (1879). Administration of Justice Act, 1 & 2 George VI, c. 63, s. 12 (1938). Civil Justice (Scotland) Act, 12, 13, & 14, George VI, c. 94, s. 14, 15 (2) (1949).

NEWSPAPERS

Arkansas Gazette (Little Rock).

Boulder County News (Colorado).

Daily Oklahoman (Oklahoma City).

Daily Times Herald (Dallas, Texas).

Dallas Morning News (Texas).

Evening Review (Albuquerque, New Mexico).

Kansas City Times (Missouri).

New York Times (New York).

Oakland Tribune (California).

San Francisco Chronicle (California).

Sunday Times (London, England).
USA Today (Washington, D.C.).
Wall Street Journal (New York).
Weekly New Mexican—El Nuevo Mejicano (Santa Fe).

GENERAL WORKS

Abbott, John S. C. *Captain William Kidd.* New York: Dodd and Mead, 1874.

Adamic, Louis. *Dynamite: The Story of Class Violence in America.* New York: Viking Press, 1935.

Adams, Ramon F. *A Fitting Death for Billy the Kid.* Norman: University of Oklahoma Press, 1960.

————. *Six-Guns and Saddle Leather: A Bibliography of Books and Pamphlets on Western Outlaws and Gunmen.* Norman: University of Oklahoma Press, 1969.

————. *Western Words: A Dictionary of the American West.* Norman: University of Oklahoma Press, 1968.

American Indians and the Law. New Brunswick, N.J.: Transaction Books, 1976.

Andrist, Ralph K. *The Long Death: The Last Days of the Plains Indians.* New York: Macmillan, 1964.

Angiolillo, Paul F. *A Criminal as Hero: Angelo Duca.* Lawrence: Regents Press of Kansas, 1979.

Athearn, Robert G. *The Mythic West in Twentieth-Century America.* Lawrence: University Press of Kansas, 1986.

————. *Thomas Francis Meagher: An Irish Revolutionary in America.* Boulder: University of Colorado Press, 1949.

Baker, Pearl. *Robbers Roost Recollections.* Logan: Utah State University Press, 1976.

Ball, Larry D. *The United States Marshals of New Mexico and Arizona Territories, 1846–1912.* Albuquerque: University of New Mexico Press, 1978.

Bancroft, Hubert Howe. *Popular Tribunals.* 2 vols. San Francisco: History Co., 1887.

Bar, Carl Ludwig von. *A History of Continental Criminal Law.* Boston: Little, Brown, 1916.

Bartholomew, Ed. *Black Jack Ketcham.* Houston: Frontier Press, 1955.

Battis, Emery. *Saints and Sectaries.* Chapel Hill: University of North Carolina Press, 1962.

Beebe, Lucius, and Charles Clegg. *U.S. West: The Saga of Wells Fargo.* New York: E. P. Dutton, 1949.

Bellamy, John. *Crime and Public Order in England in the Later Middle Ages.* London: Routledge and Kegan Paul, 1973.

Bella Starr, the Bandit Queen, or the Female Jesse James: A Full and Authentic His-

tory of the Dashing Female Highwayman. 1889. Austin: Steck Company, 1960.

Berger, Harold L. *Science Fiction and the New Dark Age.* Bowling Green, Ohio: Bowling Green University Press, 1976.

Betenson, Lula Parker. *Butch Cassidy, My Brother.* Provo, Utah: Brigham Young University Press, 1975.

Billington, Ray Allen. *Land of Savagery Land of Promise: The European Image of the American Frontier in the Nineteenth Century.* Norman: University of Oklahoma Press, 1981.

Bird, Isabella. *A Lady's Life in the Rocky Mountains.* 1879. Norman: University of Oklahoma Press, 1960.

Blakeborough, Richard. *The Hand of Glory.* London: Grant Richards, 1924.

Bonner, Willard Hallam. *Pirate Laureate: The Life and Legends of Captain Kidd.* New Brunswick, N.J.: Rutgers University Press, 1947.

Bonney, Edward. *The Banditti of the Prairies; or, The Murderer's Doom!!* 1850. Norman: University of Oklahoma Press, 1963.

Botkin, B. A. *A Treasury of American Folklore.* New York: Crown Publishers, 1944.

Botting, Douglas. *The Pirates.* Alexandria, Va.: Time-Life Books, 1978.

Boyer, Paul, and Stephen Nissenbaum. *Salem Possessed: The Social Origins of Witchcraft.* Cambridge, Mass.: Harvard University Press, 1974.

Bracton, Henry de. *De Legibus et Consuetudininbus Angliae.* 1256. Cambridge, Mass.: Harvard University Press, 1968.

Braddy, Haldeen. *Pancho Villa at Columbus.* El Paso: Texas Western College, 1965.

Breakenridge, William M. *Helldorado: Bringing the Law to the Mesquite.* Boston: Houghton Mifflin, 1928.

Breihan, Carl W. *Outlaws of the Old West.* New York: Bonanza Books, 1957.

————. *Quantrill and His Civil War Guerrillas.* Denver: Sage Books, 1959.

Broehl, Wayne G. *The Molly Maguires.* Cambridge, Mass.: Harvard University Press, 1964.

Bronaugh, W. C. *The Youngers' Fight for Freedom: A Southern Soldier's Twenty Years' Campaign.* Columbia, Mo.: E. W. Stephens, 1906.

Brooks, Juanita. *The Mountain Meadows Massacre.* 1950. Norman: University of Oklahoma Press, 1962.

Brooks, Tim, and Earle March. *The Complete Directory to Prime Time Network TV Shows.* New York: Ballantine Books, 1985.

Browning, Frank, and John Gerassi. *The American Way of Crime.* New York: G. P. Putnam's Sons, 1980.

Brownlee, Richard S. *Gray Ghosts of the Confederacy: Guerrilla Warfare in the West, 1861–1865.* Baton Rouge: Louisiana State University Press, 1958.

Brownlow, Kevin. *The Parade's Gone By.* Berkeley: University of California Press, 1968.

————. *The War, the West, and the Wilderness.* New York: Alfred A. Knopf, 1979.

Buel, James William. *The Border Outlaws: An Authentic and Thrilling History.* Baltimore: I. and M. Ottenheimer, 1882.

Burns, Walter Noble. *The Robin Hood of El Dorado.* New York: Coward-McCann, 1932.

————. *The Saga of Billy the Kid.* Garden City, N.Y.: Doubleday, Page, 1926.

Burroughs, John Rolfe. *Where the Old West Stayed Young: The Remarkable History of Brown's Park.* New York: William Morrow, 1962.

Burt, Olive Woolley. *American Murder Ballads.* New York: Oxford University Press, 1958.

Butler, Anne M. *Daughters of Joy, Sisters of Misery.* Urbana: University of Illinois Press, 1985.

Butler, William Vivian. *The Durable Desperadoes.* London: Macmillan, 1973.

Byrnes, Thomas. *Professional Criminals of America.* 1886. New York: Chelsea House, 1969.

Calder, Jenni. *There Must Be a Lone Ranger.* New York: Taplinger, 1974.

Campa, Arthur L. *Hispanic Culture in the Southwest.* Norman: University of Oklahoma Press, 1979.

Campbell, Joseph. *The Hero with a Thousand Faces.* New York: Pantheon, 1949.

Canton, Frank M. *Frontier Trails: The Autobiography of Frank M. Canton.* Boston: Houghton Mifflin, 1930.

Carter, William. *Ghost Towns of the West.* Menlo Park, Calif.: Lane, 1978.

Cash, W. J. *The Mind of the South.* New York: Vintage Books, 1941.

Castel, Albert. *William Clarke Quantrill: His Life and Times.* New York: Frederick Fell, 1962.

Caughey, John W. *Their Majesties the Mob.* Chicago: University of Chicago Press, 1960.

Cawelti, John G. *Adventure, Mystery, and Romance: Formula Stories as Art and Popular Culture.* Chicago: University of Chicago Press, 1976.

————. *Focus on Bonnie and Clyde.* Englewood Cliffs, N.J.: Prentice-Hall, 1973.

Chambers, Anne. *Granuaile: The Life and Times of Grace O'Malley.* Dublin, Ireland: Wolfhound Press, 1979.

Chandler, Billy James. *The Bandit King: Lampião of Brazil.* College Station: Texas A&M University Press, 1978.

Chapin, Bradley. *Criminal Justice in Colonial America, 1606–1660.* Athens: University of Georgia Press, 1983.

Clarens, Carlos. *Crime Movies.* New York: W. W. Norton, 1980.

Clayton, Merle. *Union Station Massacre.* Indianapolis: Bobbs-Merrill, 1975.

Cline, Donald. *Alias Billy the Kid.* Santa Fe, N.M.: Sunstone Press, 1986.

Coates, Robert M. *The Outlaw Years: The History of Land Pirates of the Natchez Trace.* New York: Macaulay, 1930.

Coatman, John. *Police.* London: Oxford University Press, 1959.

Cohen, Felix S. *The Legal Conscience.* New Haven, Conn.: Yale University Press. 1960.

Collins, Francis A. *The Camera Man: His Adventures in Many Fields.* New York: Century, 1916.

Connelley, William Elsey. *Quantrill and the Border Wars.* Cedar Rapids, Iowa: Torch Press, 1910.

Cook, David J. *Hands Up.* 1882. Norman: University of Oklahoma Press, 1958.

Cook, James H. *Fifty Years on the Old Frontier, as Cowboy, Hunter, Guide, Scout and Ranchman.* New Haven, Conn.: Yale University Press, 1925.

Cooper, Courtney Riley. *Ten Thousand Public Enemies.* Boston: Little, Brown, 1935.

Cossley-Batt, Jill L. *The Last of the California Rangers.* New York: Funk and Wagnalls, 1928.

Crowther, Bosley. *The Great Films: Fifty Golden Years of Motion Pictures.* New York: G. P. Putnam's Sons, 1967.

Croy, Homer. *Jesse James Was My Neighbor.* New York: Duell, Sloan and Pearce, 1949.

Cunningham, Eugene. *Triggernometry: A Galaxy of Gunfighters.* Caldwell, Idaho: Caxton Printers, 1941.

Dale, Edward Everett. *Cow Country.* 1942. Norman: University of Oklahoma Press, 1965.

Dalton, Emmett. *When the Daltons Rode.* Garden City, N.Y.: Doubleday, Doran, 1931.

Davis, Harold E. *The Fledgling Province.* Chapel Hill: University of North Carolina Press, 1976.

Debo, Angie. *Geronimo: The Man, His Time, His Place.* Norman: University of Oklahoma Press, 1976.

――――. *A History of the Indians of the United States.* Norman: University of Oklahoma Press, 1970.

――――. *The Road to Disappearance.* Norman: University of Oklahoma Press, 1941.

Defoe, Daniel. *The Fortunes and Misfortunes of the Famous Moll Flanders.* 1722. New York: Heritage Press, 1942.

Demos, John Putnam. *Entertaining Satan.* New York: Oxford University Press, 1982.

Dewhurst, Henry Stephen. *The Railroad Police.* Springfield, Ill.: Charles C. Thomas, 1955.

Dimsdale, Thomas J. *The Vigilantes of Montana: or, Popular Justice in the Rocky Mountains.* 1865. Norman: University of Oklahoma Press, 1953.

Dobie, Charles Caldwell. *San Francisco's Chinatown*. New York: D. Appleton, 1936.

Dobie, J. Frank. *A Vaquero of the Brush Country*. Dallas: Southwest Press, 1929.

Dobson, R. B., and J. Taylor. *Rymes of Robyn Hood*. London: Heinemann, 1976.

Dolci, Danilo. *Outlaws*. New York: Orion Press, 1961.

Drago, Harry Sinclair. *The Legend Makers*. New York: Dodd, Mead, 1975.

_____. *Outlaws on Horseback: The History of the Organized Bands of Bank and Train Robbers*. New York: Dodd, Mead, 1964.

Dunn, J. B. John. *Perilous Trails of Texas*. Dallas: Southwest Press, 1932.

Dykstra, Robert R. *The Cattle Towns*. New York: Alfred A. Knopf, 1968.

Eberhart, Perry. *Colorado Ghost Towns and Mining Camps*. Chicago: Sage Books, 1972.

Edwards, John N. *Noted Guerrillas, or the Warfare of the Border*. Saint Louis: Bryand, Brand, 1877.

Elliott, David Stewart. *Last Raid of the Daltons: A Reliable Recital of the Battle*. 1892. Freeport, N.Y.: Books for Libraries, 1971.

Elman, Robert. *Badmen of the West: The Lives and Times of Renegades, Bandits, Rustlers, and Gunfighters*. Secaucus, N.J.: Castle Books, 1974.

Erikson, Kai T. *Wayward Puritans*. New York: John Wiley & Sons, 1966.

Evans, W. McKee. *To Die Game: The Story of the Lowry Band*. Baton Rouge: Louisiana State University Press, 1971.

Everson, William K. *American Silent Films*. New York: Oxford University Press, 1978.

_____. *The Bad Guys: A Pictorial History of the Movie Villain*. New York: Citadel Press, 1969.

_____. *A Pictorial History of the Western Film*. New York: Cadillac, 1969.

Exquemelin, Alexander O. *The Buccaneers of America*. 1678. Baltimore: Penguin Books, 1969.

Eyles, Allen. *The Western*. Cranbury, N.J.: A. S. Barnes, 1975.

Faulk, Odie B. *Tombstone: Myth and Reality*. New York: Oxford University Press, 1972.

Fenin, George N., and William K. Everson. *The Western: From Silents to Cinerama*. New York: Orion Press, 1962.

Finger, Charles J. *Frontier Ballads*. Garden City, N.Y.: Doubleday, 1927.

_____. *Highwaymen*. New York: Robert M. McBride, 1923.

Fitch, William Edward. *Some Neglected History of North Carolina*. New York: W. E. Fitch, 1914.

Fodor's Ireland. New York: Fodor's Travel Guides, 1984.

Forrest, Earle R., and Edwin B. Hill. *Lone War Trail of the Apache Kid*. Pasadena, Calif.: Trail's End, 1947.

Francisco "Pancho" Villa. Chicago: Max Stein, 1916.

Frank, Gerold. *An American Death*. Garden City, N.Y.: Doubleday, 1972.

French, Philip. *Westerns: Aspects of a Movie Genre.* New York: Viking Press, 1974.

Frost, Alan. *Convicts and Empire.* Melbourne, Australia: Oxford University Press, 1980.

Fulton, Maurice Garland. *History of the Lincoln County War.* Tucson: University of Arizona Press, 1968.

Gaddy, Jerry J. *Obituaries of the Gunfighters: Dust to Dust.* Fort Collins, Colo.: Old Army Press, 1977.

Gard, Wayne. *Frontier Justice.* Norman: University of Oklahoma Press, 1949.

――――. *Sam Bass.* Boston: Houghton Mifflin, 1936.

Garrard, Lewis H. *Wah-to-yah and the Taos Trail.* 1850. Norman: University of Oklahoma Press, 1955.

Garrett, Pat F. *The Authentic Life of Billy, the Kid.* 1882. Norman: University of Oklahoma Press, 1954.

Gaute, J. H., and Robin Odell. *The Murderer's Who's Who.* New York: Methuen, 1979.

Gayarré, Charles. *Historical Sketch of Pierre and Jean Lafitte.* c. 1890. Austin: Pemberton Press, 1964.

Gish, Anthony. *American Bandits: A Biographical History of the Nation's Outlaws.* Girard, Kans.: Haldeman-Julius, 1938.

Goldman, William. *Butch Cassidy and the Sundance Kid.* New York: Bantam Books, 1969.

Gollomb, Joseph. *Master Highwaymen.* New York: Macaulay, 1927.

Goodenow, John Milton. *Historical Sketches of American Jurisprudence.* 1819. New York: Arno Press, 1972.

Gosse, Philip. *The History of Piracy.* London: Longmans, Green, 1932.

Graves, Richard S. *Oklahoma Outlaws: A Graphic History of the Early Days in Oklahoma.* Oklahoma City: State Printing Co., 1915.

Grebler, Leo, Joan W. Moore, and Ralph C. Guzman. *The Mexican-American People.* New York: Free Press, 1970.

Green, Donald E. *The Creek People.* Phoenix: Indian Tribal Series, 1973.

Green, Jonathan H. *The Secret Band of Brothers: or, The American Outlaws.* Philadelphia: G. B. Zieber, 1847.

Greenberg, Douglas. *Crime and Law Enforcement in the Colony of New York 1691–1776.* Ithaca, N.Y.: Cornell University Press, 1974.

Greenwood, Robert. *The California Outlaw Tiburcio Vásquez.* Los Gatos, Calif.: Talisman Press, 1960.

Grey, Zane. *Riders of the Purple Sage.* 1912. Roslyn, N.Y.: Walter J. Black, 1940.

Grummond, Jane Lucas de. *The Baratarians and the Battle of New Orleans.* Baton Rouge: Louisiana State University Press, 1961.

Guns and the Gunfighters. New York: Bonanza Books, 1975.

Hagan, William T. *Indian Police and Judges: Experiments in Acculturation and Control.* New Haven: Conn.: Yale University Press, 1966.

Halaas, David Fridtjof. *Boom Town Newspapers, 1859–1881.* Albuquerque: University of New Mexico Press, 1981.

Hanawalt, Barbara A. *Crime and Conflict in English Communities, 1300–1348.* Cambridge, Mass.: Harvard University Press, 1979.

Hanes, Bailey C. *Bill Doolin, Outlaw, O.T.* Norman: University of Oklahoma Press, 1968.

Hardin, John Wesley. *The Life of John Wesley Hardin as Written by Himself.* 1896. Norman: University of Oklahoma Press, 1961.

Haring, C. H. *The Buccaneers in the West Indies in the XVII Century.* London: Methuen, 1910.

Haskell, Molly. *From Reverence to Rape: The Treatment of Women in the Movies.* Chicago: University of Chicago Press, 1987.

Hazlitt, W. Caren. *Old English Plays.* 15 vols. London: Reeves and Turner, 1874.

Hearst, Patricia Campbell. *Every Secret Thing.* New York: Doubleday, 1982.

Hendricks, George D. *The Bad Man of the West.* 1941. San Antonio, Texas: Naylor, 1950.

Henry, H. M. *Police Control of the Slave in South Carolina.* Emory, Va.: H. M. Henry, 1914.

Hibbert, Christopher. *Highwaymen.* New York: Delacorte, 1967.

Hicks, Edwin P. *Belle Starr and Her Pearl.* Little Rock, Ark.: Pioneer Press, 1963.

Higashi, Sumiko. *Virgins, Vamps, and Flappers: The American Silent Movie Heroine.* Montreal: Eden Press, 1978.

Hirsch, Foster, *The Dark Side of the Screen: Film Noir.* San Diego, Calif.: A. S. Barnes, 1981.

Hobsbawm, Eric. *Bandits.* New York: Delacorte, 1969.

―――. *Primitive Rebels.* New York: Praeger, 1963.

Hogan, William Ransom. *The Texas Republic.* Norman: University of Oklahoma Press, 1946.

Holbrook, Stuart H. *Murder Out Yonder.* New York: Macmillan, 1941.

―――. *The Rocky Mountain Revolution.* New York: Henry Holt, 1956.

Holdsworth, W. S. *A History of English Law.* 16 vols. London: Methuen, 1908.

Holmes, Ronald. *Witchcraft in British History.* London: Frederick Muller, 1974.

Holt, J. C. *Robin Hood.* London: Thames and Hudson, 1982.

Hoover, J. Edgar. *Persons in Hiding.* London: J. M. Dent & Sons, 1938.

Hoppe, E. O. *Pirates, Buccaneers, and Gentlemen Adventurers.* New York: A. S. Barnes, 1972.

Horan, James D. *Desperate Men.* Garden City, N.Y.: Doubleday, 1962.

―――. *The Outlaws.* New York: Crown, 1977.

―――. *The Wild Bunch.* New York: New American Library, 1958.

―――, and Paul Sann. *Pictorial History of the Wild West: A True Account of the*

Bad Men, Desperados, Rustlers, and Outlaws of the Old West. New York: Crown, 1954.

————, and Howard Swiggett. *The Pinkerton Story.* New York: G. P. Putnam's Sons, 1951.

Horn, Calvin. *New Mexico's Troubled Years.* Albuquerque: Horn and Wallace, 1963.

Horn, Tom. *Life of Tom Horn: Government Scout and Interpreter Written by Himself.* 1904. Norman: University of Oklahoma Press, 1964.

Hough, Emerson. *The Passing of the Frontier.* New Haven, Conn.: Yale University Press, 1918.

————. *The Story of the Outlaw: A Study of the Western Desperado.* New York: Grosset and Dunlap, 1905.

Hughes, Robert. *The Fatal Shore.* New York: Alfred A. Knopf, 1987.

Huie, William Bradford. *He Slew the Dreamer.* New York: Delacorte Press, 1968.

Inciardi, James A., Alan A. Block, and Lyle A. Hollowell. *Historical Approaches to Crime.* Beverly Hills, Calif.: Sage, 1977.

Inglis, K. S. *The Australian Colonists.* Carlton, Australia: Melbourne University Press, 1974.

Jackson, Joseph Henry. *Anybody's Gold: The Story of California's Mining Towns.* New York: D. Appleton-Century, 1941.

Jameson, J. Franklin. *Privateering and Piracy in the Colonial Period.* 1923. New York: Augustus M. Kelley, 1970.

Jenkins, John H., and Gordon H. Frost. *I'm Frank Hamer.* Austin, Texas: Pemberton Press, 1968.

Jennings, Al. *Through the Shadows with O. Henry.* New York: A. L. Burt, 1921.

Jennings, N. A. *A Texas Ranger.* New York: Charles Scribner's Sons, 1899.

Jeudwine, J. W. *Tort, Crime, and Police in Mediaeval England.* London: Williams and Norgate, 1917.

Johnson, Captain Charles. *A General History of the Robberies and Murders of the Most Notorious Pirates.* 1724. New York: Dodd, Mead, 1927.

Johnson, Dorothy M. *Western Badmen.* New York: Dodd, Mead, 1970.

Jolliffe, J. E. A. *The Constitutional History of Medieval England.* London: Adam and Charles Black, 1947.

Jordan, Philip D. *Frontier Law and Order.* Lincoln: University of Nebraska Press, 1970.

Kaminsky, Stuart M. *American Film Genres: Approaches to a Critical Theory of Popular Film.* New York: Dell, 1974.

Karpis, Alvin. *The Alvin Karpis Story.* New York: Coward, McCann & Geoghegan, 1971.

Karsner, David. *John Brown: Terrible 'Saint.'* New York: Dodd, Mead, 1934.

Katz, Jack. *Seductions of Crime: Moral and Sensual Attractions in Doing Evil.* New York: Basic Books, 1988.

Katz, William Loren. *Black Indians.* New York: Atheneum, 1986.

Kee, Robert. *Ireland: A History.* London: Abacus, 1982.

Keen, Maurice. *The Outlaws of Medieval Legend.* Toronto: University of Toronto Press, 1961.

Kelly, Charles. *The Outlaw Trail: A History of Butch Cassidy and His Wild Bunch.* 1938. New York: Devin-Adair, 1959.

―――, and Hoffman Birney. *Holy Murder: The Story of Porter Rockwell.* New York: Minton, Balch, 1934.

Kennedy, Capt., U.S.A. *The Life and History of Francisco Villa.* Baltimore: I. and M. Ottenheimer, 1916.

Kephart, William M. *Extraordinary Groups.* New York: St. Martin's Press, 1982.

Kitses, Jim. *Horizons West.* Bloomington: Indiana University Press, 1969.

Klasner, Lily. *My Girlhood Among Outlaws.* Tucson: University of Arizona Press, 1972.

Kohn, George C. *Dictionary of Culprits and Criminals.* Metuchen, N.J.: Scarecrow Press, 1986.

Kooistra, Paul. *Criminals as Heroes: Structure, Power and Identity.* Bowling Green, Ohio: Bowling Green University Press, 1989.

Lamar, Howard R., ed. *The Reader's Encyclopedia of the American West.* New York: Thomas Y. Crowell, 1977.

Lane, Mark, and Dick Gregory. *Code Name "Zorro."* Englewood Cliffs, N.J.: Prentice-Hall, 1977.

Lane, Roger. *Policing the City: Boston 1882–1885.* Cambridge, Mass.: Harvard University Press, 1967.

Lange, J. de. *The Relation and Development of English and Icelandic Outlaw Traditions.* Haarlem, Netherlands: Willink and Zoon, 1935.

Langlois, Janet L. *Belle Gunness: The Lady Bluebeard.* Bloomington: Indiana University Press, 1985.

Langum, David J. *Law and Community on the Mexican California Frontier, 1821–1846.* Norman: University of Oklahoma Press, 1987.

Latta, Frank. *Joaquin Murrieta and His Horse Gangs.* Santa Cruz, Calif.: Bear State Books, 1980.

The Laws Respecting Women. 1777. Dobbs Ferry, N.Y.: Oceana Publications, 1974.

Lee, Robert E. *Blackbeard the Pirate.* Winston-Salem, N.C.: John F. Blair, 1974.

Lee, W. L. Melville. *A History of Police in England.* London: Methuen, 1901.

LeFors, Joe. *Wyoming Peace Officer: An Autobiography.* Laramie, Wyo.: Laramie Printing Co., 1953.

Life and Adventures of Sam Bass. Dallas: Dallas Commercial Steam Press, 1878.

Llewellyn, Karl N., and E. Adamson Hoebel. *The Cheyenne Way: Conflict and Case Law in Primitive Jurisprudence.* Norman: University of Oklahoma Press, 1941.

Lloyd, A. L. *Folk Song in England.* New York: International Publishers, 1967.

Lomax, Alan. *The Folk Songs of North America.* Garden City, N.Y.: Doubleday, 1960.

Lomax, John A., and Alan Lomax. *Best-Loved American Folk Songs.* New York: Grosset and Dunlap, 1947.

Long, Jeff. *Outlaw: The True Story of Claude Dallas.* New York: William Morrow, 1985.

Love, Robertus. *The Rise and Fall of Jesse James.* New York: G. P. Putnam's Sons, 1926.

Loyalist Americans. Tarrytown, N.Y.: Sleepy Hollow Restorations, 1975.

Lyon, Peter. *The Wild, Wild West.* New York: Funk and Wagnalls, 1969.

McArthur, Colin. *Underworld U.S.A.* New York: Viking Press, 1972.

McDonald, Archie P. *Shooting Stars: Heroes and Heroines of Western Film.* Bloomington: Indiana University Press, 1987.

McGrath, Roger D. *Gunfighters Highwaymen & Vigilantes.* Berkeley: University of California Press, 1984.

McKechnie, William Sharp. *Magna Carta.* Glasgow: James Maclehose and Sons, 1914.

McKinley, James. *Assassination in America.* New York: Harper and Row, 1977.

Magill, Frank N. *Magill's Survey of Cinema.* 3 vols. Englewood Cliffs, N.J.: Salem Press, 1982.

Mannheim, Hermann. *Comparative Criminology.* Boston: Houghton Mifflin, 1965.

Martin, Charles L. *A Sketch of Sam Bass, the Bandit.* 1880. Norman: University of Oklahoma Press, 1956.

Mason, Herbert Molloy. *The Great Pursuit.* New York: Random House, 1970.

Mercer, A. S. *The Banditti of the Plains: Or the Cattlemen's Invasion of Wyoming in 1892 (The Crowning Infamy of the Ages).* 1894. Norman: University of Oklahoma Press, 1954.

Meyer, Duane. *The Heritage of Missouri.* Saint Louis: State Publishing Co., 1973.

Monkkonen, Eric H. *Police in Urban America.* Cambridge, England: Cambridge University Press, 1981.

Morn, Frank. *The Eye That Never Sleeps.* Bloomington: Indiana University Press, 1982.

Mullin, Gerald W. *Flight and Rebellion: Slave Resistance in Eighteenth Century Virginia.* New York: Oxford University Press, 1972.

Myers, Albert Cook, ed. *Narratives of Early Pennsylvania West New Jersey and Delaware, 1630–1707.* New York: Charles Scribner's Sons, 1912.

Nash, Jay Robert, *Bloodletters and Badmen.* New York: M. Evans, 1973.

Nettle, Reginald. *Sing a Song of England.* Denver: Alan Swallow, 1950.

Newark, Peter. *The Crimson Book of Highwaymen.* London: Jupiter Books, 1979.

Newcomb, Horace. *TV: The Most Popular Art.* Garden City, N.Y.: Anchor Press, 1974.

Nolan, Frederick W. *The Life and Death of John Henry Tunstall.* Albuquerque: University of New Mexico Press, 1965.

Oates, Stephen B. *To Purge This Land with Blood.* New York: Harper and Row, 1970.

O'Connor, John E. *The Hollywood Indian: Stereotypes of Native Americans in Films.* Trenton: New Jersey State Museum, 1980.

Olsen, Jack. *Give a Boy a Gun: A True Story of Law and Disorder in the American West.* New York: Delacorte, 1985.

O'Neal, Bill. *Encyclopedia of Western Gunfighters.* Norman: University of Oklahoma Press, 1979.

Orlando [N. E. Paxton]. *The Brigand, or, A Tale of the West Done into Ryme.* Georgetown, Ky.: Wise and French, 1845.

Osawatomie, Kansas. Osawatomie, Kans.: n.p., 1982.

O'Shaughnessy, Edith. *A Diplomat's Wife in Mexico.* New York: Harper & Brothers, 1916.

Paredes, Americo. *With His Pistol in His Hand: A Border Ballad and Its Hero.* Austin: University of Texas Press, 1958.

Parish, James R., and Don E. Stanke. *Swashbucklers.* New Rochelle, N.Y.: Arlington House, 1976.

Parker, Emma, and Nell Barrow Cowan. *Fugitives: The Story of Clyde Barrow and Bonnie Parker.* Dallas: Ranger Press, 1934.

Patridge, Eric. *Pirates, Highwaymen and Adventurers.* London: Scholartis Press, 1927.

Patterson, Richard. *Historical Atlas of the Outlaw West.* Boulder, Colo.: Johnson Books, 1985.

———. *Train Robbery: The Birth, Flowering and Decline of a Notorious Western Enterprise.* Boulder, Colo.: Johnson Books, 1981.

Penick, James Lal, Jr. *The Great Western Land Pirate: John A. Murrell in Legend and History.* Columbia: University of Missouri Press, 1981.

Phares, Ross. *Reverend Devil.* New Orleans: Pelican, 1941.

Pickard, Ray. *Who Played Who in the Movies.* New York: Schocken Books, 1981.

Pinchon, Edgcumb. *Viva Villa!* 1933. New York: Arno Press, 1970.

Pinkerton, William A. *Train Robberies and Train Robbers.* Jamestown, Va.: International Association of Chiefs of Police, 1907.

Pioneer Days in the Southwest. Guthrie, Okla.: State Capital Company, 1909.

Place, J. A. *The Western Films of John Ford.* Secaucus, N.J.: Citadel Press, 1974.

Pointer, Larry. *In Search of Butch Cassidy.* Norman: University of Oklahoma Press, 1977.

Pollack, Otto. *The Criminality of Women.* Philadelphia: University of Pennsylvania Press, 1950.

Pollock, Frederick, and Frederic William Maitland. *The History of English Law: Before the Time of Edward I.* 2 vols. 1895. Cambridge, England: Cambridge University Press, 1968.

Pound, Louise, ed. *American Ballads and Songs.* New York: Charles Scribner's Sons, 1922.

Powell, William S., James K. Huhta, and Thomas J. Farnham. *The Regulators of North Carolina: 1759–1776.* Raleigh, N.C.: State Department of Archives, 1971.

Powers, Richard Gid. *G-Men.* Carbondale: Southern Illinois University Press, 1983.

Prassel, Frank Richard. *The Western Peace Officer: A Legacy of Law and Order.* Norman: University of Oklahoma Press, 1972.

Preece, Harold. *The Dalton Gang: End of an Outlaw Era.* New York: Hastings House, 1963.

Proveda, Tony. *Lawlessness and Reform: The FBI in Transition.* Pacific Grove, Calif.: Brooks/Cole, 1990.

Pyle, Howard. *The Buccaneers and Marooners of America.* 1891. Ann Arbor, Mich.: Gryphon Books, 1971.

Quimby, Myron J. *The Devil's Emissaries.* Cranbury, N.J.: A. S. Barnes, 1969.

Raine, William MacLeod. *Famous Sheriffs and Western Outlaws.* Garden City, N.Y.: Doubleday, 1929.

Ramsaye, Terry. *A Million and One Nights.* 2 vols. New York: Simon & Schuster, 1926.

Rankin, Hugh F. *The Golden Age of Piracy.* New York: Colonial Williamsburg Press, 1969.

Rascoe, Burton. *Belle Starr, "The Bandit Queen."* New York: Random House, 1941.

Rascoe, Jesse Ed. *The Treasure Album of Pancho Villa.* Toyahvale, Texas: Frontier Book Company, 1962.

Rayner, J. L., and G. T. Crook. *The Complete Newgate Calendar.* 5 vols. 1734–1841. London: Navarre Society, 1926.

Recent Social Trends in the United States. New York: McGraw-Hill, 1933.

Redford, Robert. *The Outlaw Trail: A Journey Through Time.* New York: Grosset and Dunlap, 1978.

Rediker, Marcus. *Between the Devil and the Deep Blue Sea.* Cambridge, England: Cambridge University Press, 1987.

Reed, John. *Insurgent Mexico.* 1914. New York: International Publishers, 1969.

Richardson, Albert D. *Beyond the Mississippi.* Hartford, Conn.: American Publishing Co., 1869.

Richardson, James D., ed. *A Compilation of the Messages and Papers of the Presidents, 1789–1902.* 11 vols. Washington: Bureau of National Literature and Art, 1904.

Ridge, John Rollin [Yellow Bird]. *The Life and Adventures of Joaquin Murieta: The Celebrated California Bandit.* 1854. Norman: University of Oklahoma Press, 1955.

Ritchie, Robert C. *Captain Kidd and the War Against the Pirates.* Cambridge, Mass.: Harvard University Press, 1986.

Robinson, W. Stitt. *The Southern Colonial Frontier, 1607–1763.* Albuquerque: University of New Mexico Press, 1979.

Robinson, William Henry. *The Story of Arizona.* Phoenix: Berryhill Company, 1919.

Roddy, W. Lee. *Wanted!* Ceres, Calif.: Genie, 1970.

Rosa, Joseph G. *The Gunfighter: Man or Myth?* Norman: University of Oklahoma Press, 1969.

————. *They Called Him Wild Bill: The Life and Adventures of James Butler Hickok.* Norman: University of Oklahoma Press, 1974.

————. *The West of Wild Bill Hickok.* Norman: University of Oklahoma Press, 1982.

Rosenberg, Bruce A. *The Code of the West.* Bloomington: Indiana University Press, 1982.

Rosow, Eugene. *Born to Lose.* New York: Oxford University Press, 1978.

Rothert, Otto A. *The Outlaws of Cave-In-Rock.* Cleveland: Arthur H. Clark, 1923.

Rovin, Jeff. *The Great Television Series.* Cranbury, N.J.: A. S. Barnes, 1977.

Ruíz, Ramón Eduardo. *The Great Rebellion: Mexico, 1905–1924.* New York: W. W. Norton, 1980.

Russell, Don. *The Lives and Legends of Buffalo Bill.* Norman: University of Oklahoma Press, 1960.

————. *The Wild West, or, A History of the Wild West Shows Which Created a Wonderfully Imaginative and Unrealistic Image of the American West.* Fort Worth, Texas: Amon Carter Museum, 1970.

Rynning, Thomas H. *Gun Notches: The Life Story of a Cowboy-Soldier.* New York: Frederick A. Stokes 1931.

Sabin, Edwin L. *Wild Men of the Wild West.* New York: Thomas Y. Crowell, 1929.

Sanders, Leonard. *How Fort Worth Became the Texasmost City.* Fort Worth, Texas: Amon Carter Museum, 1973.

Saxon, Lyle. *Lafitte the Pirate.* New Orleans: Robert L. Crager, 1930.

Schellie, Don. *Vast Domain of Blood.* Los Angeles: Westernlore Press, 1968.

Schultz, William Eben. *Gay's Beggar's Opera.* New Haven, Conn.: Yale University Press, 1923.

Schuster, Ernest Otto. *Pancho Villa's Shadow.* New York: Exposition Press, 1947.

Seagle, William. *The Quest for Law.* New York: Alfred A. Knopf, 1941.

Senkewicz, Robert M. *Vigilantes in Gold Rush San Francisco.* Stanford, Calif.: Stanford University Press, 1985.

Settle, William A., Jr. *Jesse James Was His Name.* Lincoln: University of Nebraska Press, 1966.

Shadoian, Jack. *Dreams and Dead Ends.* Cambridge, Mass.: M.I.T. Press, 1977.

Shinn, Charles Howard. *Mining Camps: A Study in American Frontier Government.* 1885. New York: Alfred A. Knopf, 1948.

Shirley, Glenn. *Belle Starr and Her Times.* Norman: University of Oklahoma Press, 1982.

————. *Henry Starr: Last of the Real Badmen.* Lincoln: University of Nebraska Press, 1965.

————. *Law West of Fort Smith: A History of Frontier Justice in the Indian Territory, 1834–1896.* New York: Henry Holt, 1957.

————. *Shotgun for Hire: The Story of "Deacon" Jim Miller.* Norman: University of Oklahoma Press, 1970.

Sifakis, Carl. *The Encyclopedia of American Crime.* New York: Facts on File, 1982.

Simmons, Lee. *Assignment Huntsville: Memoirs of a Texas Prison Official.* Austin: University of Texas Press, 1957.

Siringo, Charles. *Two Evil Isms: Pinkertonism and Anarchism.* Chicago: Charles A. Siringo, 1915.

Slotkin, Richard. *The Fatal Environment, 1800–1890.* New York: Atheneum, 1985.

————. *Regeneration Through Violence: The Mythology of the American Frontier, 1600–1860.* Middletown, Conn.: Wesleyan University Press, 1973.

Smith, Henry Nash. *Virgin Land: The American West as Symbol and Myth.* Cambridge, Mass.: Harvard University Press, 1950.

Songs of the American West. Berkeley: University of California Press, 1968.

Sonnichsen, C. L. *Tucson: The Life and Times of an American City.* Norman: University of Oklahoma Press, 1982.

————, and William V. Morrison. *Alias Billy the Kid.* Albuquerque: University of New Mexico Press, 1955.

Speed, P. F. *Police and Prisons.* Hong Kong, B.C.C.: Longman Group, 1968.

Stanley, F. *Satanta and the Kiowas.* Borger, Texas: F. Stanley, 1968.

Steckmesser, Kent Ladd. *The Western Hero in History and Legend.* Norman: University of Oklahoma Press, 1965.

————. *Western Outlaws: The "Good Badman" in Fact, Film, and Folklore.* Claremont, Calif.: Regina Books, 1983.

Stedman, Raymond W. *The Serials: Suspense and Drama by Installment.* Norman: University of Oklahoma Press, 1977.

————. *Shadows of the Indian: Stereotypes in American Culture.* Norman: University of Oklahoma Press, 1982.

Stephen, James Fitzjames. *A History of the Criminal Law of England.* 3 vols. London: Macmillan, 1883.

Stratton, Porter A. *The Territorial Press of New Mexico, 1834–1912*. Albuquerque: University of New Mexico Press, 1969.

Strickland, Rennard. *Fire and the Spirits: Cherokee Law from Clan to Court*. Norman: University of Oklahoma Press, 1975.

Sutton, Fred E. *Hands Up! Stories of the Six-Gun Fighters of the Old Wild West*. Indianapolis: Bobbs-Merrill, 1927.

Swallow, Alan. *The Wild Bunch*. Denver: Sage Books, 1966.

Tatum, Stephen. *Inventing Billy the Kid: Visions of the Outlaw in America, 1881–1981*. Albuquerque: University of New Mexico Press, 1982.

Thelen, David. *Paths of Resistance: Tradition and Dignity in Industrializing Missouri*. New York: Oxford University Press, 1986.

They Went That-A-Way. London: Orbis, 1982.

Thrasher, Frederic M. *The Gang: A Study of 1,313 in Chicago*. 1927. Chicago: University of Chicago Press, 1963.

Thrower, Rayner. *The Pirate Picture*. London: Phillimore, 1980.

Tilghman, Zoe A. *Marshal of the Last Frontier: Life and Service of William Matthew (Bill) Tilghman*. Glendale, Calif.: Arthur H. Clark, 1949.

Tocqueville, Alexis de: *Democracy in America*. 1835. New York: New American Library, 1956.

Toland, John. *The Dillinger Days*. New York: Random House, 1963.

Torre, Lillian de la: *Villainy Detected*. New York: D. Appleton, 1947.

Trachtman, Paul. *The Gunfighters*. New York: Time-Life Books, 1974.

Treherne, John. *The Strange History of Bonnie and Clyde*. New York: Stein and Day, 1984.

Turner, Frederick Jackson. *The Frontier in American History*. New York: Henry Holt, 1920.

Turner, John Peter. *The North-West Mounted Police, 1873–1893*. 2 vols. Ottawa: Edmond Cloutier, 1950.

Tuska, Jon. *Billy the Kid: A Handbook*. Lincoln: University of Nebraska Press, 1983.

———. *Dark Cinema: American Film Noir in Cultural Perspective*. Westport, Conn.: Greenwood Press, 1984.

Underhill, Ruth M. *The Navajos*. Norman: University of Oklahoma Press, 1956.

Utley, Robert M. *Billy the Kid: A Short and Violent Life*. Lincoln: University of Nebraska Press, 1989.

———. *High Noon in Lincoln: Violence on the Western Frontier*. Albuquerque: University of New Mexico Press, 1987.

———. *The Indian Frontier of the American West, 1846–1890*. Albuquerque: University of New Mexico Press, 1984.

Vanderwood, Paul J. *Disorder and Progress: Bandits, Police and Mexican Development*. Lincoln: University of Nebraska Press, 1981.

Wagner, Anthony. *Heralds and Ancestors*. London: British Museum, 1978.

Wagoner, Jay J. *Arizona Territory, 1863–1912.* Tucson: University of Arizona Press, 1970.

Wake, Sandra, and Nicola Hayden. *The Bonnie and Clyde Book.* New York: Simon & Schuster, 1972.

Warshow, Robert. *The Immediate Experience: Movies, Comics, Theater, and Other Aspects of Popular Culture. 1946–55.* New York: Atheneum, 1970.

Washburn, Wilcomb E. *The Governor and the Rebel: A History of Bacon's Rebellion in Virginia.* Chapel Hill: University of North Carolina Press, 1957.

Watson, Edward James. *Pleas of the Crown for Bristol, A.D. 1221.* Bristol, England: W. Crofton Hemmons, 1902.

Webb, Walter Prescott. *The Great Plains.* New York: Grosset & Dunlap, 1931.

———. *The Texas Rangers: A Century of Frontier Defense. 1935.* Austin: University of Texas Press, 1965.

Wecter, Dixon. *The Hero in America.* New York: Charles Scribner's Sons, 1941.

Weir, Robert W. *Colonial South Carolina.* Millwood, N.Y.: KTO Press, 1983.

Wellman, Paul I. *A Dynasty of Western Outlaws.* Garden City, N.Y.: Doubleday, 1961.

———. *Spawn of Evil: The Invincible Empire of Soulless Men.* New York: Doubleday, 1964.

Wells, Evelyn Kendrick. *The Ballad Tree.* New York: Ronald Press, 1950.

Wertenbaker, Thomas J. *Virginia Under the Stuarts, 1607–1688.* Princeton, N.J.: Princeton University Press, 1914.

West, Gerald Montgomery. *The Status of the Negro in Virginia During the Colonial Period.* New York: William R. Jenkins, n.d.

Williams, Neville. *Captains Outrageous: Seven Centuries of Piracy.* New York: Macmillan, 1962.

Williams, Selma R. *Divine Rebel: The Life of Anne Marbury Hutchinson.* New York: Holt, Rinehart, and Winston, 1981.

———, and Pamela J. Williams. *Riding the Nightmare: Women and Witches.* New York: Atheneum, 1978.

Wilson, Colin. *A Criminal History of Mankind.* New York: G. P. Putnam's Sons, 1984.

Wilson, Helen. *The Treatment of the Misdemeanant in Indiana, 1816–1936.* Chicago: University of Chicago Press, 1938.

Winstock, Lewis. *Songs & Music of the Redcoats, 1642–1902.* Harrisburg, Pa.: Stackpole, 1970.

Winston, Alexander. *No Man Knows My Grave.* Boston: Houghton Mifflin, 1969.

Wise, William. *Massacre at Mountain Meadows: An American Legend and a Monumental Crime.* New York: Thomas Y. Crowell, 1976.

Woll, Allen L. *The Latin Image in American Film.* Los Angeles: University of California, 1980.

Wood, Betty. *Slavery in South Carolina, 1730–1775.* Athens: University of Georgia Press, 1984.

Wood, Peter H. *Black Majority: Negroes in Colonial South Carolina from 1670 Through the Stono Rebellion.* New York: Alfred A. Knopf, 1974.

Worcester, Donald E. *The Apaches: Eagles of the Southwest.* Norman: University of Oklahoma Press, 1979.

Wright, James, Peter H. Rossi, and Kathleen Daly. *Under the Gun: Weapons, Crime, and Violence in America.* New York: Aldine de Gruyter, 1983.

Wright, Thomas. *The Life of Daniel Defoe.* New York: Anson D. F. Randolph, 1894.

Wright, Will. *Six Guns and Society.* Berkeley: University of California Press, 1975.

Wycherley, George. *Buccaneers of the Pacific.* Indianapolis: Bobbs-Merrill, 1928.

Young, John V. *The State Parks of New Mexico.* Albuquerque: University of New Mexico Press, 1984.

PERIODICALS

Adams, James Truslow. "Our Lawless Heritage." *Atlantic Monthly* 142 (December 1928): 732–40.

"Administration of Justice in California [1850]." *California Pamphlets* 26, no. 1 (n.d.): 354–56.

Allen, Barbara. "The Heroic Ride in Western Popular Historical Tradition." *Western Historical Quarterly* 19 (November 1988): 397–412.

Arnett, R. E. "A Young Cowboy Detective." *Colorado Magazine* 24 (November 1947): 250–58.

"Bender Mounds." *Kansas Historical Quarterly* 13 (Summer 1957): 146.

Block, Anton. "The Peasant and the Brigand." *Comparative Studies in Society and History* 14 (September 1972): 494–503.

Burrows, Jack. "Ringo: 'No human being could match the draw of Ringo.' " *American West* 7 (January 1970): 17–21.

Butler, Anne M. "Still in Chains: Black Women in Western Prisons, 1865–1910." *Western Historical Quarterly* 20 (February 1989): 19–35.

Cahalan, Margaret. "Trends in Incarceration in the United States since 1880." *Crime and Delinquency* 25 (January 1979): 9–41.

Calhoun, Daniel. "Studying American Violence." *Journal of Interdisciplinary History* 1 (Autumn 1970): 163–85.

Callan, Austin. "Sheriffing in the Old Days." *Sheriffs' Association of Texas Magazine* 1, no. 1 (1930): 9–10.

Calloway, Colin G. "Neither White nor Red: White Renegades on the American Indian Frontier." *Western Historical Quarterly* 17 (January 1986): 43–66.

Canlis, Michael N. "The Evolution of Law Enforcement in California." *The Far-Westerner* 2 (July 1961): 1–13.

Chambers, Anne. "A Most Famous Feminine Sea Captain." *Ireland* 33 (May–June 1984): 38–42.

Chatwin, Bruce. "In Patagonia." *American Way* 21 (15 May 1988): 90–94.

Chrisman, Harry E. "The Damndest Story That Ever Was." *The Westerners Brand Book* 23 (1968): 71–101.

Davis, Roger H. "Outlaw Motorcyclists." *FBI Law Enforcement Bulletin* 51 (October 1982): 12–16.

Deakin, Thomas J. "The FBI Law Enforcement Bulletin." *FBI Law Enforcement Bulletin* 54 (October 1985): 2–9.

Deaver, Bobby G. "Outlawry: Another Gothic Column in North Carolina." *North Carolina Law Review* 41 (Spring 1963): 634–47.

Douglas, Norman. "The Brigands' Forest." *Cornhill Magazine* 26 (February 1909): 246–53.

Einstadter, Werner J. "Crime News in the Old West." *Urban Life* 8 (October 1979): 317–34.

Ekirch, Roger. "Bound for America: A Profile of British Convicts Transported to the Colonies, 1718–1775." *William and Mary Quarterly,* 3d ser., 62 (April 1985): 184–200.

Elliott, Mabel A. "Crime and the Frontier Mores." *American Sociological Review* 9 (April 1944): 185–92.

Ethington, Philip J. "Vigilantes and Police." *Journal of Social History* 21 (Winter 1987): 197–227.

Hansen, George W. "True Story of Wild Bill–McCanles Affray." *Nebraska History* 10 (April–June 1927): 71–112.

Hentig, Hans von. "Redhead and Outlaw." *Journal of Criminal Law and Criminology* 38 (May–June 1947): 1–6.

Hickey, Neil, and Edward Sorel. "The Warner Mob." *American Heritage* 35 (December 1983): 32–39.

Hindus, Michael S. "Black Justice Under White Law: Criminal Prosecutions of Blacks in Antebellum South Carolina." *Journal of American History* 62 (December 1976): 575–99.

Hobsbawm, Eric. "Social Bandits." *Comparative Studies in Society and History* 14 (September 1972): 503–4.

House, Lamar. "A Dark and Evil World." *Arkansas Times* 13, no. 5 (January–February 1987): 26–88; 13, no. 6 (February 1987): 42–70.

Hughson, Shirley Carter. "The Carolina Pirates and Colonial Commerce, 1670–1740." *John Hopkins University Studies in Historical and Political Science* 12 (May–July 1894): 1–134.

Hume, C. Ross. "Oklahoma History Embedded in the Law." *Chronicles of Oklahoma* 25 (Summer 1947): 92–101.

Johnson, David R. "The Origins and Structure of Intercity Criminal Activity: 1840–1920." *Journal of Social History* 15 (Summer 1982): 593–605.

Klapp, Orrin E. "The Folk Hero." *Journal of American Folklore* 62 (January–March 1949): 17–25.

Langum, David J. "Pioneer Justice on the Overland Trails." *Western Historical Quarterly* 5 (October 1974): 421–39.

Little, Craig B., and Christopher P. Sheffield. "Frontiers and Criminal Justice." *American Sociological Review* 48 (December 1983): 796–808.

Margetson, Stella. "Bold, Brave and Brilliant." *Country Life* 178 (5 December 1985): 1781–82.

————. "Sweet-Tempered Satirist." *Country Life* 178 (19 September 1985): 832–33.

McNeil, Irving. "Indian Justice." *New Mexico Historical Review* 19 (October 1944): 261–70.

Melbin, Murray. "Night as Frontier." *American Sociological Review* 43 (February 1978): 3–22.

Michelson, Charles. "Stage Robbers of the West." *Munsey's Magazine* 25 (July 1901): 448–59.

Mondy, R. W. "Analysis of Frontier Social Instability." *Southwestern Social Science Quarterly* 24 (September 1943): 167–77.

Morris, Christopher. "An Event in Community Organization: The Mississippi Slave Insurrection Scare of 1835." *Journal of Social History* 22 (Fall 1988): 93–111.

Mottram, Eric. "The Persuasive Lips: Men and Guns in America, the West." *Journal of American Studies* 10 (April 1976): 53–84.

Mueller, Oscar C. "The Central Montana Vigilante Raids of 1884." *Montana Magazine of History* 1 (January 1951): 23–56.

Nash, A. E. Keir. "Fairness and Formalism in the Trials of Blacks in the State Supreme Courts of the Old South." *Virginia Law Review* 56 (February 1970): 64–100.

Olmstead, Roger. "San Francisco and the Vigilante Style." *American West* 7 (January 1970): 6–64; 7 (March 1970): 20–62.

Outland, Charles F. "San Buenaventura Justice, 1870–1871." *Ventura County Historical Society Quarterly* 7 (November 1961): 10–18.

"Outlaws." *TV Guide* 35, no. 2 (10 January 1987): A-27.

Pool, Frank M. "The Apache Kid." *The Sheriff* 6 (March 1947): 18–24.

Pugh, Ralph B. "Early Registers of English Outlaws." *American Journal of Legal History* 27 (October 1983): 319–29.

Rigler, Erik. "Frontier Justice: In the Days Before NCIC." *FBI Law Enforcement Bulletin* 54 (July 1985): 16–22.

Rister, Carl Coke. "Outlaws and Vigilantes on the Southern Plains: 1865–1885." *Mississippi Valley Historical Review* 19 (March 1933): 537–54.

Roberts, Gary L. "The West's Gunmen." *American West* 8 (January 1971): 10–64; 8 (March 1971): 18–62.

Roberts, John W. " 'Railroad Bill' and the American Outlaw Tradition." *Western Folklore* 40 (October 1981): 315–28.

Rowe, G. S. *"Femmes Covert* and Criminal Prosecutions in Eighteenth Century Pennsylvania." *American Journal of Legal History* 32 (April 1988): 138–156.

———. "Outlawry in Pennsylvania, 1782–1788." *American Journal of Legal History* 20 (July 1976): 227–44.

"Sam Bass, Famous Desperado Was Likable Outlaw." *Sheriffs' Association of Texas Magazine* 1 (July 1931): 14.

Schaefer, Jack. "Real Heroes of the West." *Holiday* 2 (December 1957): 76–77, 184–200.

Sill, Geoffrey M. "Defoe's Two Versions of the Outlaw." *English Studies* 64 (April 1983): 122–28.

Simeone, W. E. "Robin Hood and Some Other Outlaws." *Journal of American Folklore* 71 (January–March 1958): 27–35.

Smith, Abbot Emerson. "The Transportation of Convicts to the North American Colonies in the Seventeenth Century." *American Historical Review* 39 (January 1934): 232–49.

Spindel, Donna A. "The Administration of Criminal Justice in North Carolina, 1720–1740." *American Journal of Legal History* 25 (April 1981): 141–62.

Steckmesser, Kent L. "Robin Hood and the American Outlaw." *Journal of American Folklore* 79 (April–June 1966): 348–55.

Stoeltje, Beverly J. "A Helpmate for Man Indeed." *Journal of American Folklore* 88 (January–March 1975): 25–41.

Traub, Stuart H. "Rewards, Bounty Hunting, and Criminal Justice in the West." *Western Historical Quarterly* 19 (August 1988): 287–301.

"27 Years for 'Top Ten.' " *FBI Law Enforcement Bulletin* 46 (March 1977): 31.

"Wanted by the FBI." *FBI Law Enforcement Bulletin* 43 (November 1974): 16–17.

White, Richard. "Outlaw Gangs of the Middle Border: American Social Bandits." *Western Historical Quarterly* 12 (October 1981): 387–408.

Windsor, Mulford. "The Arizona Rangers." *Our Sheriff and Police Journal* 31 (June 1936): 49–61.

Wunder, John R. "The Chinese and Courts in the Pacific Northwest: Justice Denied?" *Pacific Historical Review* 52 (May 1983): 191–211.

Index